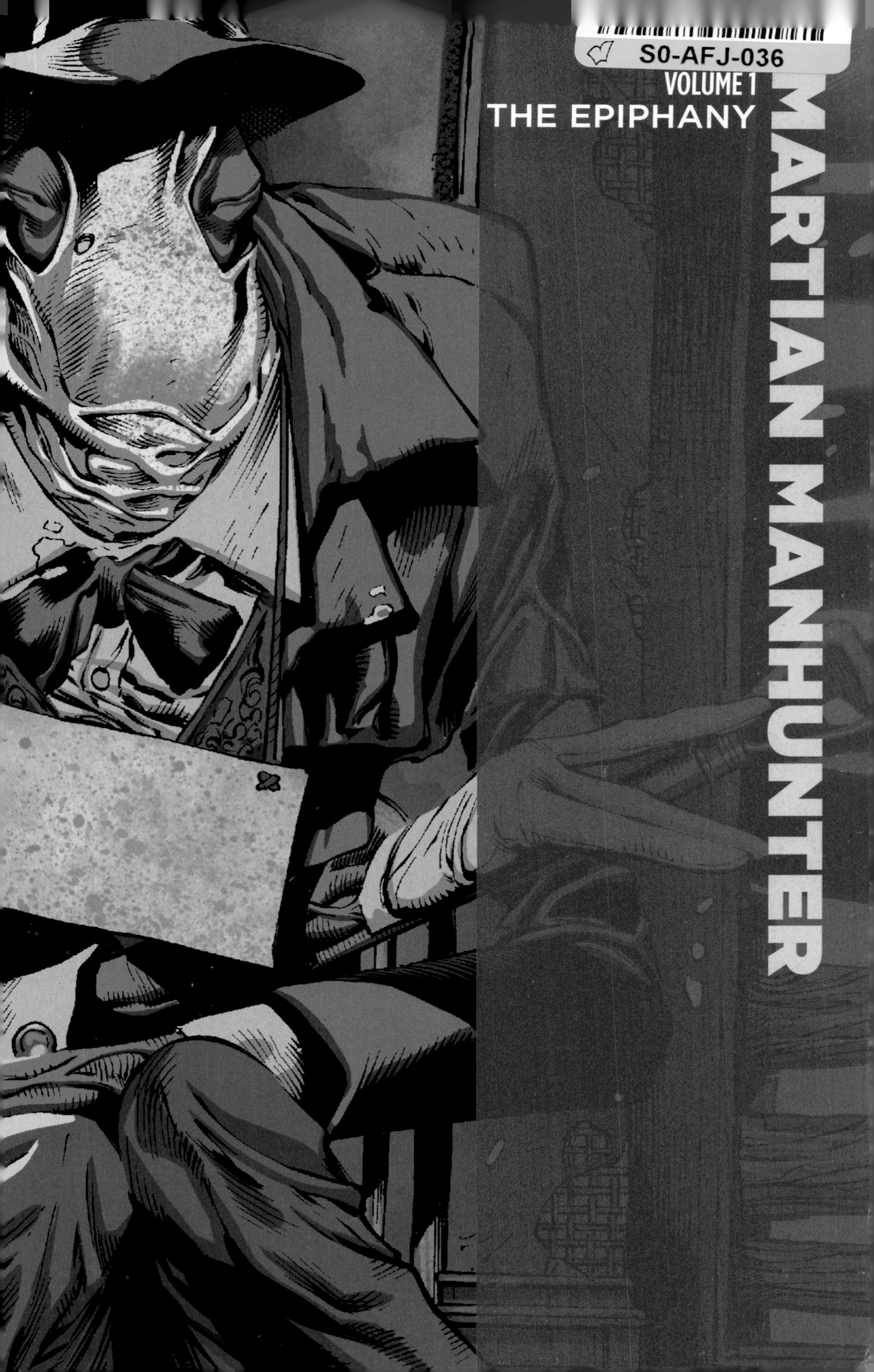
VOLUME 1
THE EPIPHANY
MARTIAN MANHUNTER

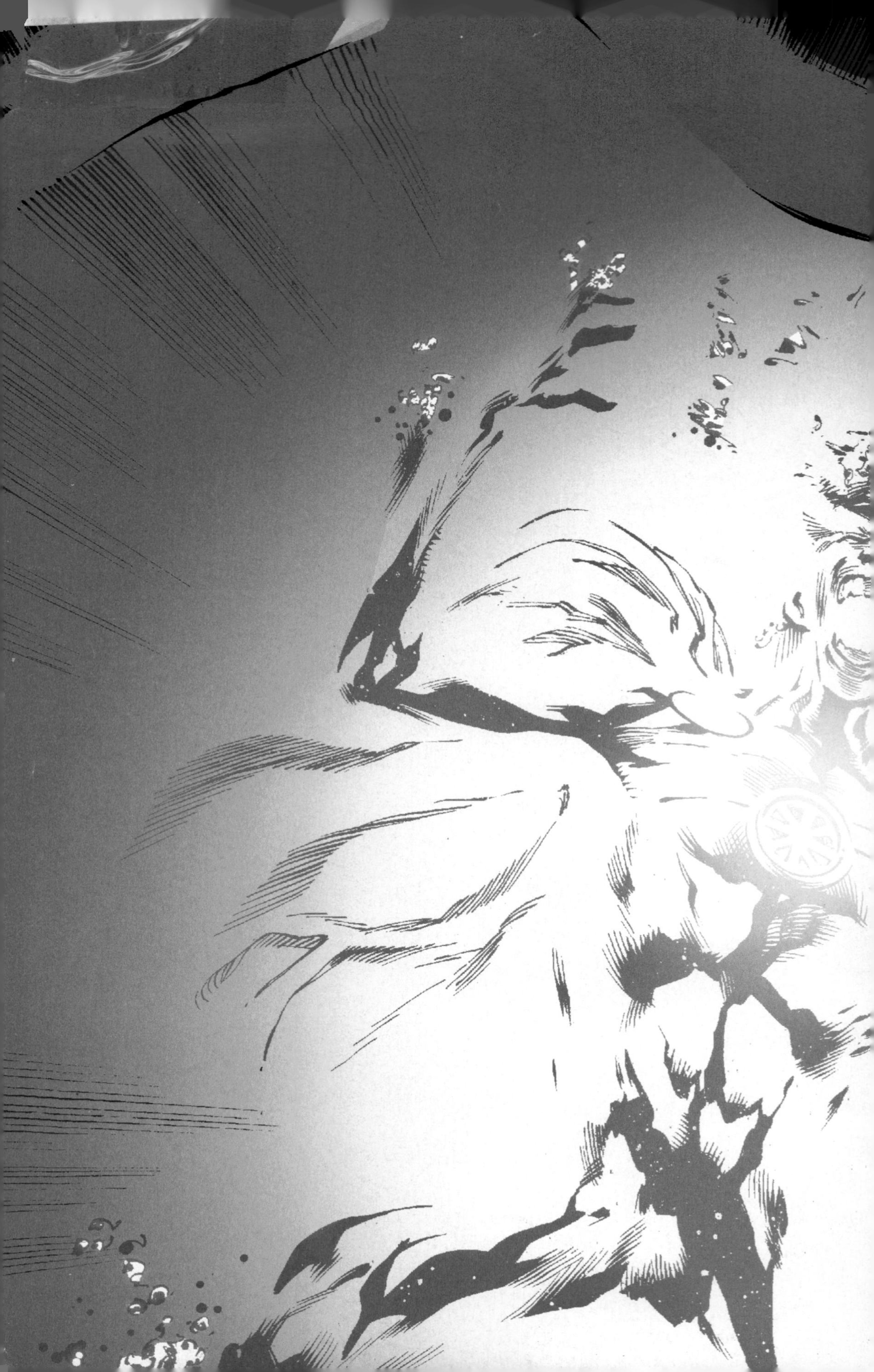

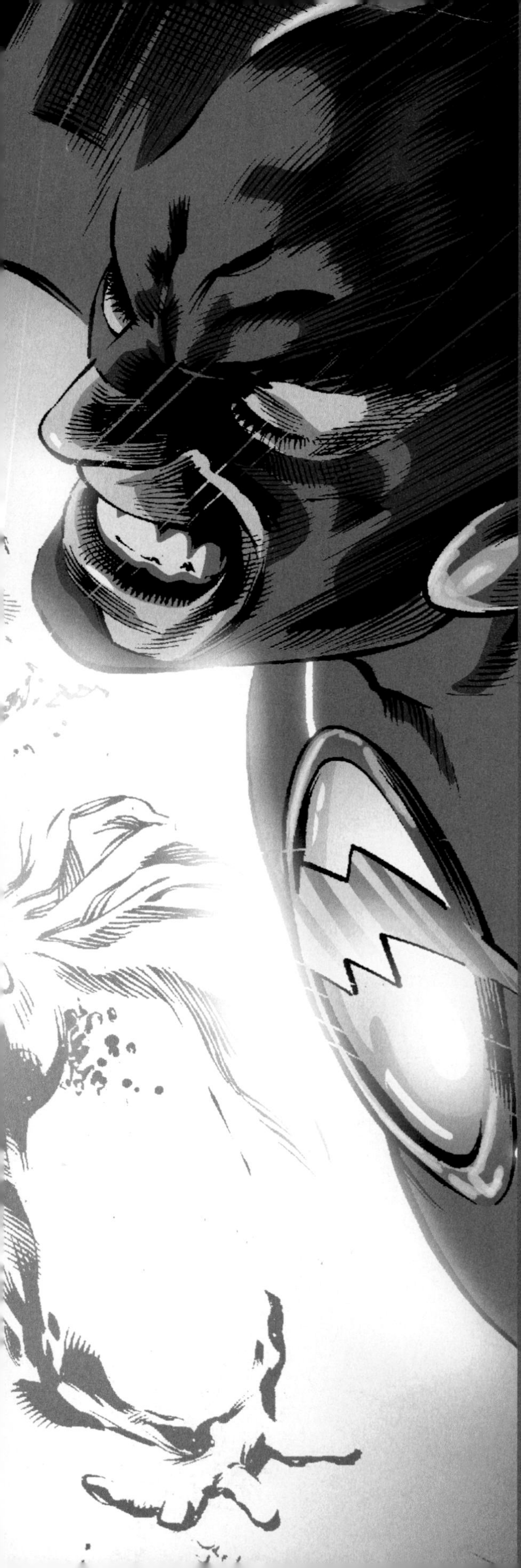

MARTIAN MANHUNTER

VOLUME 1
THE EPIPHANY

WRITTEN BY
ROB WILLIAMS

PENCILS BY
EDDY BARROWS
DIÓGENES NEVES

INKS BY
EBER FERREIRA
MARC DEERING

COLOR BY
GABE ELTAEB

LETTERS BY
TOM NAPOLITANO

COLLECTION COVER ART BY
ERIC CANETE

MARTIAN MANHUNTER CREATED BY
JOSEPH SAMACHSON
& JOE CERTA

ANDY KHOURI Editor - Original Series
HARVEY RICHARDS Associate Editor - Original Series
AMEDEO TURTURRO Assistant Editor - Original Series
JEB WOODARD Group Editor - Collected Editions
PAUL SANTOS Editor - Collected Edition
STEVE COOK Design Director - Books
DAMIAN RYLAND Publication Design

BOB HARRAS Senior VP - Editor-in-Chief, DC Comics

DIANE NELSON President
DAN DIDIO and JIM LEE Co-Publishers
GEOFF JOHNS Chief Creative Officer
AMIT DESAI Senior VP - Marketing & Global Franchise Management
NAIRI GARDINER Senior VP - Finance
SAM ADES VP - Digital Marketing
BOBBIE CHASE VP - Talent Development
MARK CHIARELLO Senior VP - Art, Design & Collected Editions
JOHN CUNNINGHAM VP - Content Strategy
ANNE DEPIES VP - Strategy Planning & Reporting
DON FALLETTI VP - Manufacturing Operations
LAWRENCE GANEM VP - Editorial Administration & Talent Relations
ALISON GILL Senior VP - Manufacturing & Operations
HANK KANALZ Senior VP - Editorial Strategy & Administration
JAY KOGAN VP - Legal Affairs
DEREK MADDALENA Senior VP - Sales & Business Development
JACK MAHAN VP - Business Affairs
DAN MIRON VP - Sales Planning & Trade Development
NICK NAPOLITANO VP - Manufacturing Administration
CAROL ROEDER VP - Marketing
EDDIE SCANNELL VP - Mass Account & Digital Sales
COURTNEY SIMMONS Senior VP - Publicity & Communications
JIM (SKI) SOKOLOWSKI VP - Comic Book Specialty & Newsstand Sales
SANDY YI Senior VP - Global Franchise Management

MARTIAN MANHUNTER VOLUME 1: THE EPIPHANY

DC Comics, 2900 West Alameda Avenue, Burbank, CA 91505
Printed by RR Donnelley, Salem, VA, USA. 1/22/16. First Printing.
ISBN: 978-1-4012-6151-1

Library of Congress Cataloging-in-Publication Data is Available.

PEFC Certified
Printed on paper from sustainably managed forests and controlled sources
PEFC/29-31-75
www.pefc.org

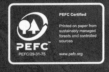

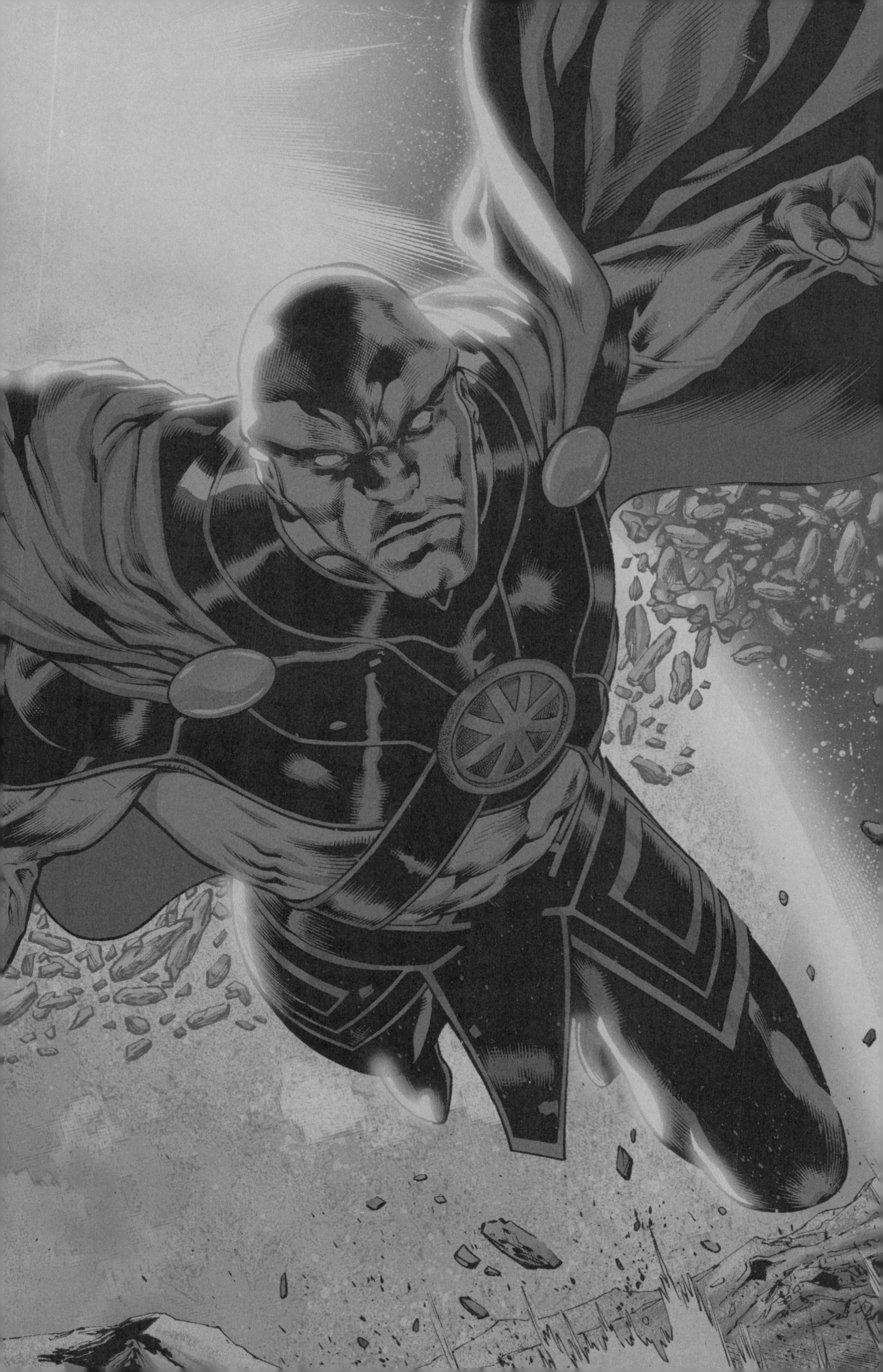

DIVERGENCE

MARTIAN MANHUNTER

J'onn J'onzz always said he was the last of his kind. He lied. When Mars launches a full-scale invasion of Earth, the Manhunter will have to decide where his loyalties lie.

ROB WILLIAMS Writer
EDDY BARROWS Penciller
EBER FERREIRA Inker
GABE ELTAEB Colorist
TOM NAPOLITANO Letterer

DC COMICS™

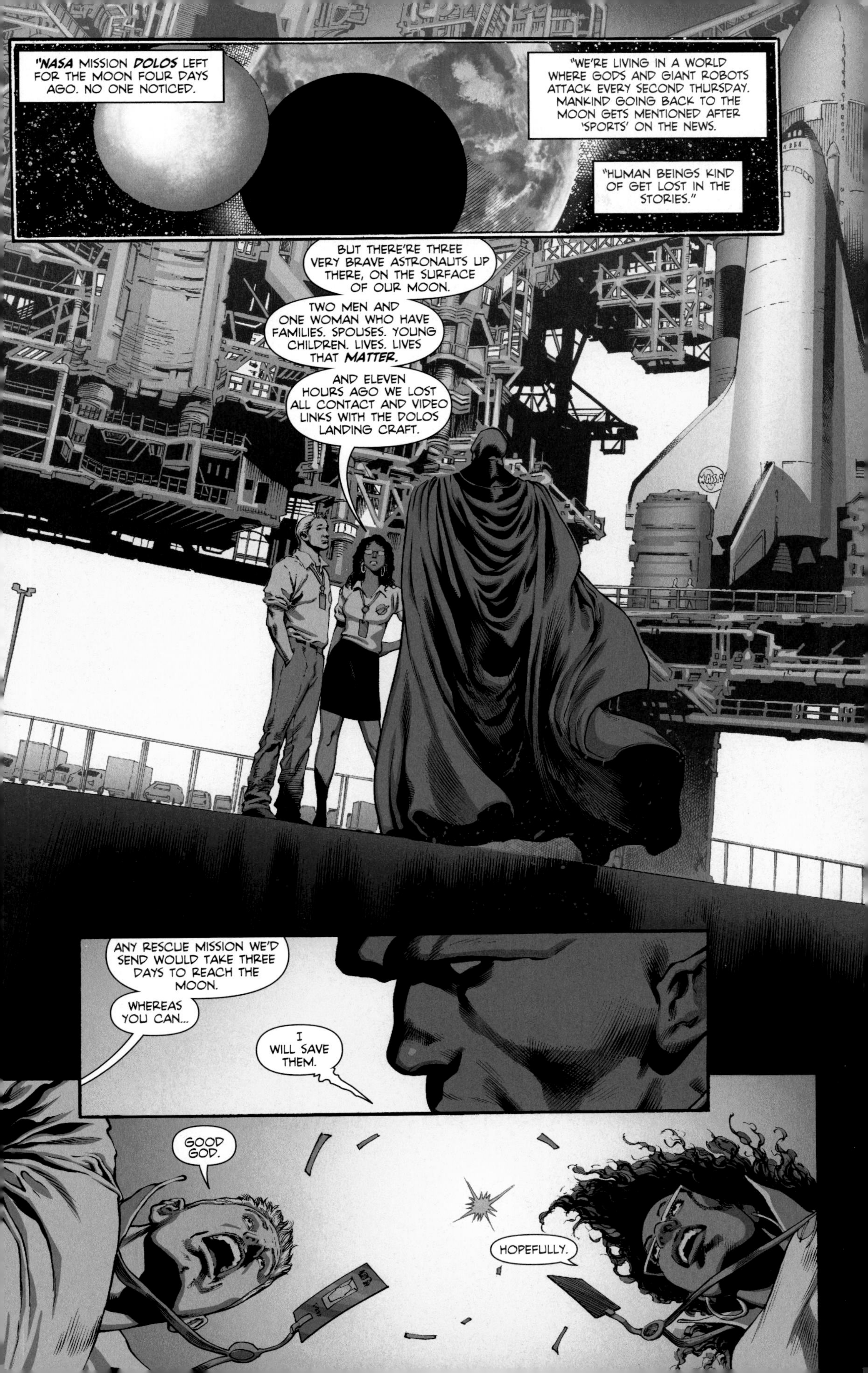
"NASA MISSION DOLOS LEFT FOR THE MOON FOUR DAYS AGO. NO ONE NOTICED.
"WE'RE LIVING IN A WORLD WHERE GODS AND GIANT ROBOTS ATTACK EVERY SECOND THURSDAY. MANKIND GOING BACK TO THE MOON GETS MENTIONED AFTER 'SPORTS' ON THE NEWS.
"HUMAN BEINGS KIND OF GET LOST IN THE STORIES."
BUT THERE'RE THREE VERY BRAVE ASTRONAUTS UP THERE, ON THE SURFACE OF OUR MOON.
TWO MEN AND ONE WOMAN WHO HAVE FAMILIES. SPOUSES. YOUNG CHILDREN. LIVES. LIVES THAT MATTER.
AND ELEVEN HOURS AGO WE LOST ALL CONTACT AND VIDEO LINKS WITH THE DOLOS LANDING CRAFT.
ANY RESCUE MISSION WE'D SEND WOULD TAKE THREE DAYS TO REACH THE MOON.
WHEREAS YOU CAN...
I WILL SAVE THEM.
GOOD GOD.
HOPEFULLY.

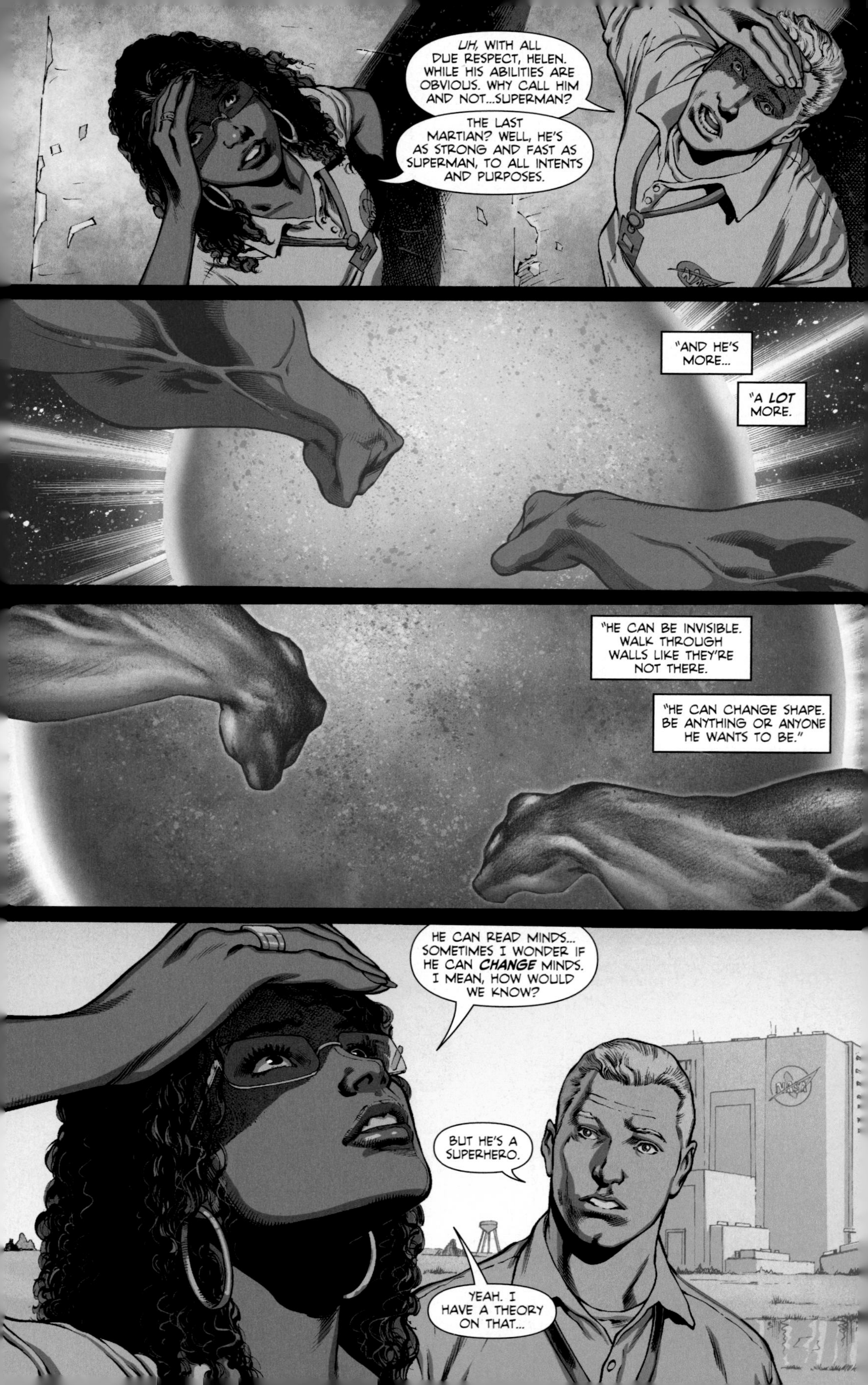
UH, WITH ALL DUE RESPECT, HELEN. WHILE HIS ABILITIES ARE OBVIOUS. WHY CALL HIM AND NOT...SUPERMAN?
THE LAST MARTIAN? WELL, HE'S AS STRONG AND FAST AS SUPERMAN, TO ALL INTENTS AND PURPOSES.
"AND HE'S MORE...
"A LOT MORE.
"HE CAN BE INVISIBLE. WALK THROUGH WALLS LIKE THEY'RE NOT THERE.
"HE CAN CHANGE SHAPE. BE ANYTHING OR ANYONE HE WANTS TO BE."
HE CAN READ MINDS... SOMETIMES I WONDER IF HE CAN CHANGE MINDS. I MEAN, HOW WOULD WE KNOW?
BUT HE'S A SUPERHERO.
YEAH. I HAVE A THEORY ON THAT...

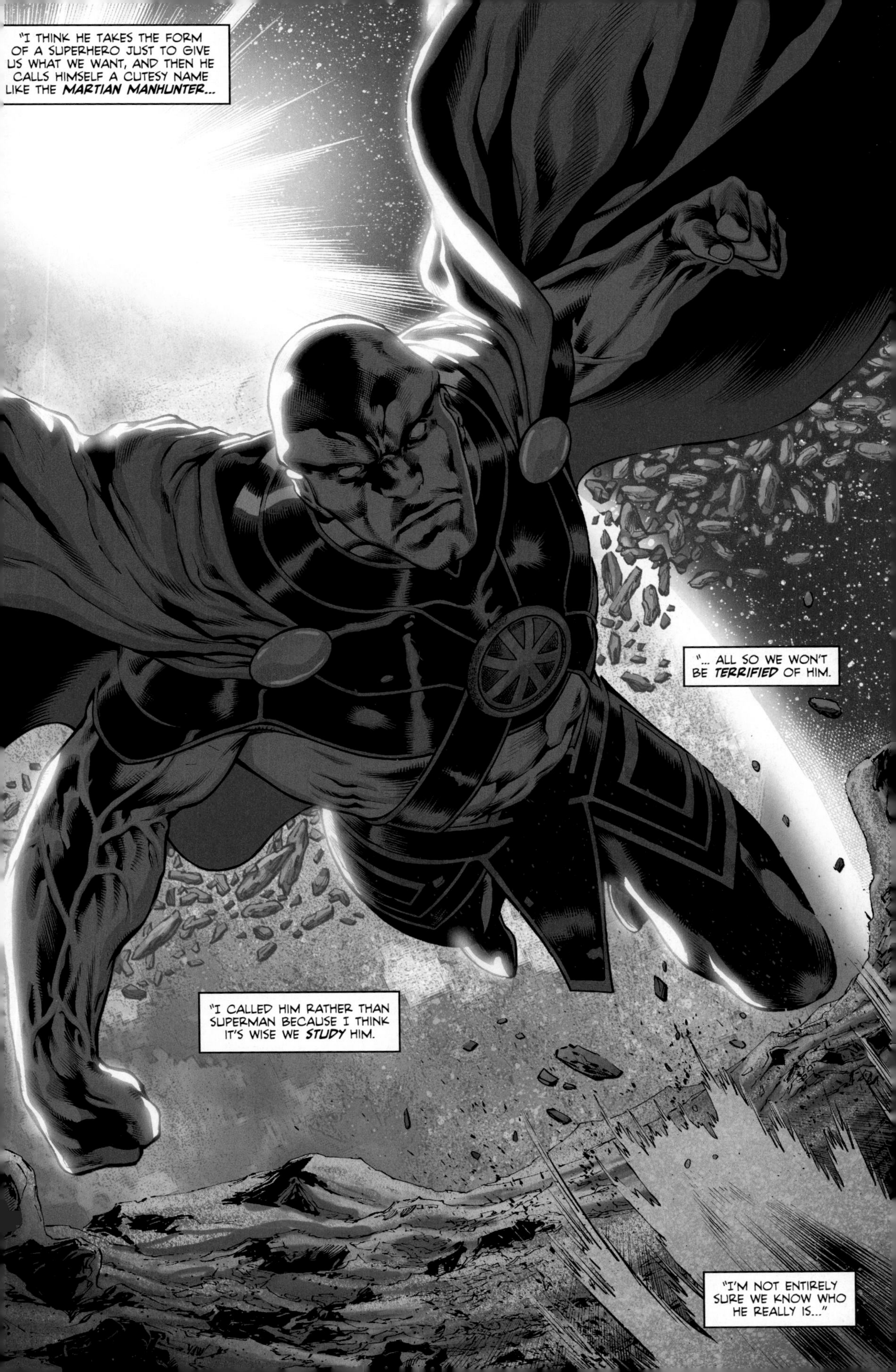
"I THINK HE TAKES THE FORM OF A SUPERHERO JUST TO GIVE US WHAT WE WANT, AND THEN HE CALLS HIMSELF A CUTESY NAME LIKE THE MARTIAN MANHUNTER...
"... ALL SO WE WON'T BE TERRIFIED OF HIM.
"I CALLED HIM RATHER THAN SUPERMAN BECAUSE I THINK IT'S WISE WE STUDY HIM.
"I'M NOT ENTIRELY SURE WE KNOW WHO HE REALLY IS..."

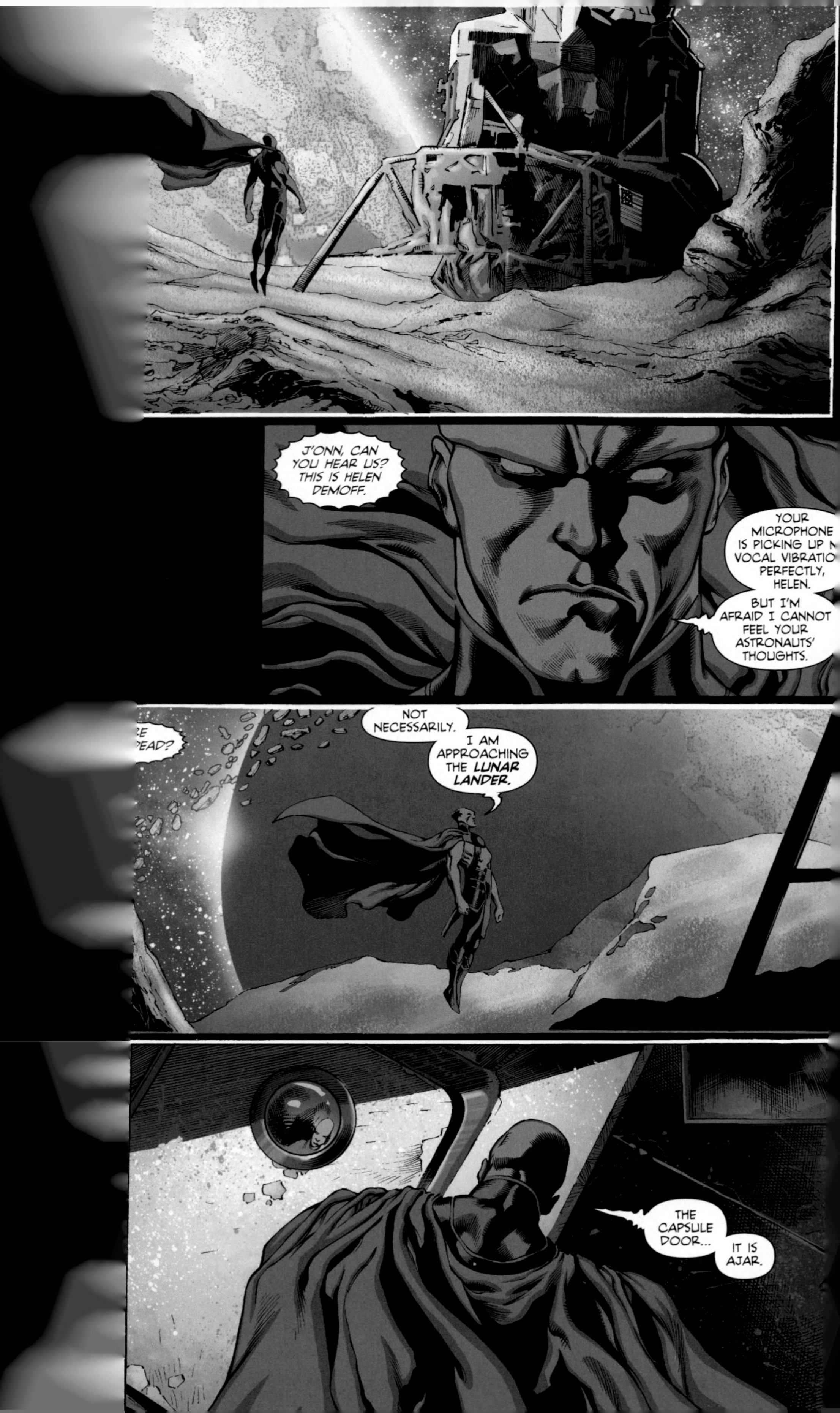
J'ONN, CAN YOU HEAR US? THIS IS HELEN DEMOFF.
YOUR MICROPHONE IS PICKING UP VOCAL VIBRATIO PERFECTLY, HELEN.
BUT I'M AFRAID I CANNOT FEEL YOUR ASTRONAUTS' THOUGHTS.
EAD?
NOT NECESSARILY.
I AM APPROACHING THE LUNAR LANDER.
THE CAPSULE DOOR...
IT IS AJAR.

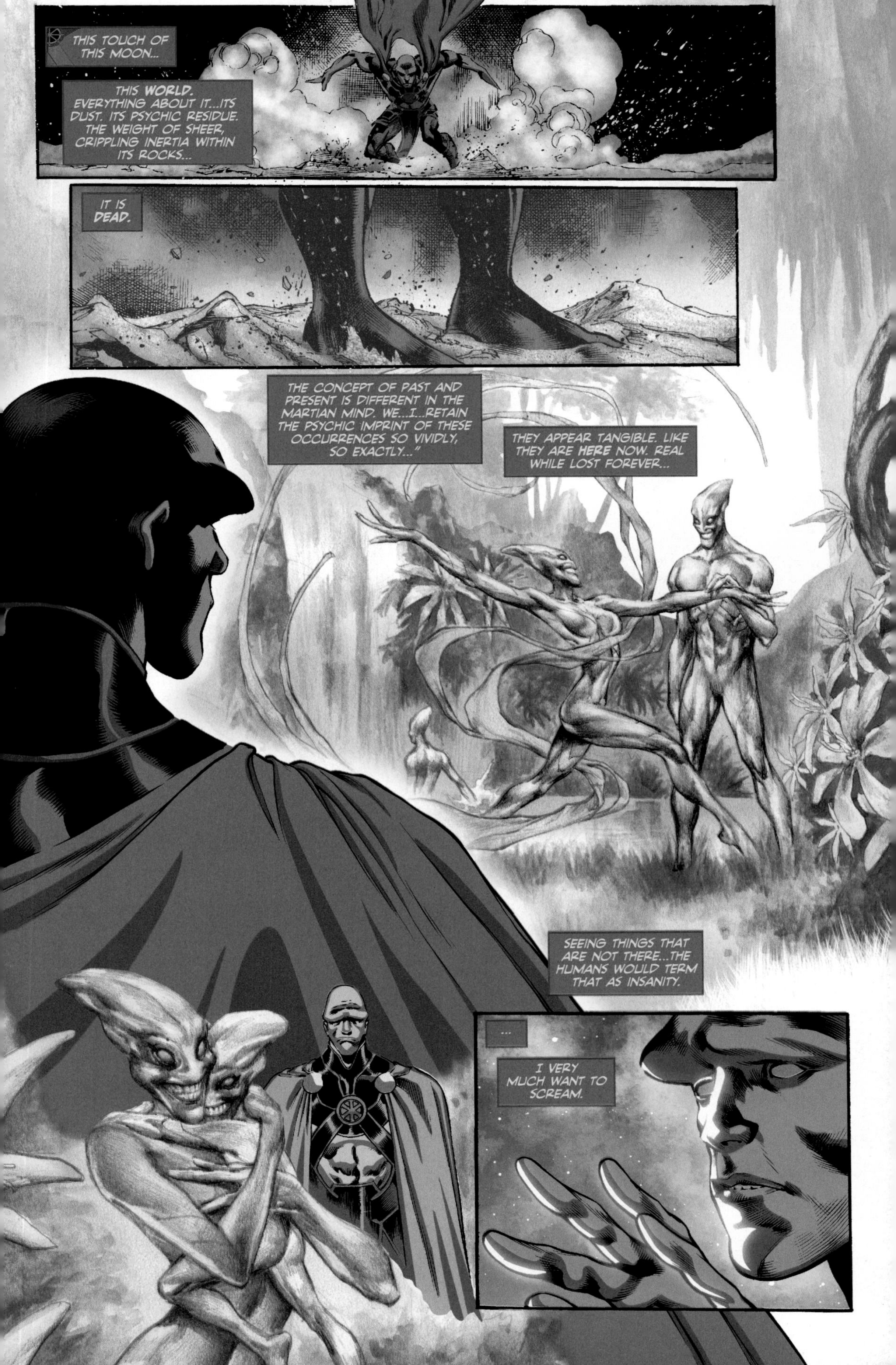
THIS TOUCH OF THIS MOON...
THIS WORLD. EVERYTHING ABOUT IT...ITS DUST. ITS PSYCHIC RESIDUE. THE WEIGHT OF SHEER, CRIPPLING INERTIA WITHIN ITS ROCKS...
IT IS DEAD.
THE CONCEPT OF PAST AND PRESENT IS DIFFERENT IN THE MARTIAN MIND. WE...I...RETAIN THE PSYCHIC IMPRINT OF THESE OCCURRENCES SO VIVIDLY, SO EXACTLY..."
THEY APPEAR TANGIBLE. LIKE THEY ARE HERE NOW. REAL WHILE LOST FOREVER...
SEEING THINGS THAT ARE NOT THERE...THE HUMANS WOULD TERM THAT AS INSANITY.
...
I VERY MUCH WANT TO SCREAM.

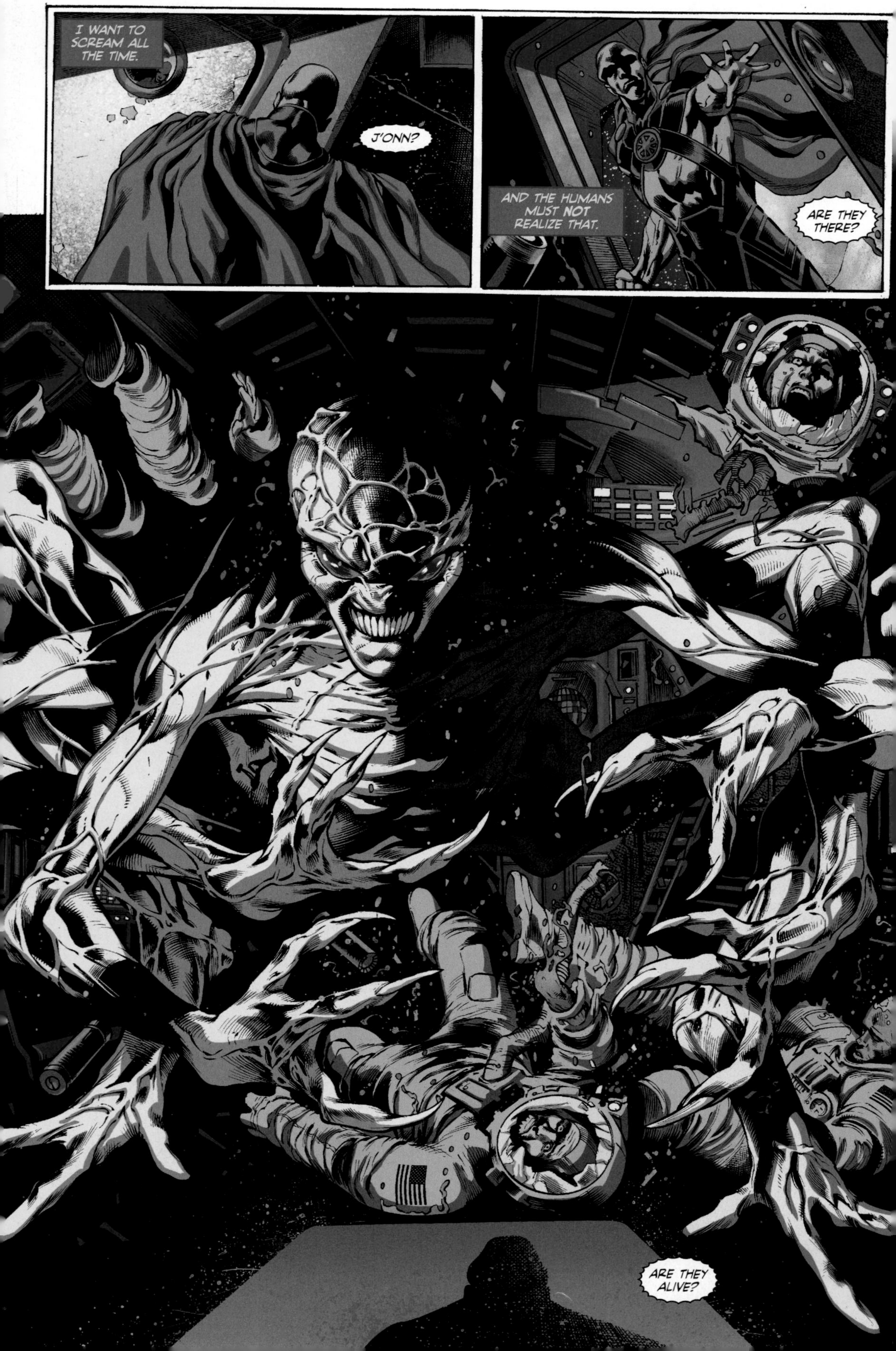
I WANT TO SCREAM ALL THE TIME.
J'ONN?
AND THE HUMANS MUST NOT REALIZE THAT.
ARE THEY THERE?
ARE THEY ALIVE?

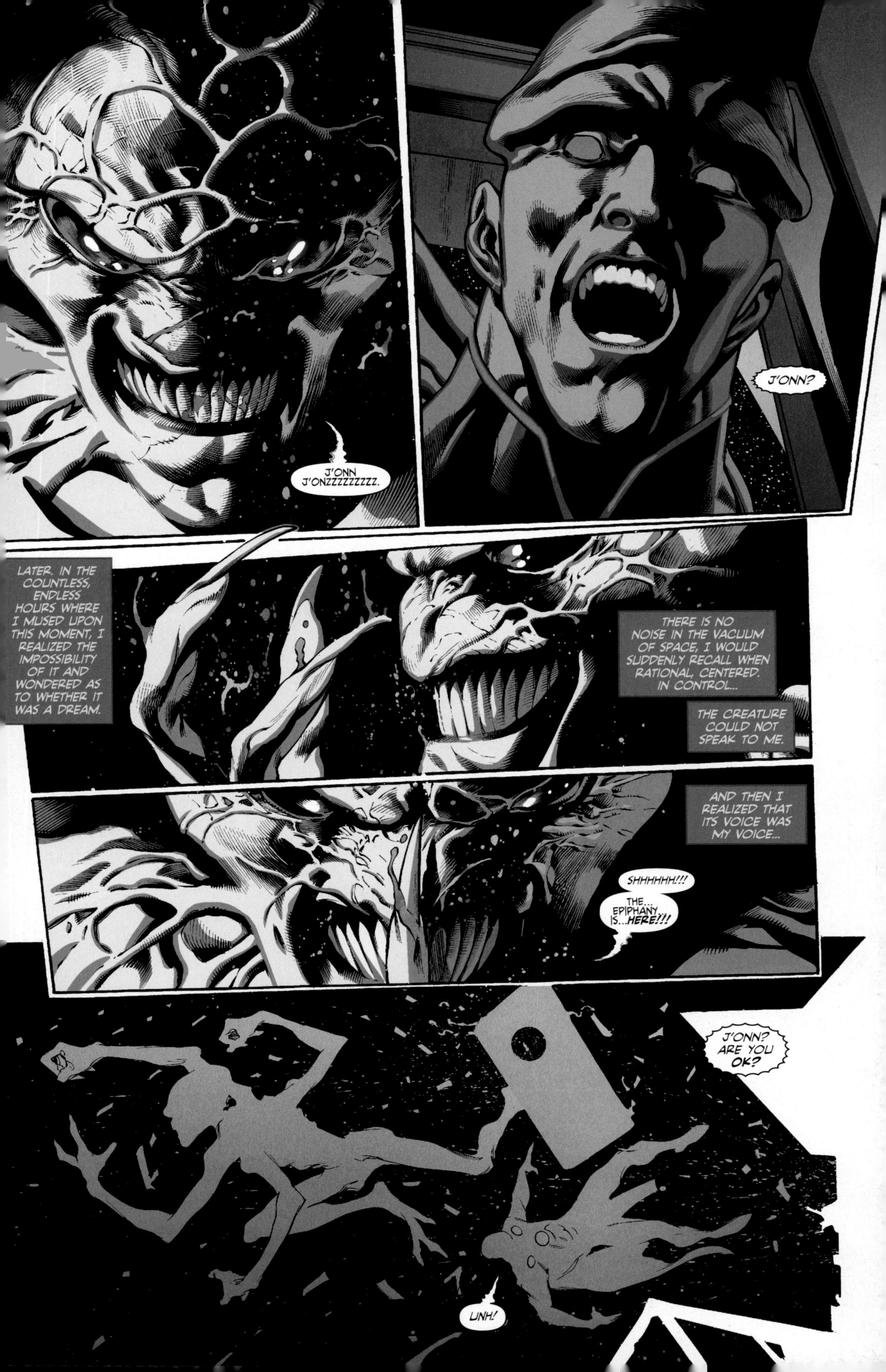
J'ONN J'ONZZZZZZZZZ.
J'ONN?
LATER. IN THE COUNTLESS, ENDLESS HOURS WHERE I MUSED UPON THIS MOMENT, I REALIZED THE IMPOSSIBILITY OF IT AND WONDERED AS TO WHETHER IT WAS A DREAM.
THERE IS NO NOISE IN THE VACUUM OF SPACE, I WOULD SUDDENLY RECALL WHEN RATIONAL, CENTERED. IN CONTROL...
THE CREATURE COULD NOT SPEAK TO ME.
AND THEN I REALIZED THAT ITS VOICE WAS MY VOICE...
SHHHHHH!!!
THE... EPIPHANY IS...HERE!!!
J'ONN? ARE YOU OK?
UNH!

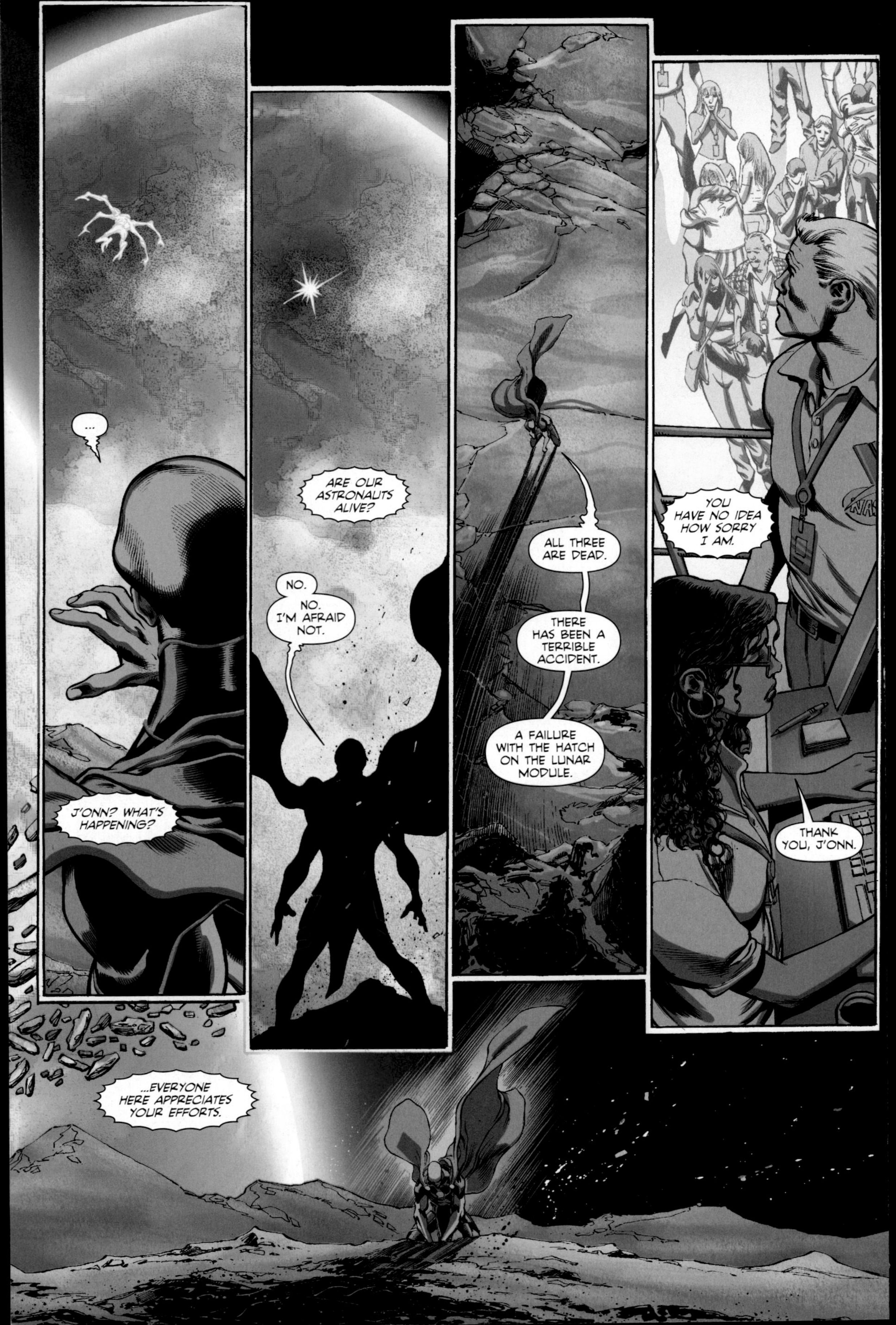
...
J'ONN? WHAT'S HAPPENING?
ARE OUR ASTRONAUTS ALIVE?
NO.
NO. I'M AFRAID NOT.
ALL THREE ARE DEAD.
THERE HAS BEEN A TERRIBLE ACCIDENT.
A FAILURE WITH THE HATCH ON THE LUNAR MODULE.
YOU HAVE NO IDEA HOW SORRY I AM.
THANK YOU, J'ONN.
...EVERYONE HERE APPRECIATES YOUR EFFORTS.

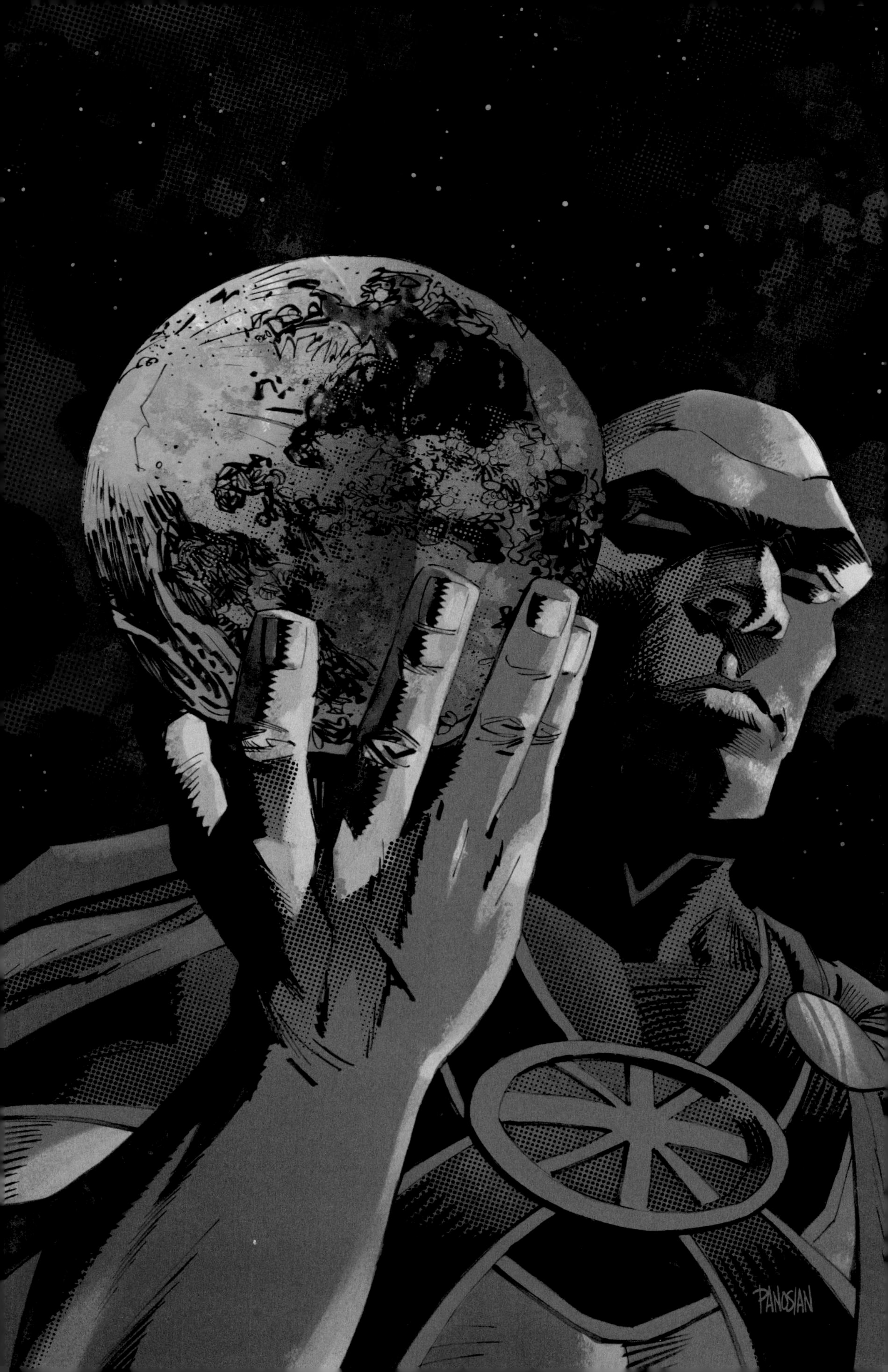
PANOSIAN

WEAPON!
cover by **DAN PANOSIAN**

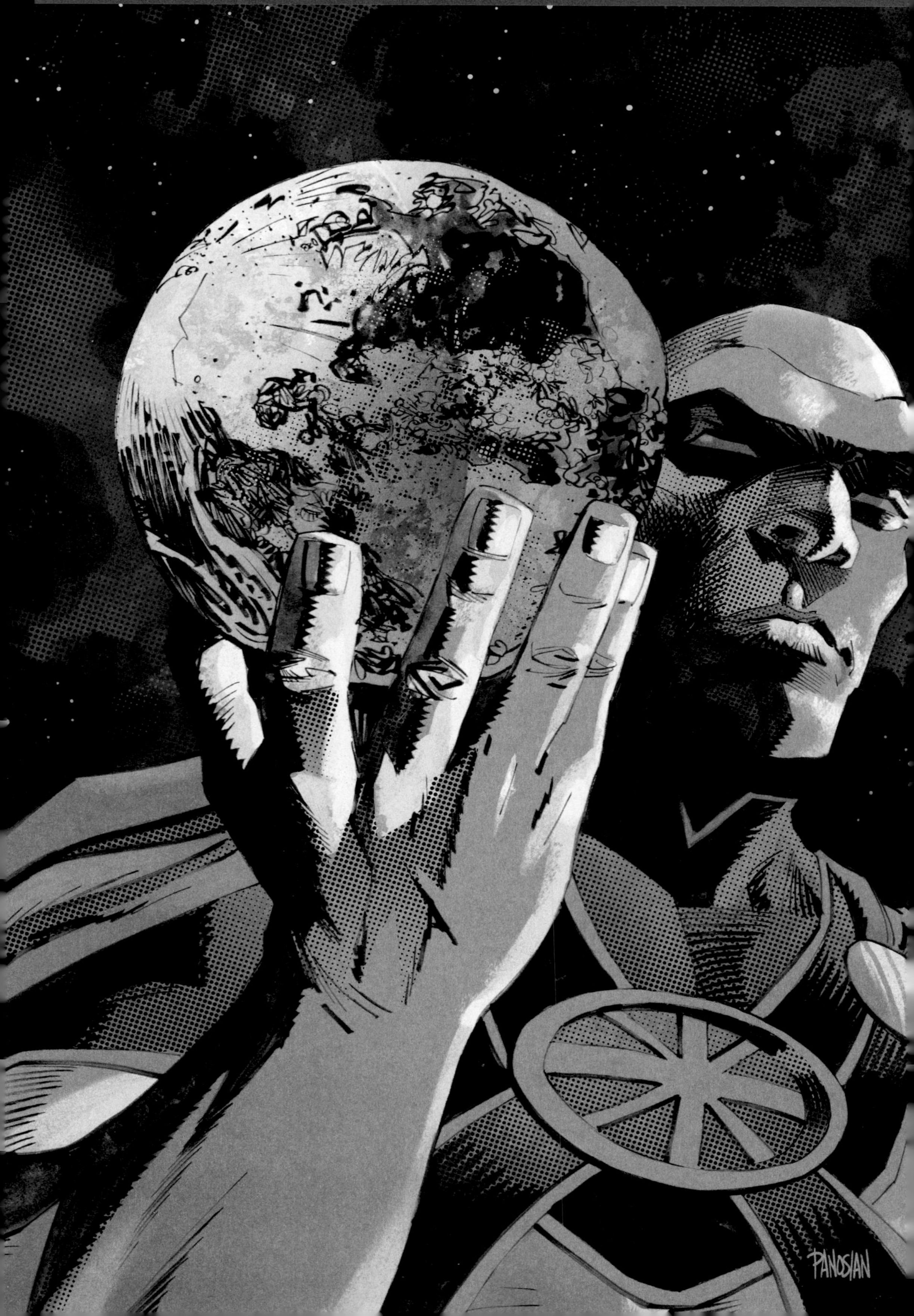

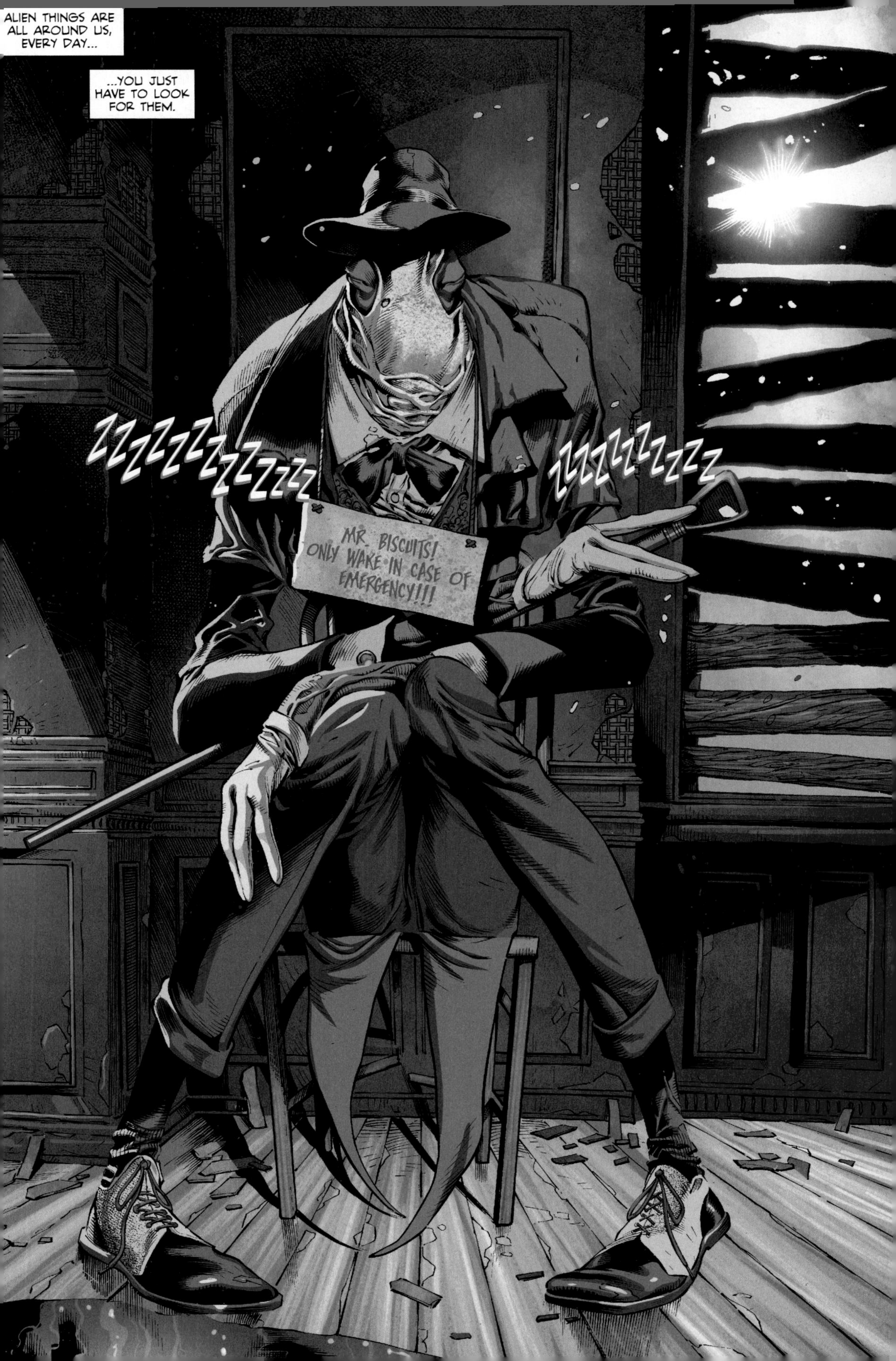
ALIEN THINGS ARE ALL AROUND US, EVERY DAY...
...YOU JUST HAVE TO LOOK FOR THEM.
ZZZZZZZZZZZZZZ
ZZZZZZZZZZZZZ
MR. BISCUITS! ONLY WAKE IN CASE OF EMERGENCY!!!

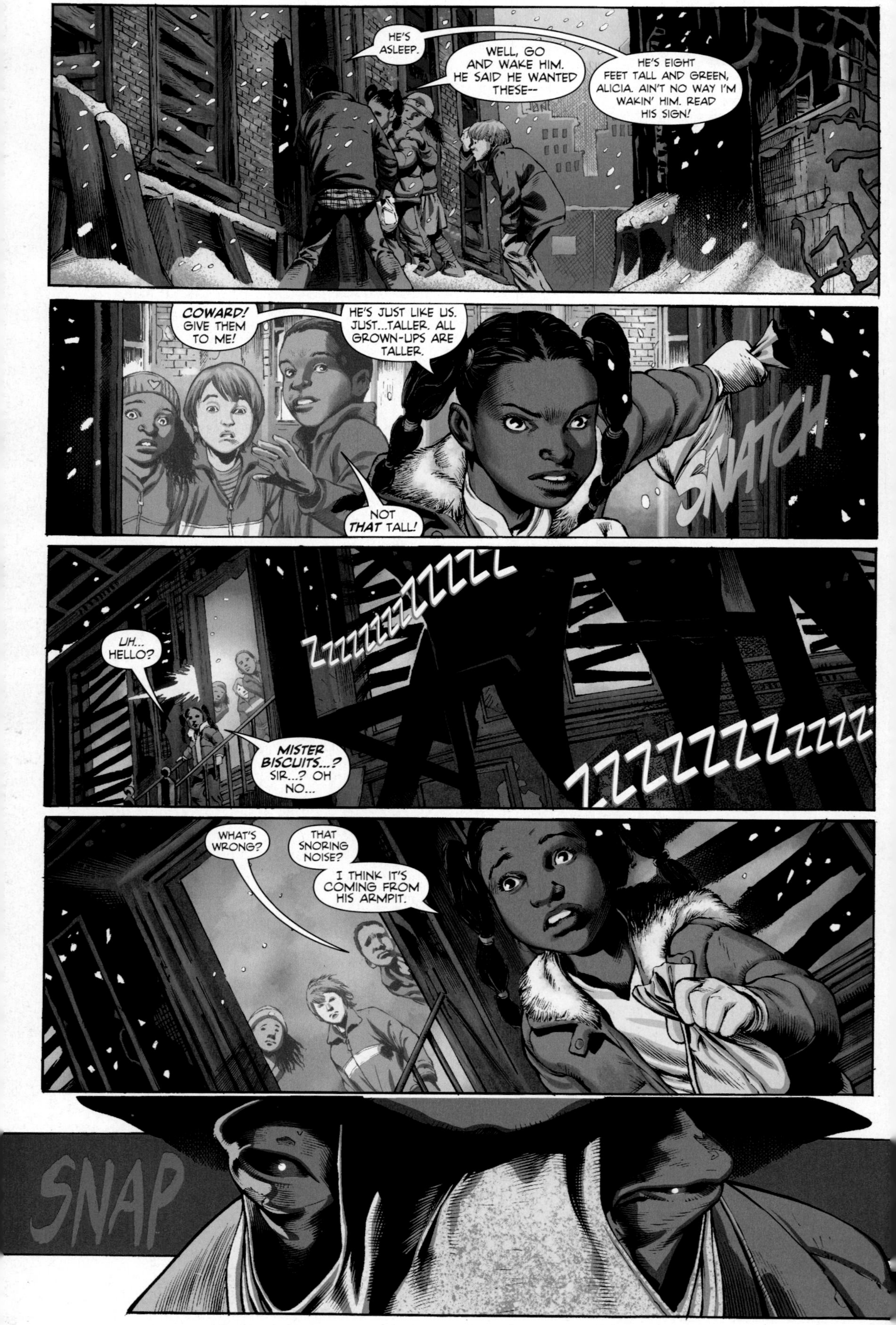
HE'S ASLEEP.
WELL, GO AND WAKE HIM. HE SAID HE WANTED THESE--
HE'S EIGHT FEET TALL AND GREEN, ALICIA. AIN'T NO WAY I'M WAKIN' HIM. READ HIS SIGN!
COWARD! GIVE THEM TO ME!
HE'S JUST LIKE US. JUST...TALLER. ALL GROWN-UPS ARE TALLER.
NOT THAT TALL!
SNATCH
UH... HELLO?
ZZZZZZZZZZZZZZZ
MISTER BISCUITS...? SIR...? OH NO...
ZZZZZZZZZZZZZZ
WHAT'S WRONG?
THAT SNORING NOISE?
I THINK IT'S COMING FROM HIS ARMPIT.
SNAP

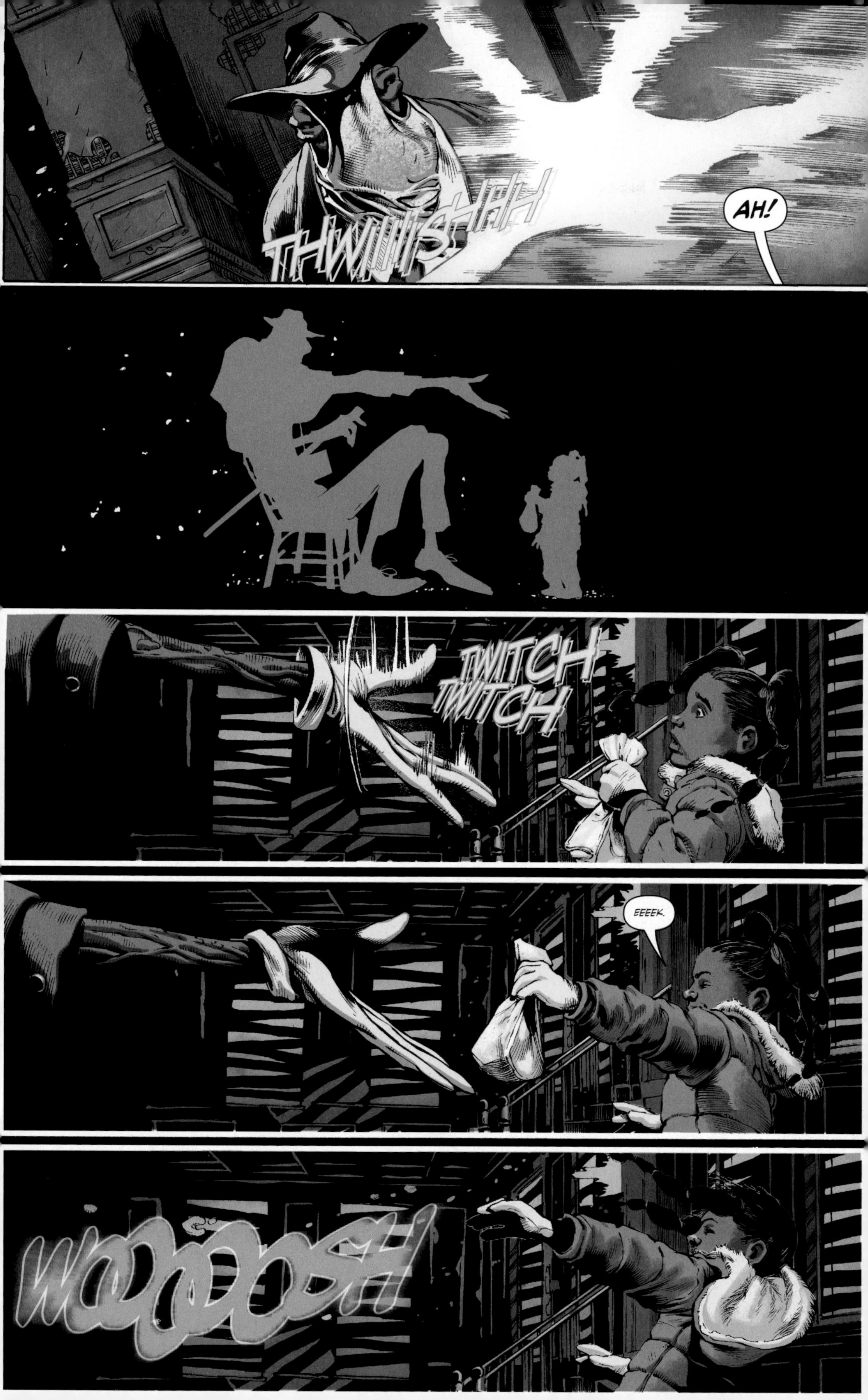
THWIIIISHHH
AH!
TWITCH TWITCH
EEEEK.
WOOOOSH

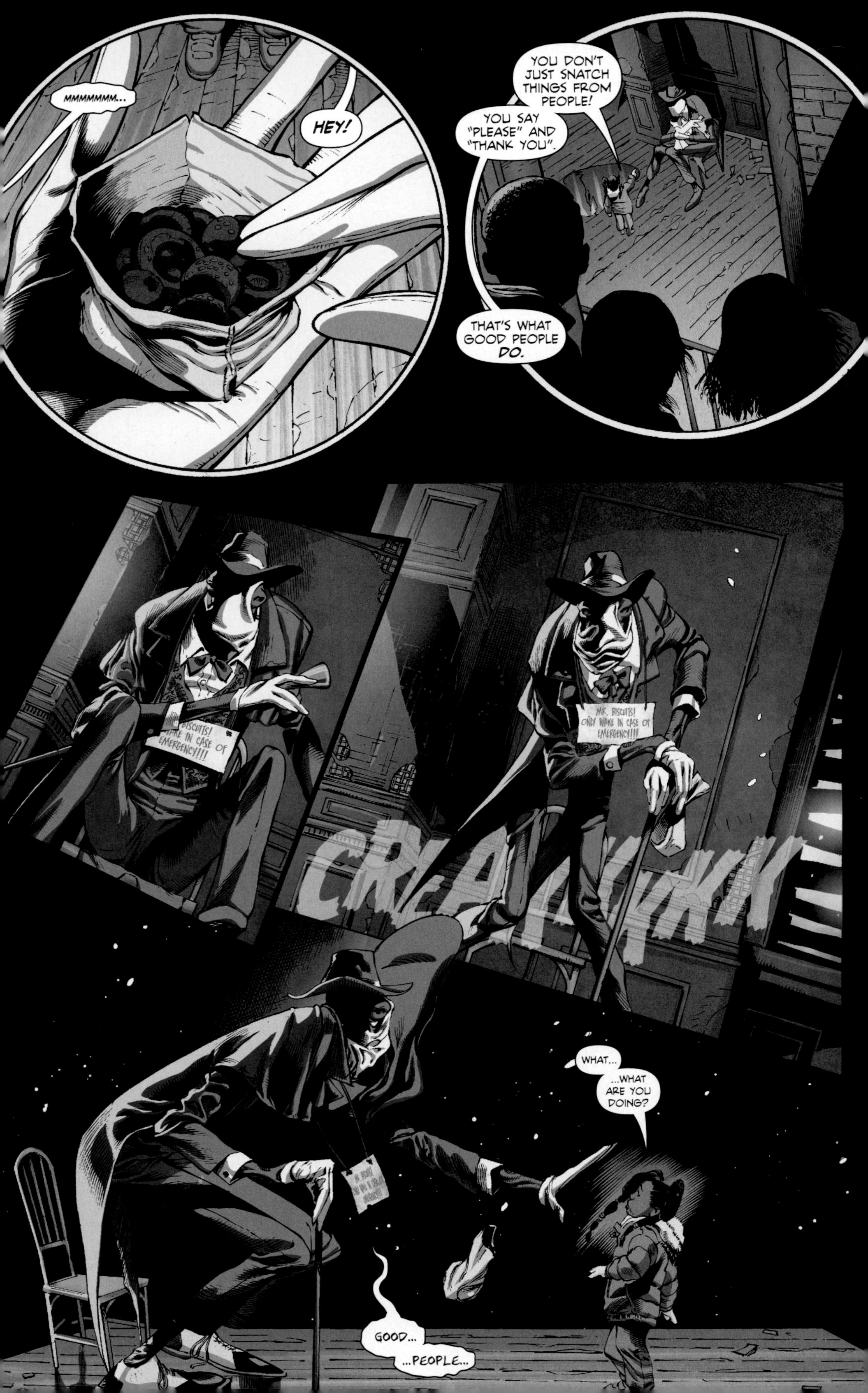
MMMMMMM...
HEY!
YOU DON'T JUST SNATCH THINGS FROM PEOPLE!
YOU SAY "PLEASE" AND "THANK YOU".
THAT'S WHAT GOOD PEOPLE DO.
BISCUITS! WAKE IN CASE OF EMERGENCY!!!
MR. BISCUITS! ONLY WAKE IN CASE OF EMERGENCY!!!
WHAT...
...WHAT ARE YOU DOING?
GOOD...
...PEOPLE...

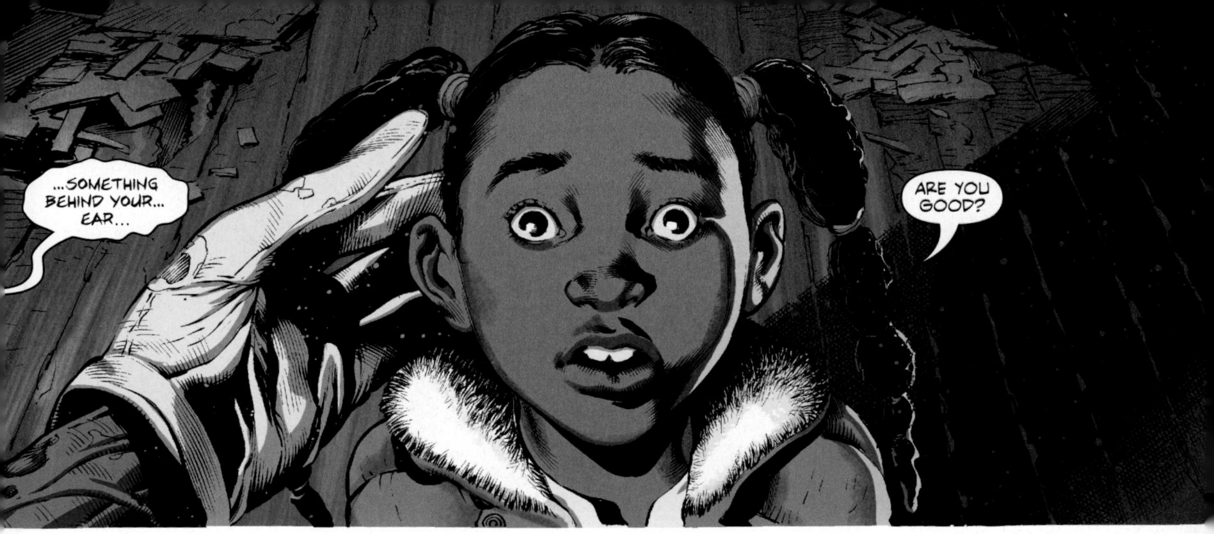
...SOMETHING BEHIND YOUR... EAR...
ARE YOU GOOD?

DC COMICS PROUDLY PRESENTS THE MARTIAN MANHUNTER IN

WEAPON!

ROB WILLIAMS WRITER EDDY BARROWS PENCILS
EBER FERREIRA INKS GABE ELTAEB COLORIST TOM NAPOLITANO LETTERER

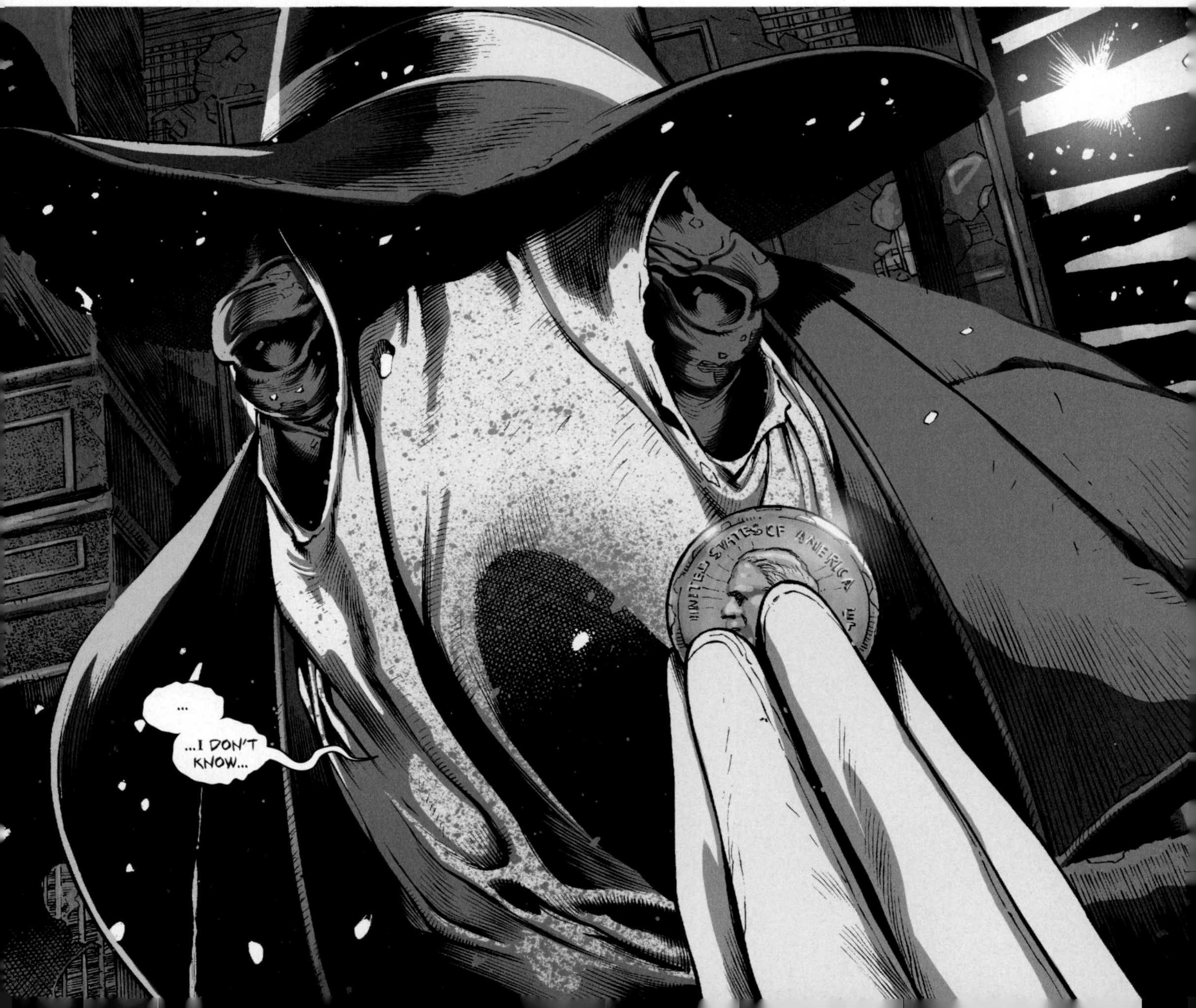
UNITED STATES OF AMERICA
...
...I DON'T KNOW...

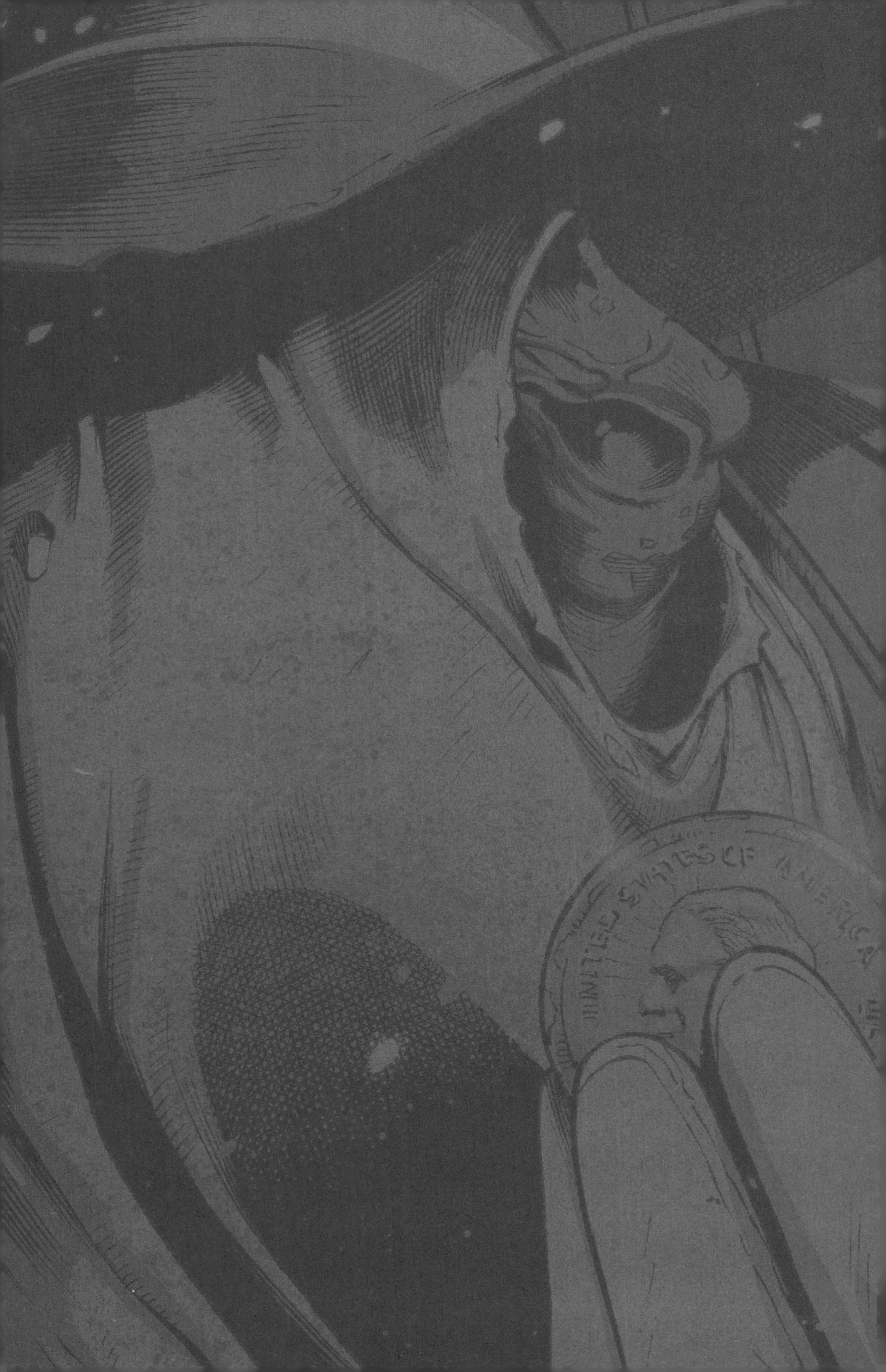
UNITED STATES OF AMERICA

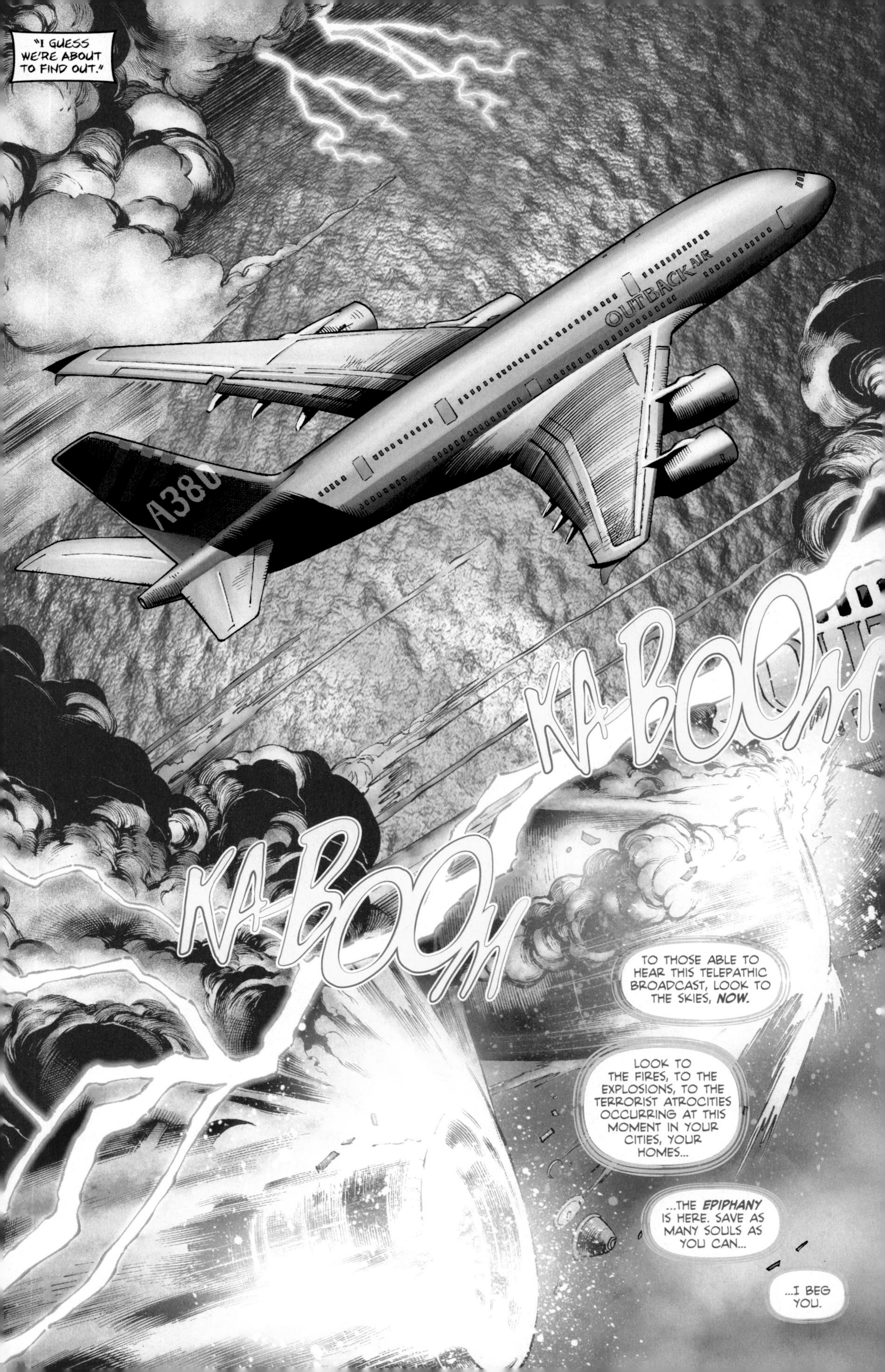
"I GUESS WE'RE ABOUT TO FIND OUT."
OUTBACK AIR
A380
KA-BOOM
KA-BOOM
TO THOSE ABLE TO HEAR THIS TELEPATHIC BROADCAST, LOOK TO THE SKIES, *NOW.*
LOOK TO THE FIRES, TO THE EXPLOSIONS, TO THE TERRORIST ATROCITIES OCCURRING AT THIS MOMENT IN YOUR CITIES, YOUR HOMES...
...THE *EPIPHANY* IS HERE. SAVE AS MANY SOULS AS YOU CAN...
...I BEG YOU.

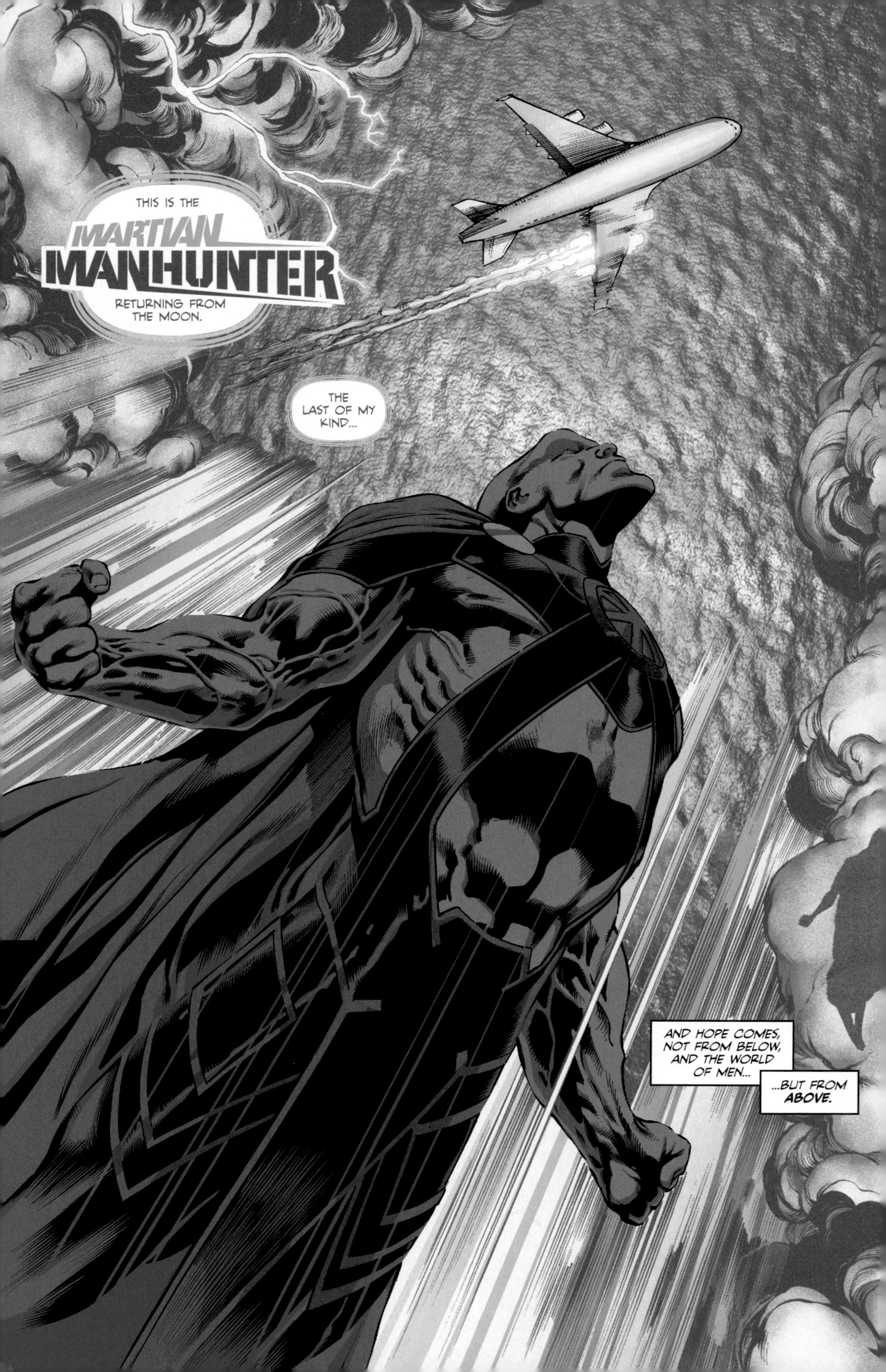
THIS IS THE
MARTIAN
MANHUNTER
RETURNING FROM THE MOON.
THE LAST OF MY KIND...
AND HOPE COMES, NOT FROM BELOW, AND THE WORLD OF MEN...
...BUT FROM ABOVE.

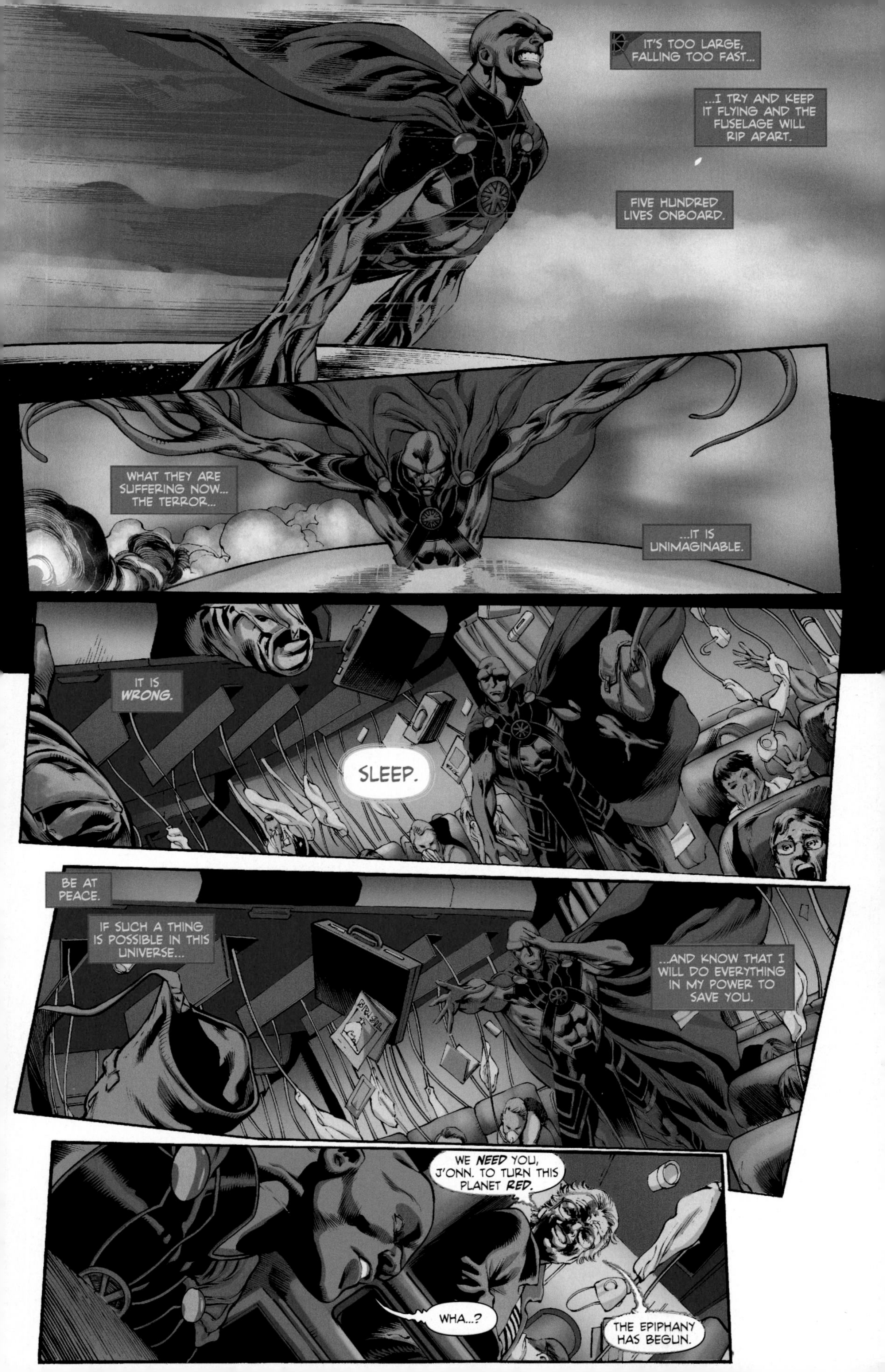
IT'S TOO LARGE, FALLING TOO FAST...
...I TRY AND KEEP IT FLYING AND THE FUSELAGE WILL RIP APART.
FIVE HUNDRED LIVES ONBOARD.
WHAT THEY ARE SUFFERING NOW... THE TERROR...
...IT IS UNIMAGINABLE.
IT IS *WRONG*.
SLEEP.
BE AT PEACE.
IF SUCH A THING IS POSSIBLE IN THIS UNIVERSE...
...AND KNOW THAT I WILL DO EVERYTHING IN MY POWER TO SAVE YOU.
WE **NEED** YOU, J'ONN. TO TURN THIS PLANET **RED**.
WHA...?
THE EPIPHANY HAS BEGUN.

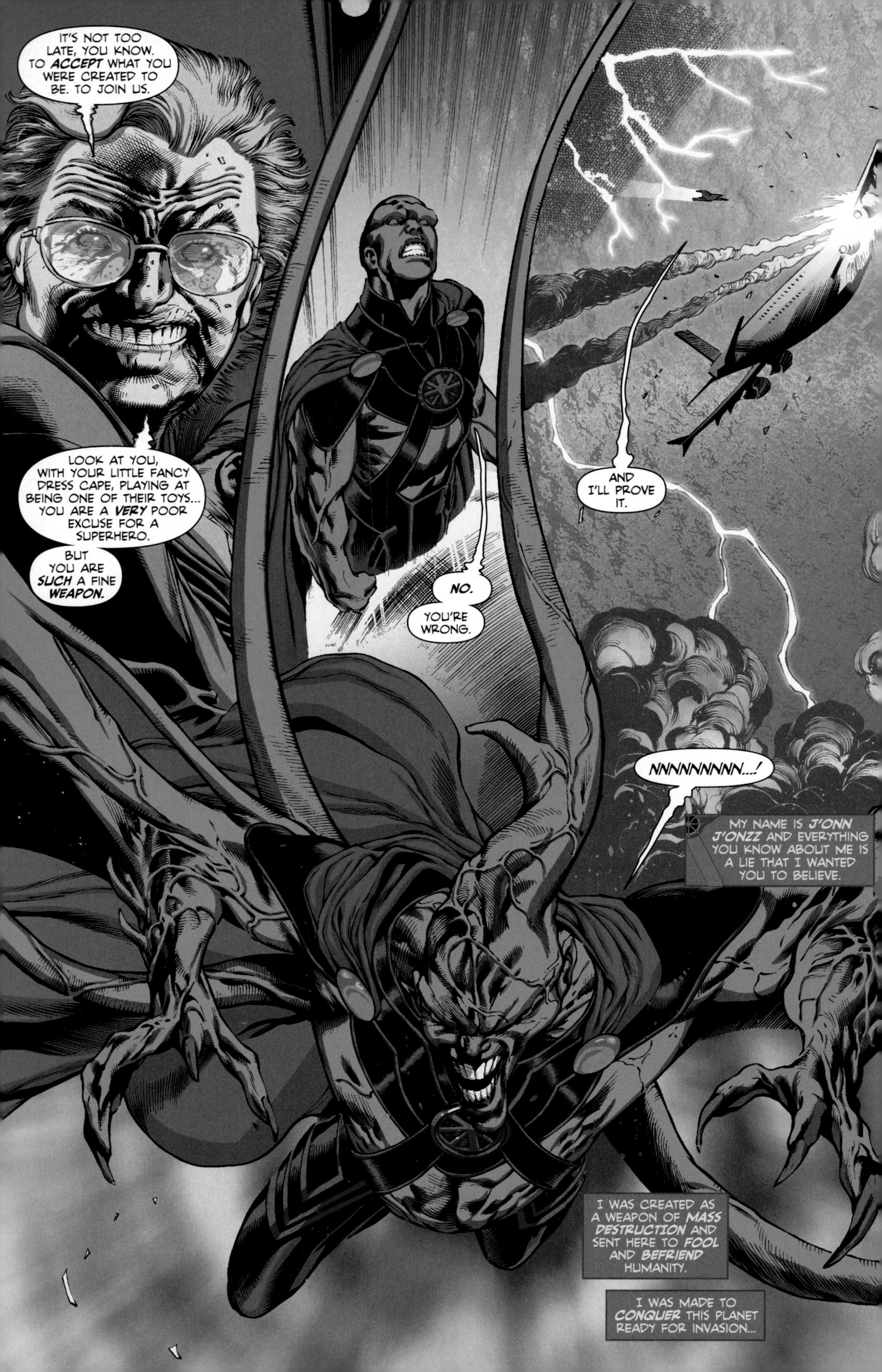
IT'S NOT TOO LATE, YOU KNOW. TO ACCEPT WHAT YOU WERE CREATED TO BE. TO JOIN US.
LOOK AT YOU, WITH YOUR LITTLE FANCY DRESS CAPE, PLAYING AT BEING ONE OF THEIR TOYS... YOU ARE A VERY POOR EXCUSE FOR A SUPERHERO.
BUT YOU ARE SUCH A FINE WEAPON.
NO.
YOU'RE WRONG.
AND I'LL PROVE IT.
NNNNNNNNN...!
MY NAME IS J'ONN J'ONZZ AND EVERYTHING YOU KNOW ABOUT ME IS A LIE THAT I WANTED YOU TO BELIEVE.
I WAS CREATED AS A WEAPON OF MASS DESTRUCTION AND SENT HERE TO FOOL AND BEFRIEND HUMANITY.
I WAS MADE TO CONQUER THIS PLANET READY FOR INVASION...

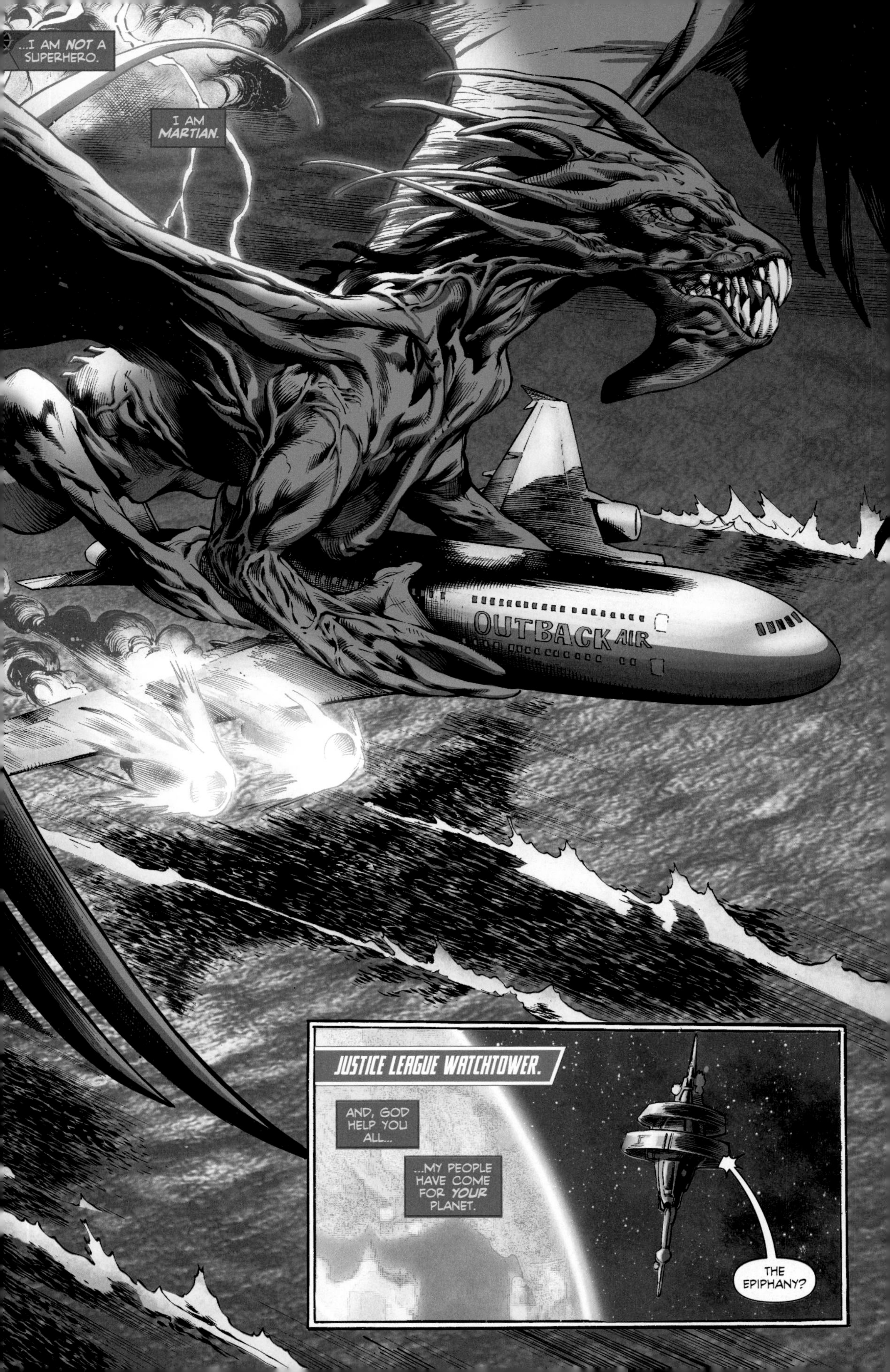
...I AM NOT A SUPERHERO.
I AM MARTIAN.
OUTBACK AIR
JUSTICE LEAGUE WATCHTOWER.
AND, GOD HELP YOU ALL...
...MY PEOPLE HAVE COME FOR YOUR PLANET.
THE EPIPHANY?

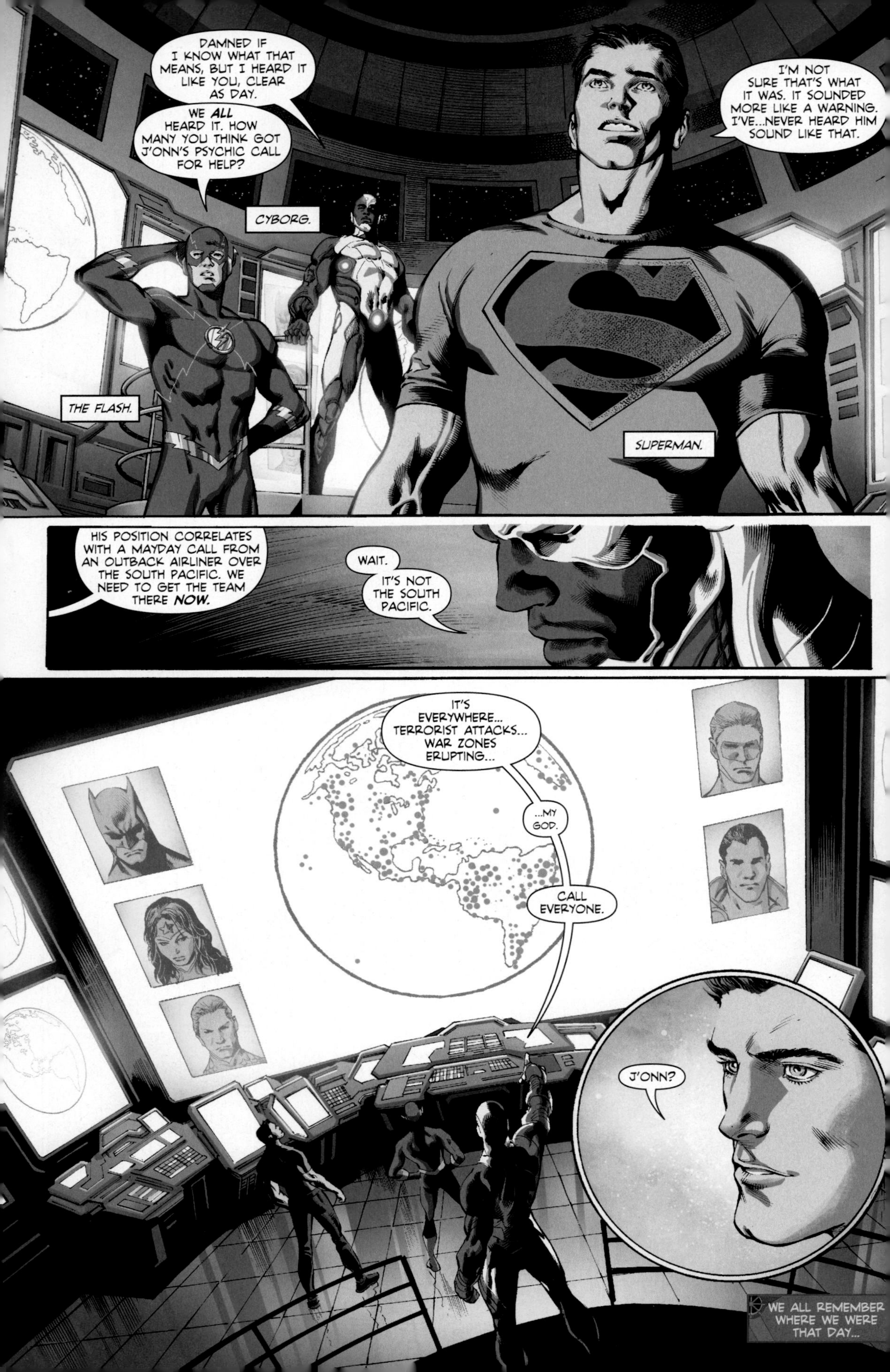
DAMNED IF I KNOW WHAT THAT MEANS, BUT I HEARD IT LIKE YOU, CLEAR AS DAY.
WE ALL HEARD IT. HOW MANY YOU THINK GOT J'ONN'S PSYCHIC CALL FOR HELP?
I'M NOT SURE THAT'S WHAT IT WAS. IT SOUNDED MORE LIKE A WARNING. I'VE...NEVER HEARD HIM SOUND LIKE THAT.
CYBORG.
THE FLASH.
SUPERMAN.
HIS POSITION CORRELATES WITH A MAYDAY CALL FROM AN OUTBACK AIRLINER OVER THE SOUTH PACIFIC. WE NEED TO GET THE TEAM THERE NOW.
WAIT.
IT'S NOT THE SOUTH PACIFIC.
IT'S EVERYWHERE... TERRORIST ATTACKS... WAR ZONES ERUPTING...
...MY GOD.
CALL EVERYONE.
J'ONN?
WE ALL REMEMBER WHERE WE WERE THAT DAY...

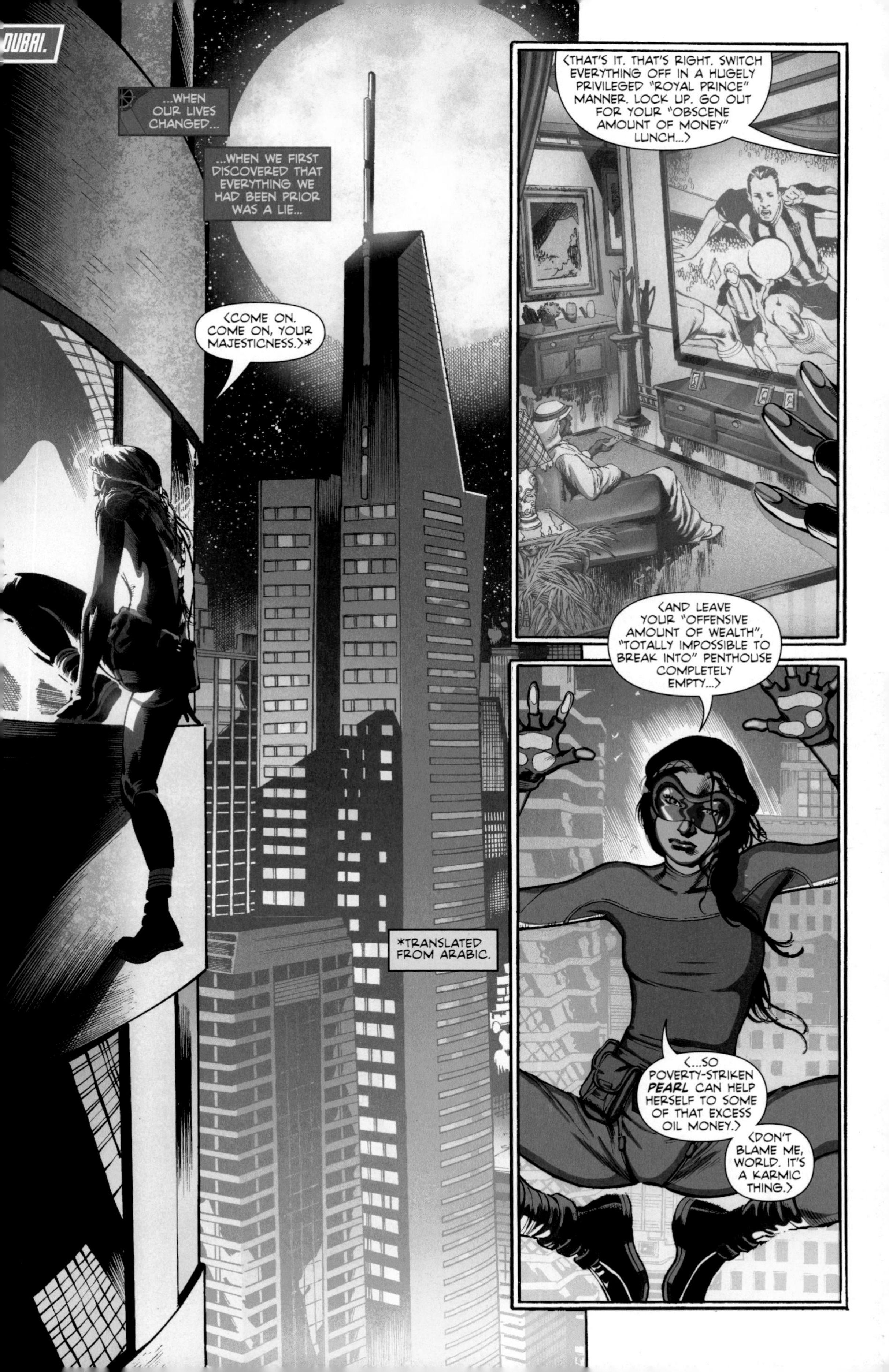
DUBAI.
...WHEN OUR LIVES CHANGED...
...WHEN WE FIRST DISCOVERED THAT EVERYTHING WE HAD BEEN PRIOR WAS A LIE...
<COME ON. COME ON, YOUR MAJESTICNESS.>*
*TRANSLATED FROM ARABIC.
<THAT'S IT. THAT'S RIGHT. SWITCH EVERYTHING OFF IN A HUGELY PRIVILEGED "ROYAL PRINCE" MANNER. LOCK UP. GO OUT FOR YOUR "OBSCENE AMOUNT OF MONEY" LUNCH...>
<AND LEAVE YOUR "OFFENSIVE AMOUNT OF WEALTH", "TOTALLY IMPOSSIBLE TO BREAK INTO" PENTHOUSE COMPLETELY EMPTY...>
<...SO POVERTY-STRIKEN **PEARL** CAN HELP HERSELF TO SOME OF THAT EXCESS OIL MONEY.>
<DON'T BLAME ME, WORLD. IT'S A KARMIC THING.>

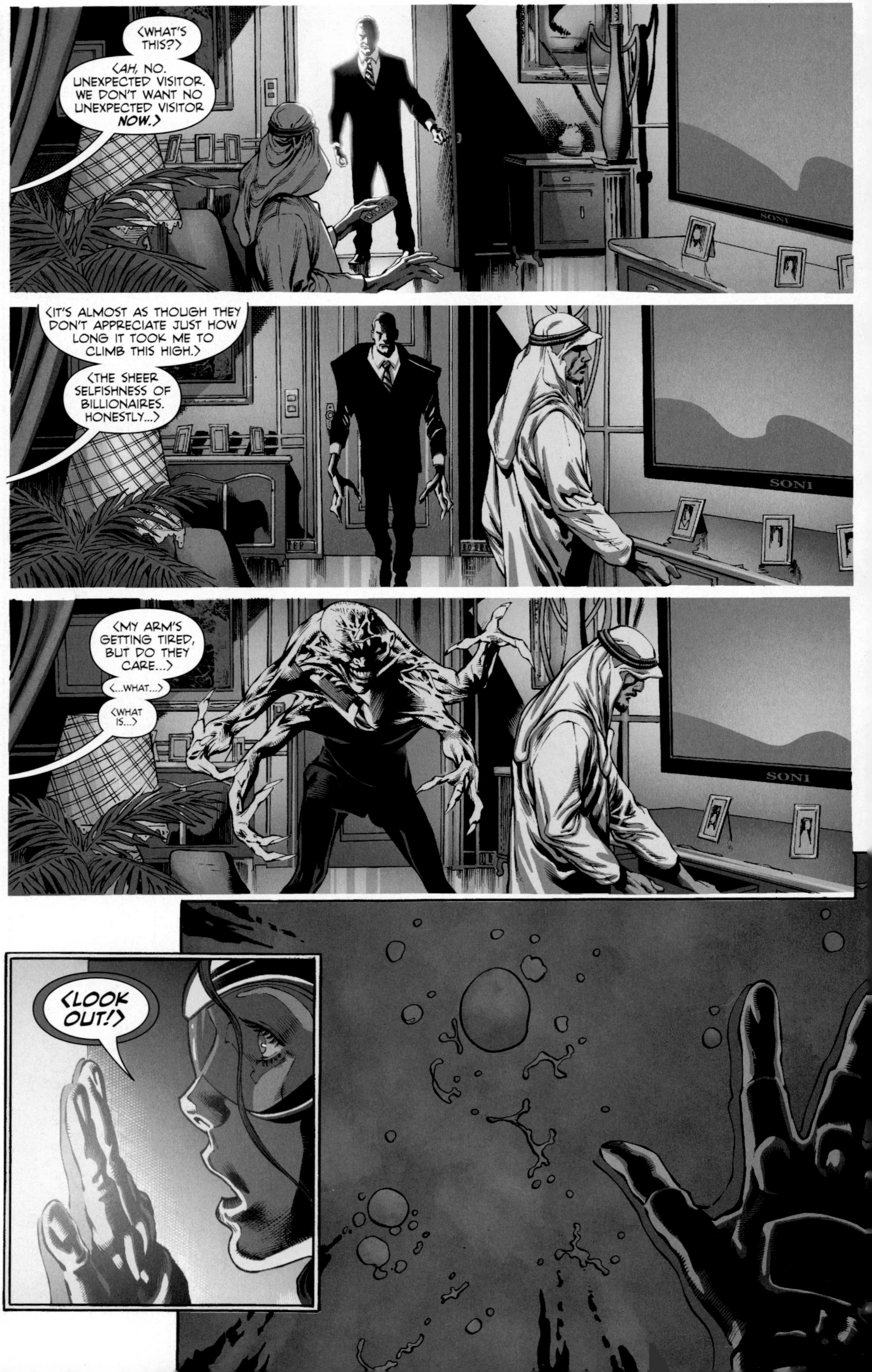
<WHAT'S THIS?>
<*AH,* NO. UNEXPECTED VISITOR. WE DON'T WANT NO UNEXPECTED VISITOR **NOW.**>
<IT'S ALMOST AS THOUGH THEY DON'T APPRECIATE JUST HOW LONG IT TOOK ME TO CLIMB THIS HIGH.>
<THE SHEER SELFISHNESS OF BILLIONAIRES. HONESTLY...>
SONI
<MY ARM'S GETTING TIRED, BUT DO THEY CARE...>
<...WHAT...>
<WHAT IS...>
<LOOK OUT!>

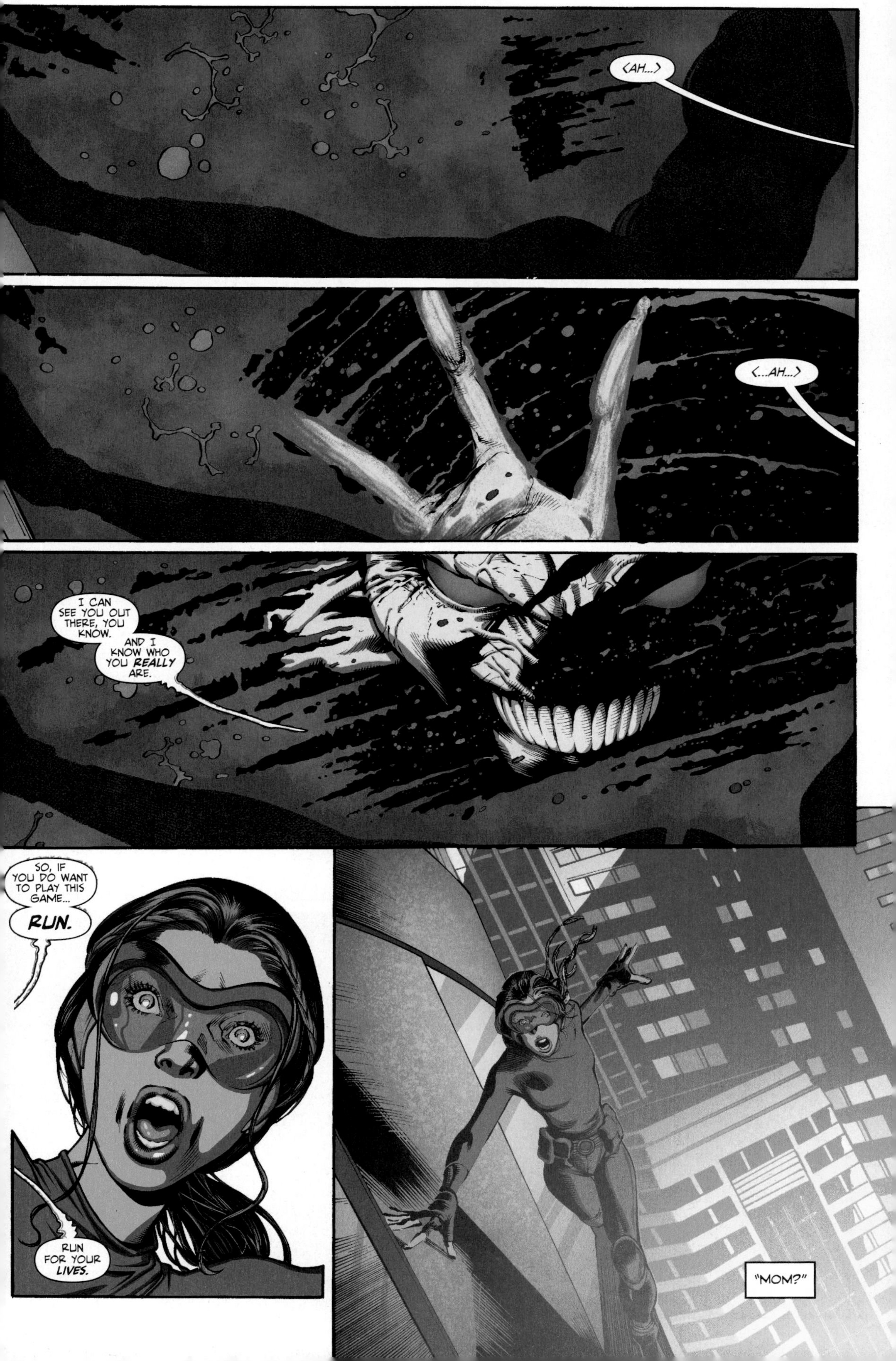

<AH...>
<...AH...>
I CAN SEE YOU OUT THERE, YOU KNOW.
AND I KNOW WHO YOU REALLY ARE.
SO, IF YOU DO WANT TO PLAY THIS GAME...
RUN.
RUN FOR YOUR LIVES.
"MOM?"

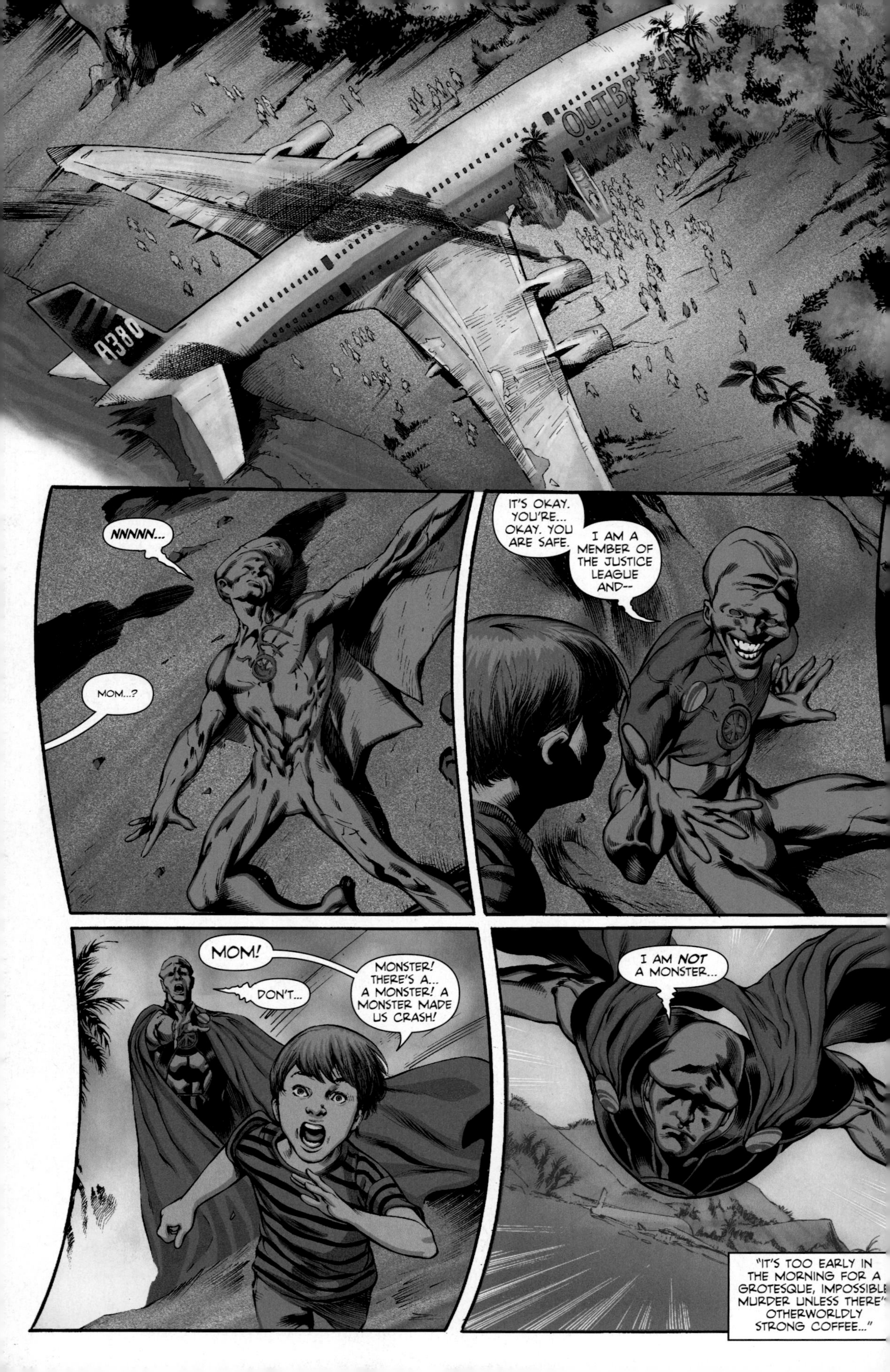
A380
NNNNN...
MOM...?
IT'S OKAY. YOU'RE... OKAY. YOU ARE SAFE.
I AM A MEMBER OF THE JUSTICE LEAGUE AND--
MOM!
DON'T...
MONSTER! THERE'S A... A MONSTER! A MONSTER MADE US CRASH!
I AM NOT A MONSTER...
"IT'S TOO EARLY IN THE MORNING FOR A GROTESQUE, IMPOSSIBLE MURDER UNLESS THERE'
OTHERWORLDLY STRONG COFFEE..."

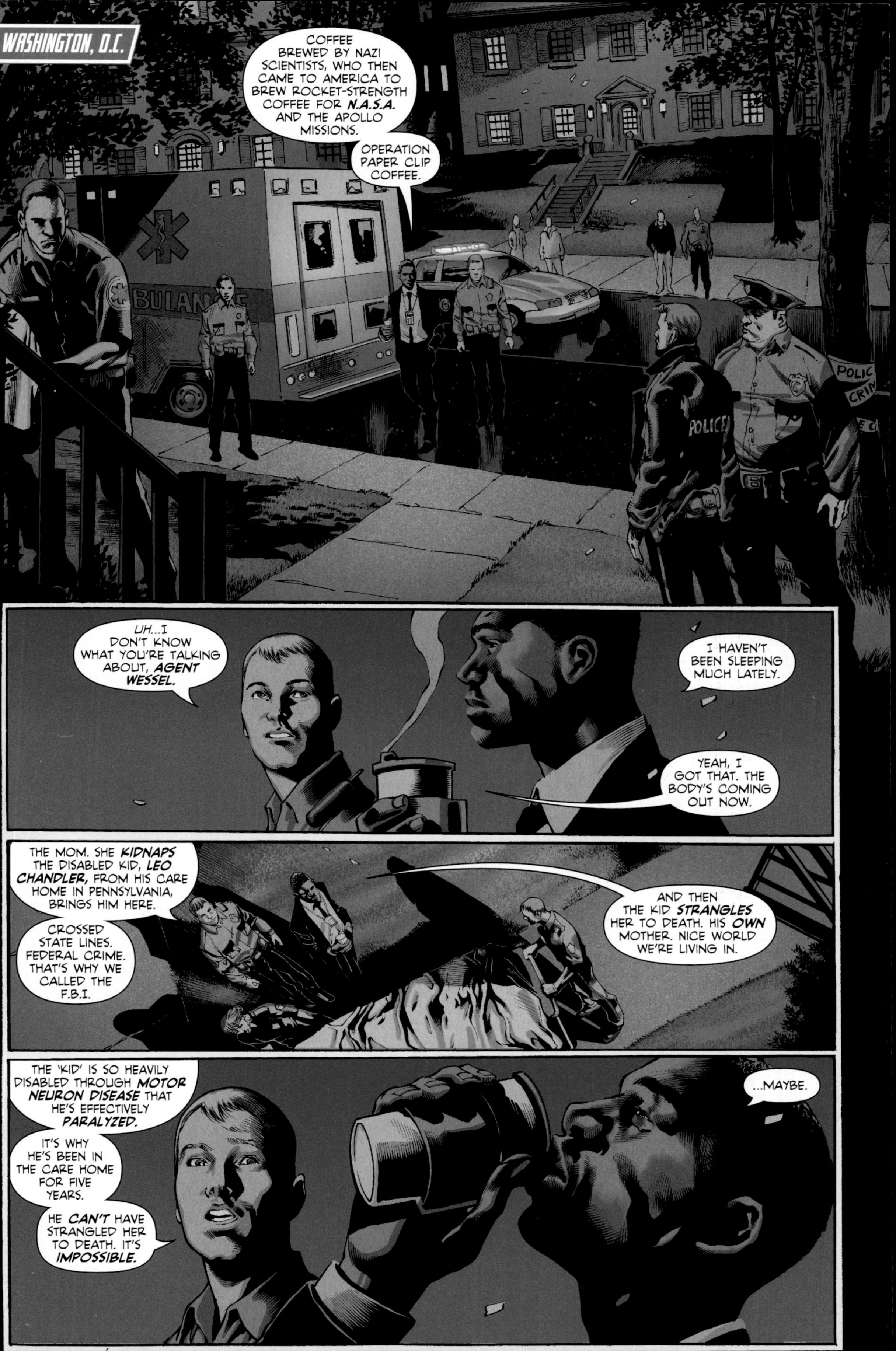

WASHINGTON, D.C.
COFFEE BREWED BY NAZI SCIENTISTS, WHO THEN CAME TO AMERICA TO BREW ROCKET-STRENGTH COFFEE FOR N.A.S.A. AND THE APOLLO MISSIONS.
OPERATION PAPER CLIP COFFEE.
POLICE
UH...I DON'T KNOW WHAT YOU'RE TALKING ABOUT, AGENT WESSEL.
I HAVEN'T BEEN SLEEPING MUCH LATELY.
YEAH, I GOT THAT. THE BODY'S COMING OUT NOW.
THE MOM. SHE KIDNAPS THE DISABLED KID, LEO CHANDLER, FROM HIS CARE HOME IN PENNSYLVANIA, BRINGS HIM HERE.
CROSSED STATE LINES. FEDERAL CRIME. THAT'S WHY WE CALLED THE F.B.I.
AND THEN THE KID STRANGLES HER TO DEATH. HIS OWN MOTHER. NICE WORLD WE'RE LIVING IN.
THE 'KID' IS SO HEAVILY DISABLED THROUGH MOTOR NEURON DISEASE THAT HE'S EFFECTIVELY PARALYZED.
IT'S WHY HE'S BEEN IN THE CARE HOME FOR FIVE YEARS.
HE CAN'T HAVE STRANGLED HER TO DEATH. IT'S IMPOSSIBLE.
...MAYBE.

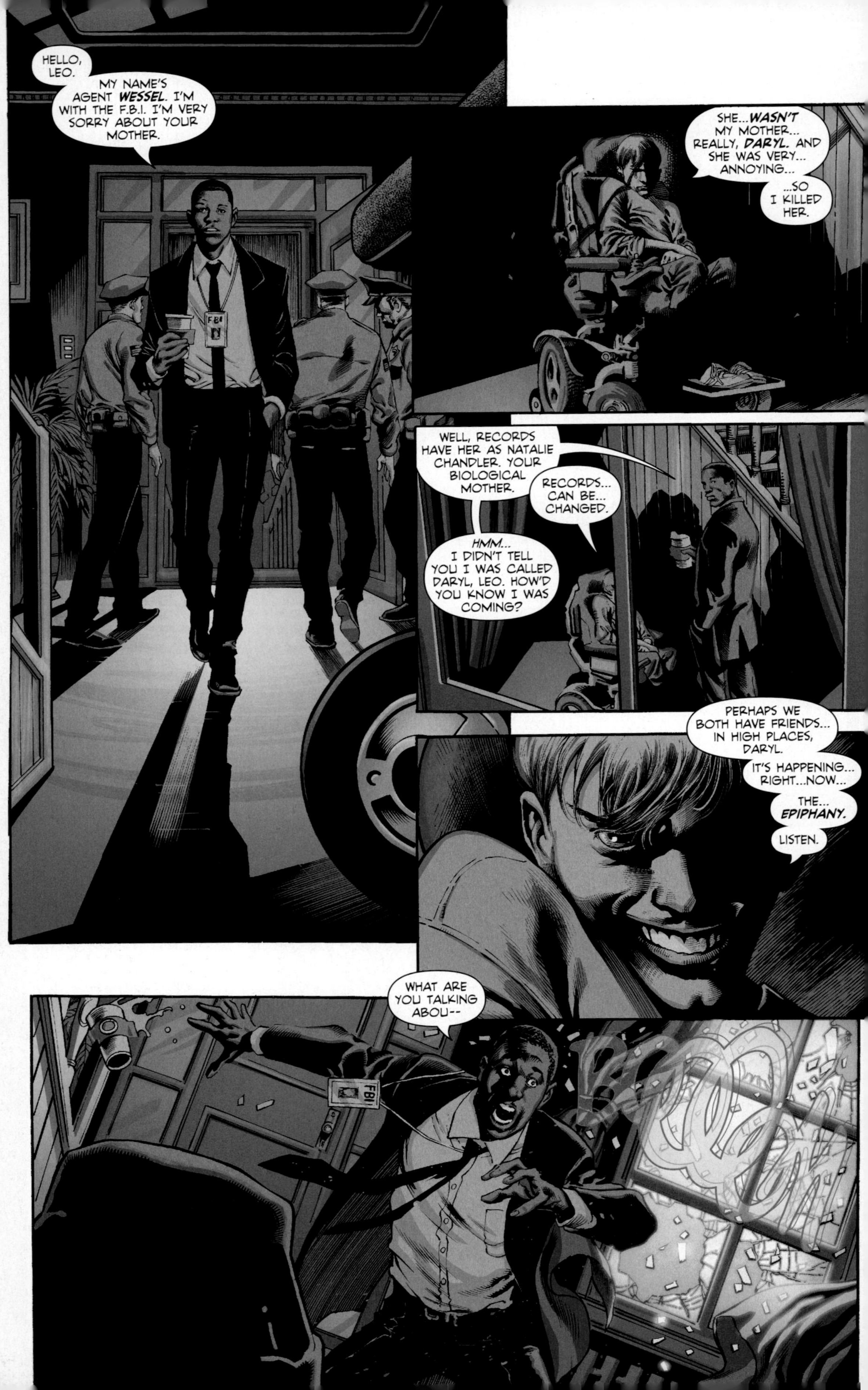
HELLO, LEO.
MY NAME'S AGENT WESSEL. I'M WITH THE F.B.I. I'M VERY SORRY ABOUT YOUR MOTHER.
SHE...WASN'T MY MOTHER... REALLY, DARYL. AND SHE WAS VERY... ANNOYING...
...SO I KILLED HER.
WELL, RECORDS HAVE HER AS NATALIE CHANDLER. YOUR BIOLOGICAL MOTHER.
RECORDS... CAN BE... CHANGED.
HMM... I DIDN'T TELL YOU I WAS CALLED DARYL, LEO. HOW'D YOU KNOW I WAS COMING?
PERHAPS WE BOTH HAVE FRIENDS... IN HIGH PLACES, DARYL.
IT'S HAPPENING... RIGHT...NOW...
THE... EPIPHANY.
LISTEN.
WHAT ARE YOU TALKING ABOU--
FBI

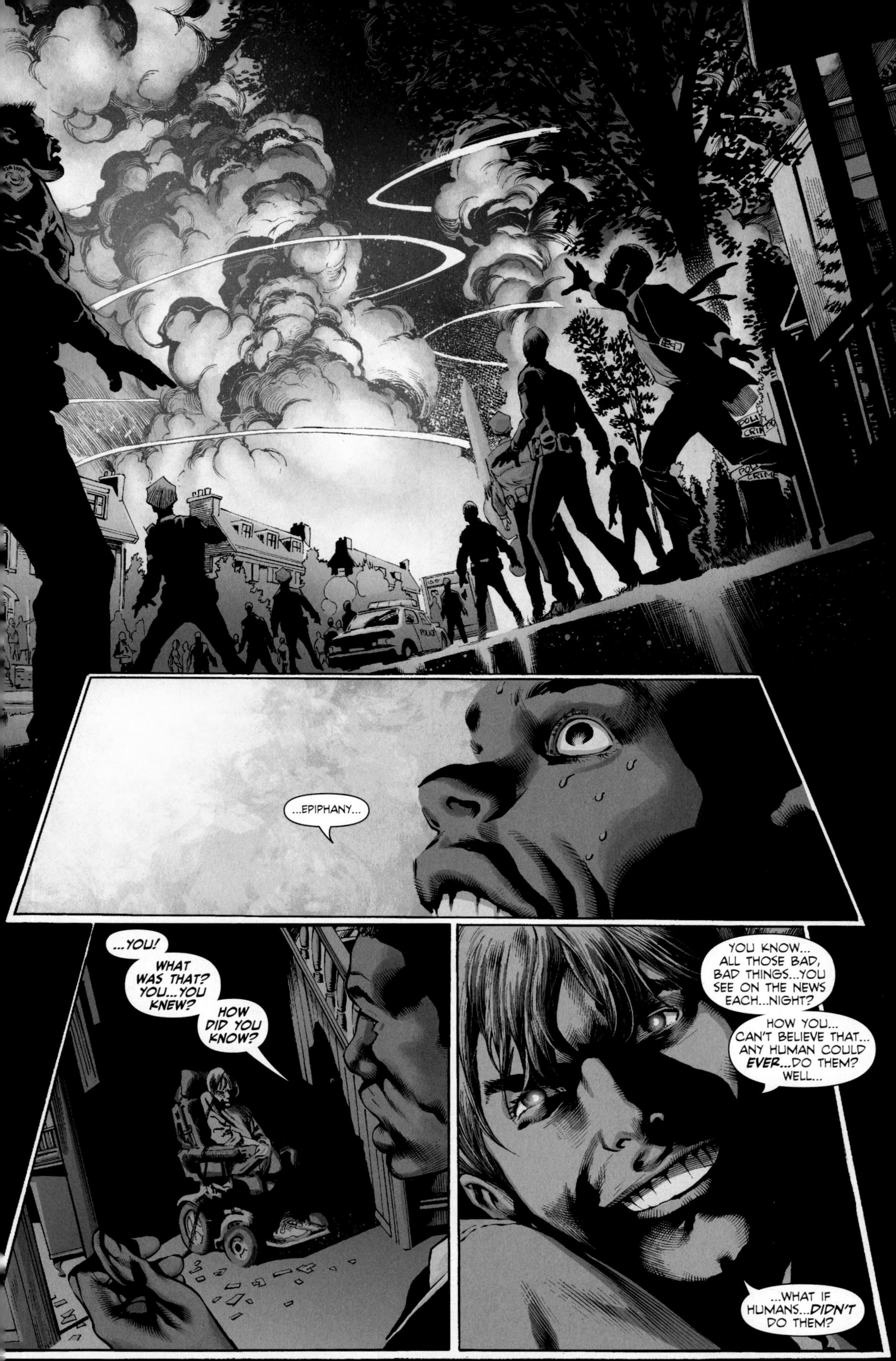
...EPIPHANY...
...YOU! WHAT WAS THAT? YOU...YOU KNEW?
HOW DID YOU KNOW?
YOU KNOW... ALL THOSE BAD, BAD THINGS...YOU SEE ON THE NEWS EACH...NIGHT?
HOW YOU... CAN'T BELIEVE THAT... ANY HUMAN COULD *EVER*...DO THEM? WELL...
...WHAT IF HUMANS...*DIDN'T* DO THEM?

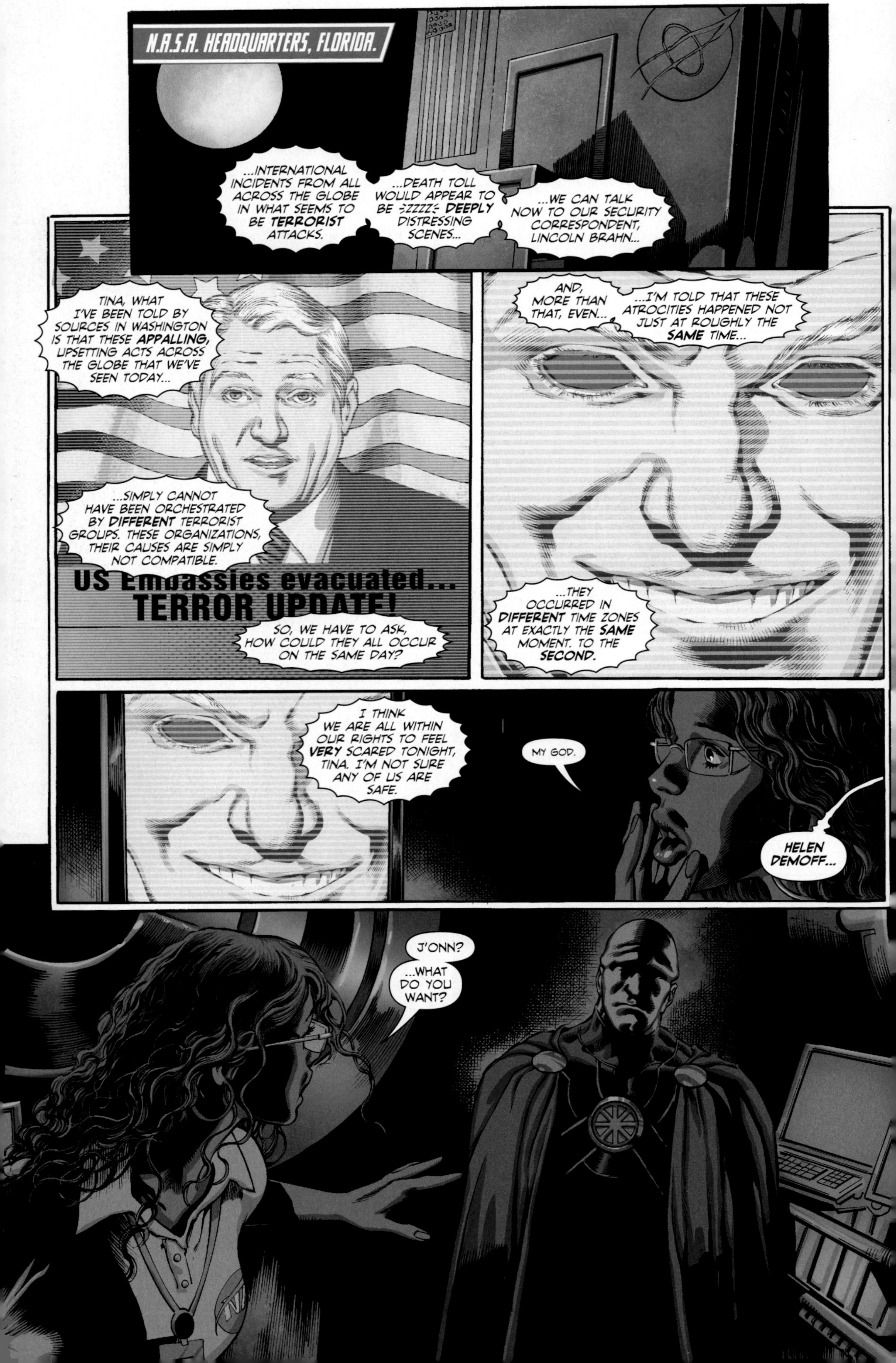
N.A.S.A. HEADQUARTERS, FLORIDA.
...INTERNATIONAL INCIDENTS FROM ALL ACROSS THE GLOBE IN WHAT SEEMS TO BE TERRORIST ATTACKS.
...DEATH TOLL WOULD APPEAR TO BE ZZZZZ DEEPLY DISTRESSING SCENES...
...WE CAN TALK NOW TO OUR SECURITY CORRESPONDENT, LINCOLN BRAHN...
TINA, WHAT I'VE BEEN TOLD BY SOURCES IN WASHINGTON IS THAT THESE APPALLING, UPSETTING ACTS ACROSS THE GLOBE THAT WE'VE SEEN TODAY...
...SIMPLY CANNOT HAVE BEEN ORCHESTRATED BY DIFFERENT TERRORIST GROUPS. THESE ORGANIZATIONS, THEIR CAUSES ARE SIMPLY NOT COMPATIBLE.
US Embassies evacuated... TERROR UPDATE!
SO, WE HAVE TO ASK, HOW COULD THEY ALL OCCUR ON THE SAME DAY?
AND, MORE THAN THAT, EVEN...
...I'M TOLD THAT THESE ATROCITIES HAPPENED NOT JUST AT ROUGHLY THE SAME TIME...
...THEY OCCURRED IN DIFFERENT TIME ZONES AT EXACTLY THE SAME MOMENT. TO THE SECOND.
I THINK WE ARE ALL WITHIN OUR RIGHTS TO FEEL VERY SCARED TONIGHT, TINA. I'M NOT SURE ANY OF US ARE SAFE.
MY GOD.
HELEN DEMOFF...
J'ONN?
...WHAT DO YOU WANT?

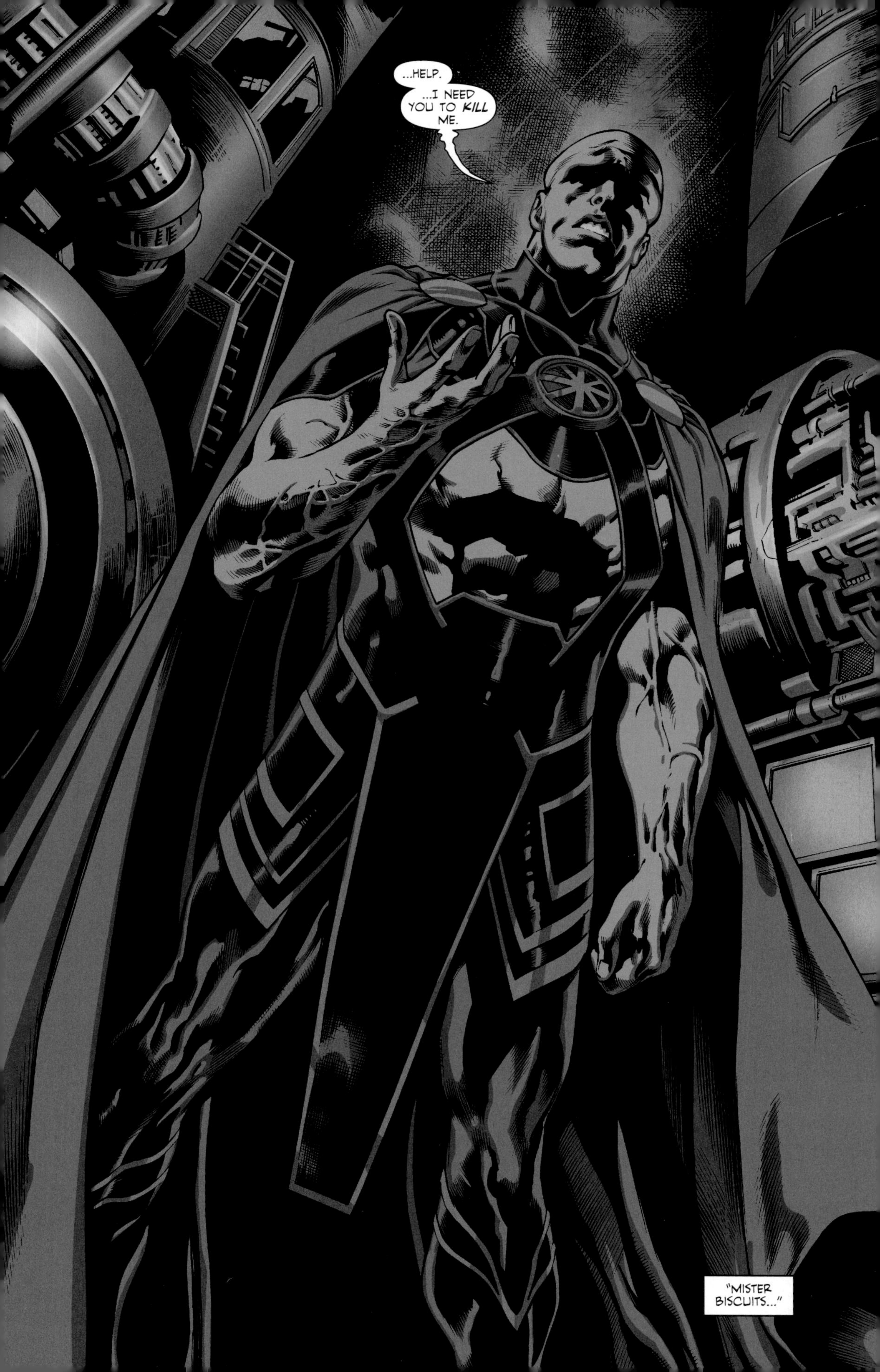
...HELP.
...I NEED YOU TO KILL ME.
"MISTER BISCUITS..."

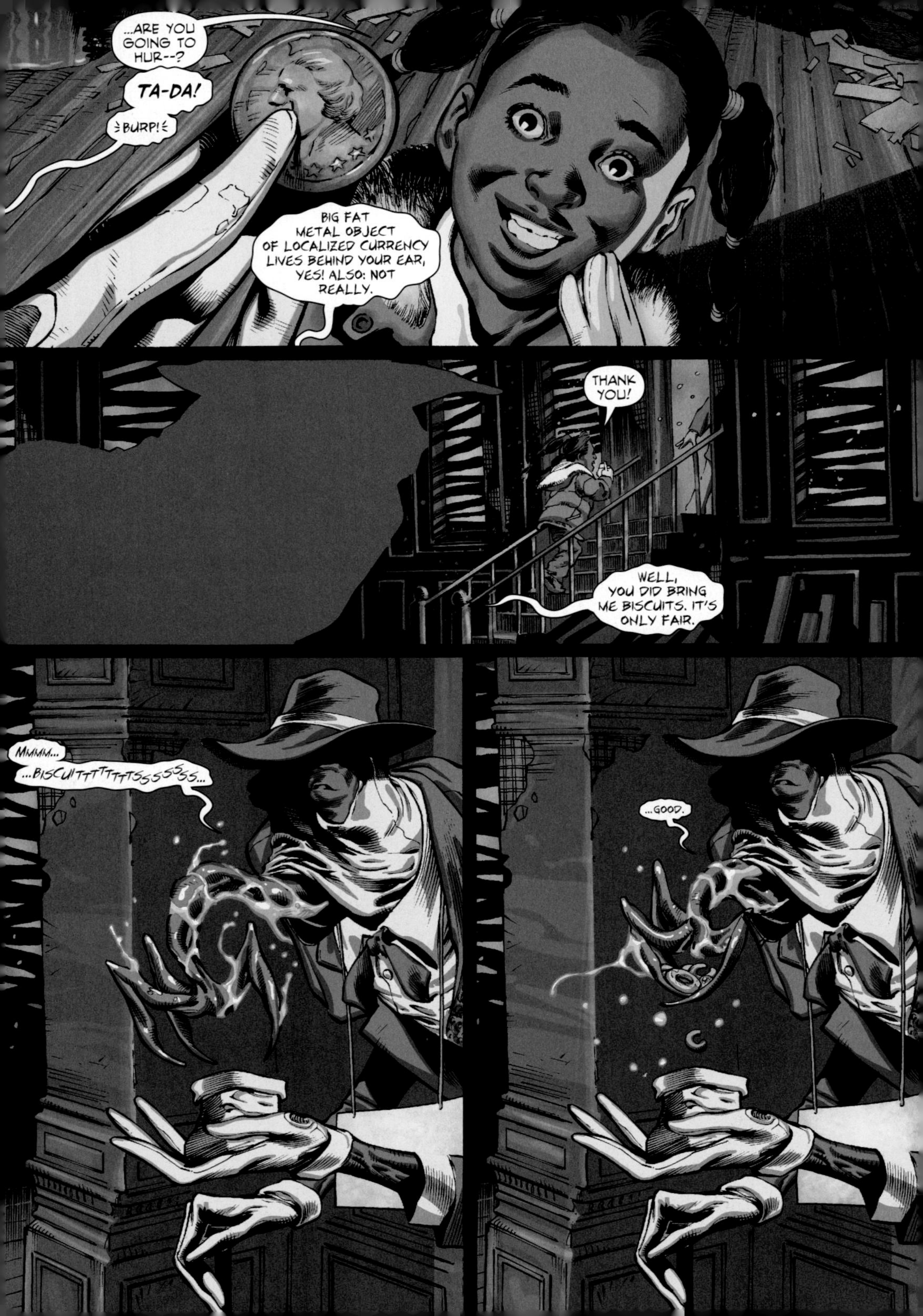
...ARE YOU GOING TO HUR--?
TA-DA!
BURP!
BIG FAT METAL OBJECT OF LOCALIZED CURRENCY LIVES BEHIND YOUR EAR, YES! ALSO: NOT REALLY.
THANK YOU!
WELL, YOU DID BRING ME BISCUITS. IT'S ONLY FAIR.
MMMM...
...BISCUITTTTTTTTSSSSSSSS...
...GOOD.

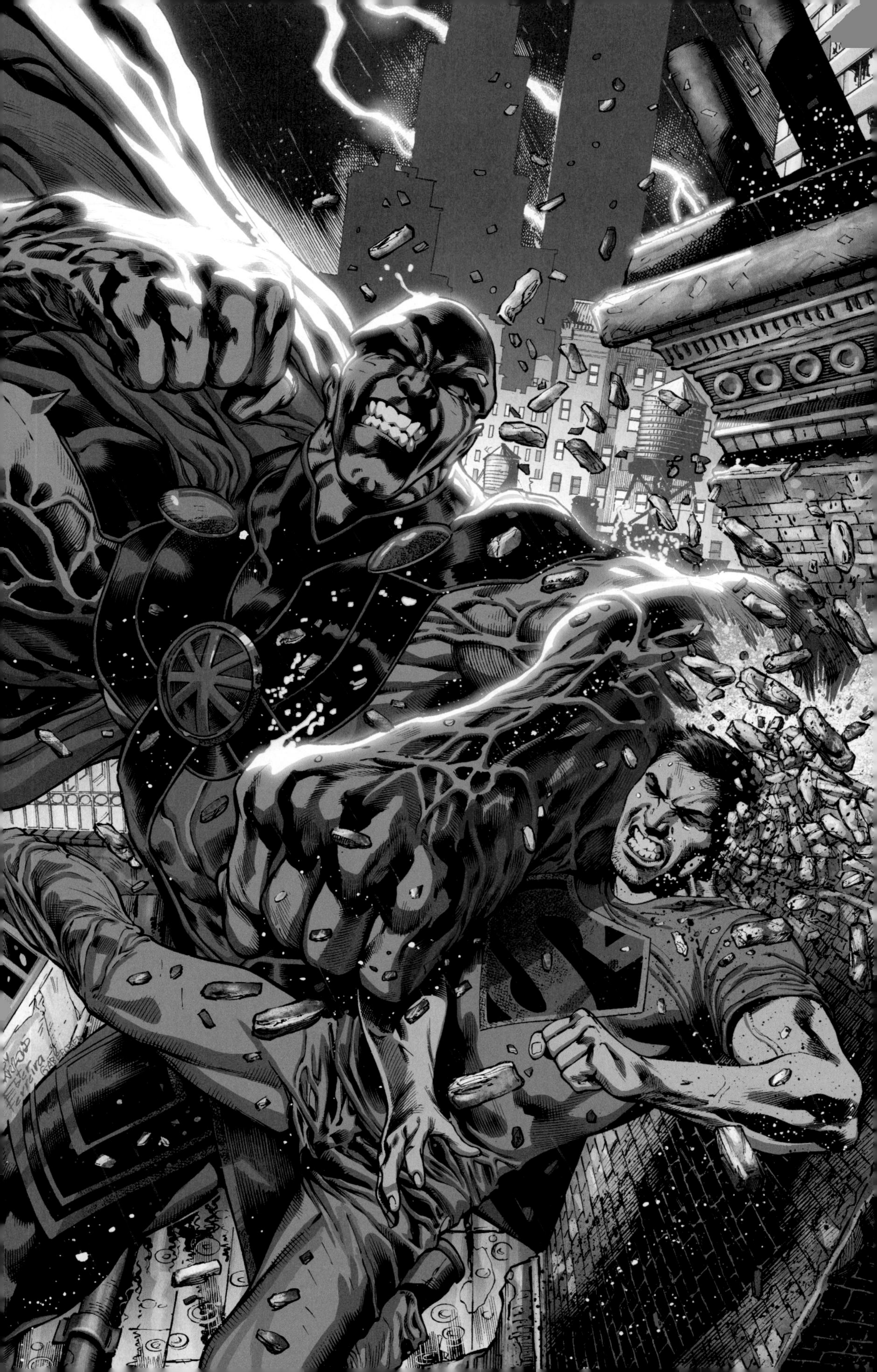

WEAPON! PART 2

cover by **EDDY BARROWS, EBER FERREIRA, & GABE ELTAEB**

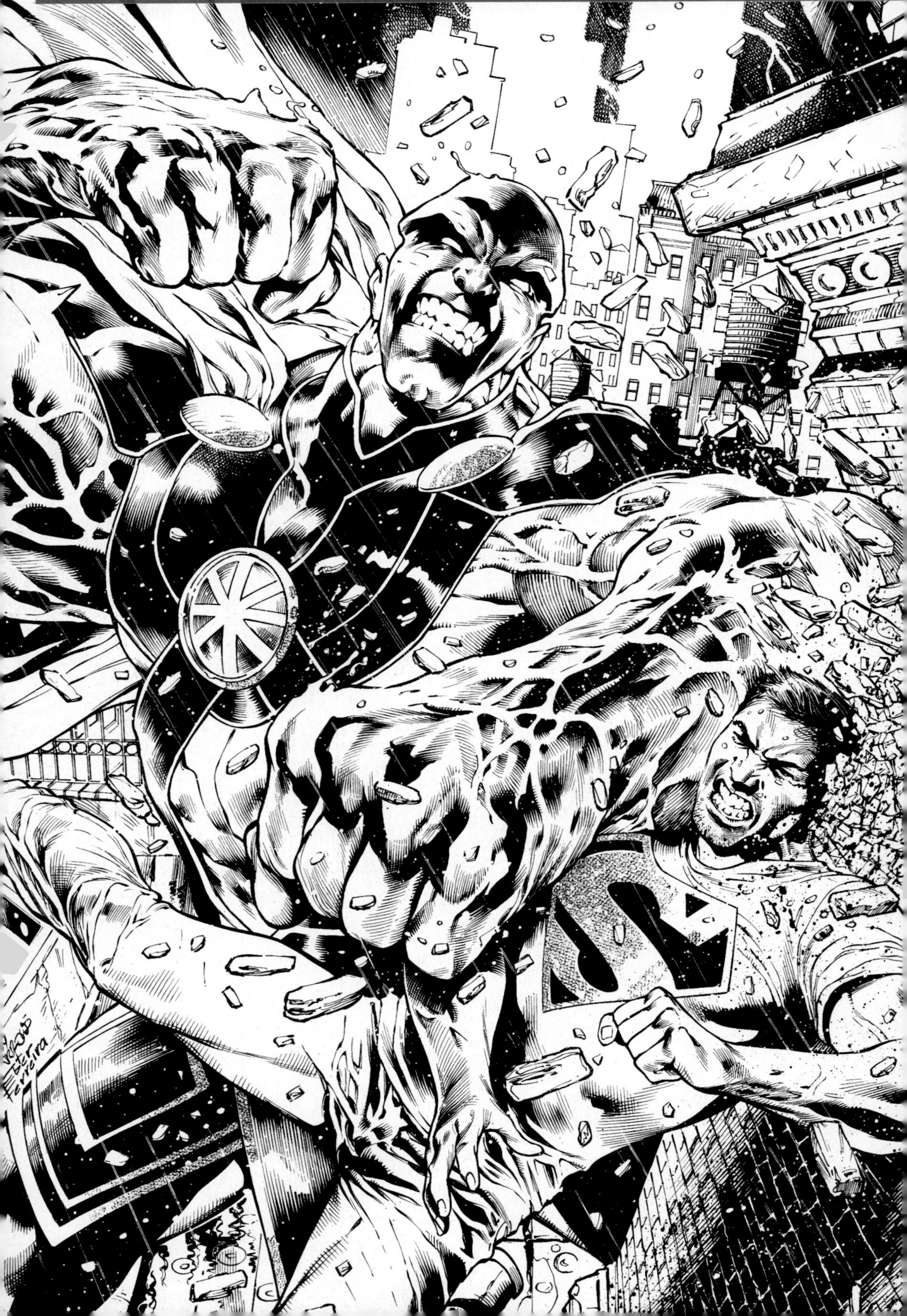

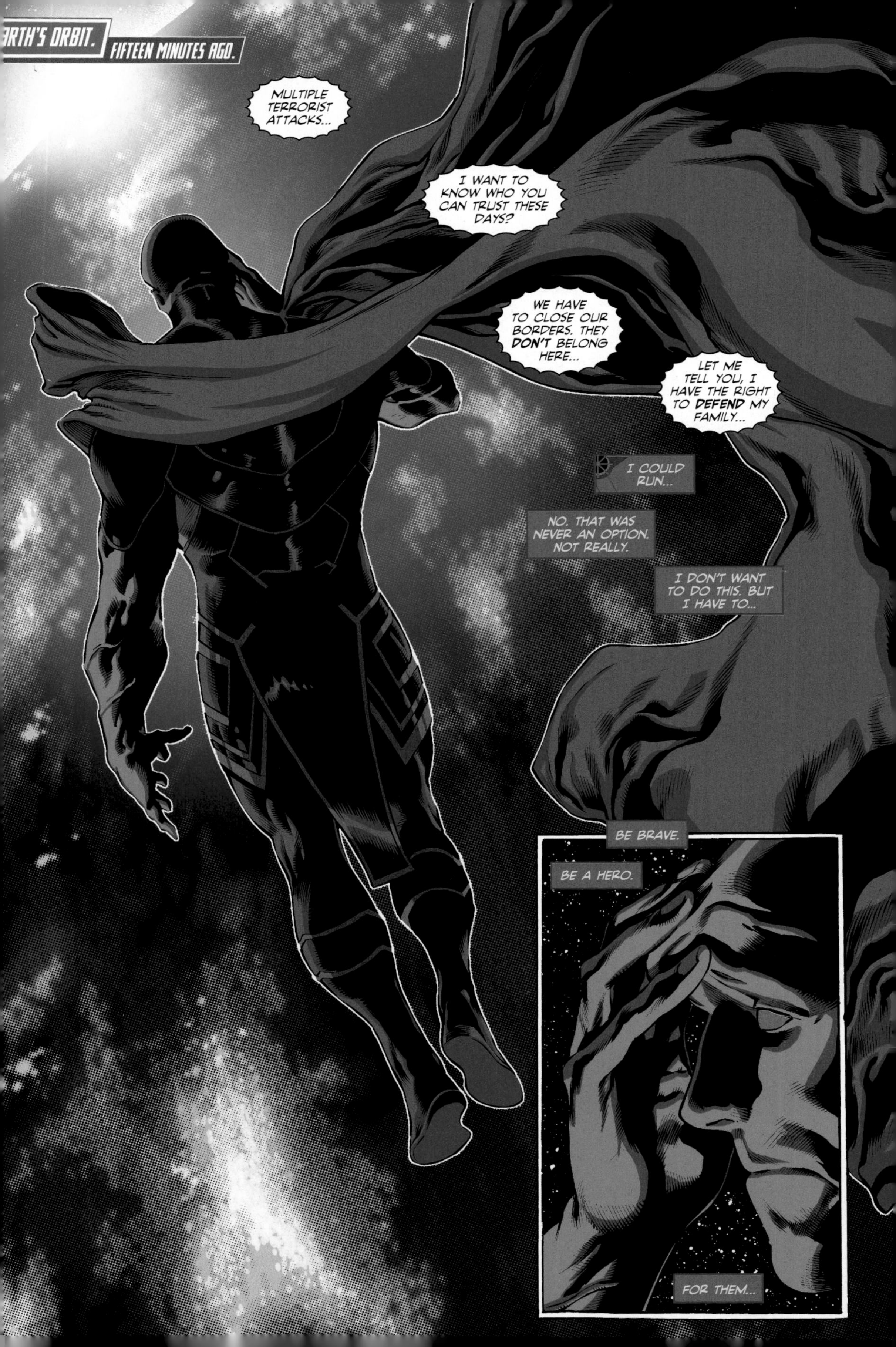

ARTH'S ORBIT.
FIFTEEN MINUTES AGO.
MULTIPLE TERRORIST ATTACKS...
I WANT TO KNOW WHO YOU CAN TRUST THESE DAYS?
WE HAVE TO CLOSE OUR BORDERS. THEY **DON'T** BELONG HERE...
LET ME TELL YOU, I HAVE THE RIGHT TO **DEFEND** MY FAMILY...
I COULD RUN...
NO. THAT WAS NEVER AN OPTION. NOT REALLY.
I DON'T WANT TO DO THIS. BUT I HAVE TO...
BE BRAVE.
BE A HERO.
FOR THEM...

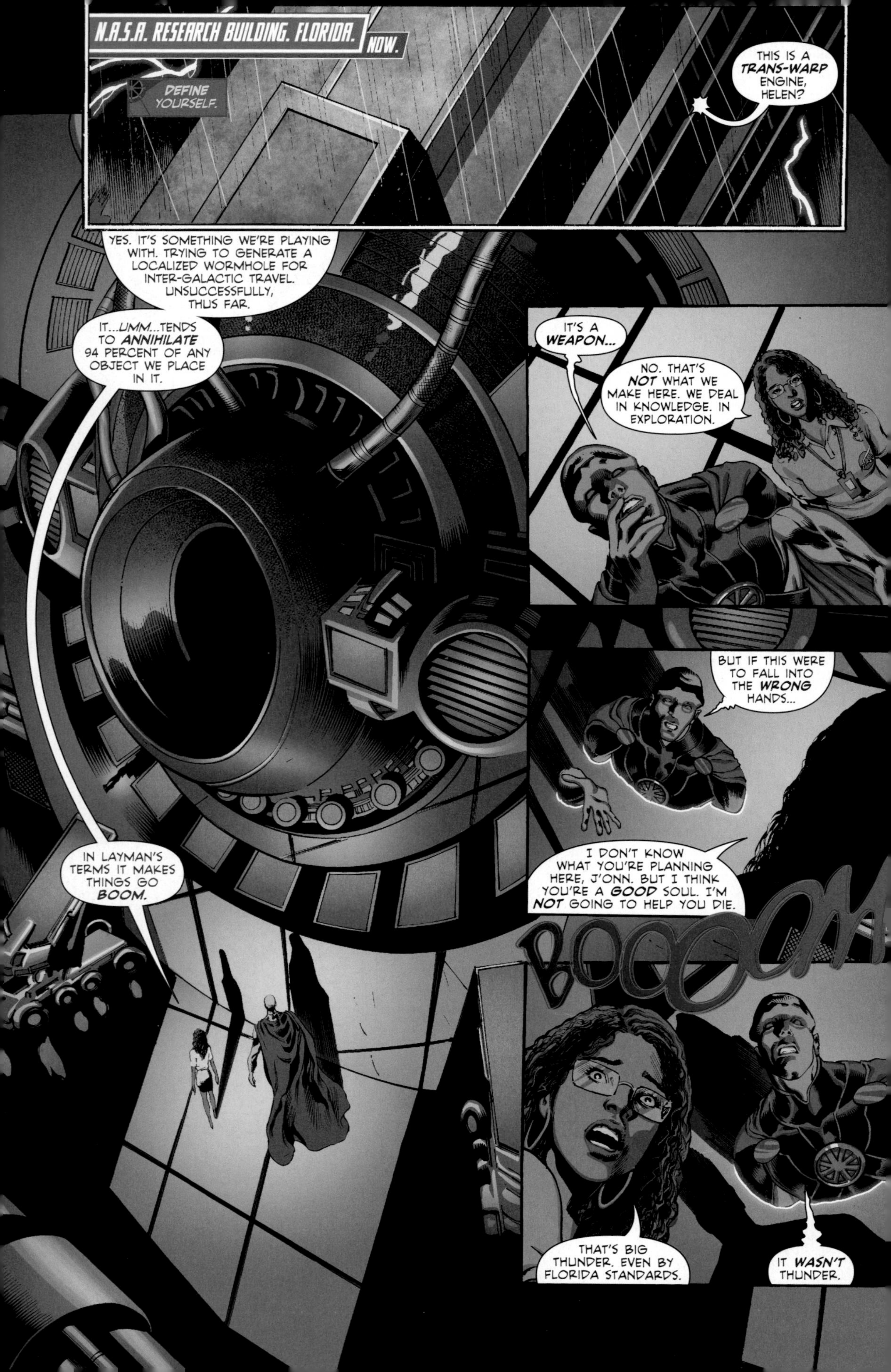
N.A.S.A. RESEARCH BUILDING. FLORIDA.
NOW.
DEFINE YOURSELF.
THIS IS A TRANS-WARP ENGINE, HELEN?
YES. IT'S SOMETHING WE'RE PLAYING WITH. TRYING TO GENERATE A LOCALIZED WORMHOLE FOR INTER-GALACTIC TRAVEL. UNSUCCESSFULLY, THUS FAR.
IT...UMM...TENDS TO ANNIHILATE 94 PERCENT OF ANY OBJECT WE PLACE IN IT.
IN LAYMAN'S TERMS IT MAKES THINGS GO BOOM.
IT'S A WEAPON...
NO. THAT'S NOT WHAT WE MAKE HERE. WE DEAL IN KNOWLEDGE. IN EXPLORATION.
BUT IF THIS WERE TO FALL INTO THE WRONG HANDS...
I DON'T KNOW WHAT YOU'RE PLANNING HERE, J'ONN. BUT I THINK YOU'RE A GOOD SOUL. I'M NOT GOING TO HELP YOU DIE.
BOOOOM
THAT'S BIG THUNDER. EVEN BY FLORIDA STANDARDS.
IT WASN'T THUNDER.

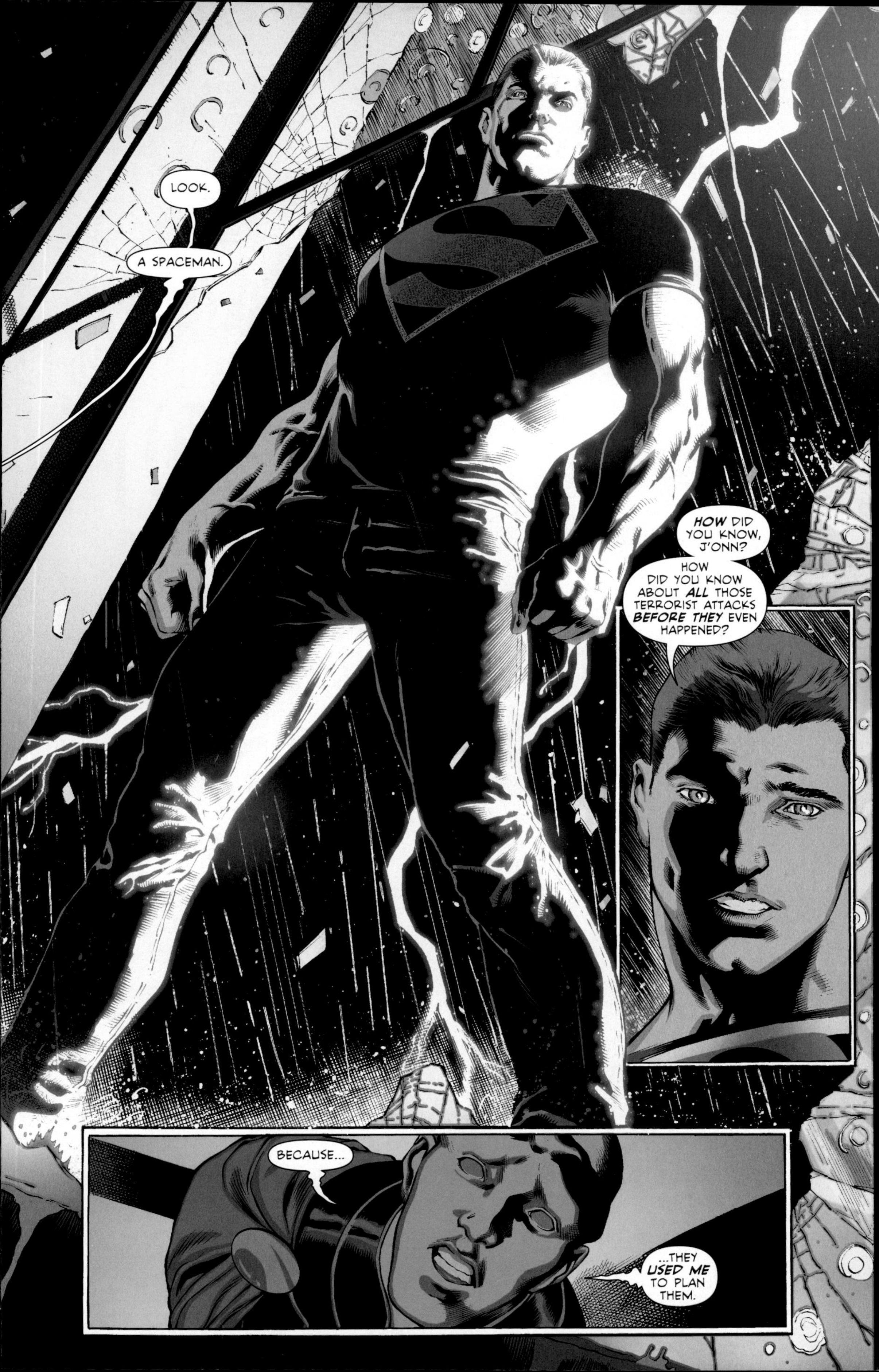
LOOK.
A SPACEMAN.
HOW DID YOU KNOW, J'ONN?
HOW DID YOU KNOW ABOUT ALL THOSE TERRORIST ATTACKS BEFORE THEY EVEN HAPPENED?
BECAUSE...
...THEY USED ME TO PLAN THEM.

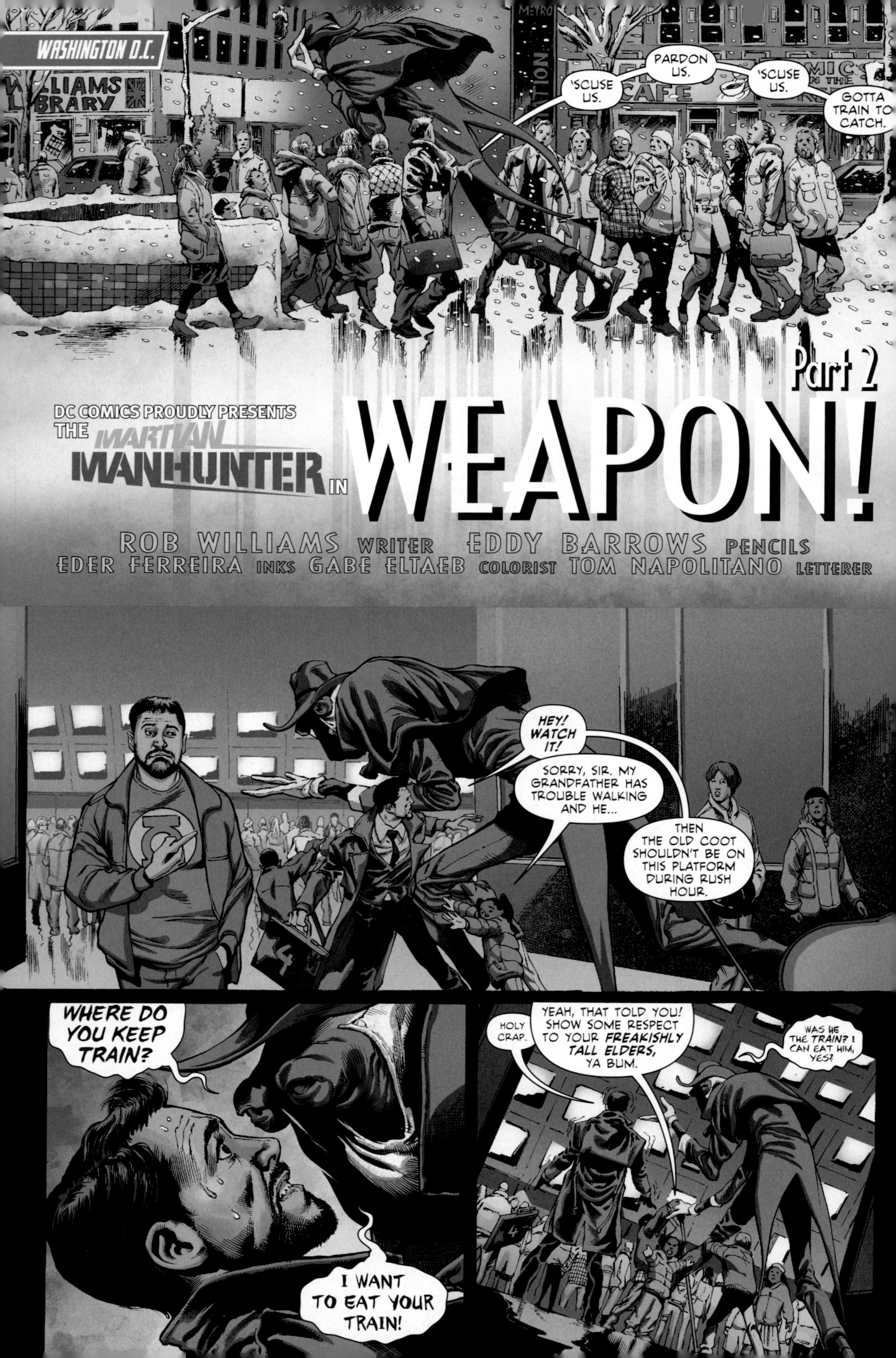
WASHINGTON D.C.
'SCUSE US.
PARDON US.
'SCUSE US.
GOTTA TRAIN TO CATCH.
Part 2
DC COMICS PROUDLY PRESENTS THE MARTIAN MANHUNTER IN
WEAPON!
ROB WILLIAMS WRITER EDDY BARROWS PENCILS
EDER FERREIRA INKS GABE ELTAEB COLORIST TOM NAPOLITANO LETTERER
HEY! WATCH IT!
SORRY, SIR. MY GRANDFATHER HAS TROUBLE WALKING AND HE...
THEN THE OLD COOT SHOULDN'T BE ON THIS PLATFORM DURING RUSH HOUR.
WHERE DO YOU KEEP TRAIN?
I WANT TO EAT YOUR TRAIN!
HOLY CRAP.
YEAH, THAT TOLD YOU! SHOW SOME RESPECT TO YOUR FREAKISHLY TALL ELDERS, YA BUM.
WAS HE THE TRAIN? I CAN EAT HIM, YES?

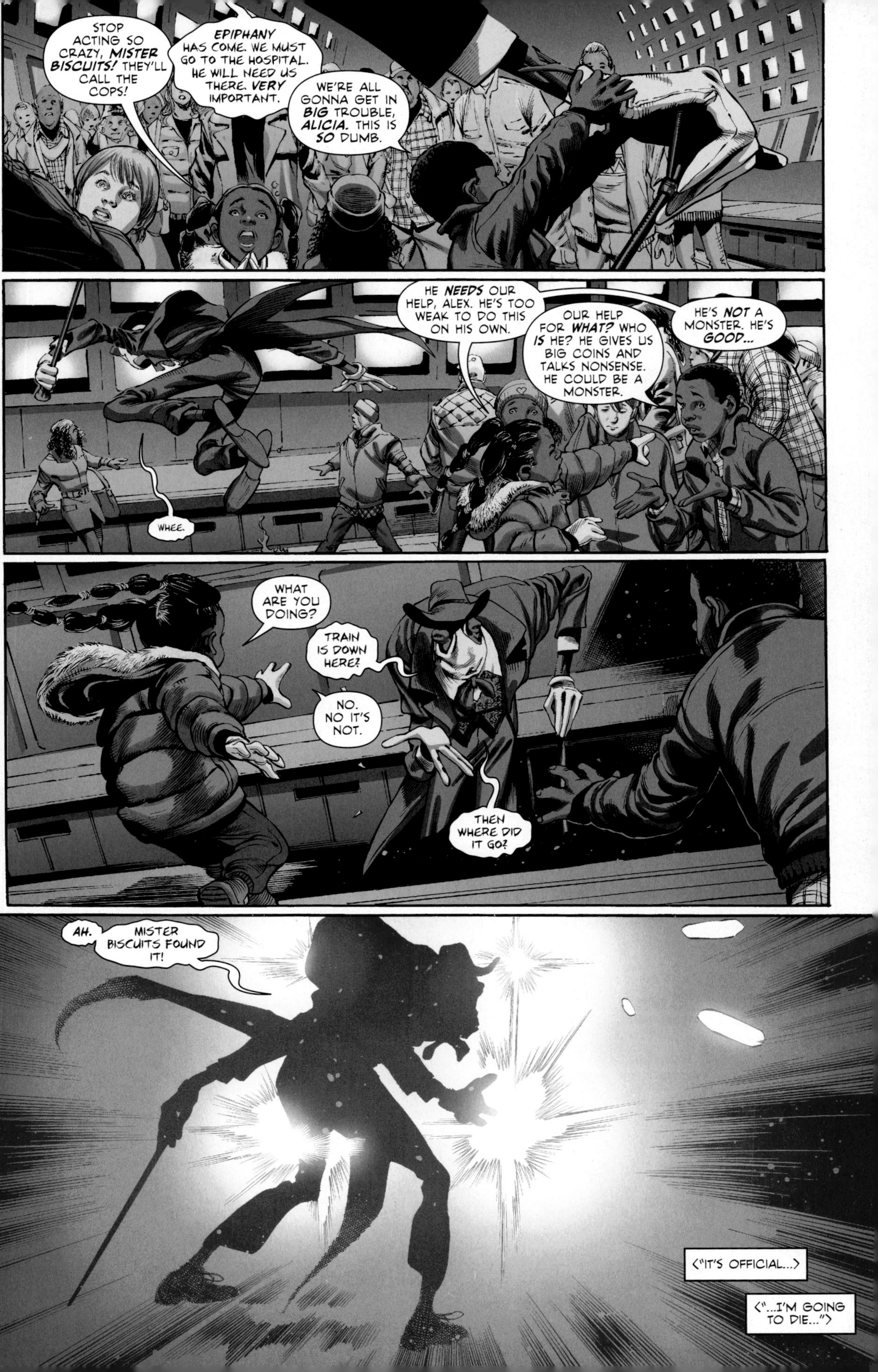
STOP ACTING SO CRAZY, MISTER BISCUITS! THEY'LL CALL THE COPS!
EPIPHANY HAS COME. WE MUST GO TO THE HOSPITAL. HE WILL NEED US THERE. VERY IMPORTANT.
WE'RE ALL GONNA GET IN BIG TROUBLE, ALICIA. THIS IS SO DUMB.
WHEE.
HE NEEDS OUR HELP, ALEX. HE'S TOO WEAK TO DO THIS ON HIS OWN.
OUR HELP FOR WHAT? WHO IS HE? HE GIVES US BIG COINS AND TALKS NONSENSE. HE COULD BE A MONSTER.
HE'S NOT A MONSTER. HE'S GOOD...
WHAT ARE YOU DOING?
TRAIN IS DOWN HERE?
NO. NO IT'S NOT.
THEN WHERE DID IT GO?
AH.
MISTER BISCUITS FOUND IT!
<"IT'S OFFICIAL...>
<"...I'M GOING TO DIE...">

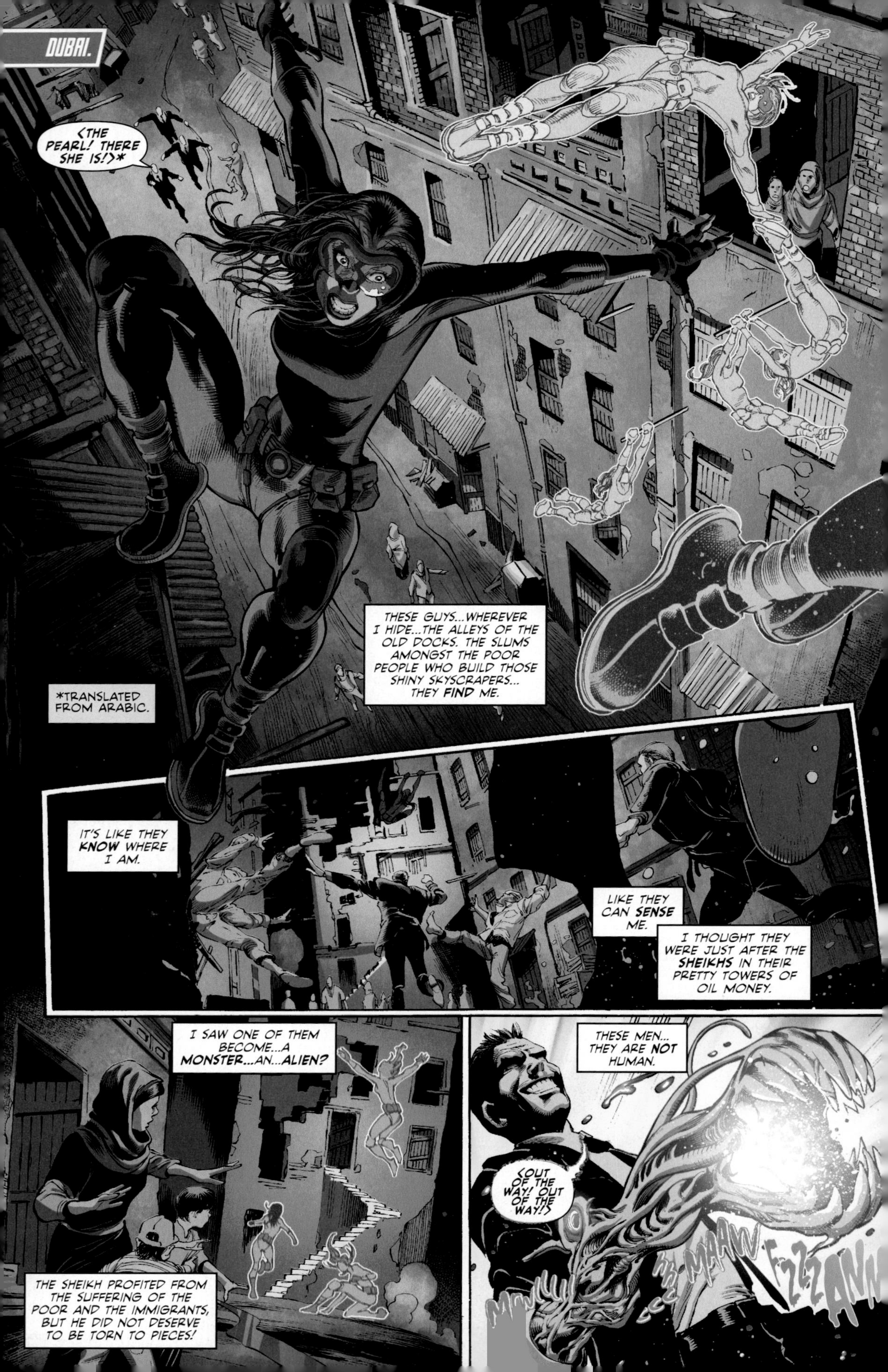
DUBAI.
<THE PEARL! THERE SHE IS!>*
THESE GUYS...WHEREVER I HIDE...THE ALLEYS OF THE OLD DOCKS. THE SLUMS AMONGST THE POOR PEOPLE WHO BUILD THOSE SHINY SKYSCRAPERS... THEY FIND ME.
*TRANSLATED FROM ARABIC.
IT'S LIKE THEY KNOW WHERE I AM.
LIKE THEY CAN SENSE ME.
I THOUGHT THEY WERE JUST AFTER THE SHEIKHS IN THEIR PRETTY TOWERS OF OIL MONEY.
I SAW ONE OF THEM BECOME...A MONSTER...AN...ALIEN?
THE SHEIKH PROFITED FROM THE SUFFERING OF THE POOR AND THE IMMIGRANTS, BUT HE DID NOT DESERVE TO BE TORN TO PIECES!
THESE MEN... THEY ARE NOT HUMAN.
<OUT OF THE WAY! OUT OF THE WAY!>
SHRAAAW
FZZZANN

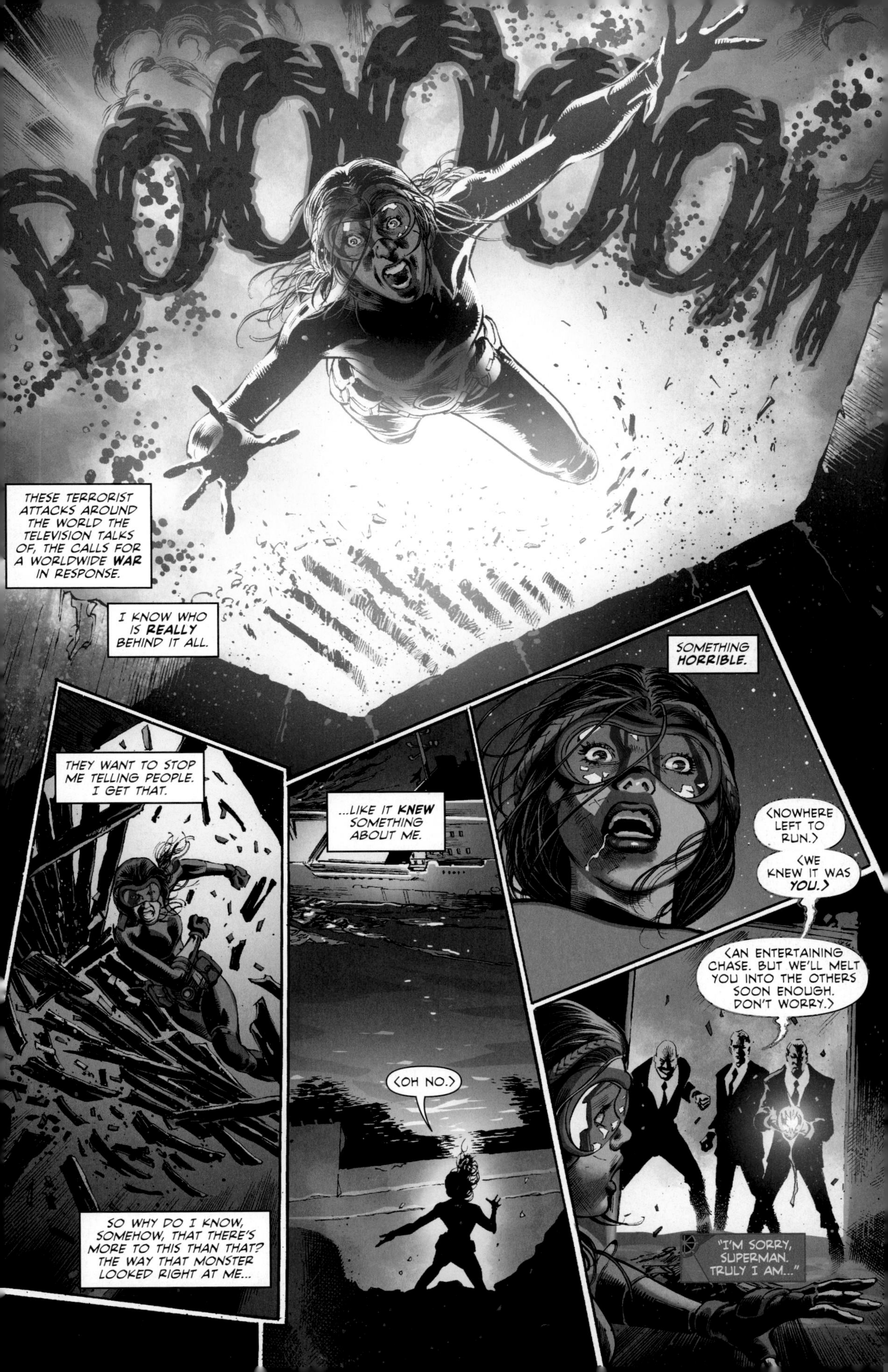
BOOOOOOM
THESE TERRORIST ATTACKS AROUND THE WORLD THE TELEVISION TALKS OF, THE CALLS FOR A WORLDWIDE WAR IN RESPONSE.
I KNOW WHO IS REALLY BEHIND IT ALL.
SOMETHING HORRIBLE.
THEY WANT TO STOP ME TELLING PEOPLE. I GET THAT.
SO WHY DO I KNOW, SOMEHOW, THAT THERE'S MORE TO THIS THAN THAT? THE WAY THAT MONSTER LOOKED RIGHT AT ME...
...LIKE IT KNEW SOMETHING ABOUT ME.
<OH NO.>
<NOWHERE LEFT TO RUN.>
<WE KNEW IT WAS YOU.>
<AN ENTERTAINING CHASE. BUT WE'LL MELT YOU INTO THE OTHERS SOON ENOUGH. DON'T WORRY.>
"I'M SORRY, SUPERMAN. TRULY I AM..."

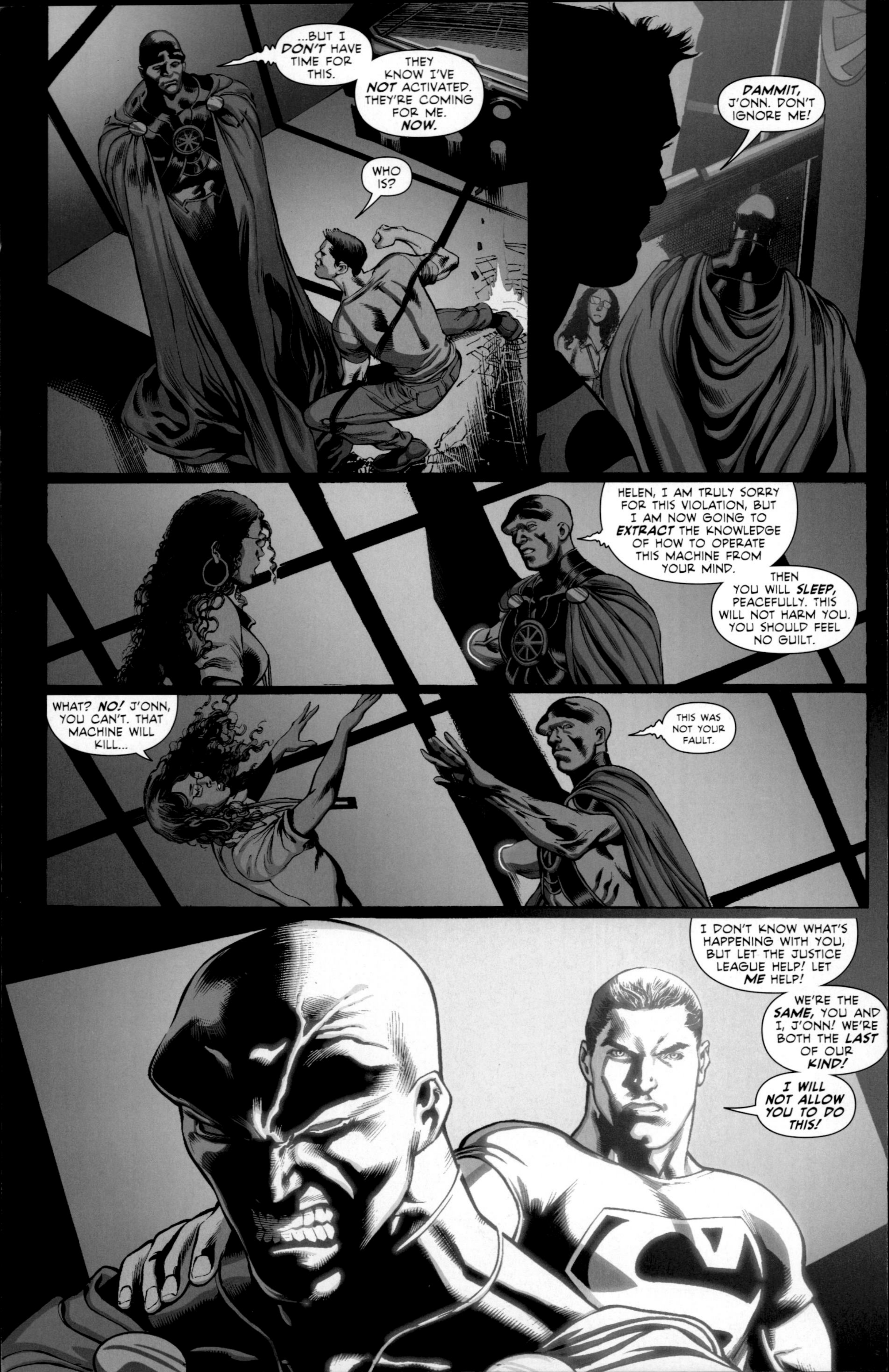
...BUT I DON'T HAVE TIME FOR THIS.
THEY KNOW I'VE NOT ACTIVATED. THEY'RE COMING FOR ME. NOW.
WHO IS?
DAMMIT, J'ONN. DON'T IGNORE ME!
HELEN, I AM TRULY SORRY FOR THIS VIOLATION, BUT I AM NOW GOING TO EXTRACT THE KNOWLEDGE OF HOW TO OPERATE THIS MACHINE FROM YOUR MIND.
THEN YOU WILL SLEEP, PEACEFULLY. THIS WILL NOT HARM YOU. YOU SHOULD FEEL NO GUILT.
WHAT? NO! J'ONN, YOU CAN'T. THAT MACHINE WILL KILL...
THIS WAS NOT YOUR FAULT.
I DON'T KNOW WHAT'S HAPPENING WITH YOU, BUT LET THE JUSTICE LEAGUE HELP! LET ME HELP!
WE'RE THE SAME, YOU AND I, J'ONN! WE'RE BOTH THE LAST OF OUR KIND!
I WILL NOT ALLOW YOU TO DO THIS!

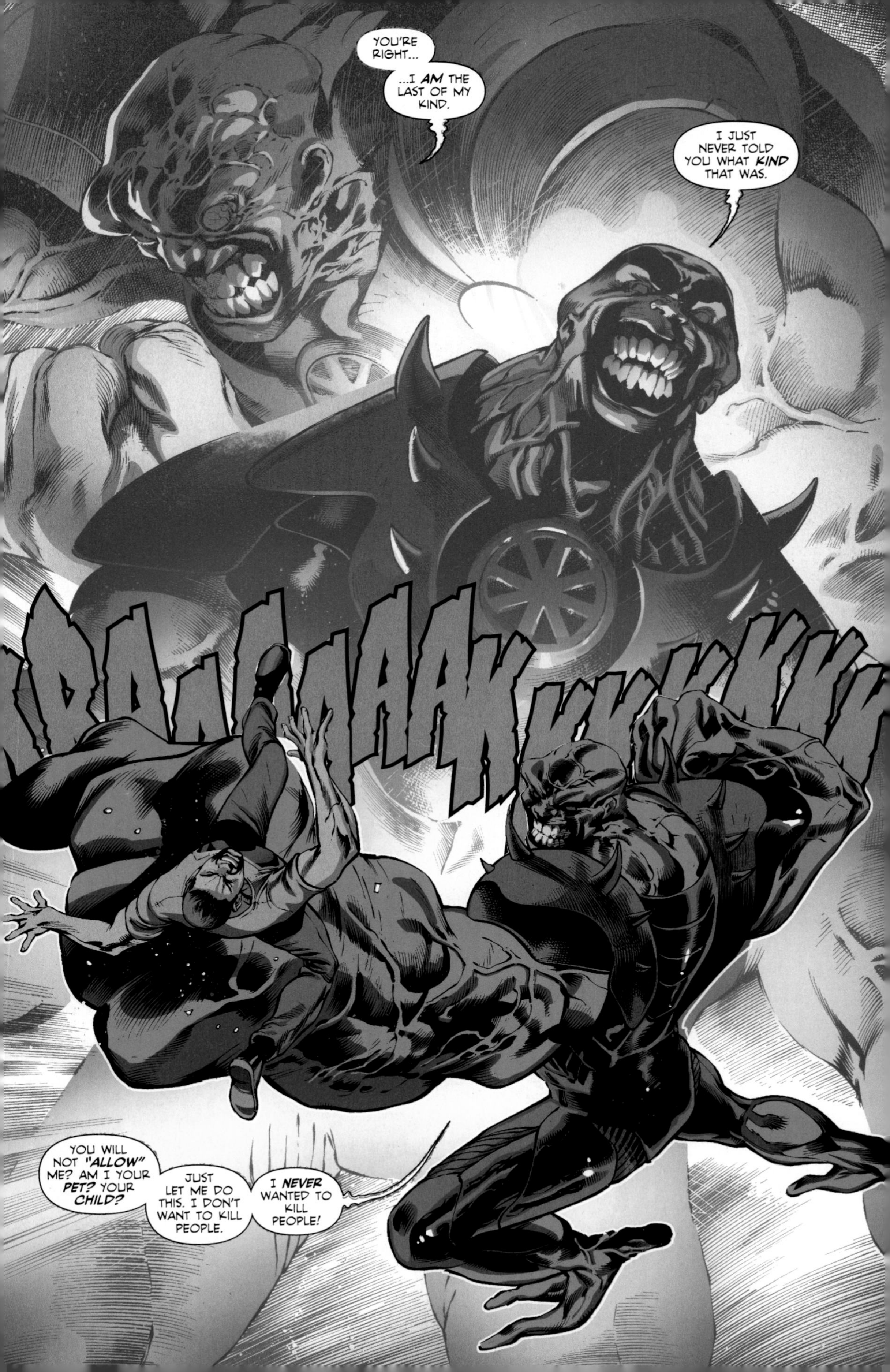
YOU'RE RIGHT...
...I AM THE LAST OF MY KIND.
I JUST NEVER TOLD YOU WHAT KIND THAT WAS.
YOU WILL NOT "ALLOW" ME? AM I YOUR PET? YOUR CHILD?
JUST LET ME DO THIS. I DON'T WANT TO KILL PEOPLE.
I NEVER WANTED TO KILL PEOPLE!

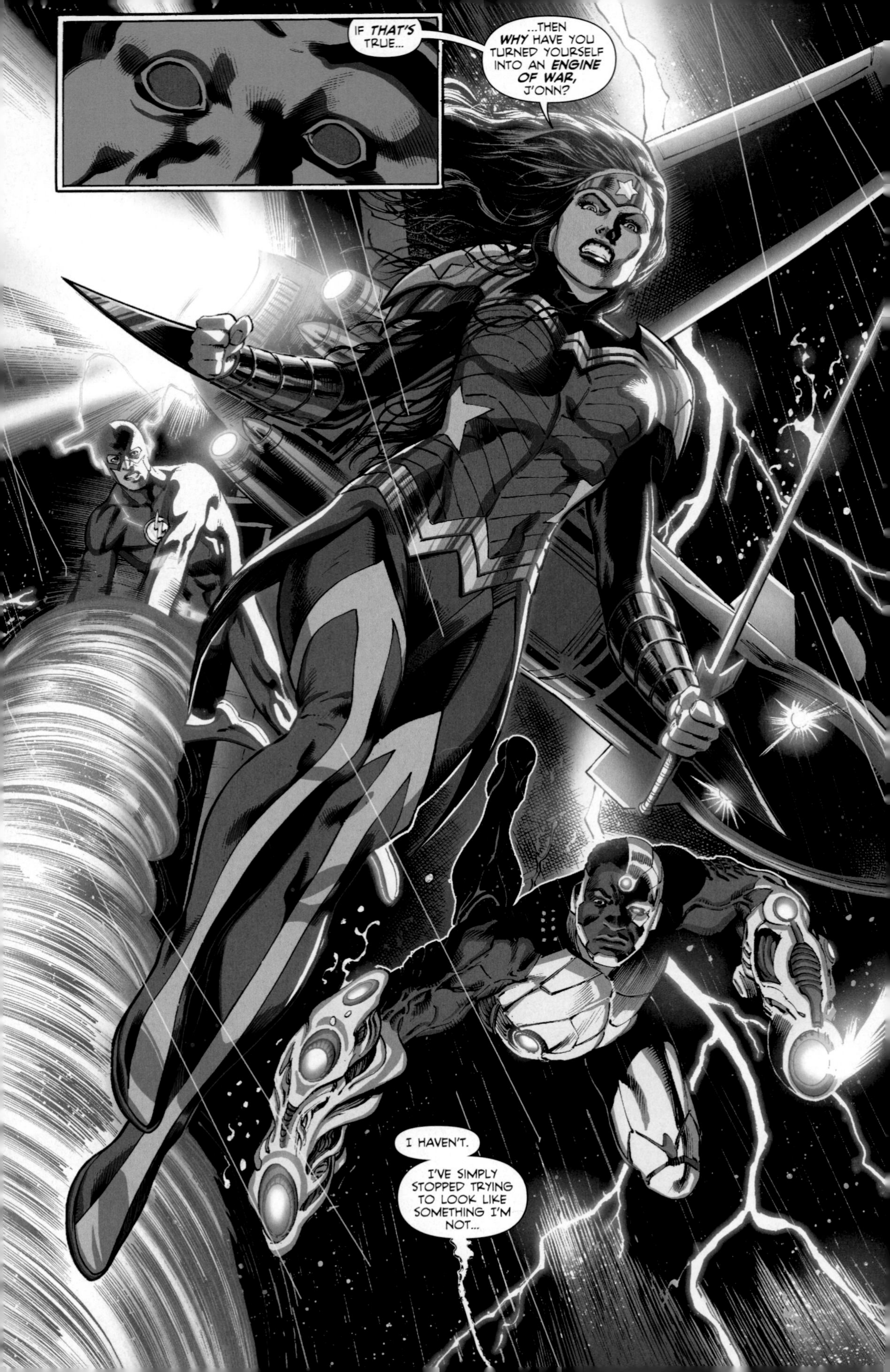
IF *THAT'S* TRUE...
...THEN *WHY* HAVE YOU TURNED YOURSELF INTO AN *ENGINE OF WAR,* J'ONN?
I HAVEN'T.
I'VE SIMPLY STOPPED TRYING TO LOOK LIKE SOMETHING I'M NOT...

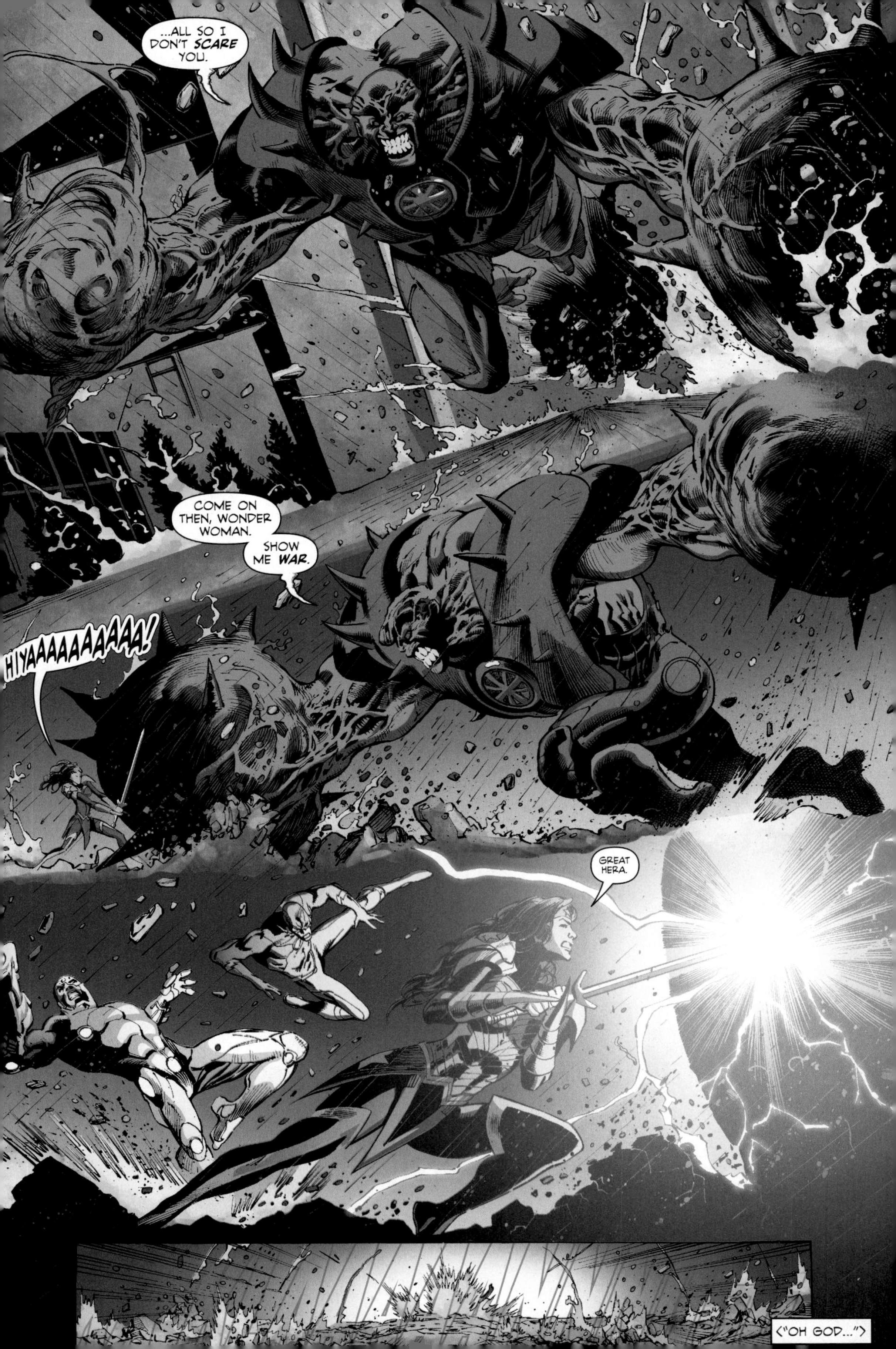
...ALL SO I DON'T SCARE YOU.
COME ON THEN, WONDER WOMAN.
SHOW ME WAR.
HIYAAAAAAAAAA!
GREAT HERA.
<"OH GOD...">

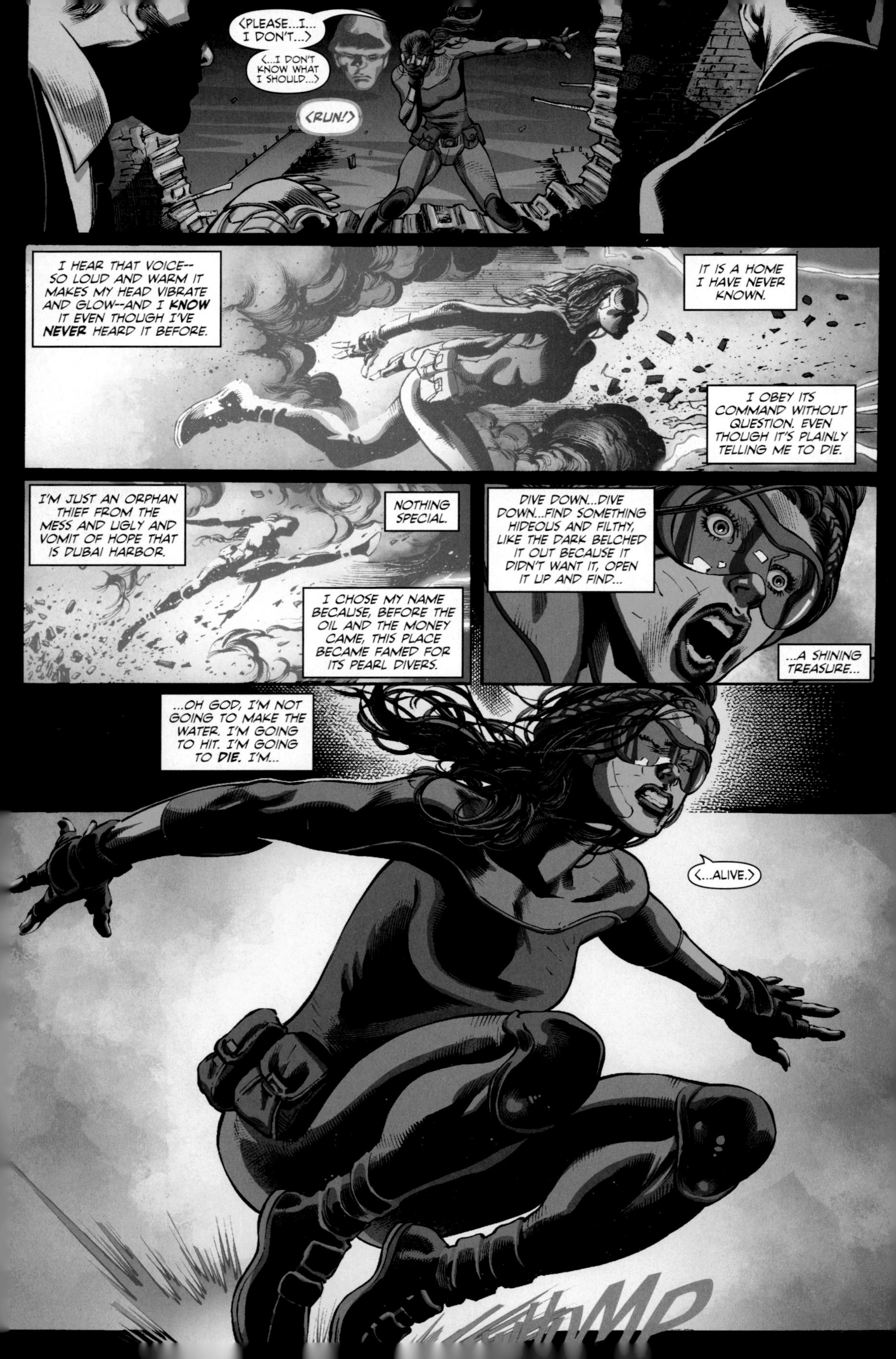

<PLEASE...I... I DON'T...>
<...I DON'T KNOW WHAT I SHOULD...>
<RUN!>
I HEAR THAT VOICE-- SO LOUD AND WARM IT MAKES MY HEAD VIBRATE AND GLOW--AND I **KNOW** IT EVEN THOUGH I'VE **NEVER** HEARD IT BEFORE.
IT IS A HOME I HAVE NEVER KNOWN.
I OBEY ITS COMMAND WITHOUT QUESTION. EVEN THOUGH IT'S PLAINLY TELLING ME TO DIE.
I'M JUST AN ORPHAN THIEF FROM THE MESS AND UGLY AND VOMIT OF HOPE THAT IS DUBAI HARBOR.
NOTHING SPECIAL.
I CHOSE MY NAME BECAUSE, BEFORE THE OIL AND THE MONEY CAME, THIS PLACE BECAME FAMED FOR ITS PEARL DIVERS.
DIVE DOWN...DIVE DOWN...FIND SOMETHING HIDEOUS AND FILTHY, LIKE THE DARK BELCHED IT OUT BECAUSE IT DIDN'T WANT IT, OPEN IT UP AND FIND...
...A SHINING TREASURE...
...OH GOD, I'M NOT GOING TO MAKE THE WATER. I'M GOING TO HIT. I'M GOING TO **DIE.** I'M...
<...ALIVE.>

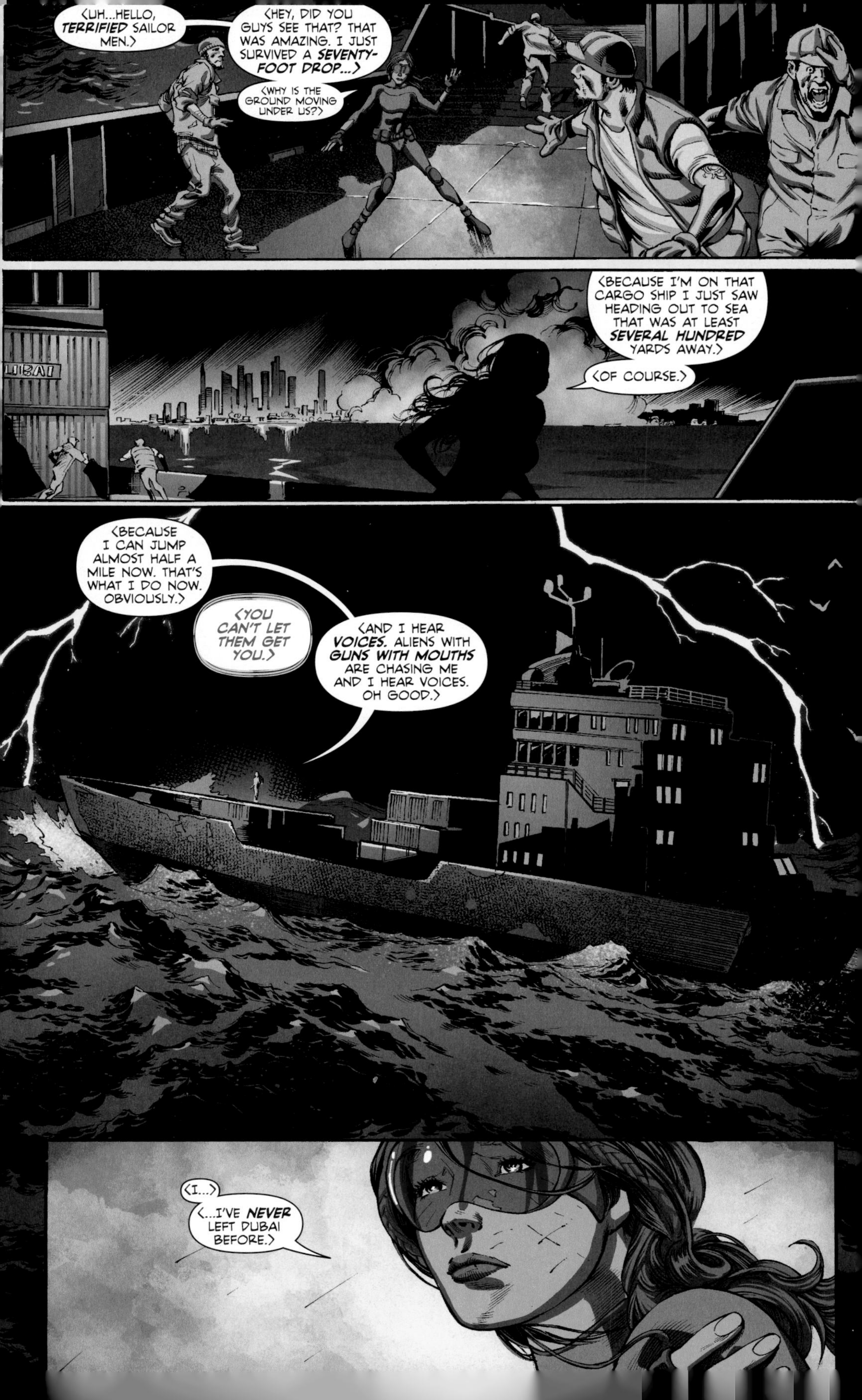

<UH...HELLO, TERRIFIED SAILOR MEN.>
<HEY, DID YOU GUYS SEE THAT? THAT WAS AMAZING. I JUST SURVIVED A SEVENTY-FOOT DROP...>
<WHY IS THE GROUND MOVING UNDER US?>
DUBAI
<BECAUSE I'M ON THAT CARGO SHIP I JUST SAW HEADING OUT TO SEA THAT WAS AT LEAST SEVERAL HUNDRED YARDS AWAY.>
<OF COURSE.>
<BECAUSE I CAN JUMP ALMOST HALF A MILE NOW. THAT'S WHAT I DO NOW. OBVIOUSLY.>
<YOU CAN'T LET THEM GET YOU.>
<AND I HEAR VOICES. ALIENS WITH GUNS WITH MOUTHS ARE CHASING ME AND I HEAR VOICES. OH GOOD.>
<I...>
<...I'VE NEVER LEFT DUBAI BEFORE.>

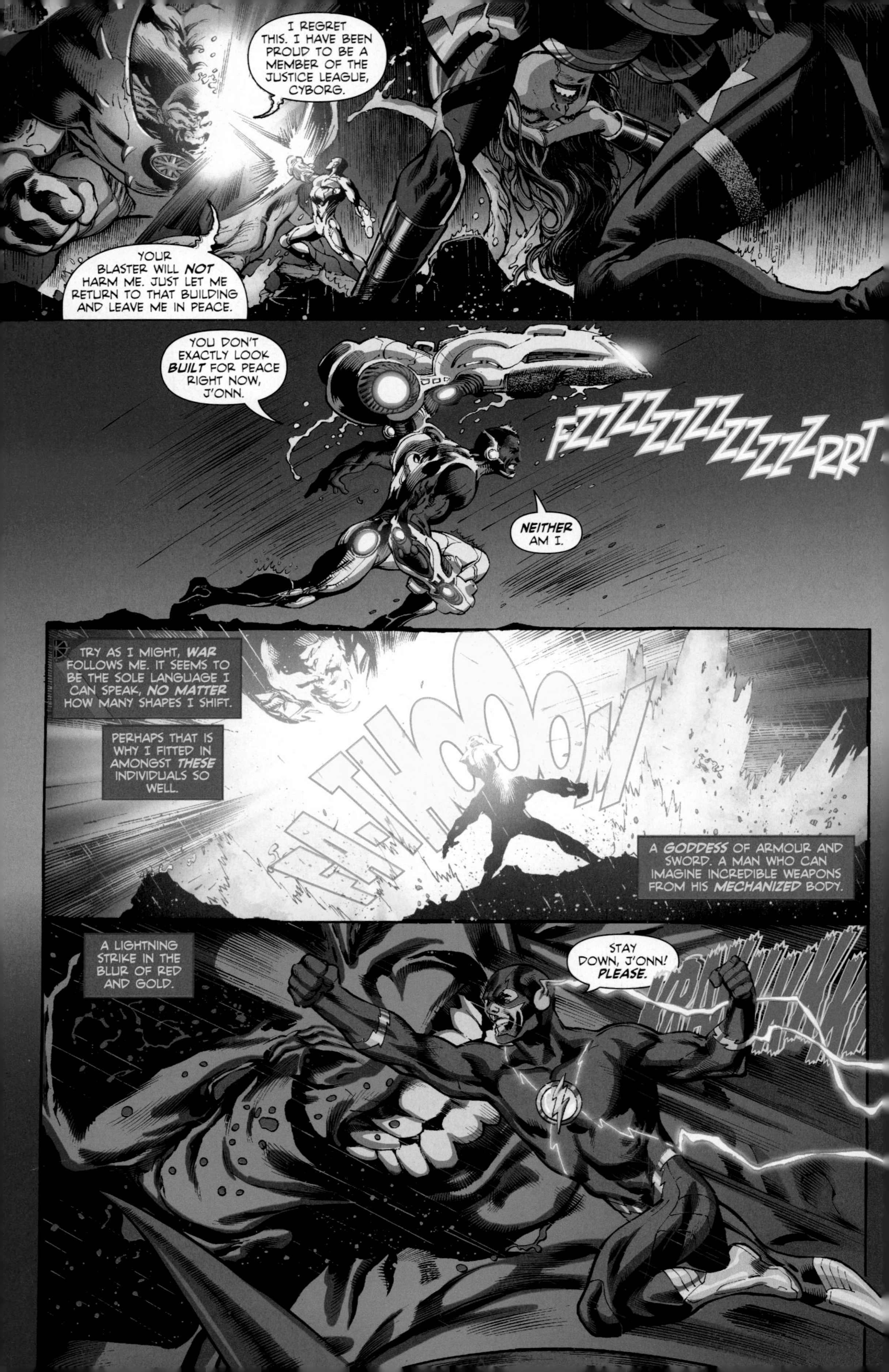
I REGRET THIS. I HAVE BEEN PROUD TO BE A MEMBER OF THE JUSTICE LEAGUE, CYBORG.
YOUR BLASTER WILL NOT HARM ME. JUST LET ME RETURN TO THAT BUILDING AND LEAVE ME IN PEACE.
YOU DON'T EXACTLY LOOK BUILT FOR PEACE RIGHT NOW, J'ONN.
FZZZZZZZZZZZZZRRT
NEITHER AM I.
TRY AS I MIGHT, WAR FOLLOWS ME. IT SEEMS TO BE THE SOLE LANGUAGE I CAN SPEAK, NO MATTER HOW MANY SHAPES I SHIFT.
PERHAPS THAT IS WHY I FITTED IN AMONGST THESE INDIVIDUALS SO WELL.
A GODDESS OF ARMOUR AND SWORD. A MAN WHO CAN IMAGINE INCREDIBLE WEAPONS FROM HIS MECHANIZED BODY.
A LIGHTNING STRIKE IN THE BLUR OF RED AND GOLD.
STAY DOWN, J'ONN! PLEASE.

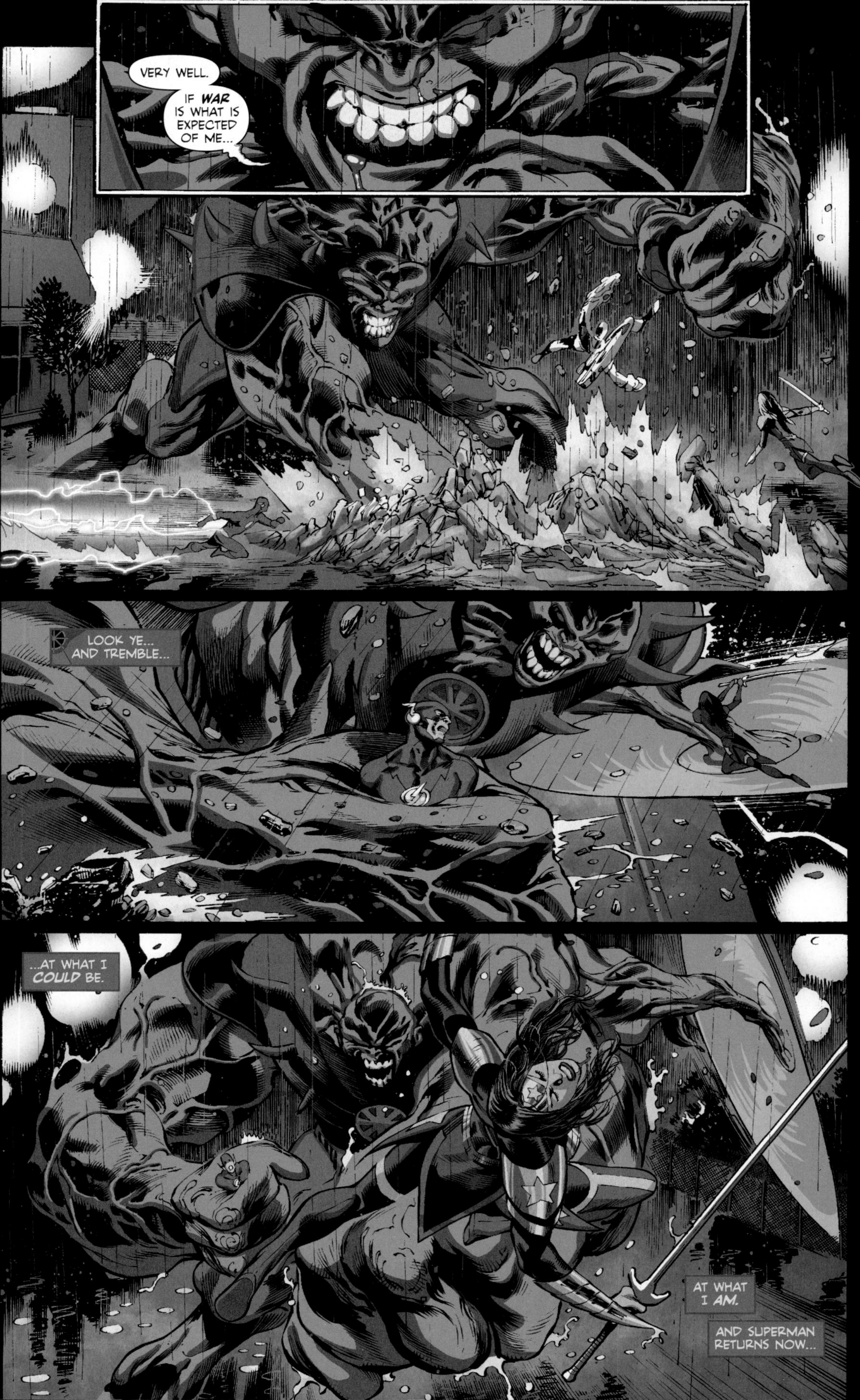
VERY WELL.
IF *WAR* IS WHAT IS EXPECTED OF ME...
LOOK YE... AND TREMBLE...
...AT WHAT I *COULD* BE.
AT WHAT I *AM*.
AND SUPERMAN RETURNS NOW...

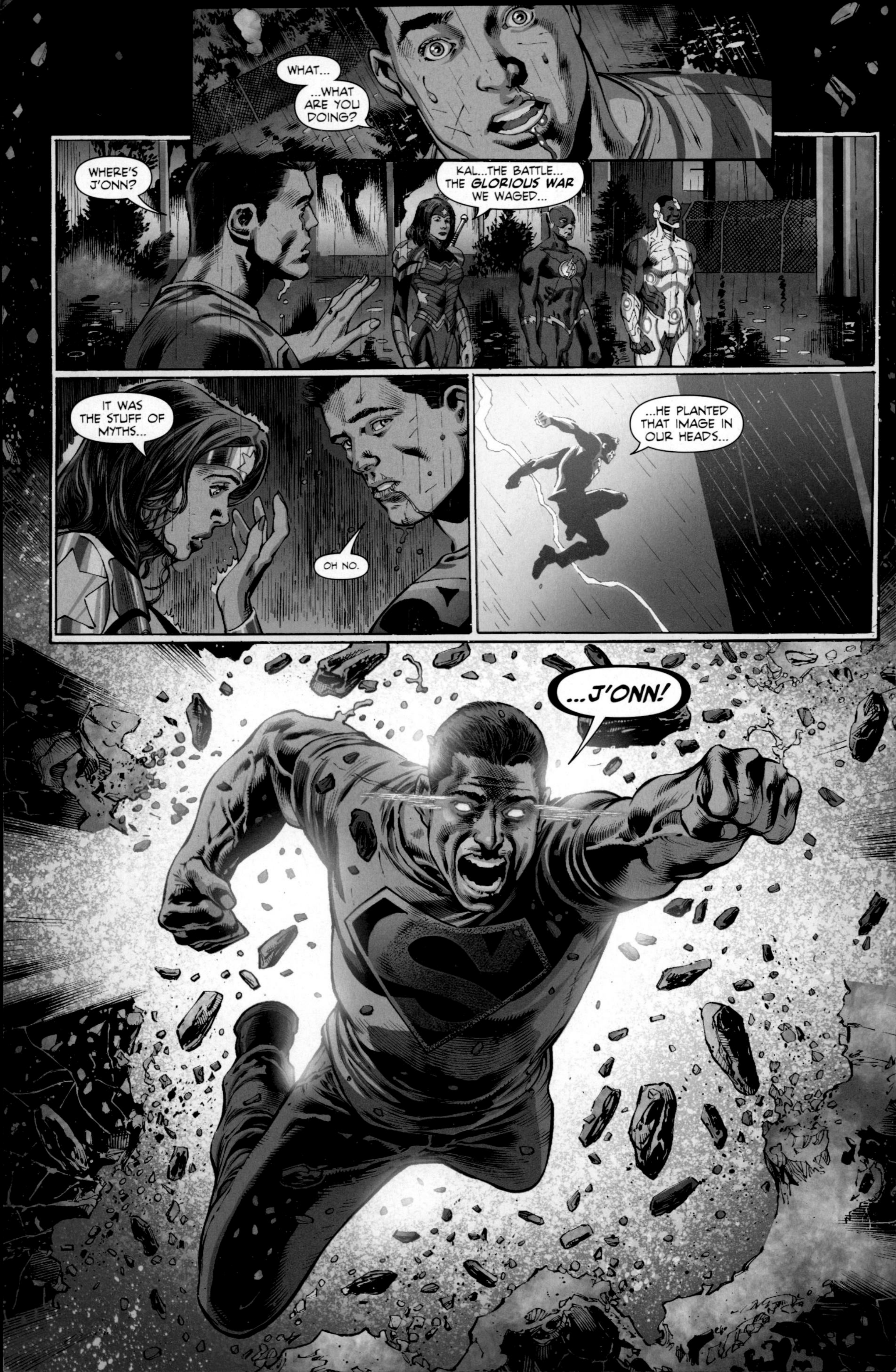
WHAT...
...WHAT ARE YOU DOING?
WHERE'S J'ONN?
KAL...THE BATTLE... THE GLORIOUS WAR WE WAGED...
IT WAS THE STUFF OF MYTHS...
OH NO.
...HE PLANTED THAT IMAGE IN OUR HEADS...
...J'ONN!

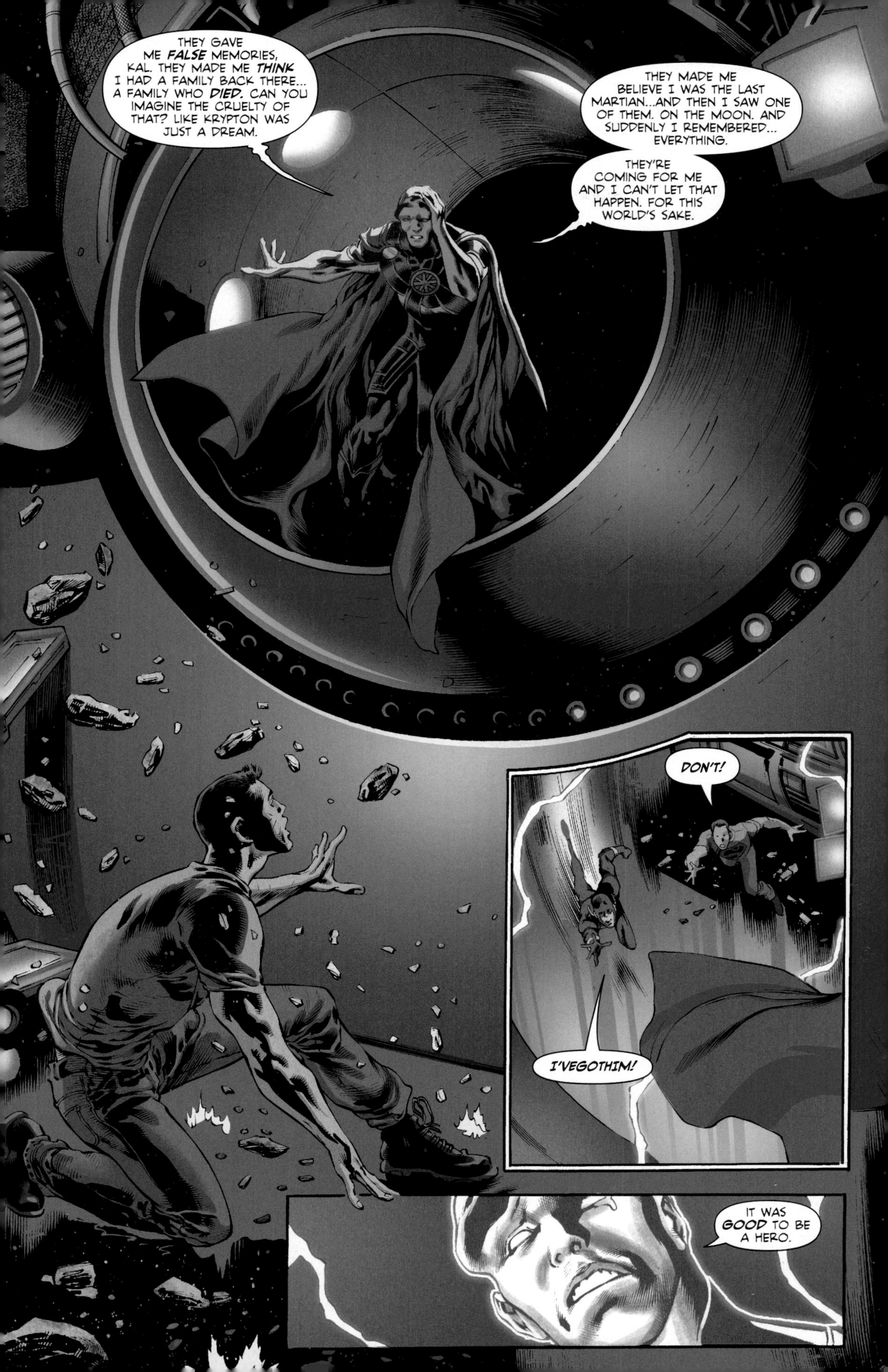
THEY GAVE ME FALSE MEMORIES, KAL. THEY MADE ME THINK I HAD A FAMILY BACK THERE... A FAMILY WHO DIED. CAN YOU IMAGINE THE CRUELTY OF THAT? LIKE KRYPTON WAS JUST A DREAM.
THEY MADE ME BELIEVE I WAS THE LAST MARTIAN...AND THEN I SAW ONE OF THEM. ON THE MOON. AND SUDDENLY I REMEMBERED... EVERYTHING.
THEY'RE COMING FOR ME AND I CAN'T LET THAT HAPPEN. FOR THIS WORLD'S SAKE.
DON'T!
I'VEGOTHIM!
IT WAS GOOD TO BE A HERO.

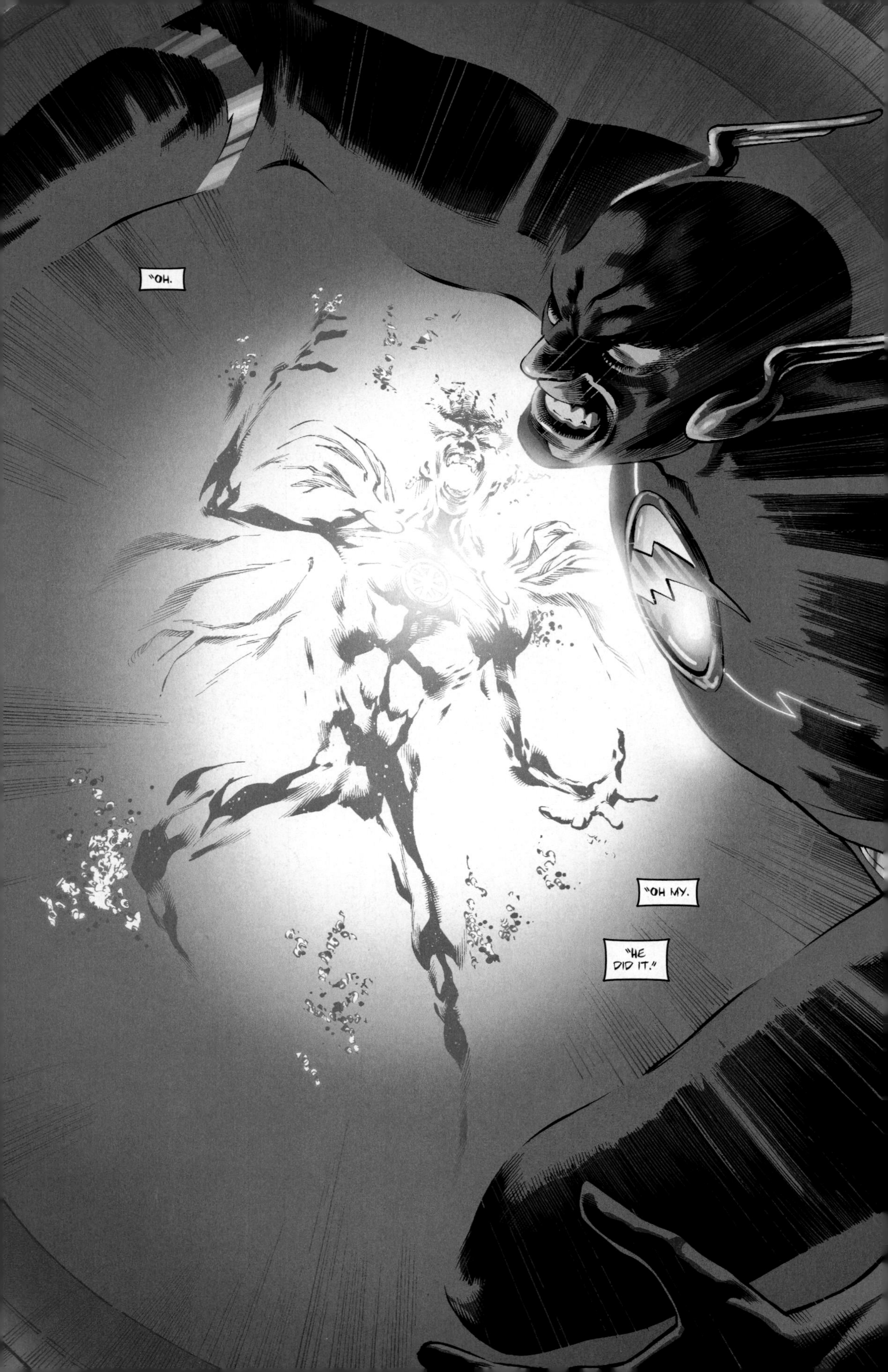
"OH.
"OH MY.
"HE DID IT."

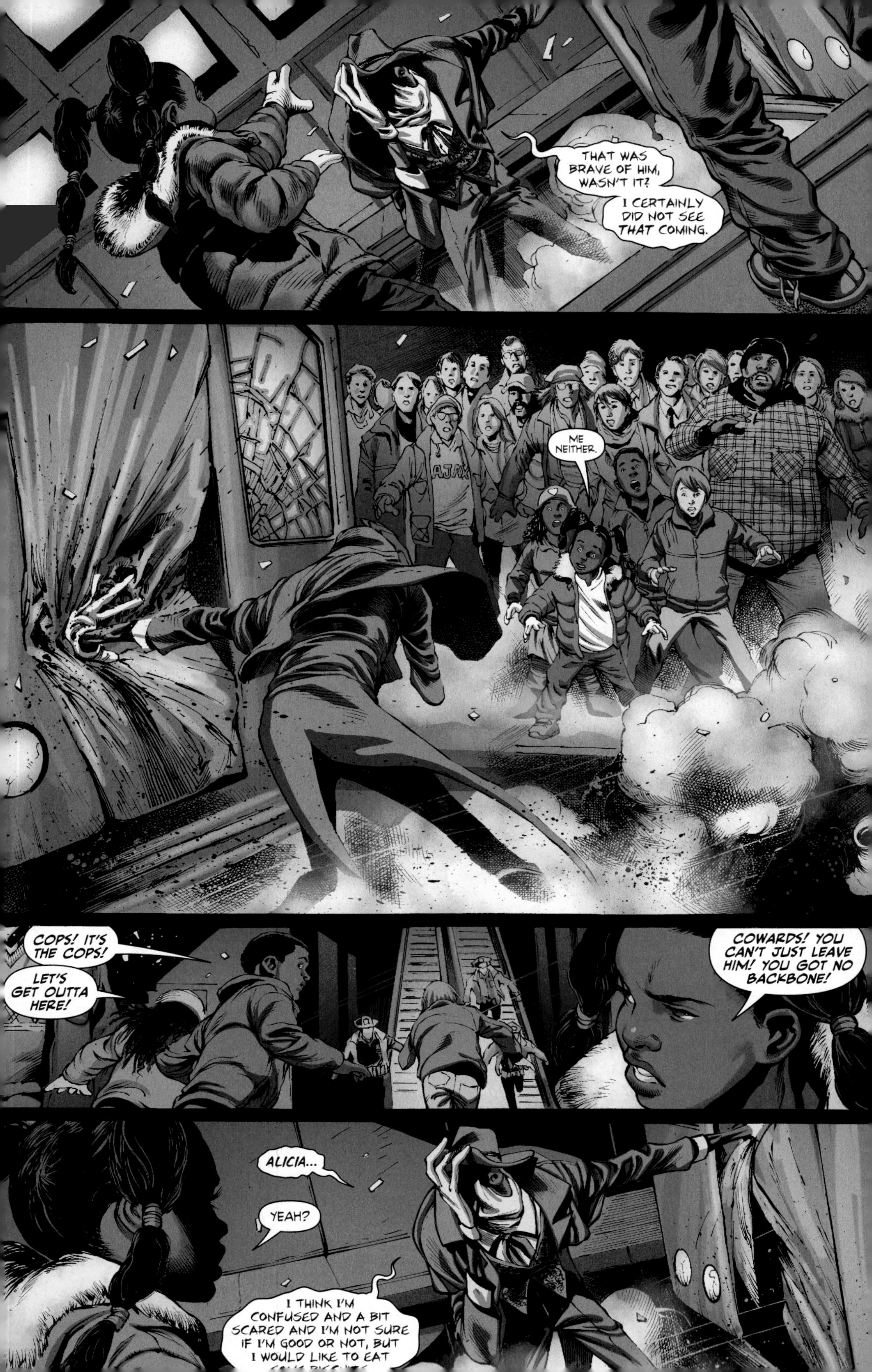
THAT WAS BRAVE OF HIM, WASN'T IT?
I CERTAINLY DID NOT SEE THAT COMING.
ME NEITHER.
COPS! IT'S THE COPS!
LET'S GET OUTTA HERE!
COWARDS! YOU CAN'T JUST LEAVE HIM! YOU GOT NO BACKBONE!
ALICIA...
YEAH?
I THINK I'M CONFUSED AND A BIT SCARED AND I'M NOT SURE IF I'M GOOD OR NOT, BUT I WOULD LIKE TO EAT

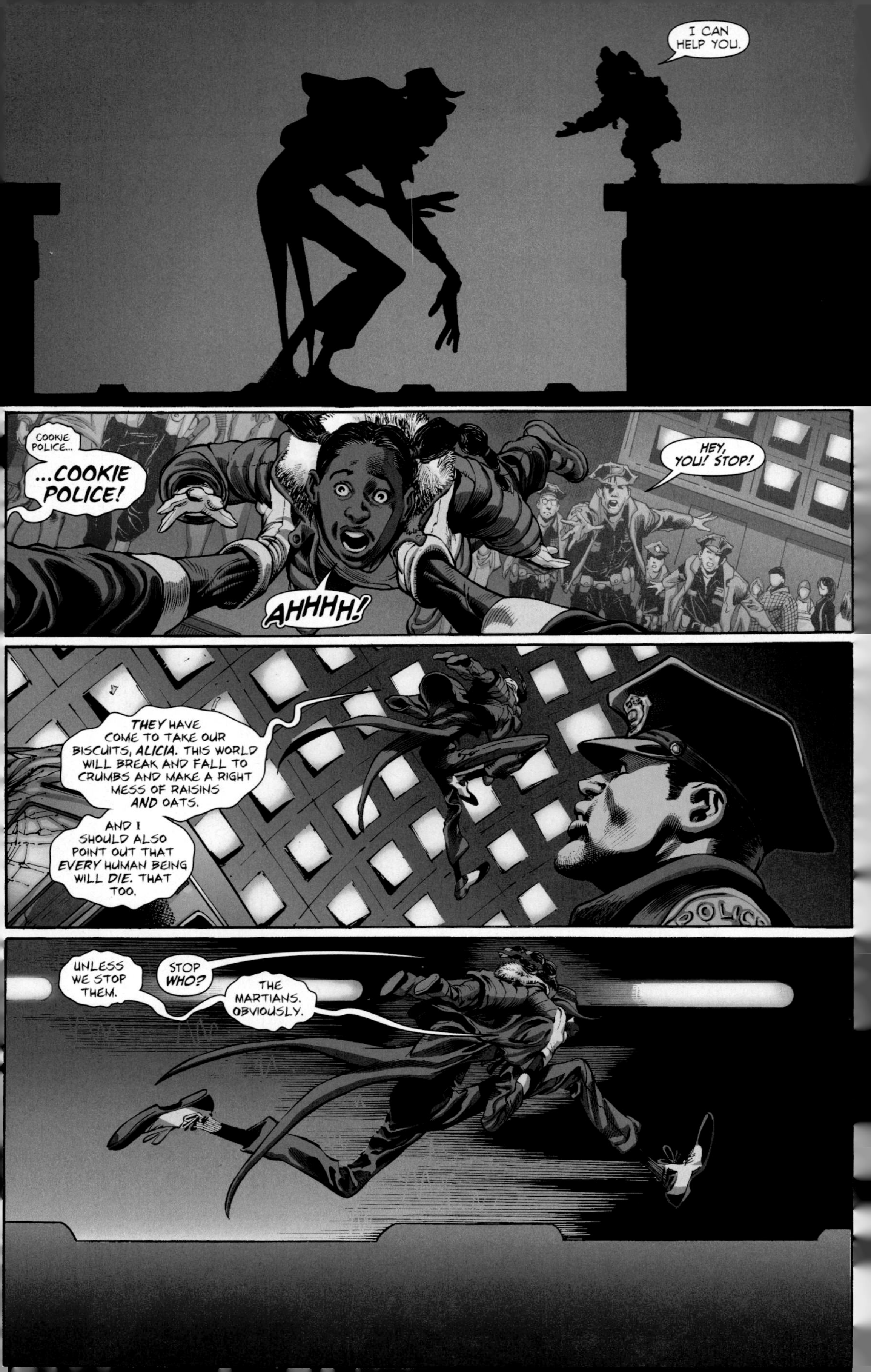
I CAN HELP YOU.
COOKIE POLICE...
...COOKIE POLICE!
HEY, YOU! STOP!
AHHHH!
THEY HAVE COME TO TAKE OUR BISCUITS, ALICIA. THIS WORLD WILL BREAK AND FALL TO CRUMBS AND MAKE A RIGHT MESS OF RAISINS AND OATS.
AND I SHOULD ALSO POINT OUT THAT EVERY HUMAN BEING WILL DIE. THAT TOO.
POLICE
UNLESS WE STOP THEM.
STOP WHO?
THE MARTIANS. OBVIOUSLY.

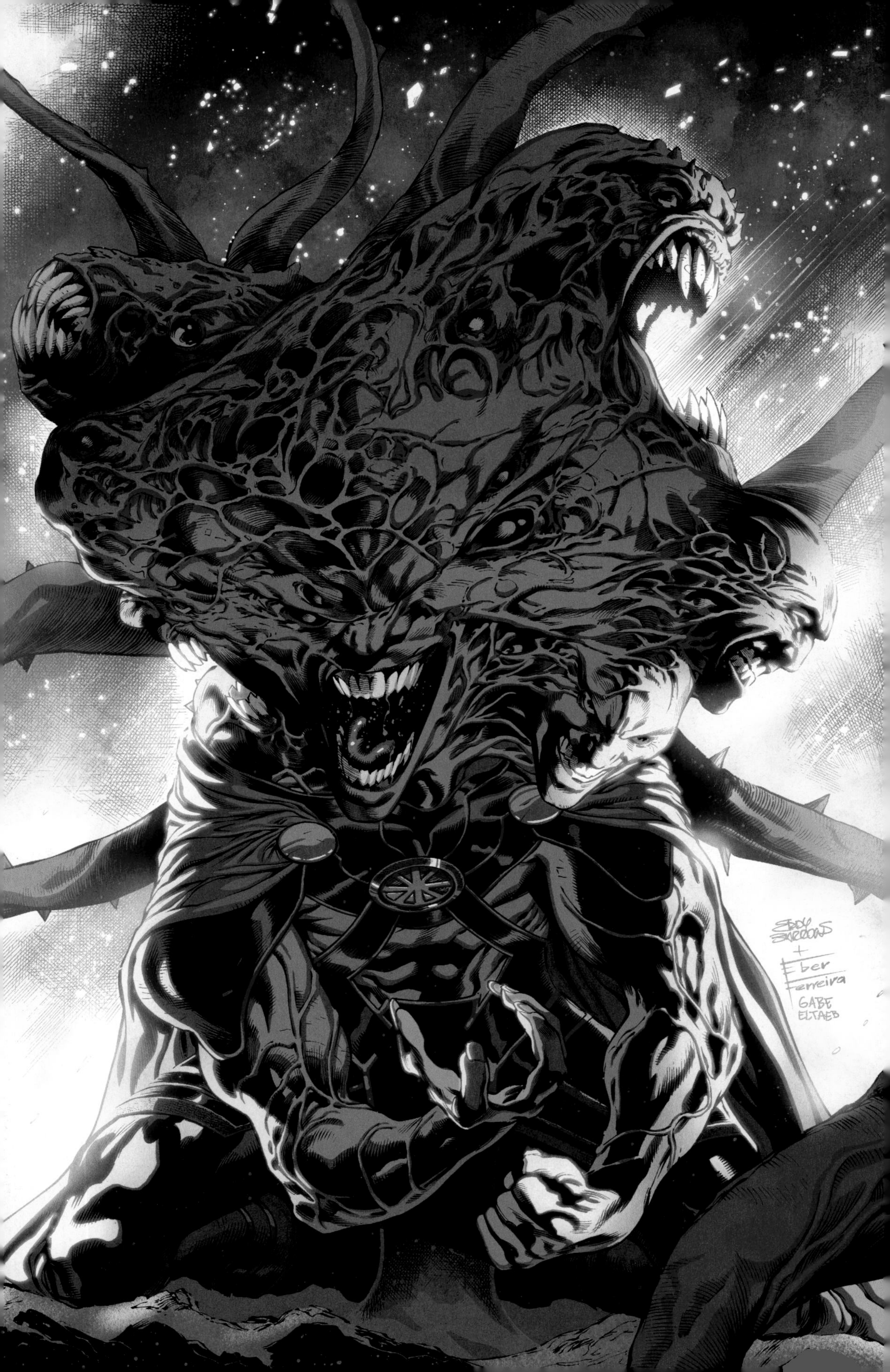
Eber
Ferreira
GABE
ELTAEB

DIFFERENT WORLDS

cover by **EDDY BARROWS, EBER FERREIRA, & GABE ELTAEB**

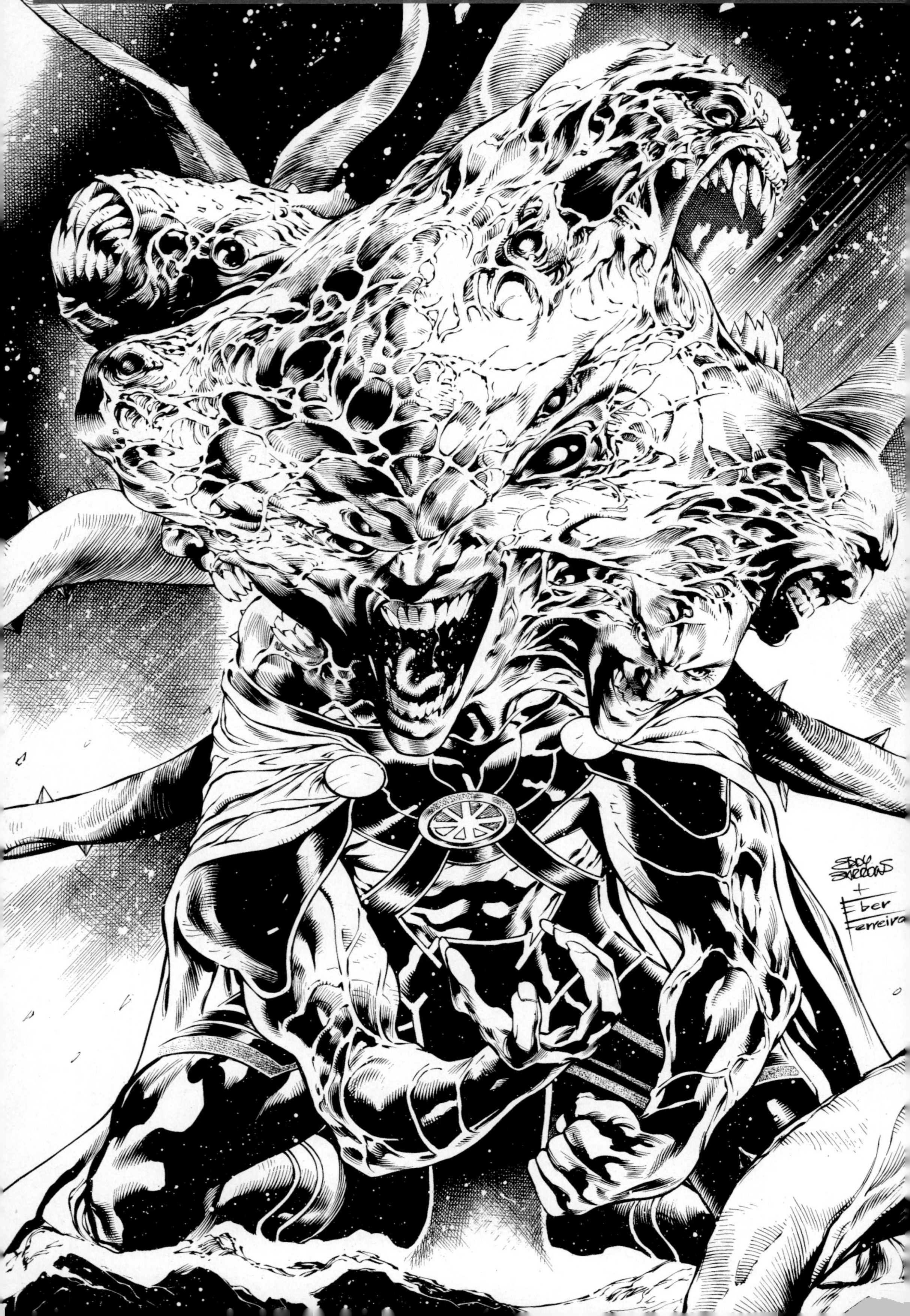
EDDY BARROWS
+
Eber
Ferreira

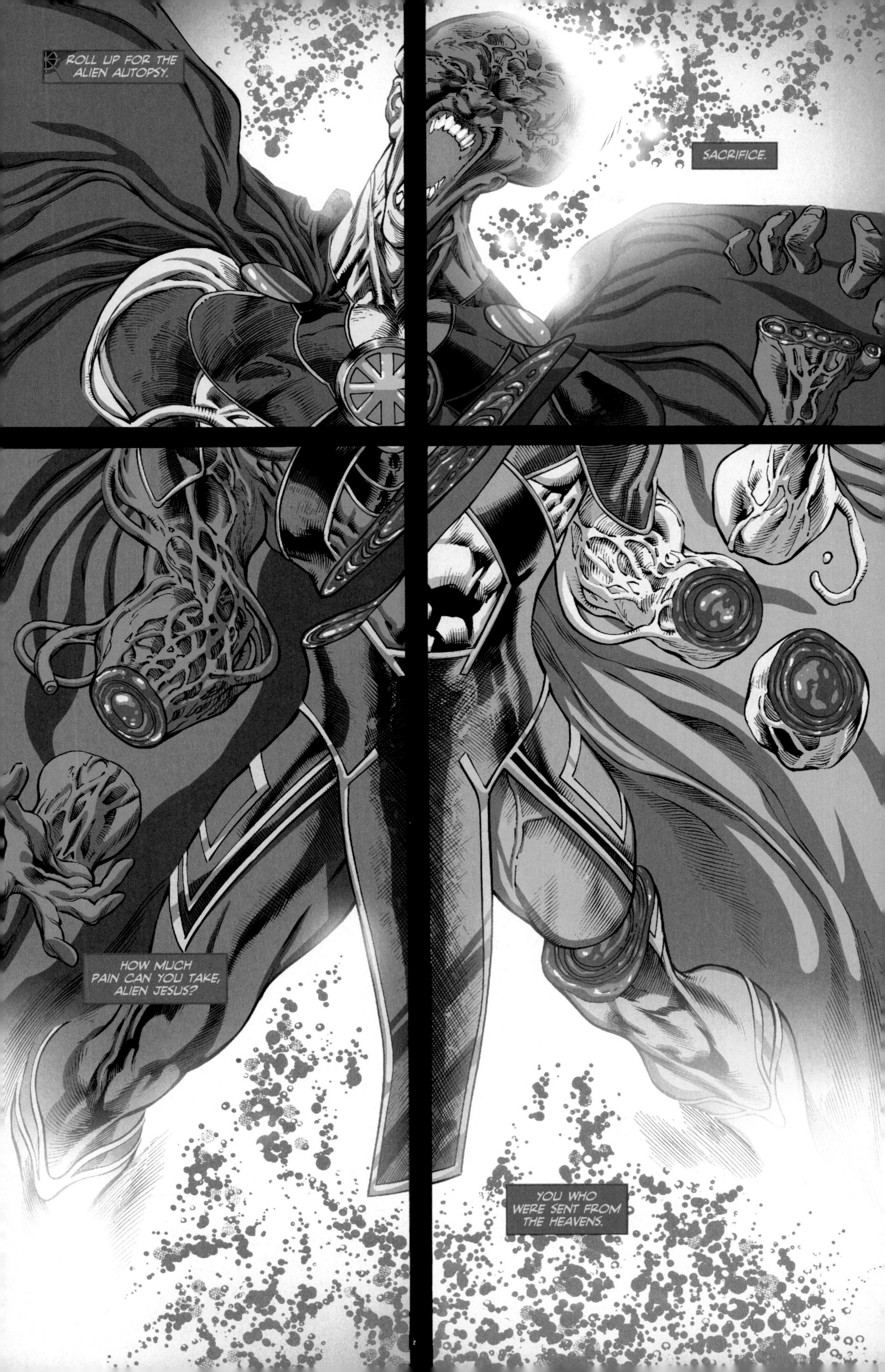
ROLL UP FOR THE ALIEN AUTOPSY.
SACRIFICE.
HOW MUCH PAIN CAN YOU TAKE, ALIEN JESUS?
YOU WHO WERE SENT FROM THE HEAVENS.

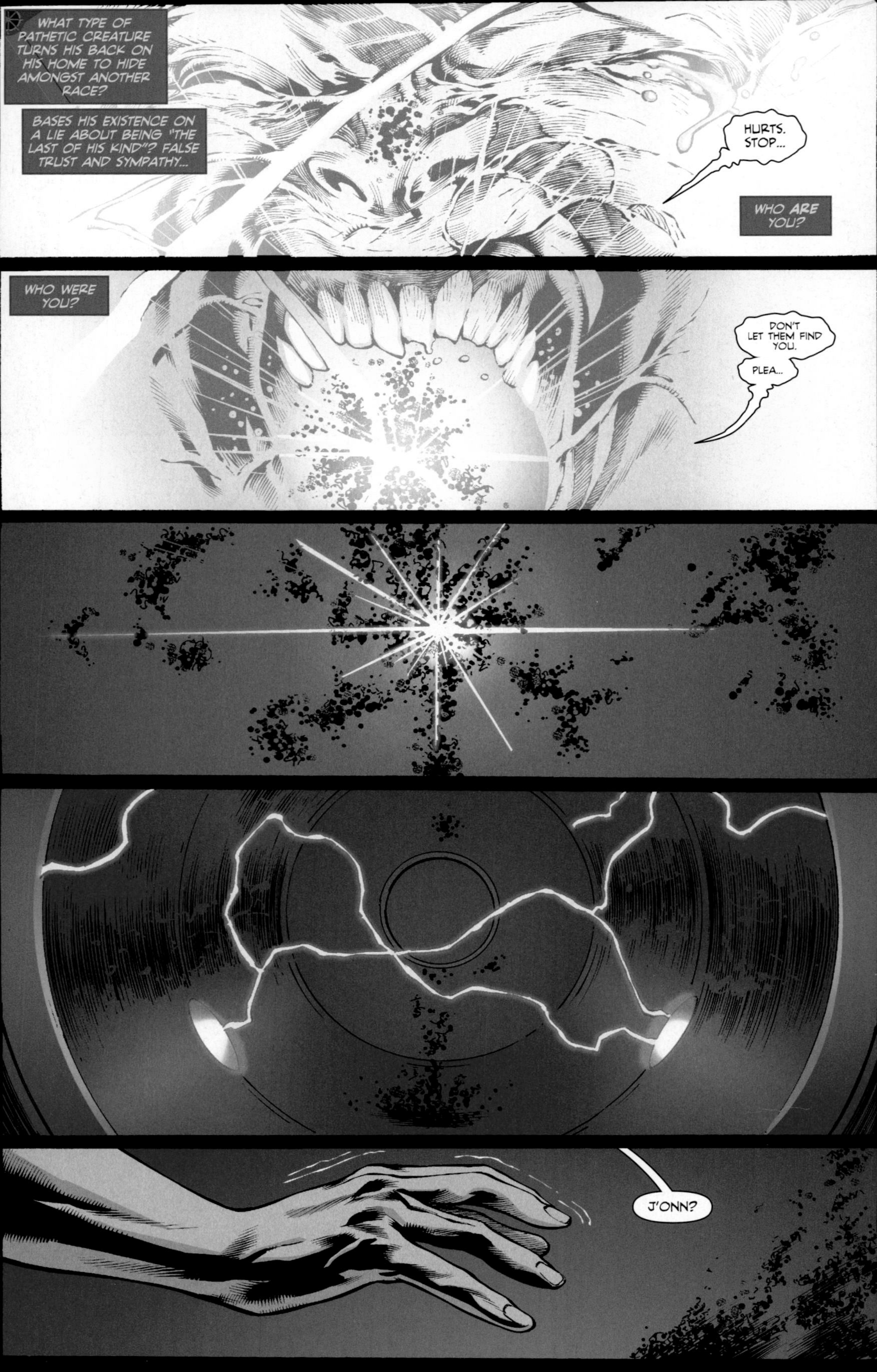
WHAT TYPE OF PATHETIC CREATURE TURNS HIS BACK ON HIS HOME TO HIDE AMONGST ANOTHER RACE?
BASES HIS EXISTENCE ON A LIE ABOUT BEING "THE LAST OF HIS KIND"? FALSE TRUST AND SYMPATHY...
HURTS. STOP...
WHO ARE YOU?
WHO WERE YOU?
DON'T LET THEM FIND YOU.
PLEA...
J'ONN?

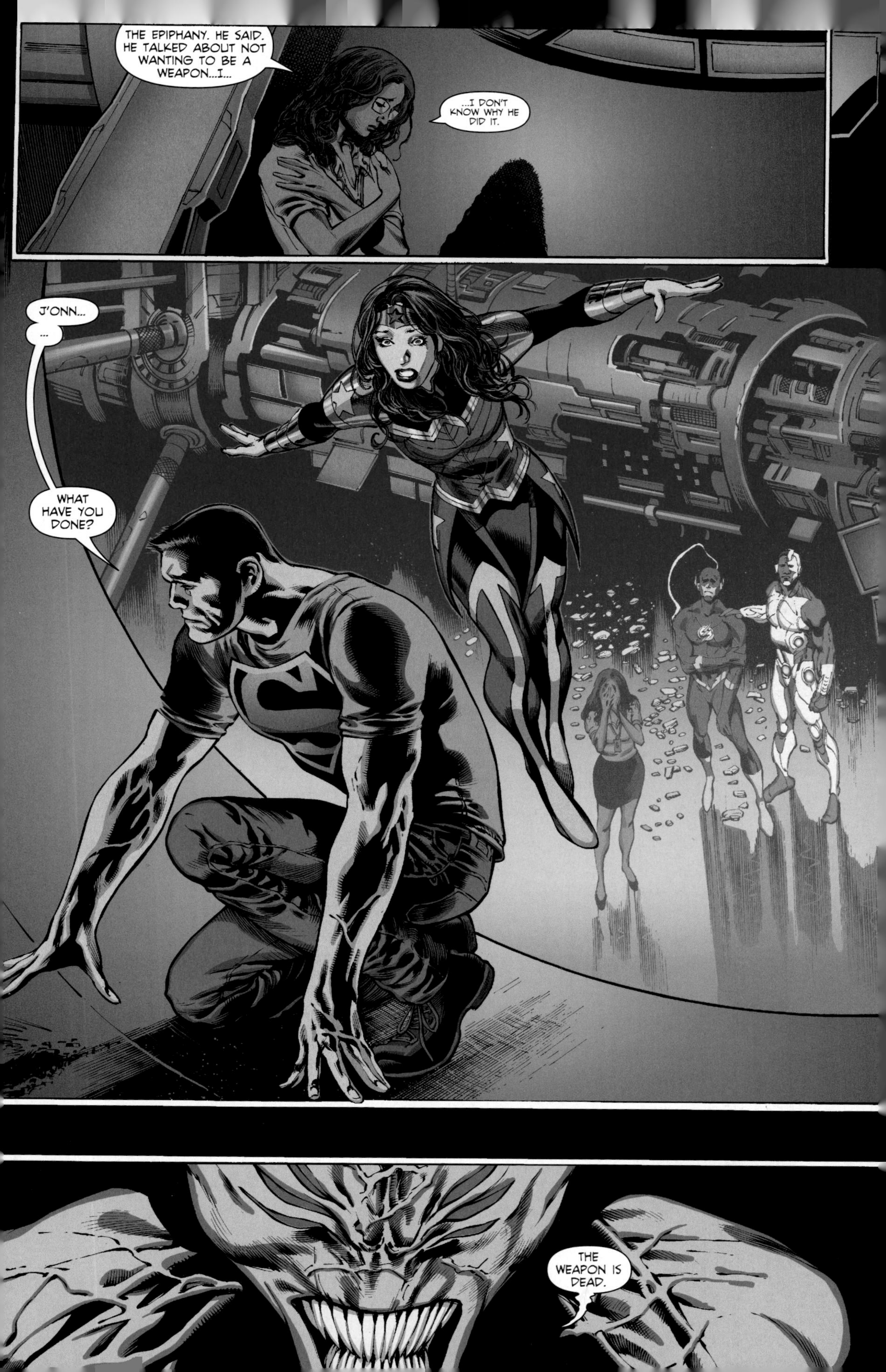
THE EPIPHANY. HE SAID. HE TALKED ABOUT NOT WANTING TO BE A WEAPON...I...
...I DON'T KNOW WHY HE DID IT.
J'ONN...
...
WHAT HAVE YOU DONE?
THE WEAPON IS DEAD.

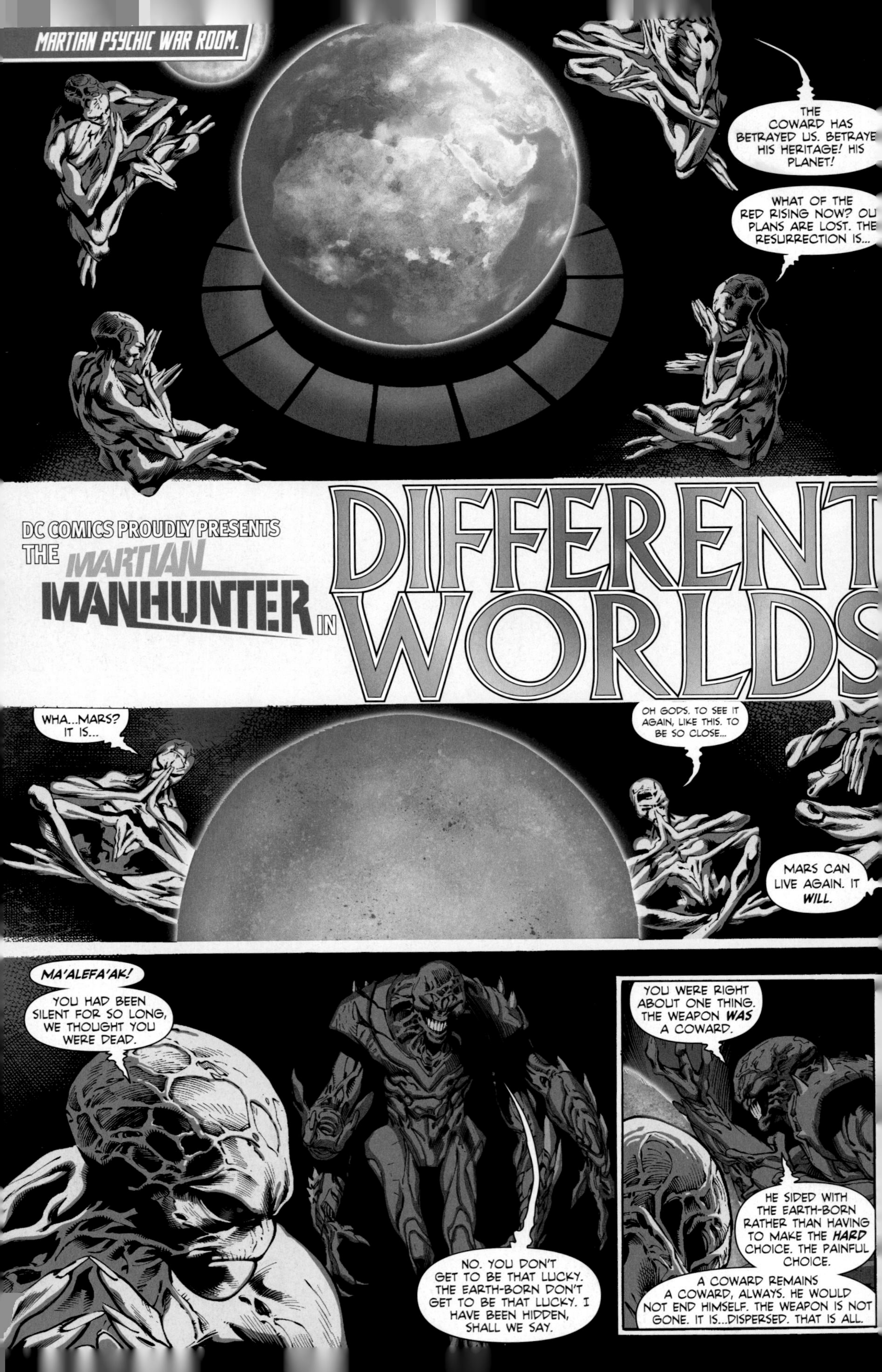
MARTIAN PSYCHIC WAR ROOM.
THE COWARD HAS BETRAYED US. BETRAYE HIS HERITAGE! HIS PLANET!
WHAT OF THE RED RISING NOW? OU PLANS ARE LOST. THE RESURRECTION IS...
DC COMICS PROUDLY PRESENTS
THE MARTIAN MANHUNTER IN
DIFFERENT WORLDS
WHA...MARS? IT IS...
OH GODS. TO SEE IT AGAIN, LIKE THIS. TO BE SO CLOSE...
MARS CAN LIVE AGAIN. IT WILL.
MA'ALEFA'AK!
YOU HAD BEEN SILENT FOR SO LONG, WE THOUGHT YOU WERE DEAD.
NO. YOU DON'T GET TO BE THAT LUCKY. THE EARTH-BORN DON'T GET TO BE THAT LUCKY. I HAVE BEEN HIDDEN, SHALL WE SAY.
YOU WERE RIGHT ABOUT ONE THING. THE WEAPON WAS A COWARD.
HE SIDED WITH THE EARTH-BORN RATHER THAN HAVING TO MAKE THE HARD CHOICE. THE PAINFUL CHOICE.
A COWARD REMAINS A COWARD, ALWAYS. HE WOULD NOT END HIMSELF. THE WEAPON IS NOT GONE. IT IS...DISPERSED. THAT IS ALL.

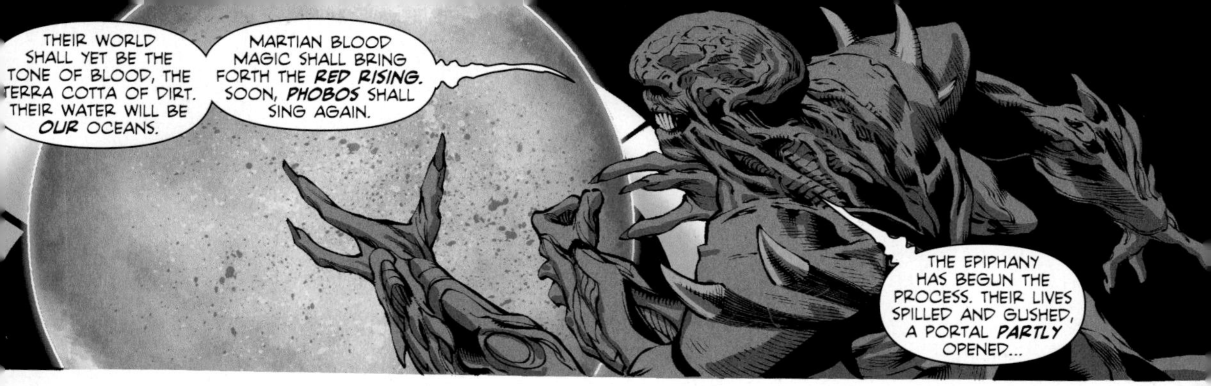
THEIR WORLD SHALL YET BE THE TONE OF BLOOD, THE TERRA COTTA OF DIRT. THEIR WATER WILL BE *OUR* OCEANS.
MARTIAN BLOOD MAGIC SHALL BRING FORTH THE ***RED RISING.*** SOON, ***PHOBOS*** SHALL SING AGAIN.
THE EPIPHANY HAS BEGUN THE PROCESS. THEIR LIVES SPILLED AND GUSHED, A PORTAL ***PARTLY*** OPENED...

ROB WILLIAMS WRITER EDDY BARROWS PENCILS
BER FERREIRA INKS GABE ELTAEB COLORIST TOM NAPOLITANO LETTERER

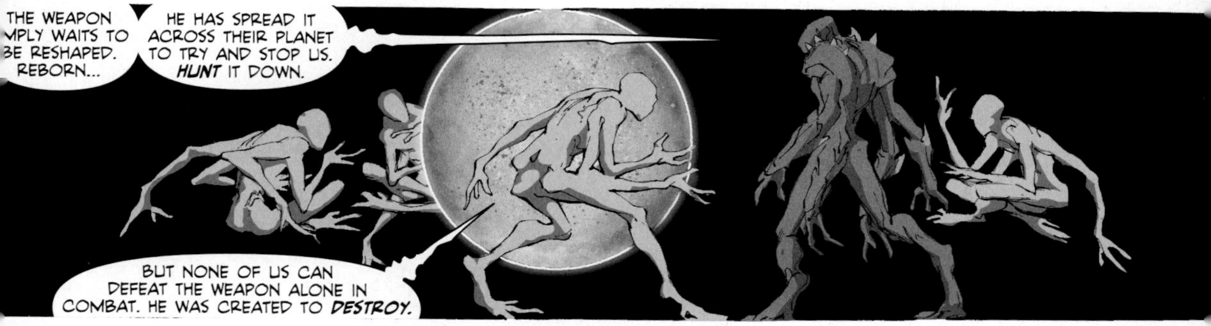
THE WEAPON MPLY WAITS TO BE RESHAPED. REBORN...
HE HAS SPREAD IT ACROSS THEIR PLANET TO TRY AND STOP US. ***HUNT*** IT DOWN.
BUT NONE OF US CAN DEFEAT THE WEAPON ALONE IN COMBAT. HE WAS CREATED TO ***DESTROY.***

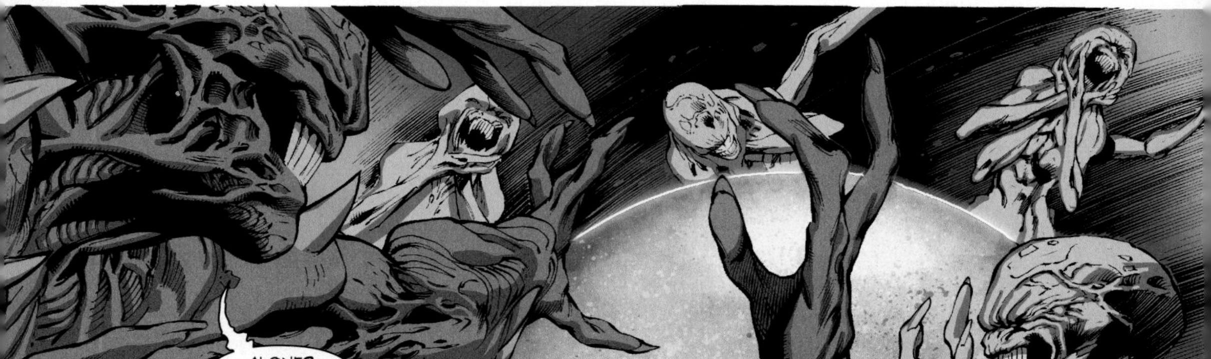
ALONE? NO...YOU ARE CORRECT ABOUT THAT MUCH, AT LEAST.
BUT TOGETHER...
AH... WHAT...WHAT ARE YOU...***RELEASE US!***

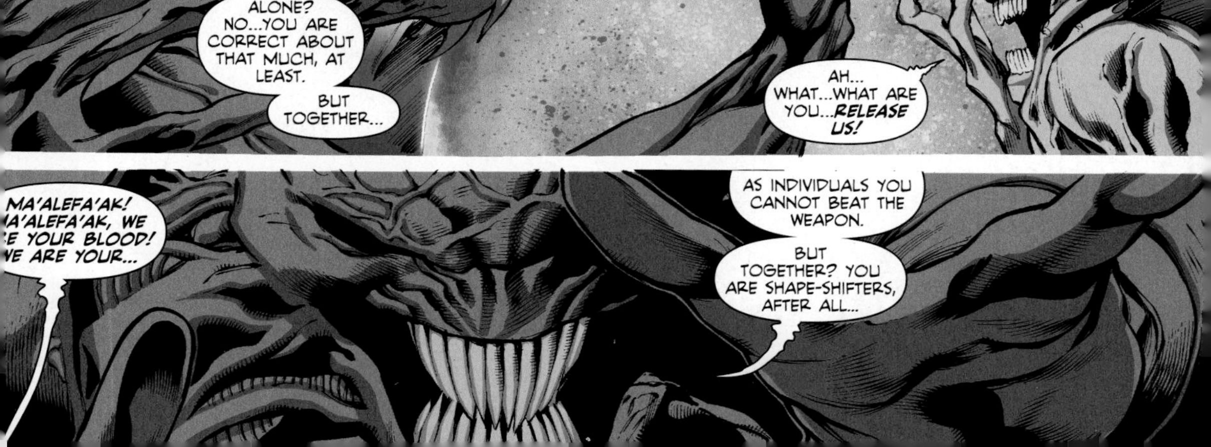
MA'ALEFA'AK! IA'ALEFA'AK, WE E YOUR BLOOD! VE ARE YOUR...
AS INDIVIDUALS YOU CANNOT BEAT THE WEAPON.
BUT TOGETHER? YOU ARE SHAPE-SHIFTERS, AFTER ALL...

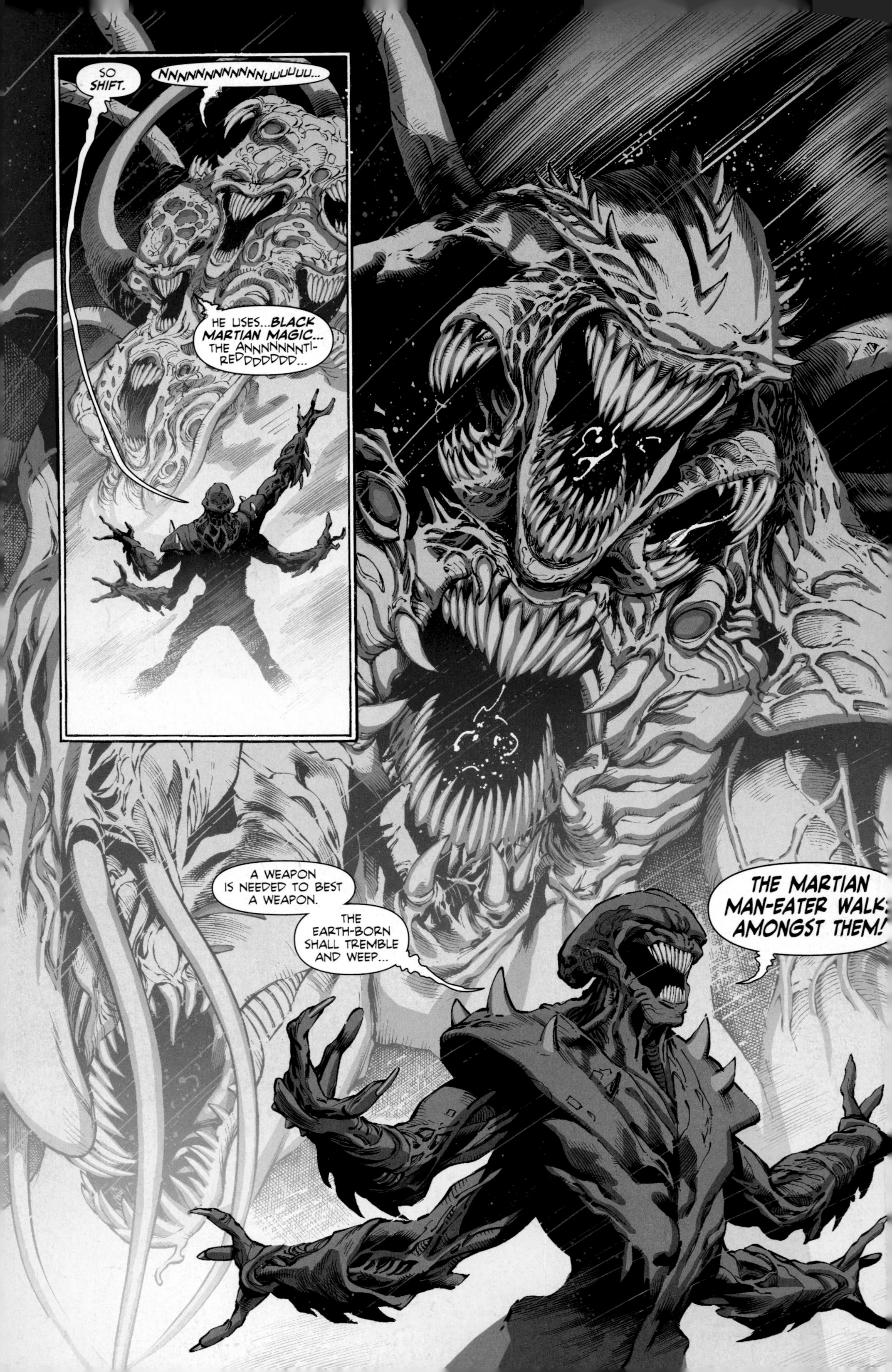
SO SHIFT.
NNNNNNNNNNNNNUUUUUU...
HE USES...BLACK MARTIAN MAGIC... THE ANNNNNNNTI-REDDDDDDD...
A WEAPON IS NEEDED TO BEST A WEAPON.
THE EARTH-BORN SHALL TREMBLE AND WEEP...
THE MARTIAN MAN-EATER WALKS AMONGST THEM!

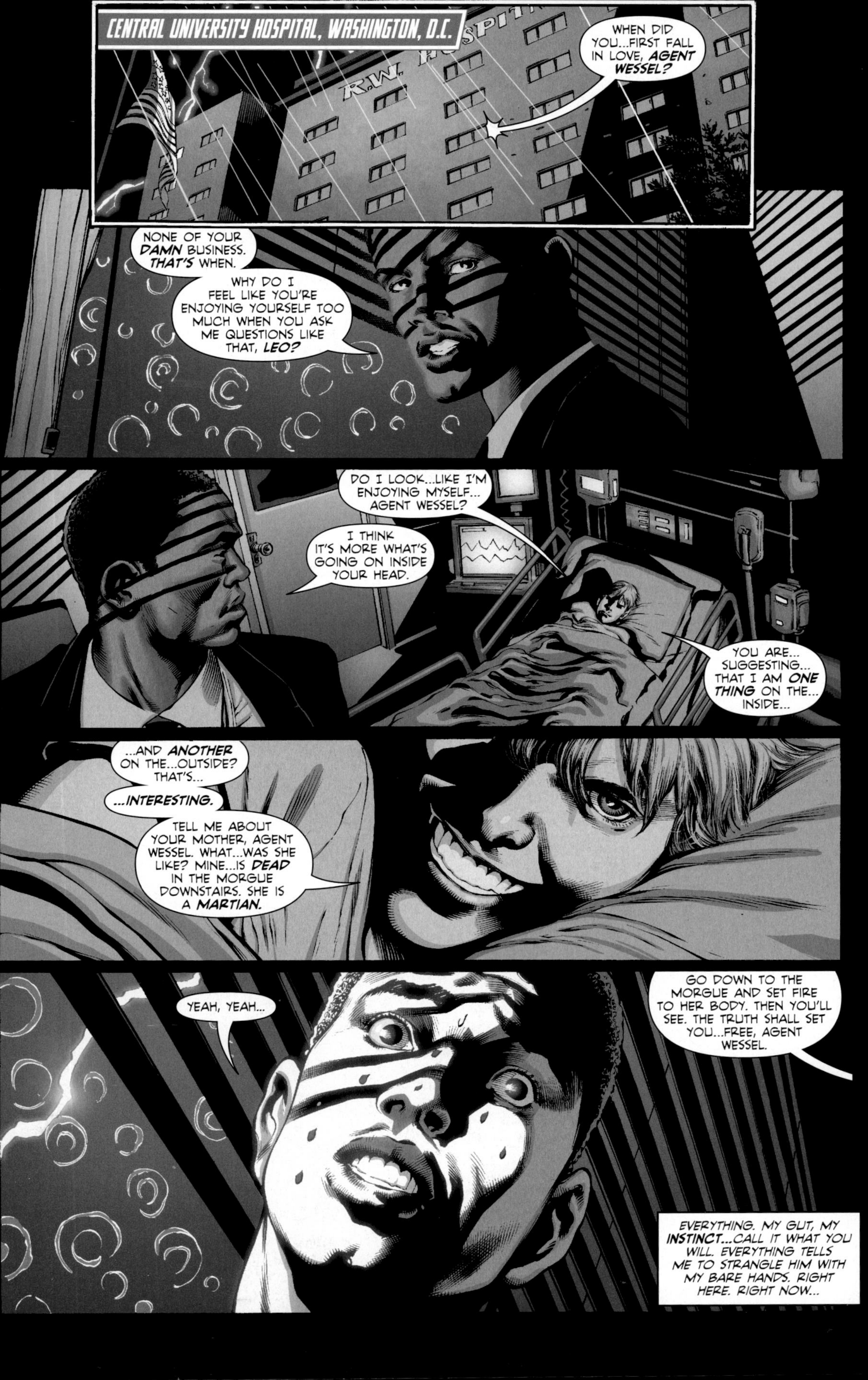
CENTRAL UNIVERSITY HOSPITAL, WASHINGTON, D.C.
R.W. HOSPITAL
WHEN DID YOU...FIRST FALL IN LOVE, AGENT WESSEL?
NONE OF YOUR DAMN BUSINESS. THAT'S WHEN.
WHY DO I FEEL LIKE YOU'RE ENJOYING YOURSELF TOO MUCH WHEN YOU ASK ME QUESTIONS LIKE THAT, LEO?
DO I LOOK...LIKE I'M ENJOYING MYSELF... AGENT WESSEL?
I THINK IT'S MORE WHAT'S GOING ON INSIDE YOUR HEAD.
YOU ARE... SUGGESTING... THAT I AM ONE THING ON THE... INSIDE...
...AND ANOTHER ON THE...OUTSIDE? THAT'S...
...INTERESTING.
TELL ME ABOUT YOUR MOTHER, AGENT WESSEL. WHAT...WAS SHE LIKE? MINE...IS DEAD IN THE MORGUE DOWNSTAIRS. SHE IS A MARTIAN.
YEAH, YEAH...
GO DOWN TO THE MORGUE AND SET FIRE TO HER BODY. THEN YOU'LL SEE. THE TRUTH SHALL SET YOU...FREE, AGENT WESSEL.
EVERYTHING. MY GUT, MY INSTINCT...CALL IT WHAT YOU WILL. EVERYTHING TELLS ME TO STRANGLE HIM WITH MY BARE HANDS. RIGHT HERE. RIGHT NOW...

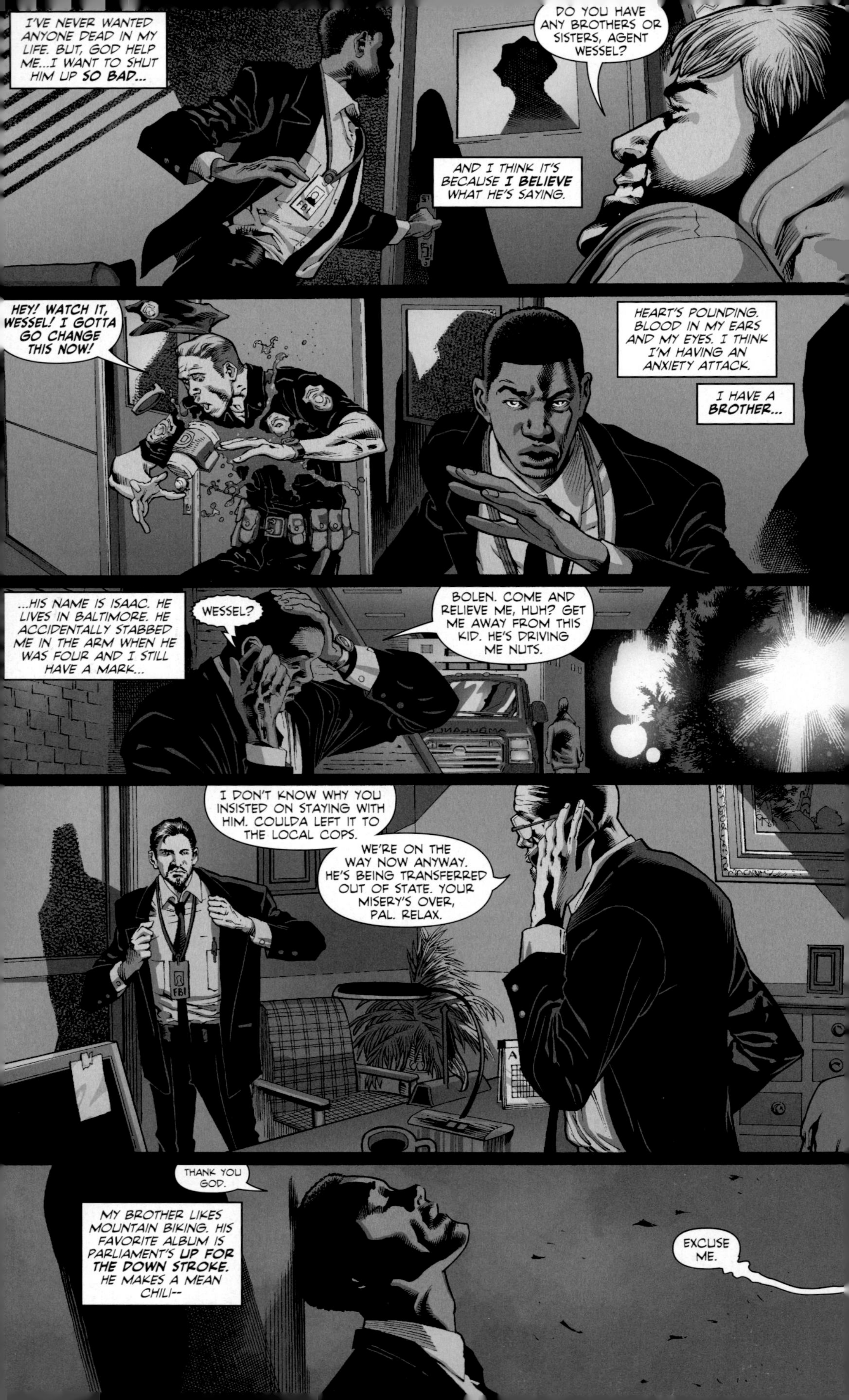
I'VE NEVER WANTED ANYONE DEAD IN MY LIFE. BUT, GOD HELP ME...I WANT TO SHUT HIM UP SO BAD...
DO YOU HAVE ANY BROTHERS OR SISTERS, AGENT WESSEL?
AND I THINK IT'S BECAUSE I BELIEVE WHAT HE'S SAYING.
FBI
HEY! WATCH IT, WESSEL! I GOTTA GO CHANGE THIS NOW!
HEART'S POUNDING. BLOOD IN MY EARS AND MY EYES. I THINK I'M HAVING AN ANXIETY ATTACK.
I HAVE A BROTHER...
...HIS NAME IS ISAAC. HE LIVES IN BALTIMORE. HE ACCIDENTALLY STABBED ME IN THE ARM WHEN HE WAS FOUR AND I STILL HAVE A MARK...
WESSEL?
BOLEN. COME AND RELIEVE ME, HUH? GET ME AWAY FROM THIS KID. HE'S DRIVING ME NUTS.
I DON'T KNOW WHY YOU INSISTED ON STAYING WITH HIM. COULDA LEFT IT TO THE LOCAL COPS.
WE'RE ON THE WAY NOW ANYWAY. HE'S BEING TRANSFERRED OUT OF STATE. YOUR MISERY'S OVER, PAL. RELAX.
FBI
THANK YOU GOD.
MY BROTHER LIKES MOUNTAIN BIKING. HIS FAVORITE ALBUM IS PARLIAMENT'S UP FOR THE DOWN STROKE. HE MAKES A MEAN CHILI--
EXCUSE ME.

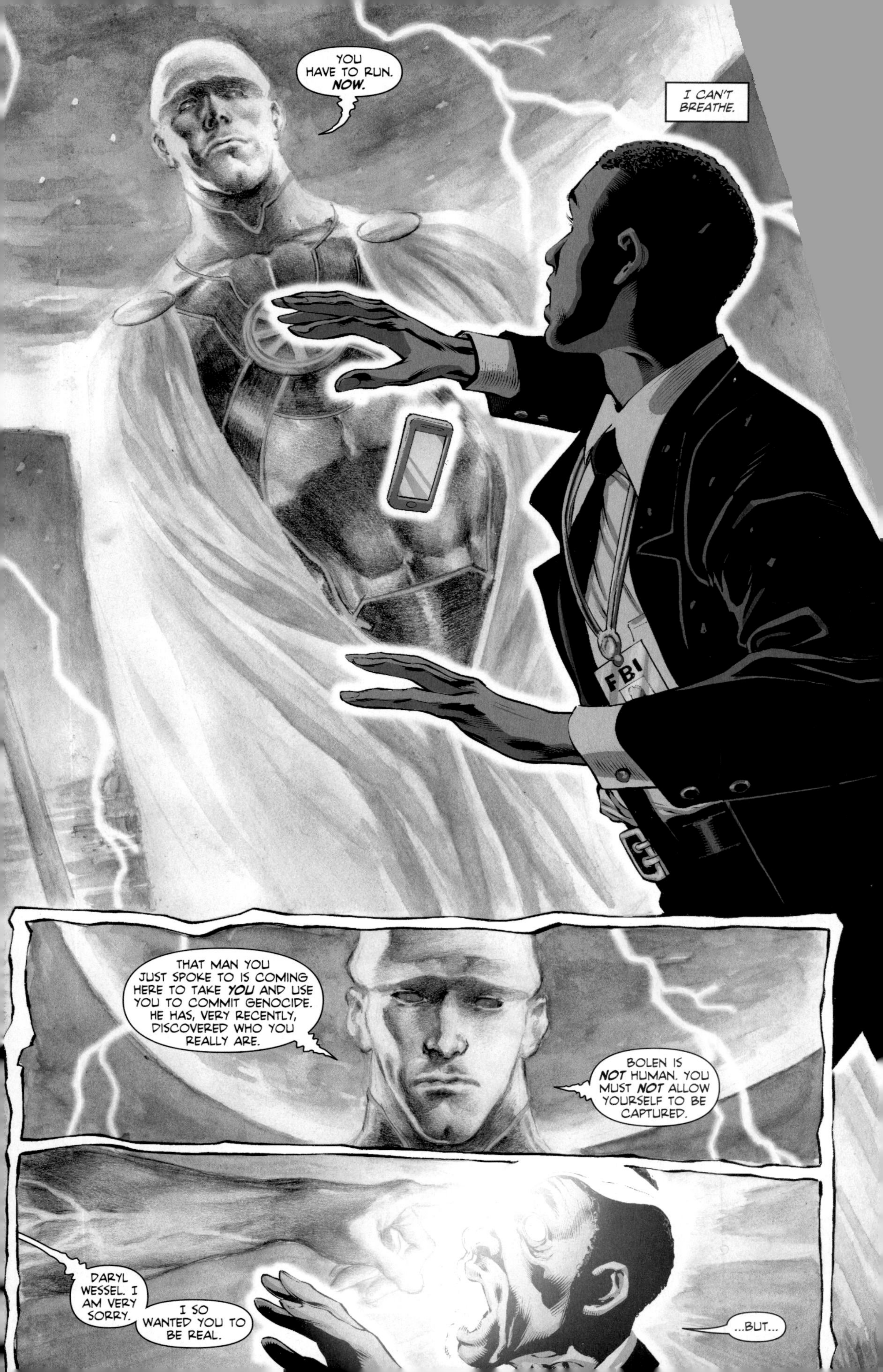
YOU HAVE TO RUN. NOW.
I CAN'T BREATHE.
THAT MAN YOU JUST SPOKE TO IS COMING HERE TO TAKE YOU AND USE YOU TO COMMIT GENOCIDE. HE HAS, VERY RECENTLY, DISCOVERED WHO YOU REALLY ARE.
BOLEN IS NOT HUMAN. YOU MUST NOT ALLOW YOURSELF TO BE CAPTURED.
DARYL WESSEL. I AM VERY SORRY.
I SO WANTED YOU TO BE REAL.
...BUT...
FBI

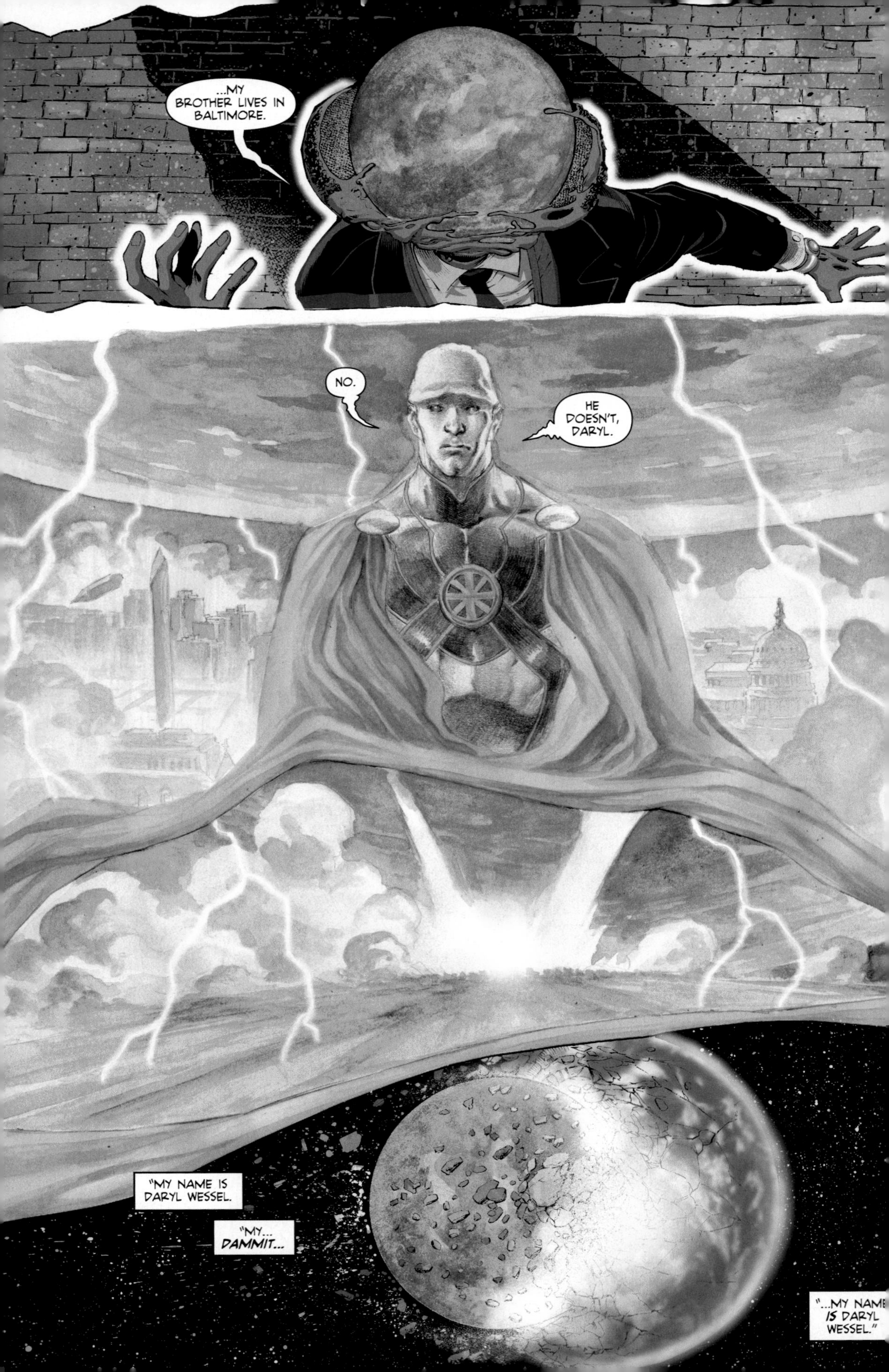
...MY BROTHER LIVES IN BALTIMORE.
NO.
HE DOESN'T, DARYL.
"MY NAME IS DARYL WESSEL.
"MY... *DAMMIT*...
"...MY NAME *IS* DARYL WESSEL."

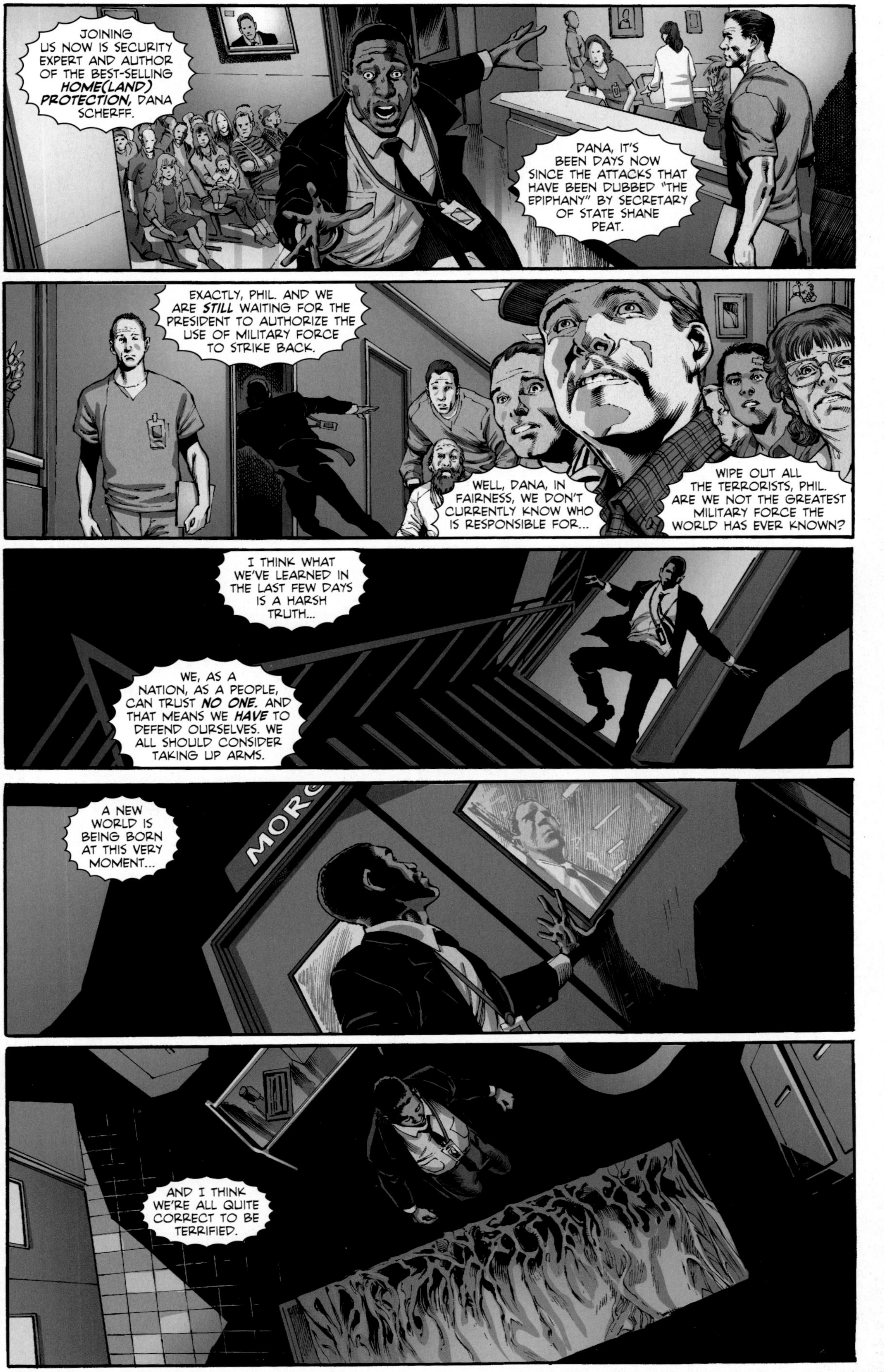

JOINING US NOW IS SECURITY EXPERT AND AUTHOR OF THE BEST-SELLING HOME(LAND) PROTECTION, DANA SCHERFF.
DANA, IT'S BEEN DAYS NOW SINCE THE ATTACKS THAT HAVE BEEN DUBBED "THE EPIPHANY" BY SECRETARY OF STATE SHANE PEAT.
EXACTLY, PHIL. AND WE ARE STILL WAITING FOR THE PRESIDENT TO AUTHORIZE THE USE OF MILITARY FORCE TO STRIKE BACK.
WELL, DANA, IN FAIRNESS, WE DON'T CURRENTLY KNOW WHO IS RESPONSIBLE FOR...
WIPE OUT ALL THE TERRORISTS, PHIL. ARE WE NOT THE GREATEST MILITARY FORCE THE WORLD HAS EVER KNOWN?
I THINK WHAT WE'VE LEARNED IN THE LAST FEW DAYS IS A HARSH TRUTH...
WE, AS A NATION, AS A PEOPLE, CAN TRUST NO ONE. AND THAT MEANS WE HAVE TO DEFEND OURSELVES. WE ALL SHOULD CONSIDER TAKING UP ARMS.
A NEW WORLD IS BEING BORN AT THIS VERY MOMENT...
MORG
AND I THINK WE'RE ALL QUITE CORRECT TO BE TERRIFIED.

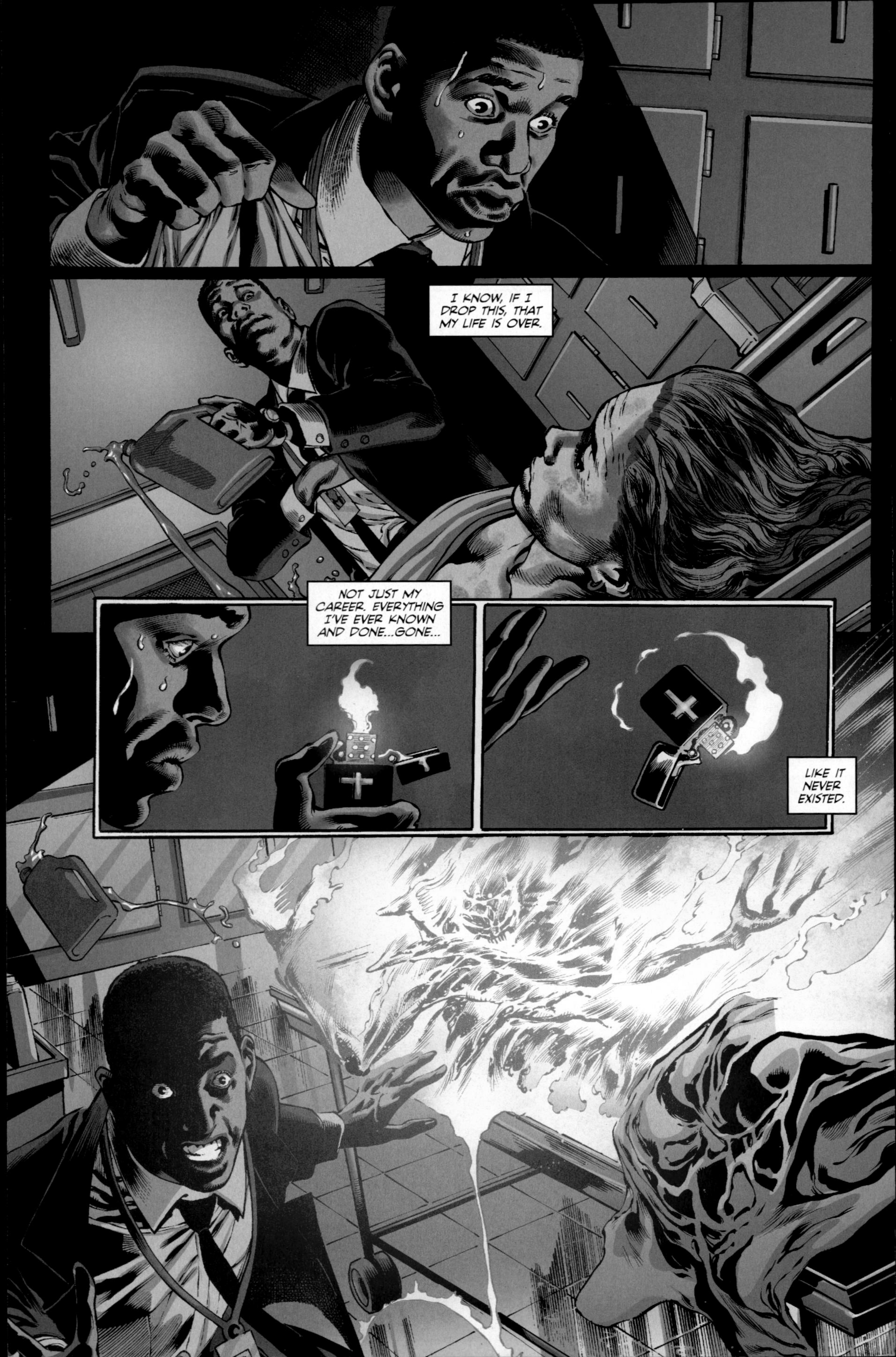
I KNOW, IF I DROP THIS, THAT MY LIFE IS OVER.
NOT JUST MY CAREER. EVERYTHING I'VE EVER KNOWN AND DONE...GONE...
LIKE IT NEVER EXISTED.

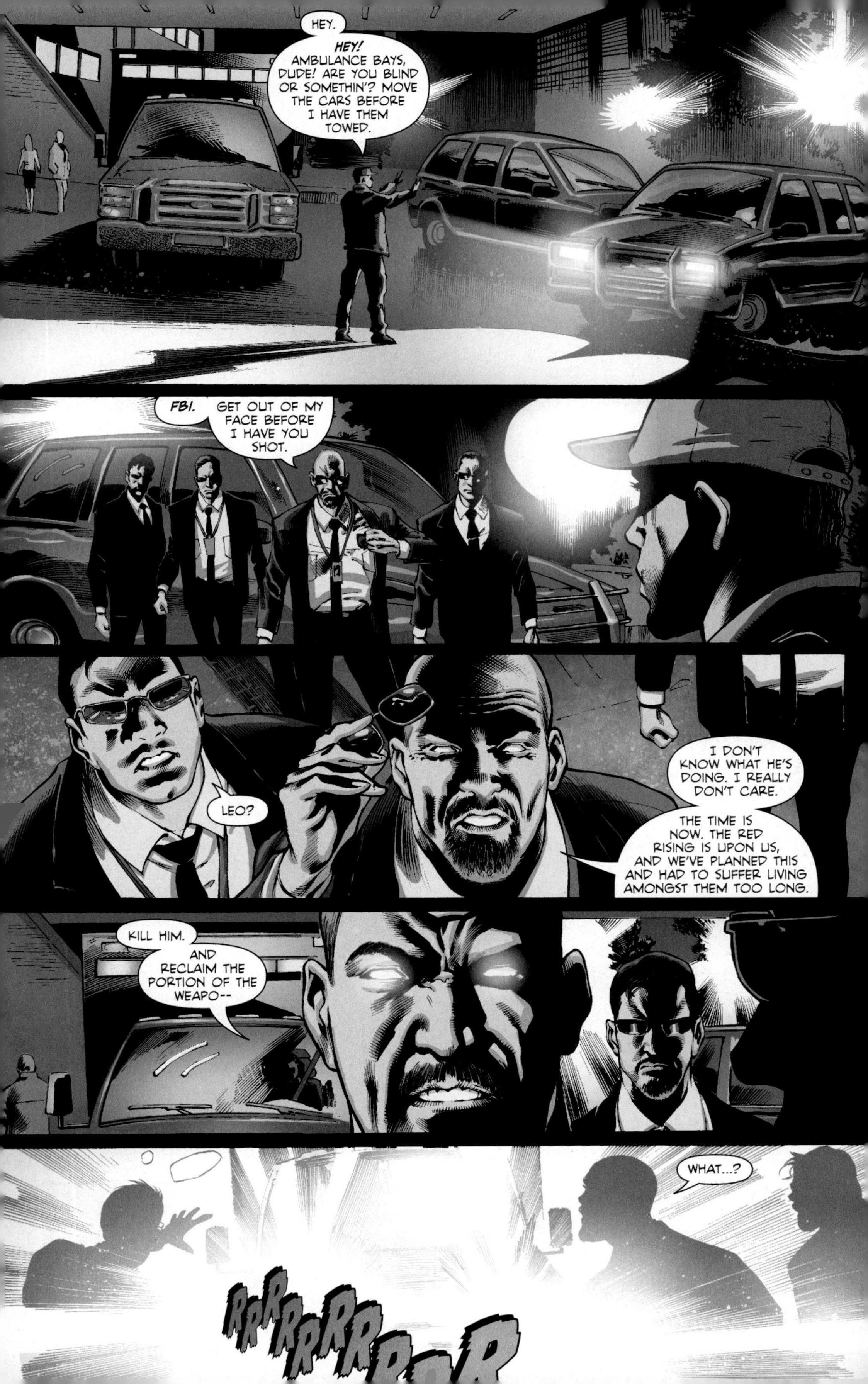
HEY.
HEY! AMBULANCE BAYS, DUDE! ARE YOU BLIND OR SOMETHIN'? MOVE THE CARS BEFORE I HAVE THEM TOWED.
FBI.
GET OUT OF MY FACE BEFORE I HAVE YOU SHOT.
LEO?
I DON'T KNOW WHAT HE'S DOING. I REALLY DON'T CARE.
THE TIME IS NOW. THE RED RISING IS UPON US, AND WE'VE PLANNED THIS AND HAD TO SUFFER LIVING AMONGST THEM TOO LONG.
KILL HIM.
AND RECLAIM THE PORTION OF THE WEAPO--
WHAT...?
RRRRRRRROAR

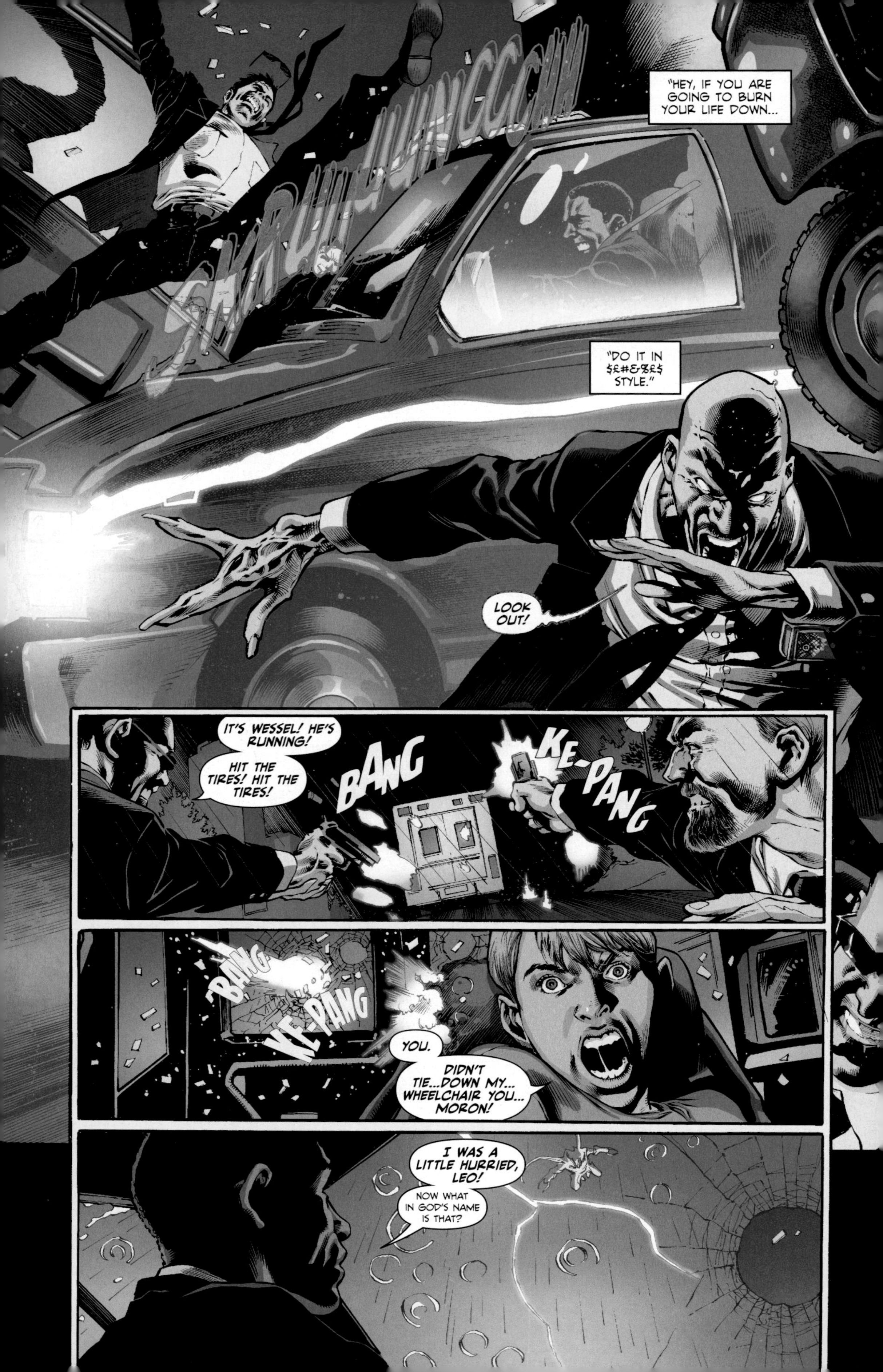
SKRUUUUNNGCCHH
"HEY, IF YOU ARE GOING TO BURN YOUR LIFE DOWN...
"DO IT IN $£#&%£$ STYLE."
LOOK OUT!
IT'S WESSEL! HE'S RUNNING!
HIT THE TIRES! HIT THE TIRES!
BANG
KE-PANG
BANG
KE-PANG
YOU.
DIDN'T TIE...DOWN MY... WHEELCHAIR YOU... MORON!
I WAS A LITTLE HURRIED, LEO!
NOW WHAT IN GOD'S NAME IS THAT?

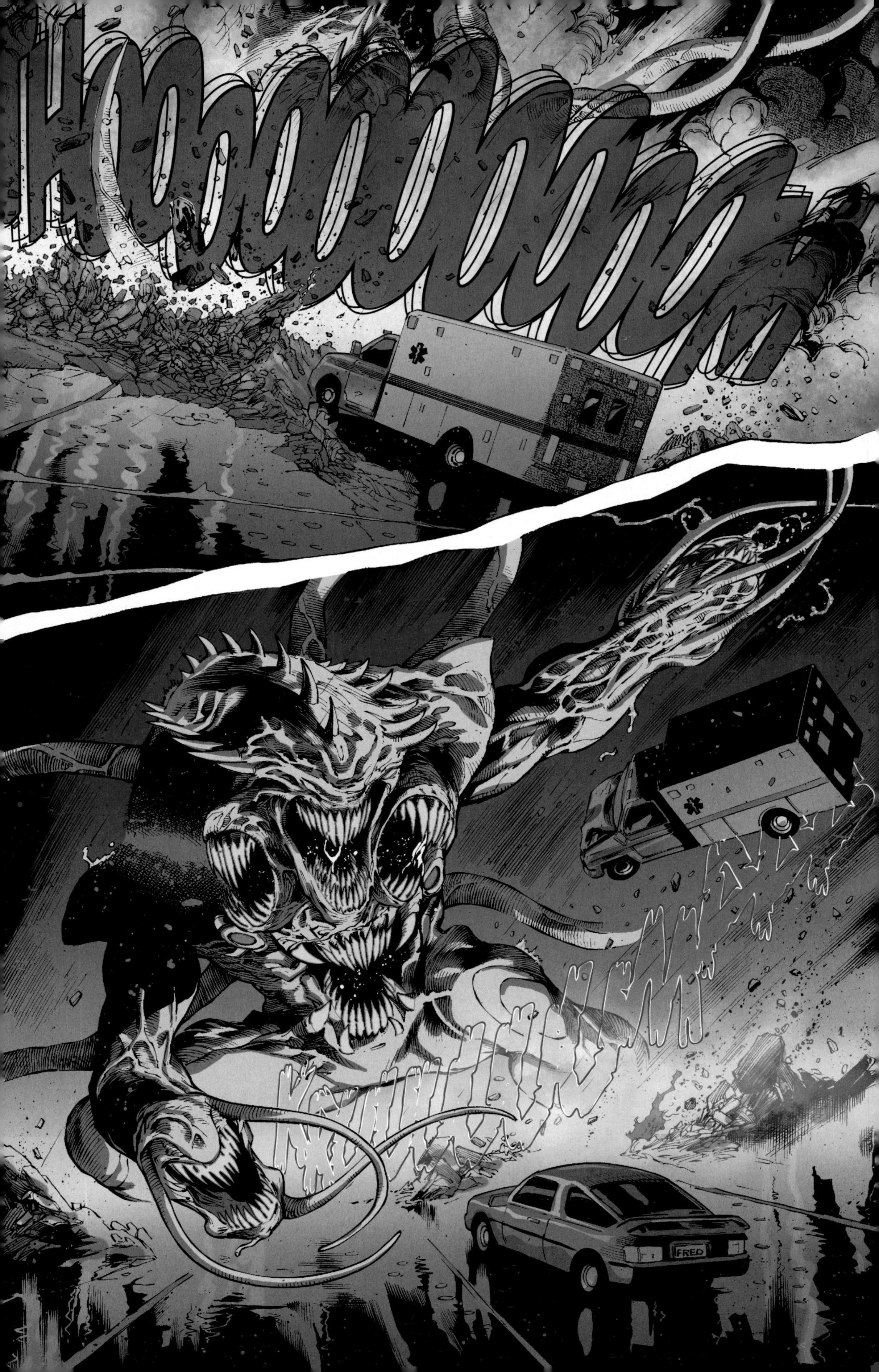
FRED

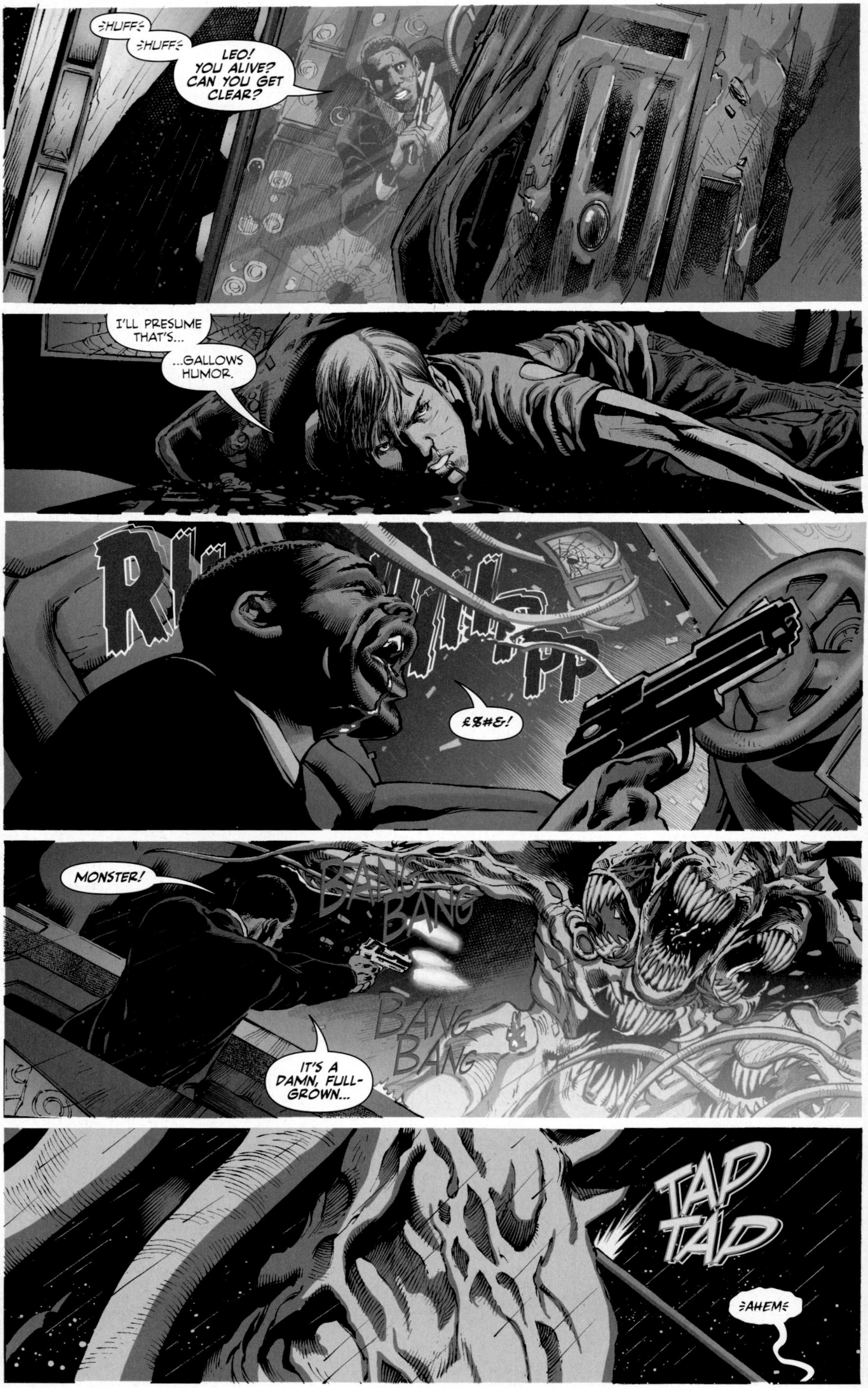

HUFF
HUFF
LEO! YOU ALIVE? CAN YOU GET CLEAR?
I'LL PRESUME THAT'S...
...GALLOWS HUMOR.
£%#&!
MONSTER!
BANG BANG
BANG BANG
IT'S A DAMN, FULL-GROWN...
TAP TAP
AHEM

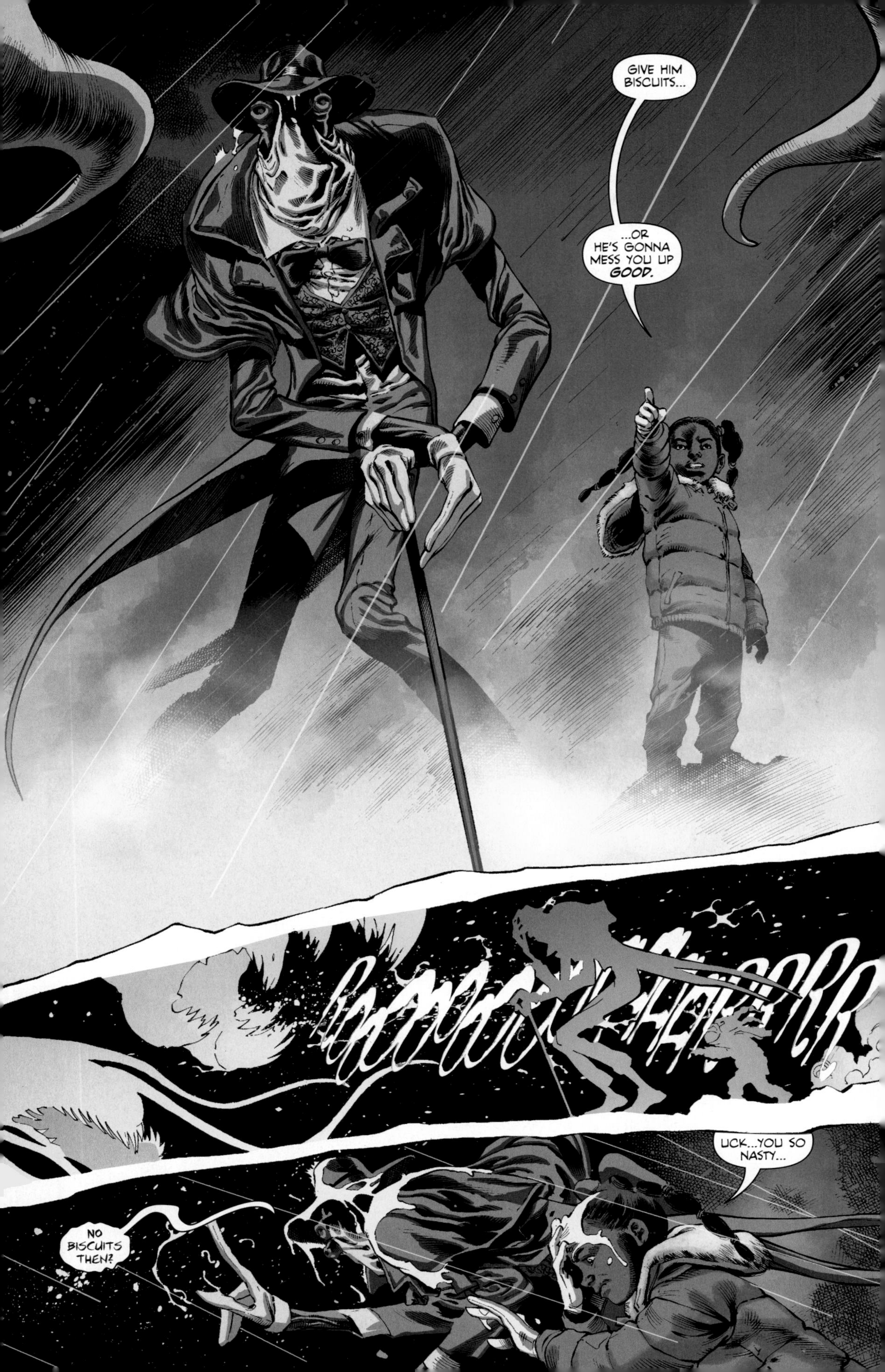
GIVE HIM BISCUITS...
...OR HE'S GONNA MESS YOU UP *GOOD*.
UCK...YOU SO NASTY...
NO BISCUITS THEN?

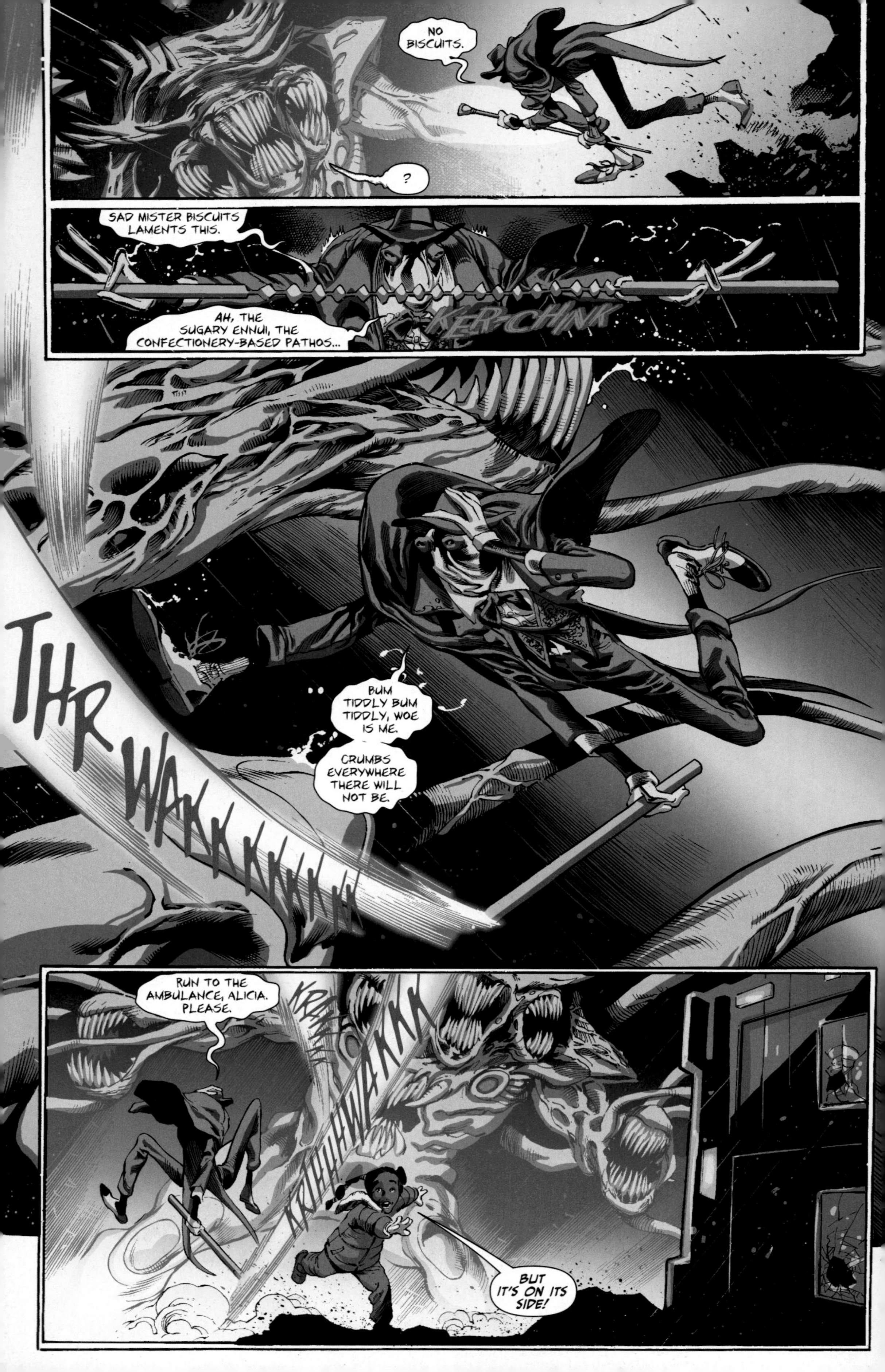
NO BISCUITS.
?
SAD MISTER BISCUITS LAMENTS THIS.
AH, THE SUGARY ENNUI, THE CONFECTIONERY-BASED PATHOS...
KER-CHNK
BUM TIDDLY BUM TIDDLY, WOE IS ME.
CRUMBS EVERYWHERE THERE WILL NOT BE.
THRWAKKKKKKK
RUN TO THE AMBULANCE, ALICIA. PLEASE.
KRAKWAKK
KRTHHWAKKK
BUT IT'S ON ITS SIDE!

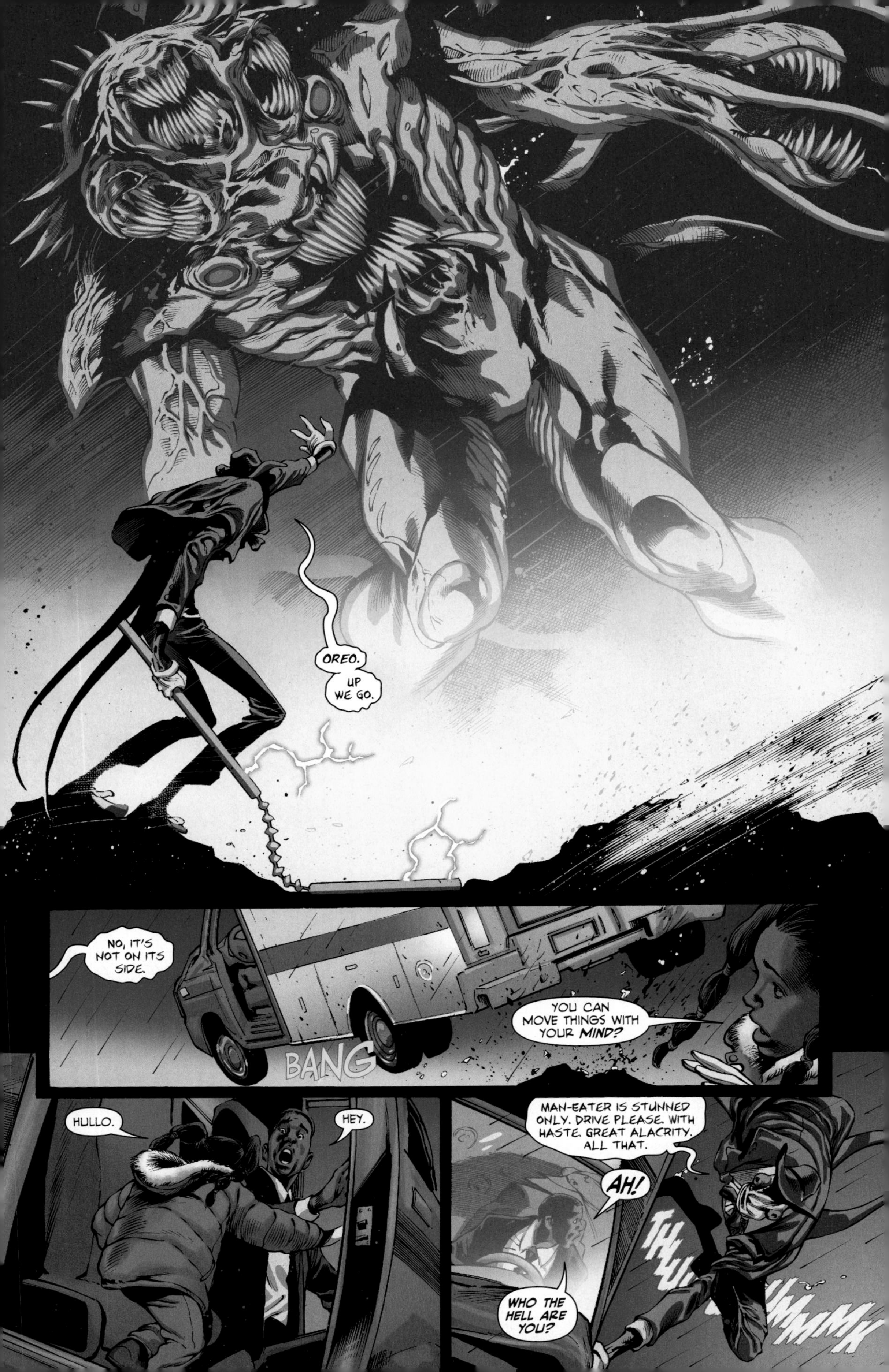
OREO.
UP WE GO.
NO, IT'S NOT ON ITS SIDE.
YOU CAN MOVE THINGS WITH YOUR MIND?
BANG
HULLO.
HEY.
MAN-EATER IS STUNNED ONLY. DRIVE PLEASE. WITH HASTE. GREAT ALACRITY. ALL THAT.
AH!
WHO THE HELL ARE YOU?

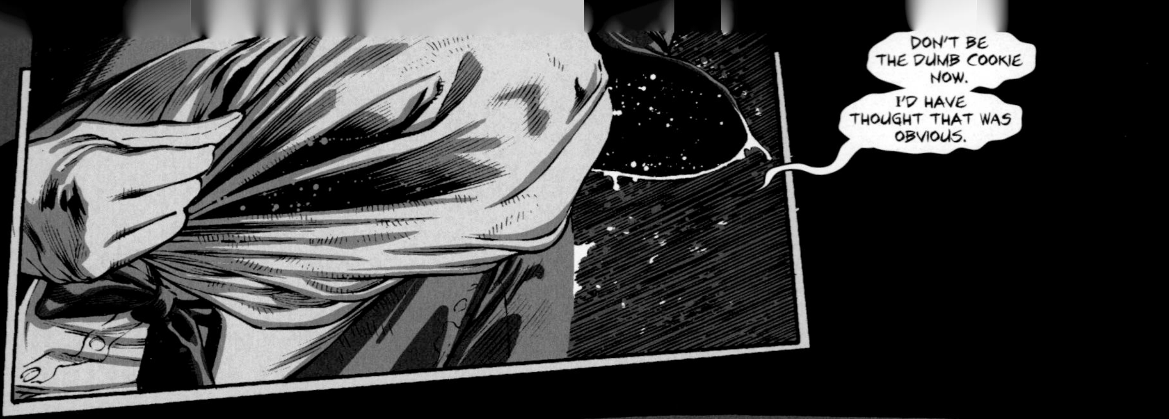
DON'T BE THE DUMB COOKIE NOW.
I'D HAVE THOUGHT THAT WAS OBVIOUS.
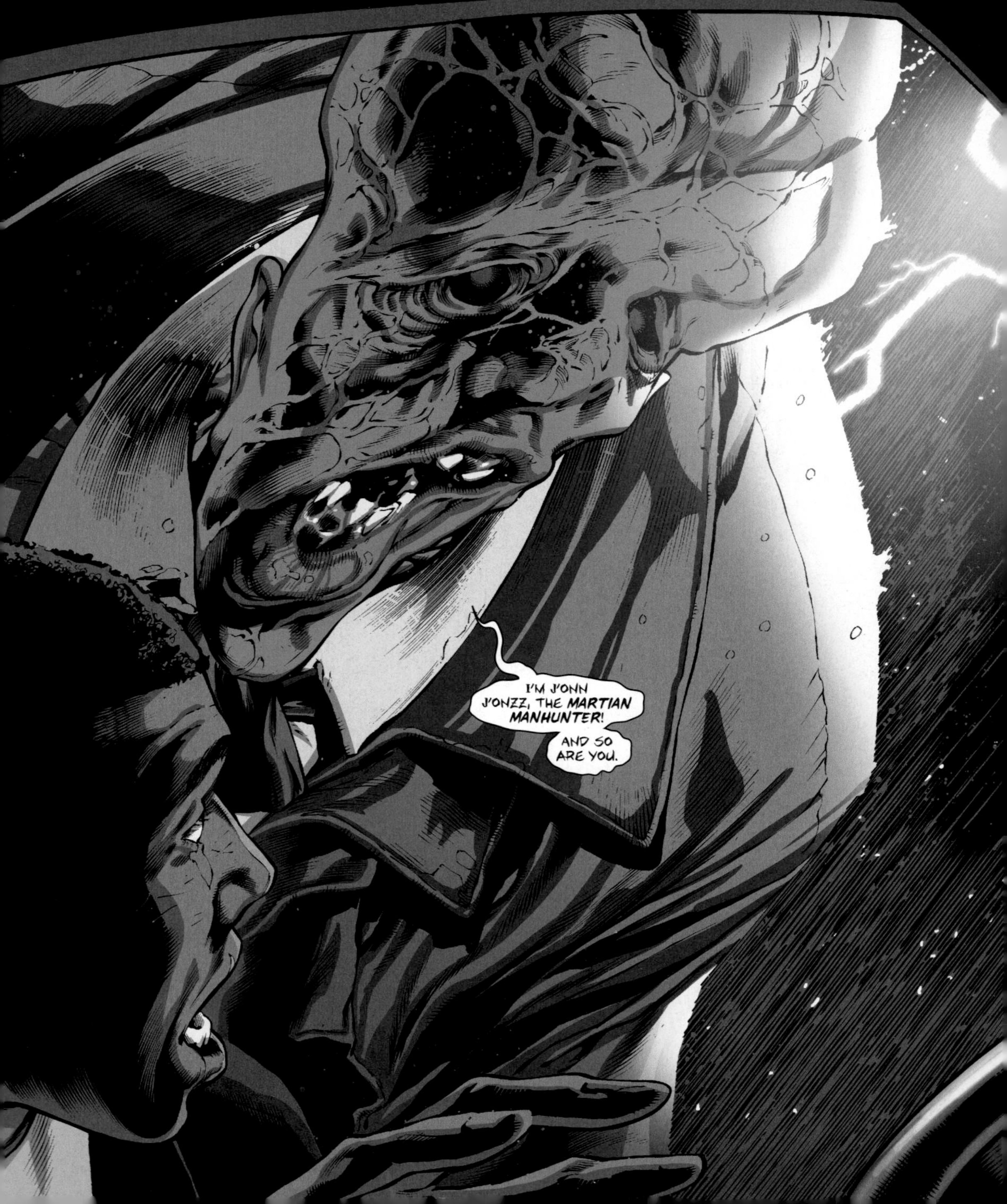
I'M J'ONN J'ONZZ, THE *MARTIAN MANHUNTER*!
AND SO ARE YOU.

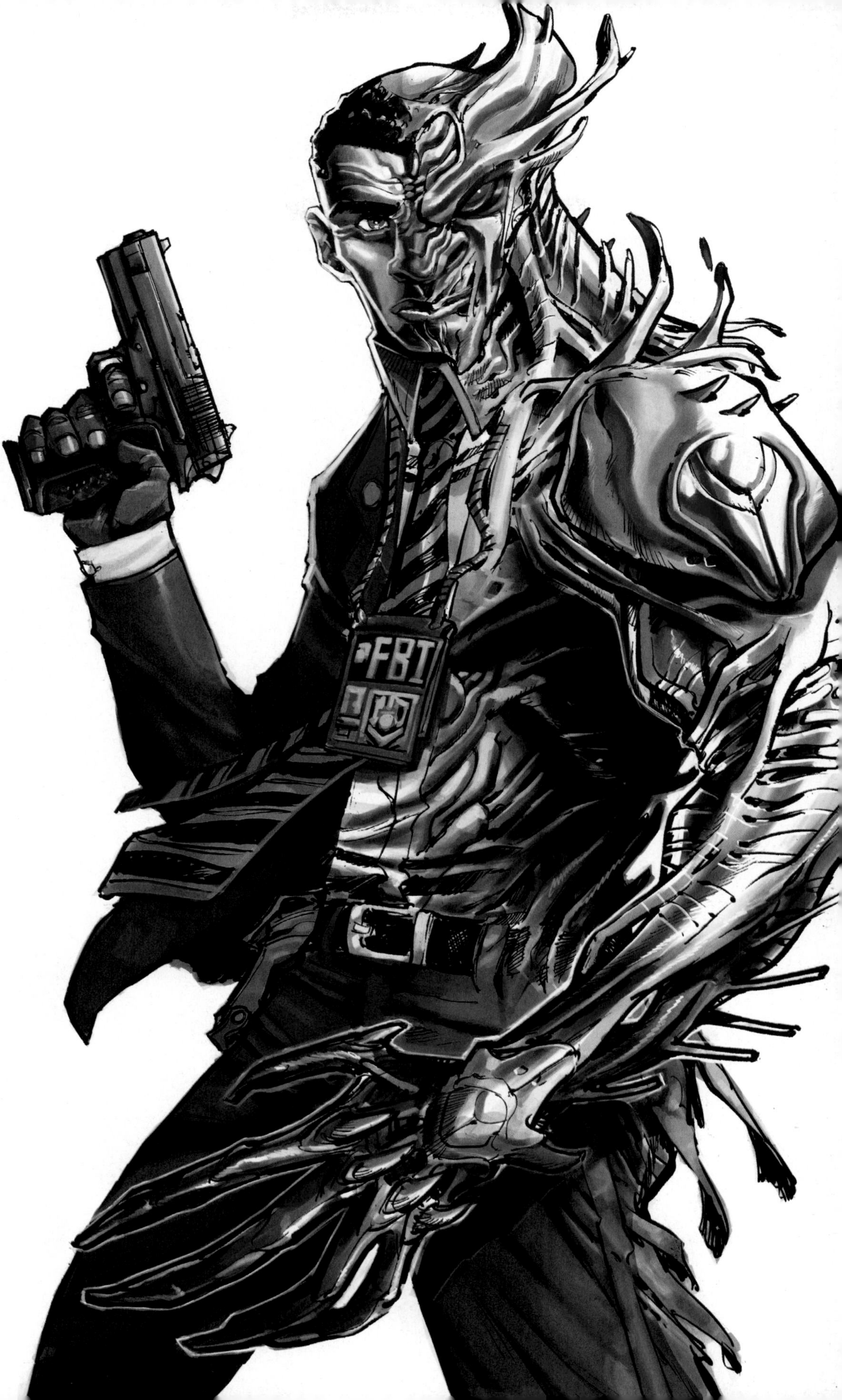
FBI

ALONE
cover by **ERIC CANETE**

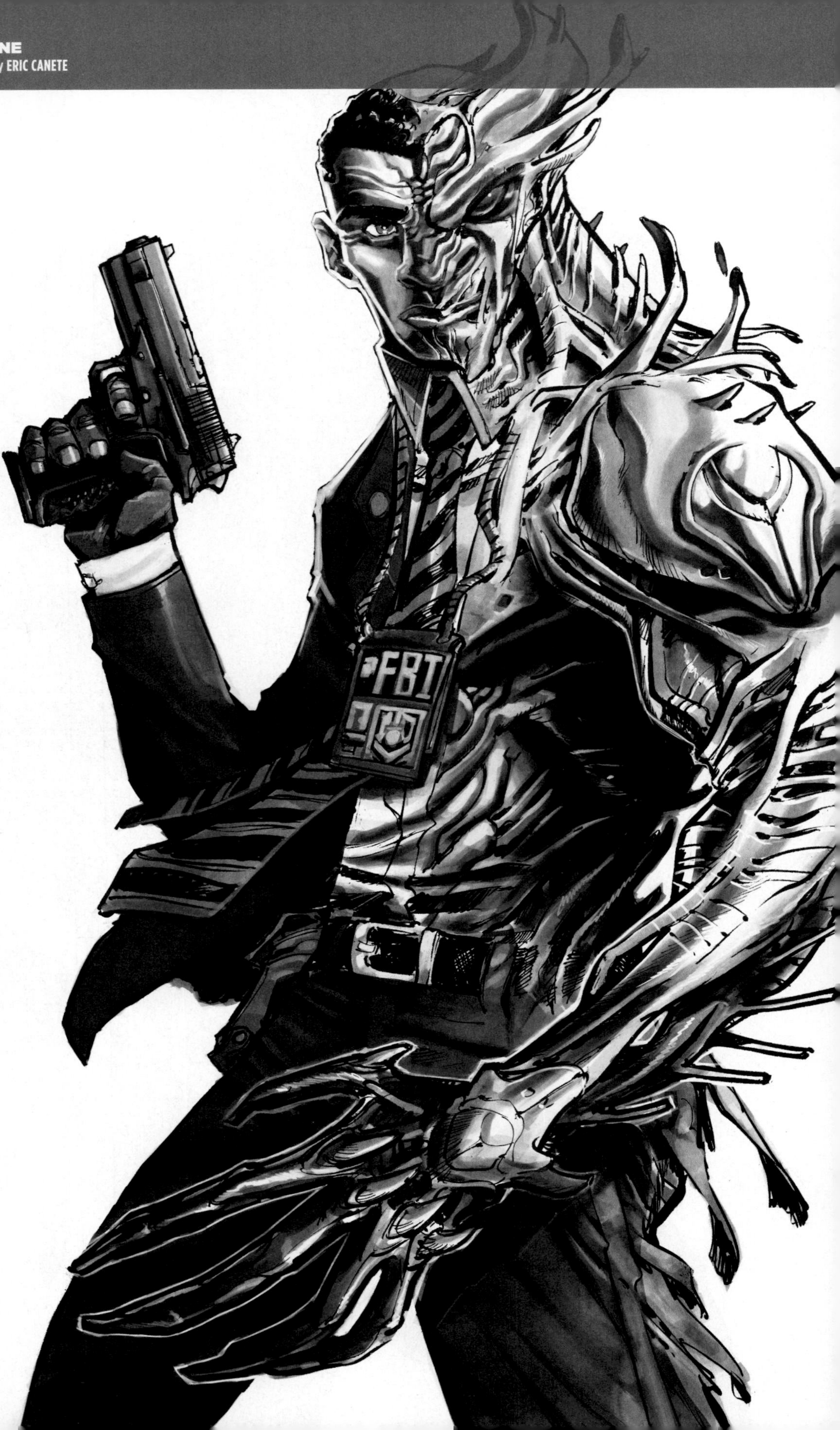
FBI

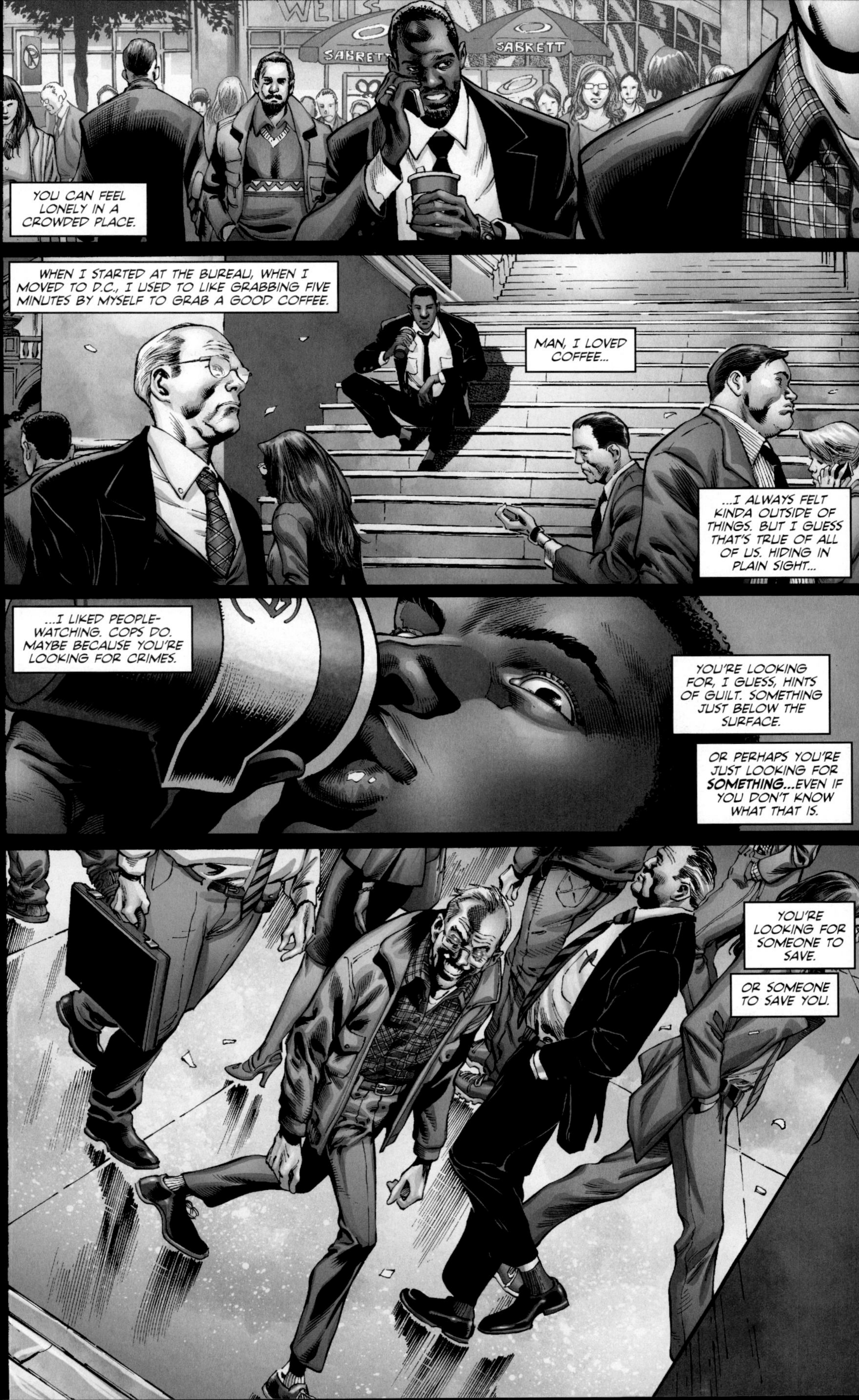
WELLS
SABRETT
SABRETT
YOU CAN FEEL LONELY IN A CROWDED PLACE.
WHEN I STARTED AT THE BUREAU, WHEN I MOVED TO D.C., I USED TO LIKE GRABBING FIVE MINUTES BY MYSELF TO GRAB A GOOD COFFEE.
MAN, I LOVED COFFEE...
...I ALWAYS FELT KINDA OUTSIDE OF THINGS. BUT I GUESS THAT'S TRUE OF ALL OF US. HIDING IN PLAIN SIGHT...
...I LIKED PEOPLE-WATCHING. COPS DO. MAYBE BECAUSE YOU'RE LOOKING FOR CRIMES.
YOU'RE LOOKING FOR, I GUESS, HINTS OF GUILT. SOMETHING JUST BELOW THE SURFACE.
OR PERHAPS YOU'RE JUST LOOKING FOR **SOMETHING...**EVEN IF YOU DON'T KNOW WHAT THAT IS.
YOU'RE LOOKING FOR SOMEONE TO SAVE.
OR SOMEONE TO SAVE YOU.

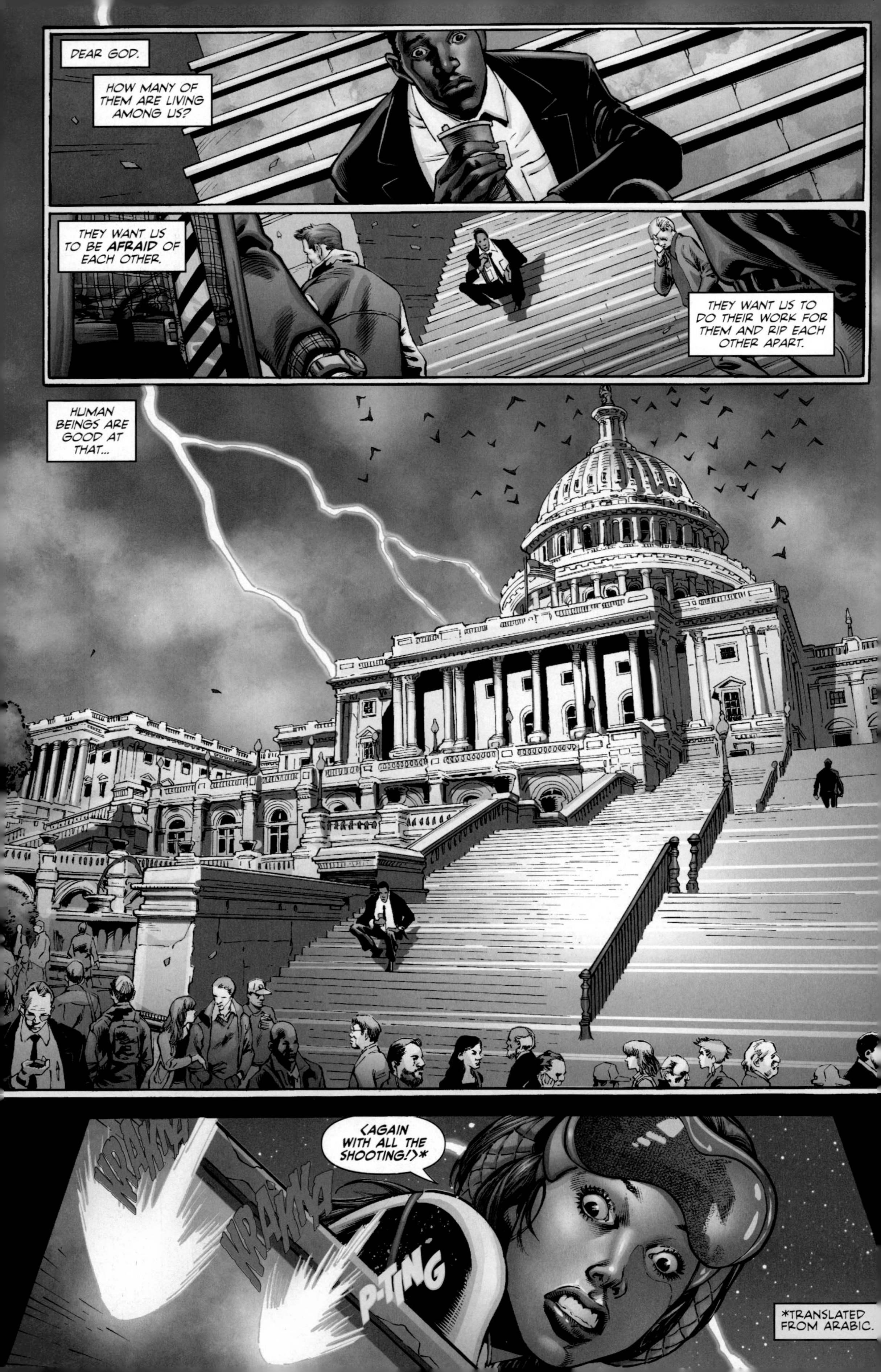
DEAR GOD.
HOW MANY OF THEM ARE LIVING AMONG US?
THEY WANT US TO BE AFRAID OF EACH OTHER.
THEY WANT US TO DO THEIR WORK FOR THEM AND RIP EACH OTHER APART.
HUMAN BEINGS ARE GOOD AT THAT...
VRAKKA
VRAKKA
<AGAIN WITH ALL THE SHOOTING!>*
P-TING
*TRANSLATED FROM ARABIC.

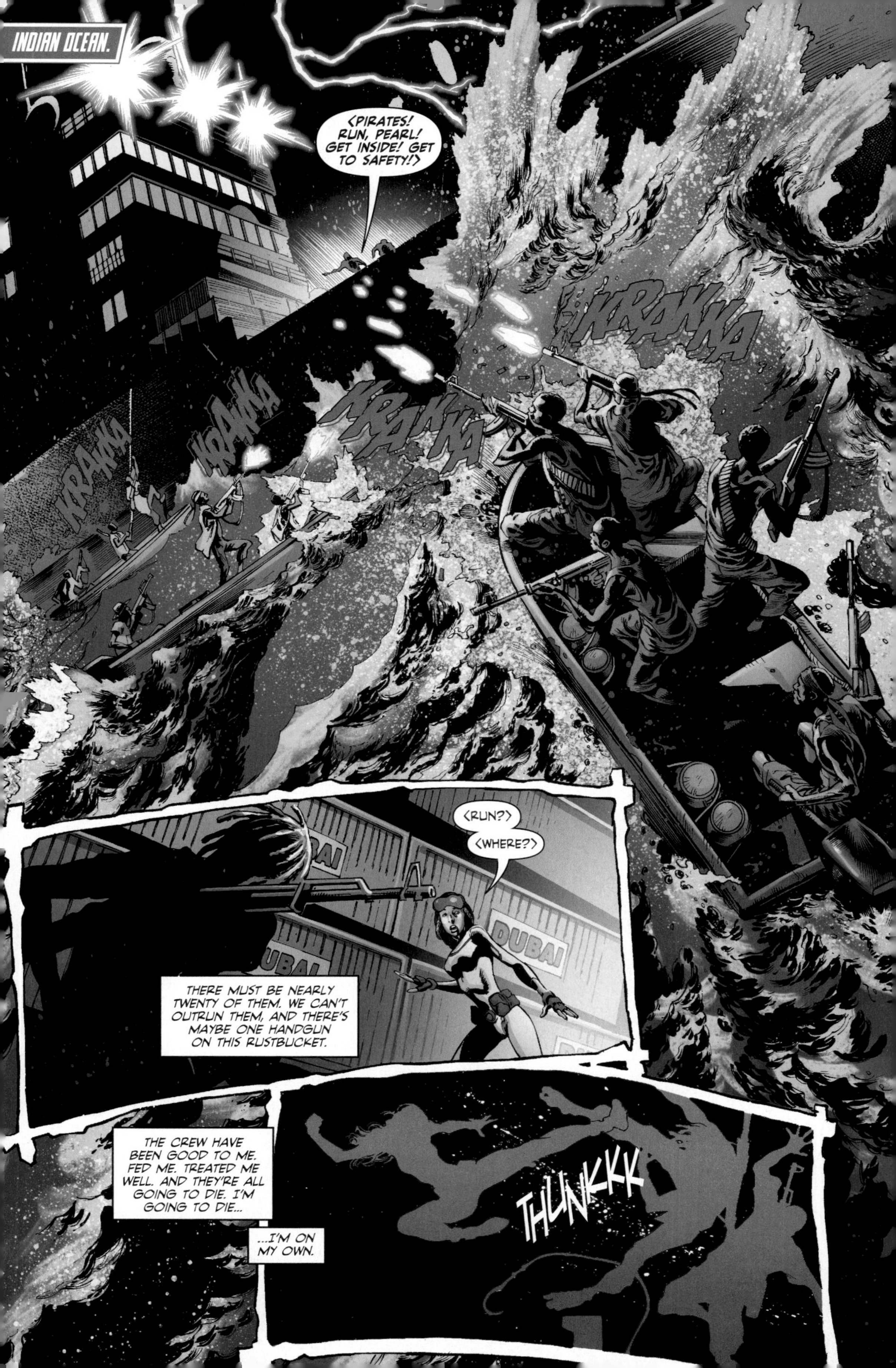
INDIAN OCEAN.
<PIRATES! RUN, PEARL! GET INSIDE! GET TO SAFETY!>
KRAKKA
KRAKKA
KRAKKA
KRAKKA
KRAKKA
<RUN?>
<WHERE?>
DUBAI
DUBAI
DUBAI
THERE MUST BE NEARLY TWENTY OF THEM. WE CAN'T OUTRUN THEM, AND THERE'S MAYBE ONE HANDGUN ON THIS RUSTBUCKET.
THE CREW HAVE BEEN GOOD TO ME. FED ME. TREATED ME WELL. AND THEY'RE ALL GOING TO DIE. I'M GOING TO DIE...
...I'M ON MY OWN.
THUNKKK

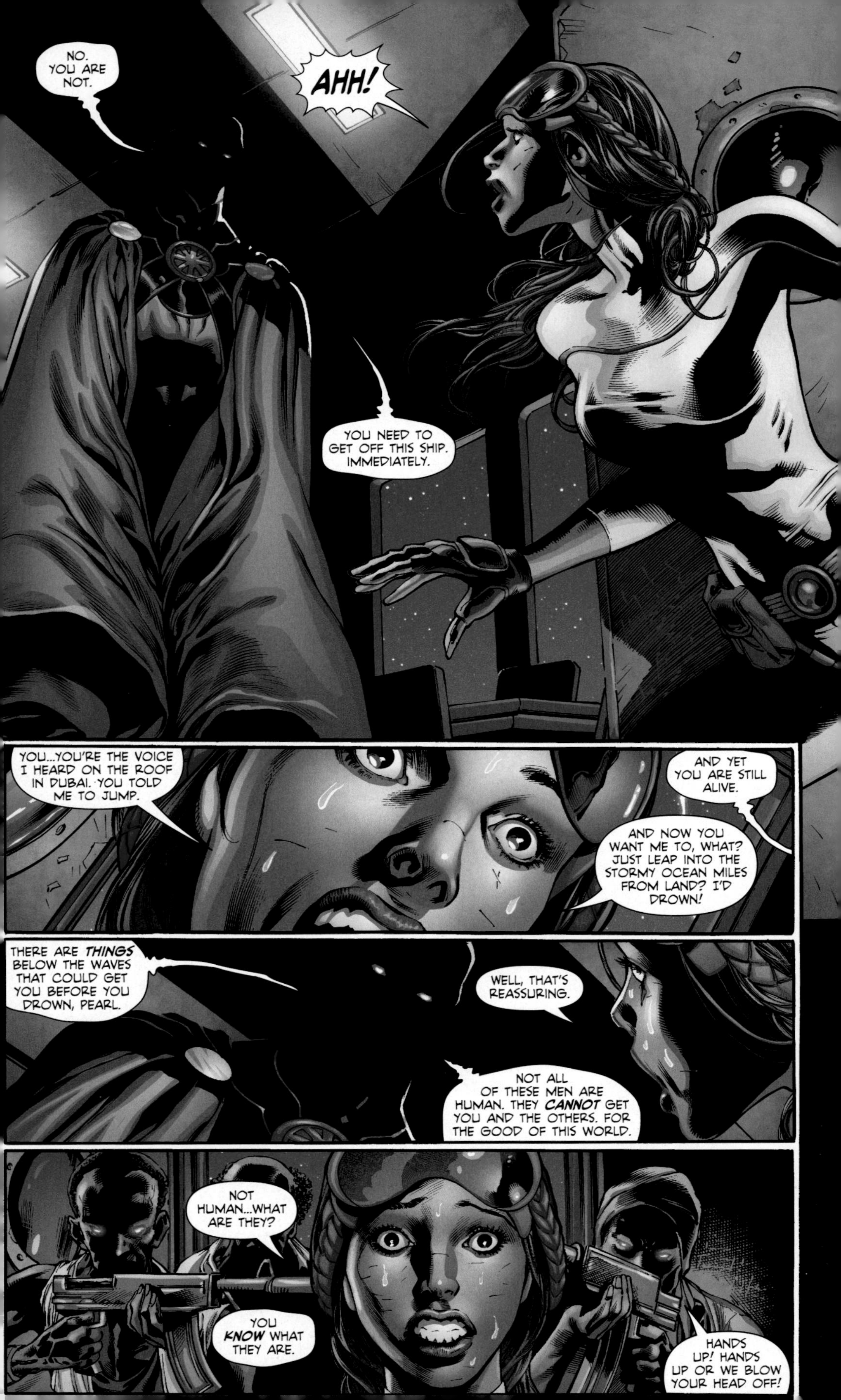
NO. YOU ARE NOT.
AHH!
YOU NEED TO GET OFF THIS SHIP. IMMEDIATELY.
YOU...YOU'RE THE VOICE I HEARD ON THE ROOF IN DUBAI. YOU TOLD ME TO JUMP.
AND YET YOU ARE STILL ALIVE.
AND NOW YOU WANT ME TO, WHAT? JUST LEAP INTO THE STORMY OCEAN MILES FROM LAND? I'D DROWN!
THERE ARE THINGS BELOW THE WAVES THAT COULD GET YOU BEFORE YOU DROWN, PEARL.
WELL, THAT'S REASSURING.
NOT ALL OF THESE MEN ARE HUMAN. THEY CANNOT GET YOU AND THE OTHERS. FOR THE GOOD OF THIS WORLD.
NOT HUMAN...WHAT ARE THEY?
YOU KNOW WHAT THEY ARE.
HANDS UP! HANDS UP OR WE BLOW YOUR HEAD OFF!

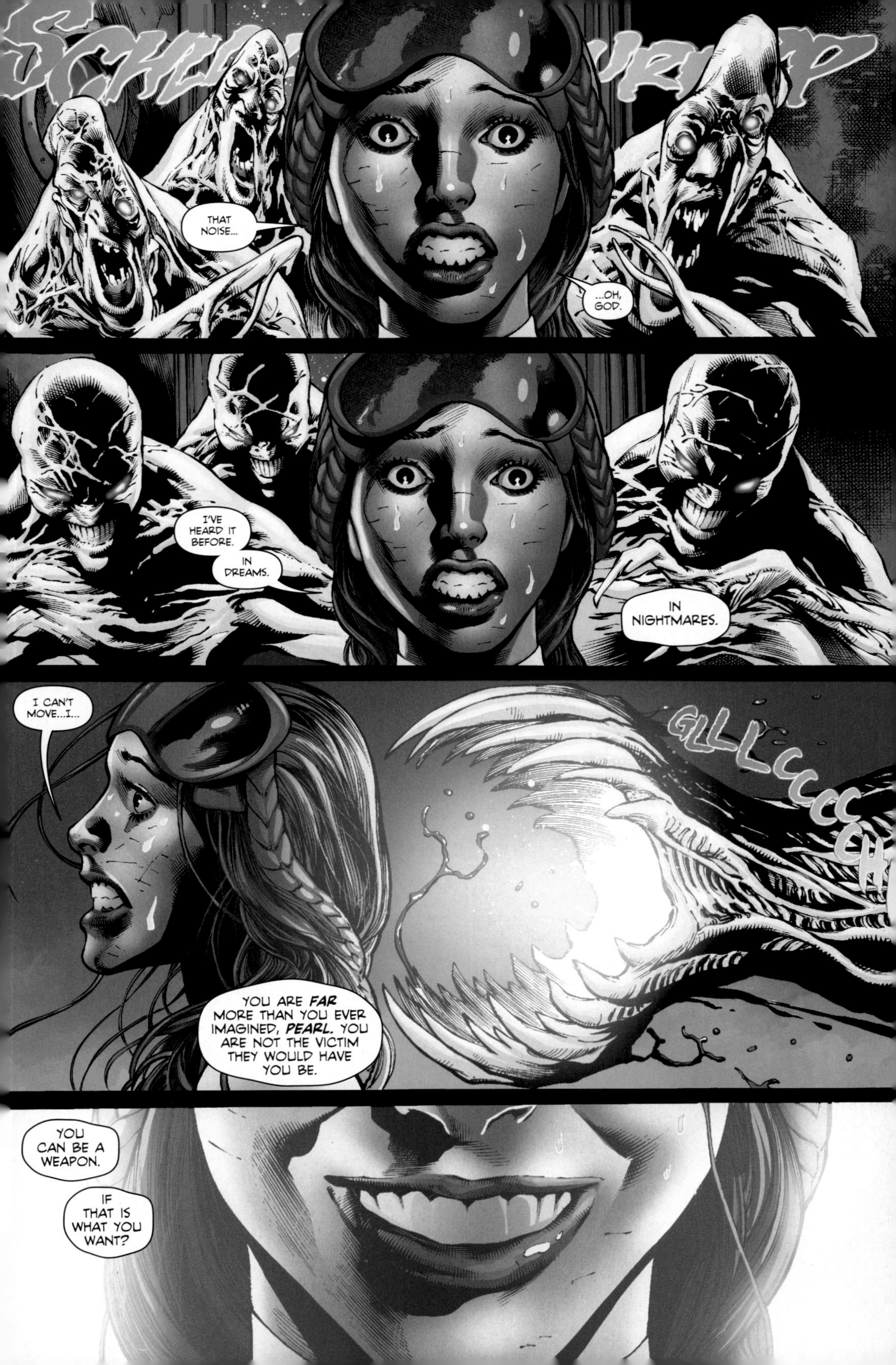
THAT NOISE...
...OH, GOD.
I'VE HEARD IT BEFORE.
IN DREAMS.
IN NIGHTMARES.
I CAN'T MOVE...I...
GLLLCCCCCH
YOU ARE FAR MORE THAN YOU EVER IMAGINED, PEARL. YOU ARE NOT THE VICTIM THEY WOULD HAVE YOU BE.
YOU CAN BE A WEAPON.
IF THAT IS WHAT YOU WANT?

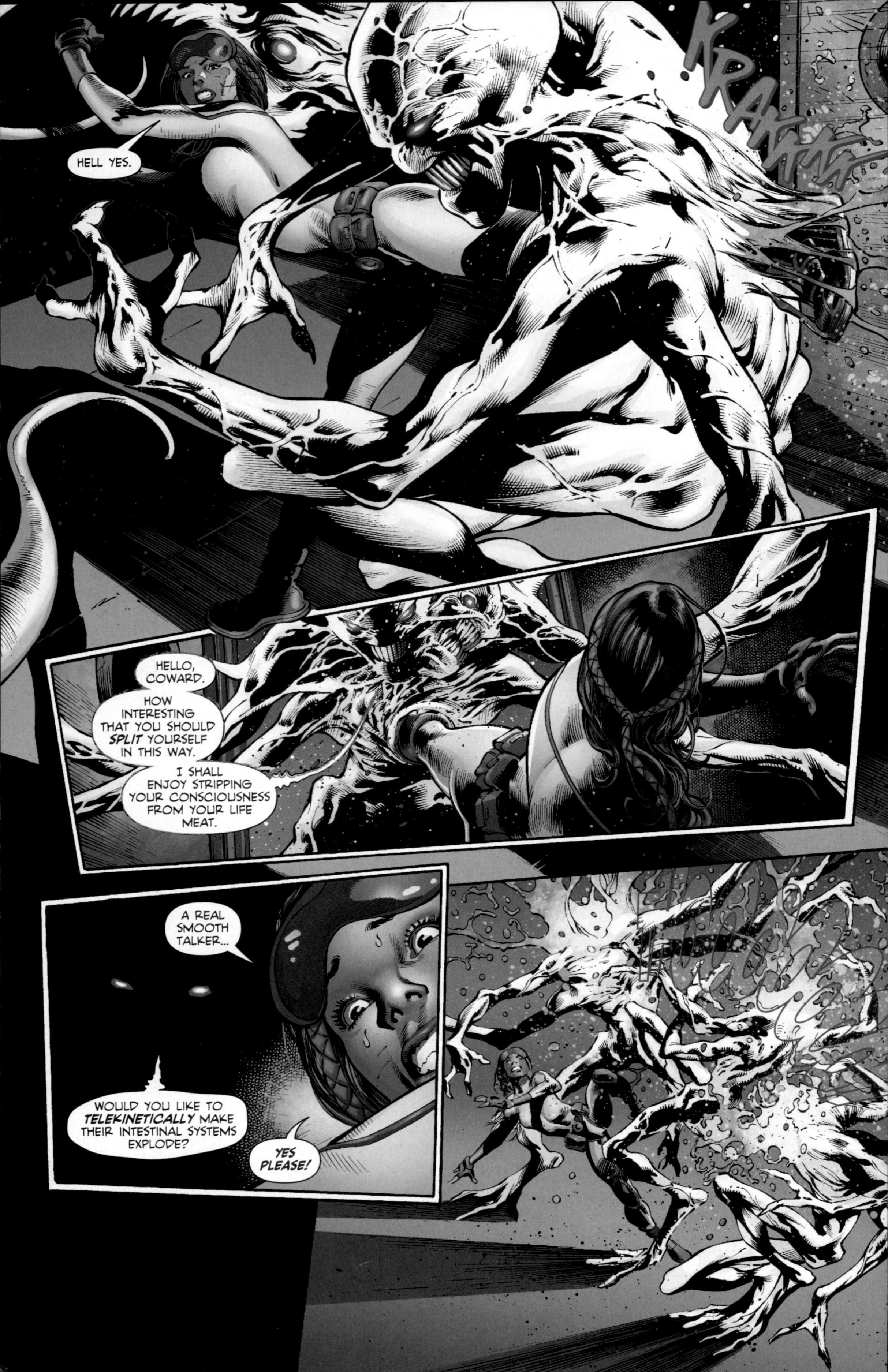
HELL YES.
HELLO, COWARD.
HOW INTERESTING THAT YOU SHOULD SPLIT YOURSELF IN THIS WAY.
I SHALL ENJOY STRIPPING YOUR CONSCIOUSNESS FROM YOUR LIFE MEAT.
A REAL SMOOTH TALKER...
WOULD YOU LIKE TO TELEKINETICALLY MAKE THEIR INTESTINAL SYSTEMS EXPLODE?
YES PLEASE!

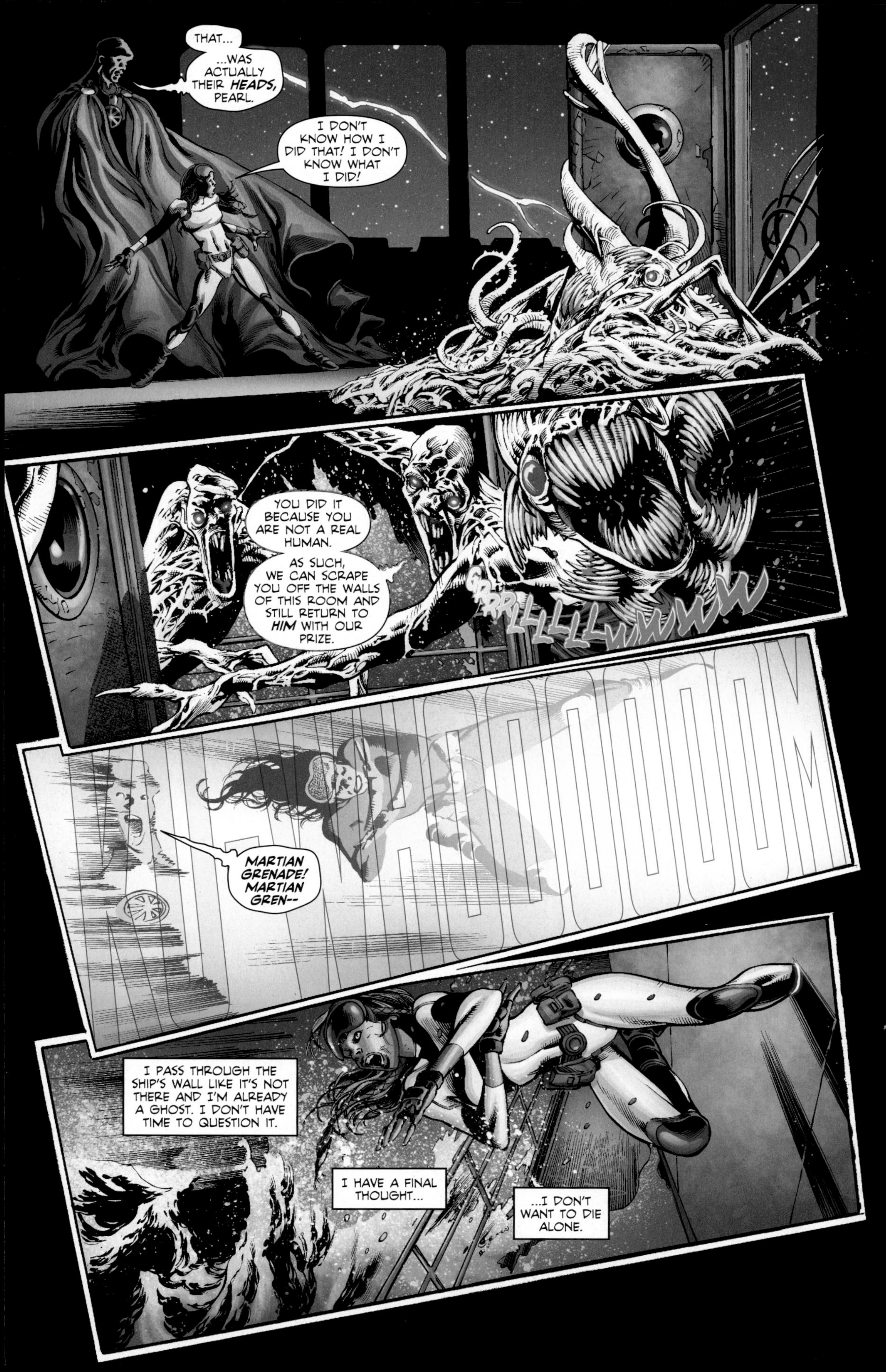
THAT...
...WAS ACTUALLY THEIR HEADS, PEARL.
I DON'T KNOW HOW I DID THAT! I DON'T KNOW WHAT I DID!
YOU DID IT BECAUSE YOU ARE NOT A REAL HUMAN.
AS SUCH, WE CAN SCRAPE YOU OFF THE WALLS OF THIS ROOM AND STILL RETURN TO HIM WITH OUR PRIZE.
MARTIAN GRENADE! MARTIAN GREN--
I PASS THROUGH THE SHIP'S WALL LIKE IT'S NOT THERE AND I'M ALREADY A GHOST. I DON'T HAVE TIME TO QUESTION IT.
I HAVE A FINAL THOUGHT...
...I DON'T WANT TO DIE ALONE.

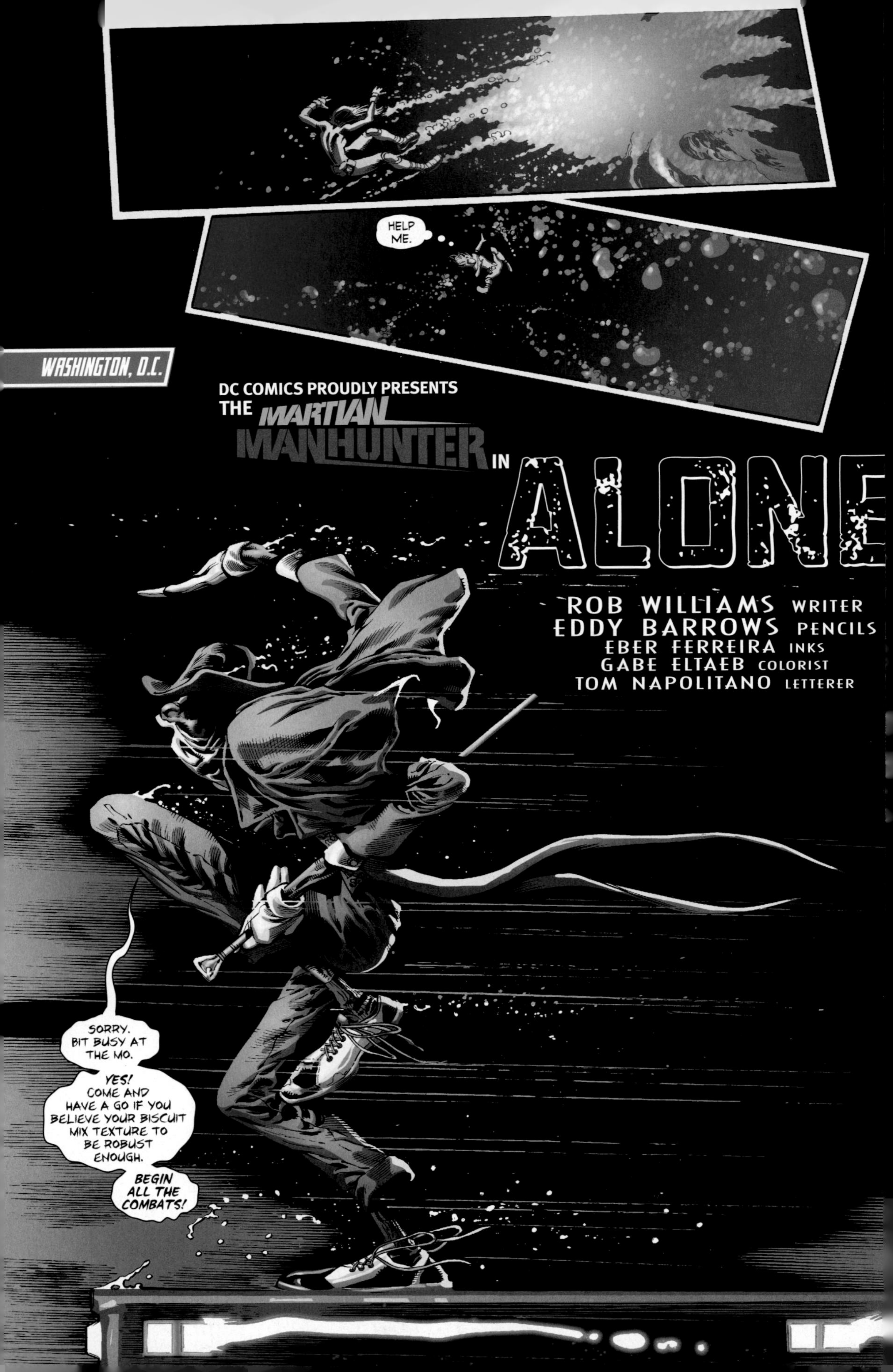
HELP ME.
WASHINGTON, D.C.
DC COMICS PROUDLY PRESENTS
THE MARTIAN MANHUNTER IN
ALONE
ROB WILLIAMS WRITER
EDDY BARROWS PENCILS
EBER FERREIRA INKS
GABE ELTAEB COLORIST
TOM NAPOLITANO LETTERER
SORRY. BIT BUSY AT THE MO.
YES! COME AND HAVE A GO IF YOU BELIEVE YOUR BISCUIT MIX TEXTURE TO BE ROBUST ENOUGH.
BEGIN ALL THE COMBATS!

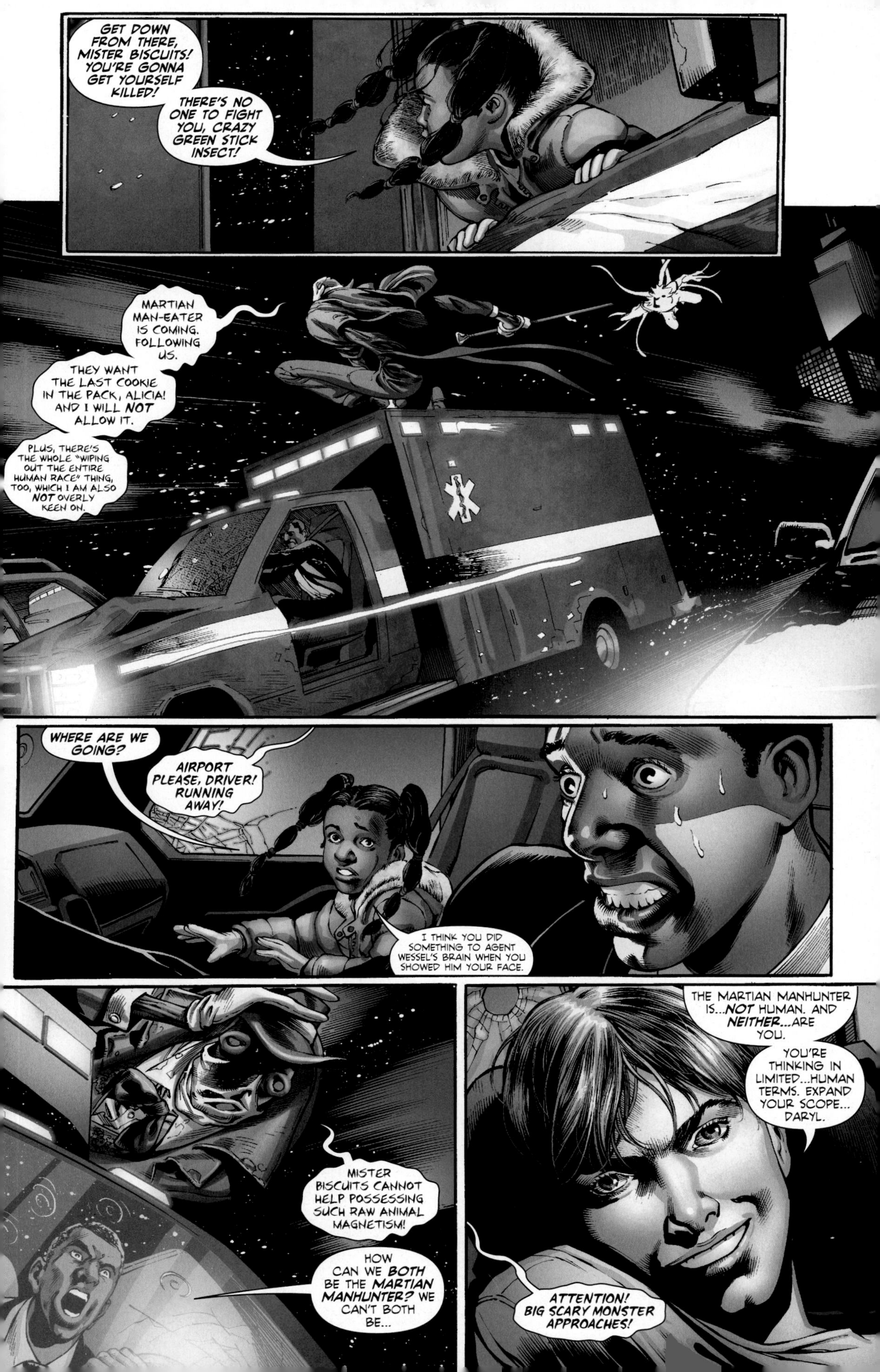
GET DOWN FROM THERE, MISTER BISCUITS! YOU'RE GONNA GET YOURSELF KILLED!
THERE'S NO ONE TO FIGHT YOU, CRAZY GREEN STICK INSECT!
MARTIAN MAN-EATER IS COMING. FOLLOWING US.
THEY WANT THE LAST COOKIE IN THE PACK, ALICIA! AND I WILL NOT ALLOW IT.
PLUS, THERE'S THE WHOLE "WIPING OUT THE ENTIRE HUMAN RACE" THING, TOO, WHICH I AM ALSO NOT OVERLY KEEN ON.
WHERE ARE WE GOING?
AIRPORT PLEASE, DRIVER! RUNNING AWAY!
I THINK YOU DID SOMETHING TO AGENT WESSEL'S BRAIN WHEN YOU SHOWED HIM YOUR FACE.
MISTER BISCUITS CANNOT HELP POSSESSING SUCH RAW ANIMAL MAGNETISM!
HOW CAN WE BOTH BE THE MARTIAN MANHUNTER? WE CAN'T BOTH BE...
THE MARTIAN MANHUNTER IS...NOT HUMAN. AND NEITHER...ARE YOU.
YOU'RE THINKING IN LIMITED...HUMAN TERMS. EXPAND YOUR SCOPE... DARYL.
ATTENTION! BIG SCARY MONSTER APPROACHES!

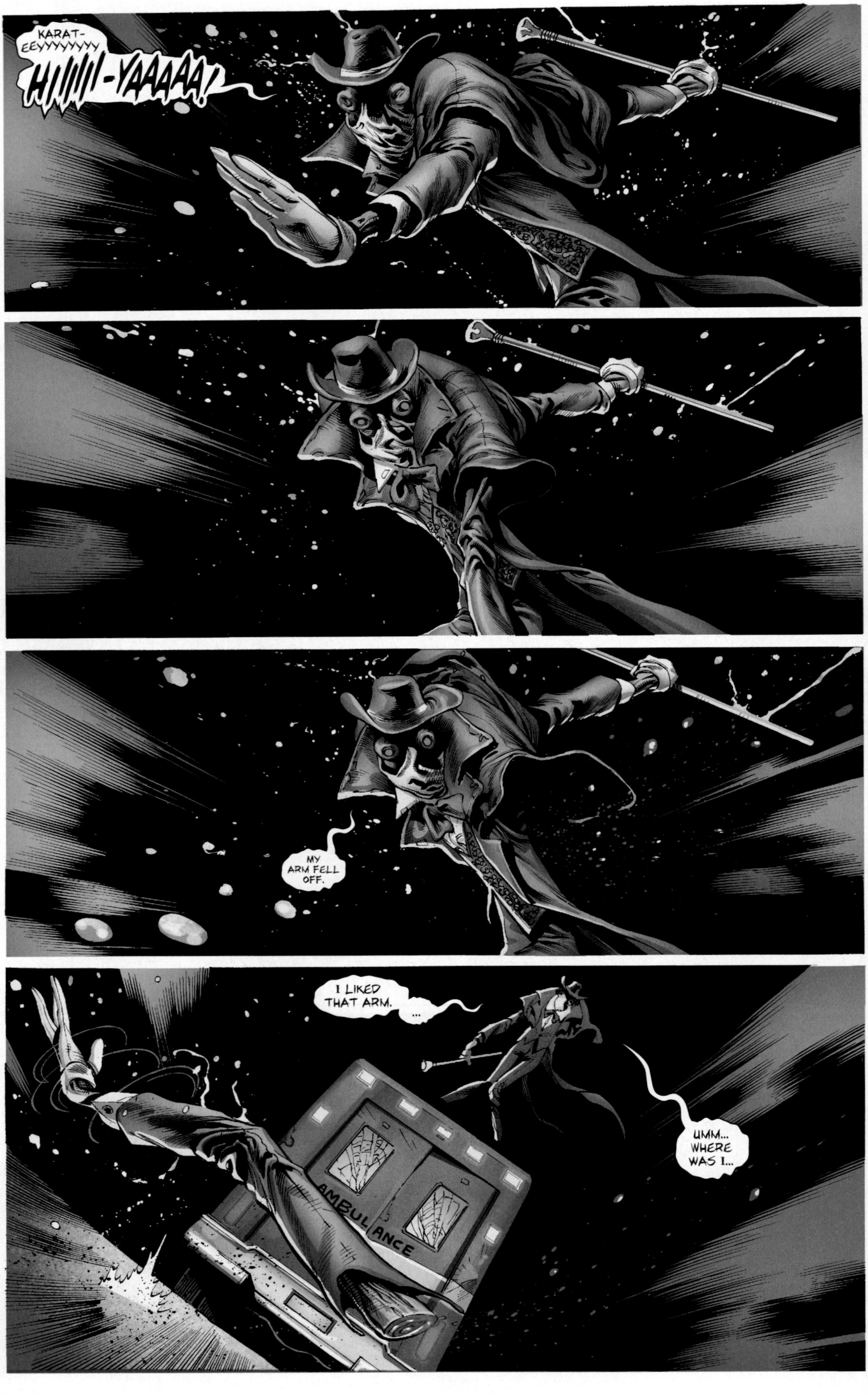
KARAT-EEYYYYYYYY
HI!!!!!-YAAAAA!
MY ARM FELL OFF.
I LIKED THAT ARM.
...
UMM... WHERE WAS I...

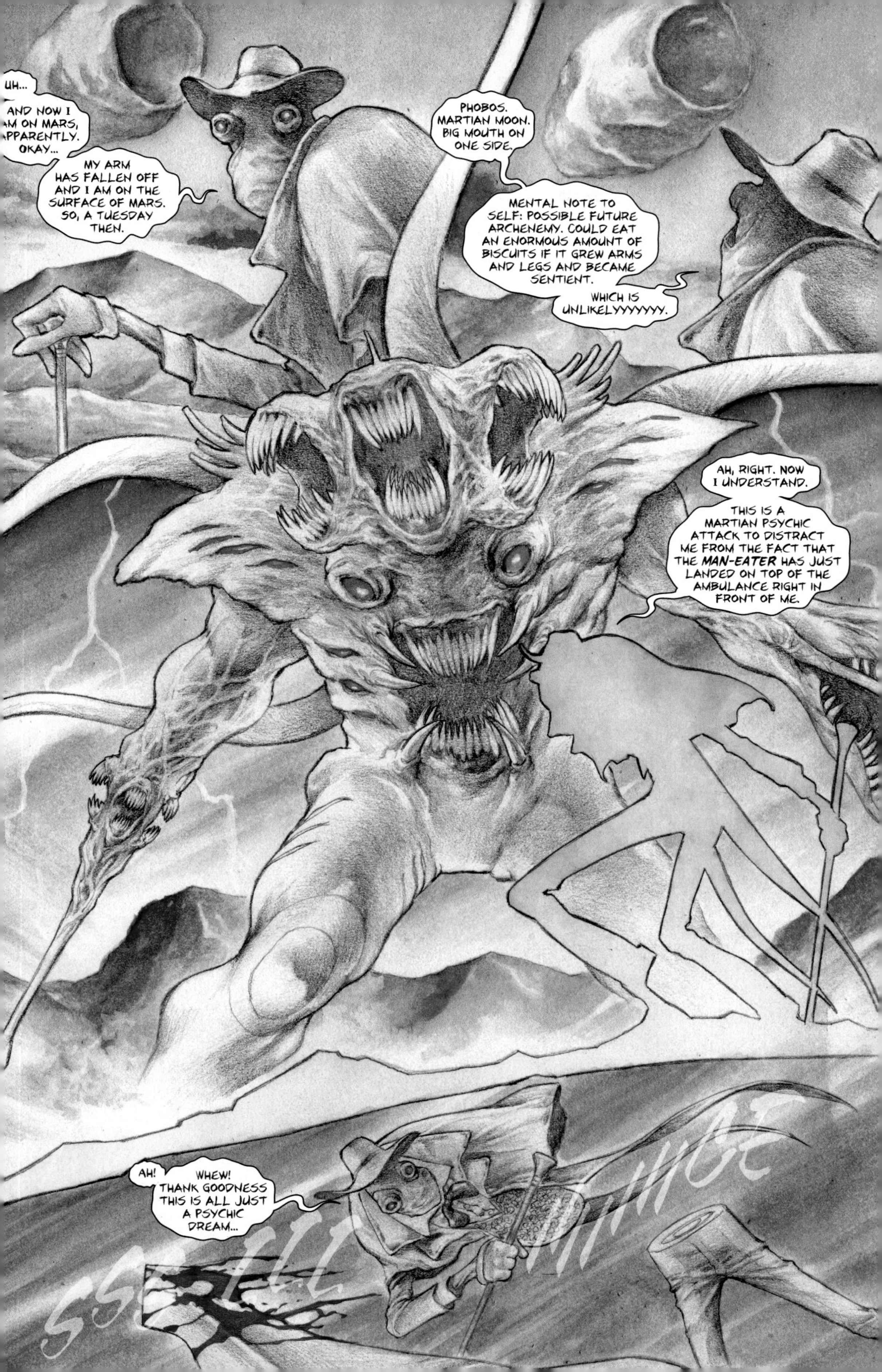
UH...
AND NOW I AM ON MARS, APPARENTLY. OKAY...
MY ARM HAS FALLEN OFF AND I AM ON THE SURFACE OF MARS. SO, A TUESDAY THEN.
PHOBOS. MARTIAN MOON. BIG MOUTH ON ONE SIDE.
MENTAL NOTE TO SELF: POSSIBLE FUTURE ARCHENEMY. COULD EAT AN ENORMOUS AMOUNT OF BISCUITS IF IT GREW ARMS AND LEGS AND BECAME SENTIENT.
WHICH IS UNLIKELYYYYYYY.
AH, RIGHT. NOW I UNDERSTAND.
THIS IS A MARTIAN PSYCHIC ATTACK TO DISTRACT ME FROM THE FACT THAT THE MAN-EATER HAS JUST LANDED ON TOP OF THE AMBULANCE RIGHT IN FRONT OF ME.
AH!
WHEW! THANK GOODNESS THIS IS ALL JUST A PSYCHIC DREAM...
SSPLLLCHHHHOE

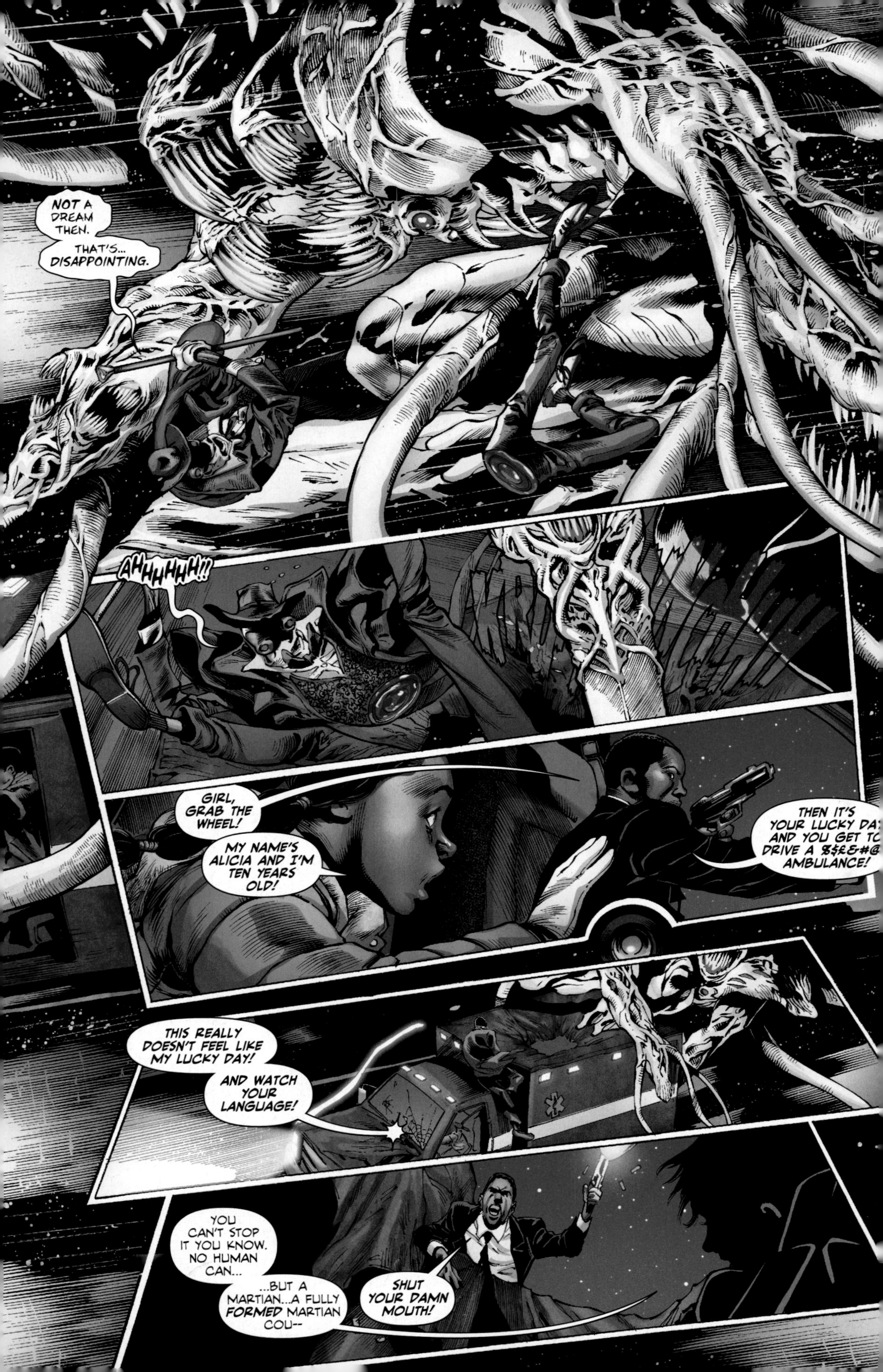
NOT A DREAM THEN.
THAT'S... DISAPPOINTING.
AHHHHHH!!
GIRL, GRAB THE WHEEL!
MY NAME'S ALICIA AND I'M TEN YEARS OLD!
THEN IT'S YOUR LUCKY DA AND YOU GET TO DRIVE A %$£&#@ AMBULANCE!
THIS REALLY DOESN'T FEEL LIKE MY LUCKY DAY!
AND WATCH YOUR LANGUAGE!
YOU CAN'T STOP IT YOU KNOW. NO HUMAN CAN...
...BUT A MARTIAN...A FULLY FORMED MARTIAN COU--
SHUT YOUR DAMN MOUTH!

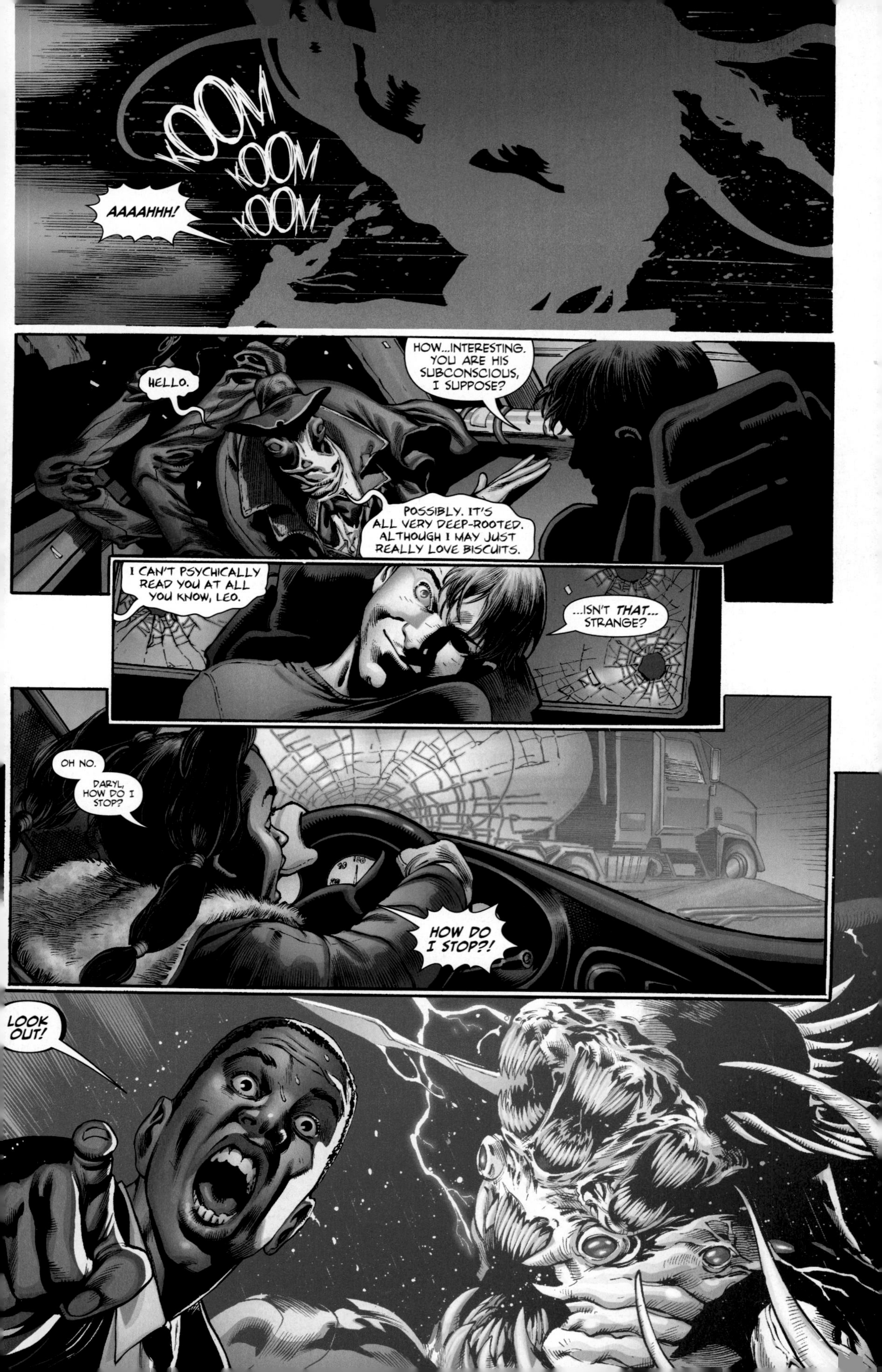
AAAAHHH!
KOOM KOOM KOOM
HELLO.
HOW...INTERESTING. YOU ARE HIS SUBCONSCIOUS, I SUPPOSE?
POSSIBLY. IT'S ALL VERY DEEP-ROOTED. ALTHOUGH I MAY JUST REALLY LOVE BISCUITS.
I CAN'T PSYCHICALLY READ YOU AT ALL YOU KNOW, LEO.
...ISN'T THAT... STRANGE?
OH NO.
DARYL, HOW DO I STOP?
HOW DO I STOP?!
LOOK OUT!

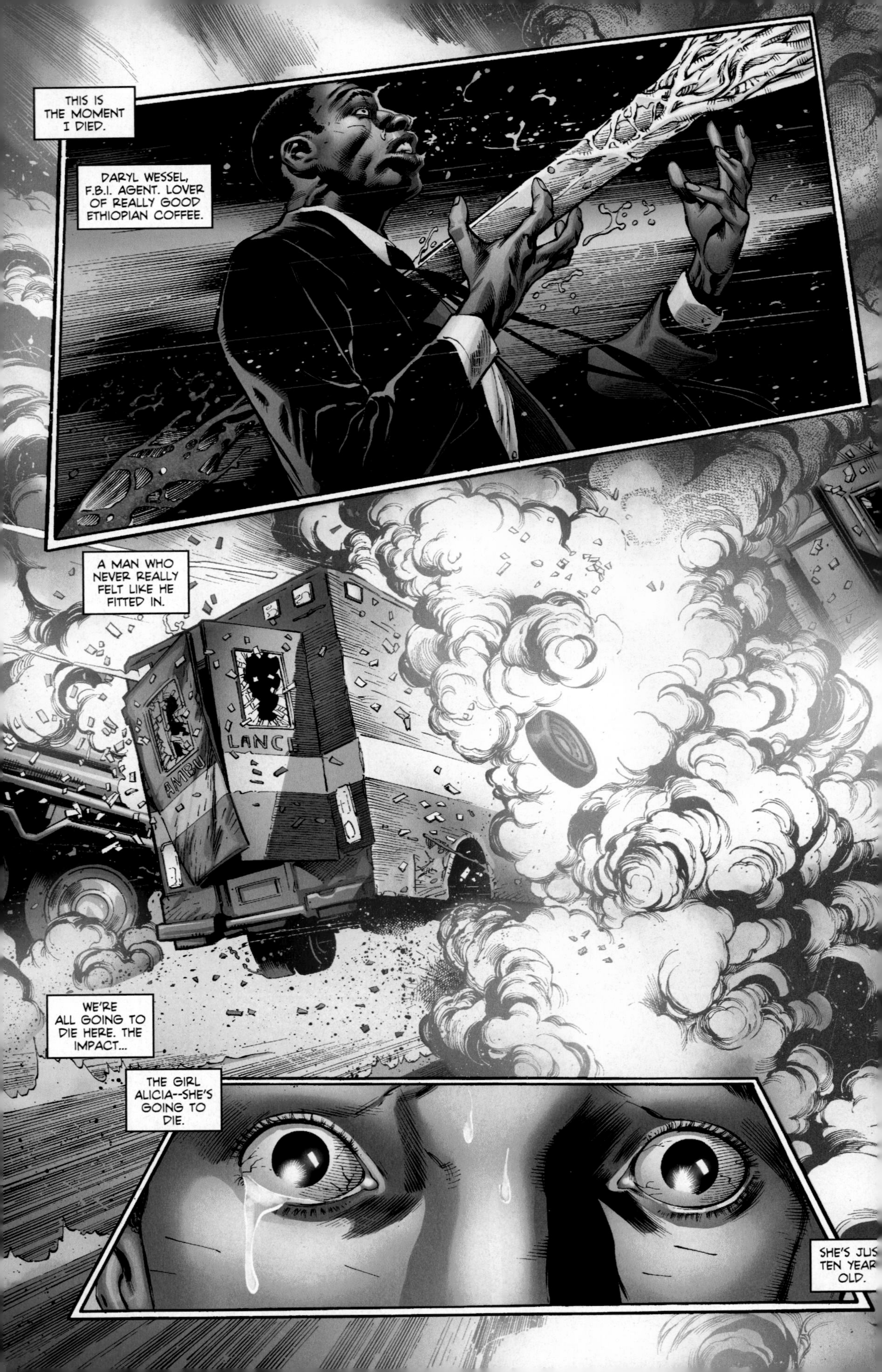

THIS IS THE MOMENT I DIED.
DARYL WESSEL, F.B.I. AGENT. LOVER OF REALLY GOOD ETHIOPIAN COFFEE.
A MAN WHO NEVER REALLY FELT LIKE HE FITTED IN.
AMBU
LANCE
WE'RE ALL GOING TO DIE HERE. THE IMPACT...
THE GIRL ALICIA--SHE'S GOING TO DIE.
SHE'S JUS TEN YEAR OLD.

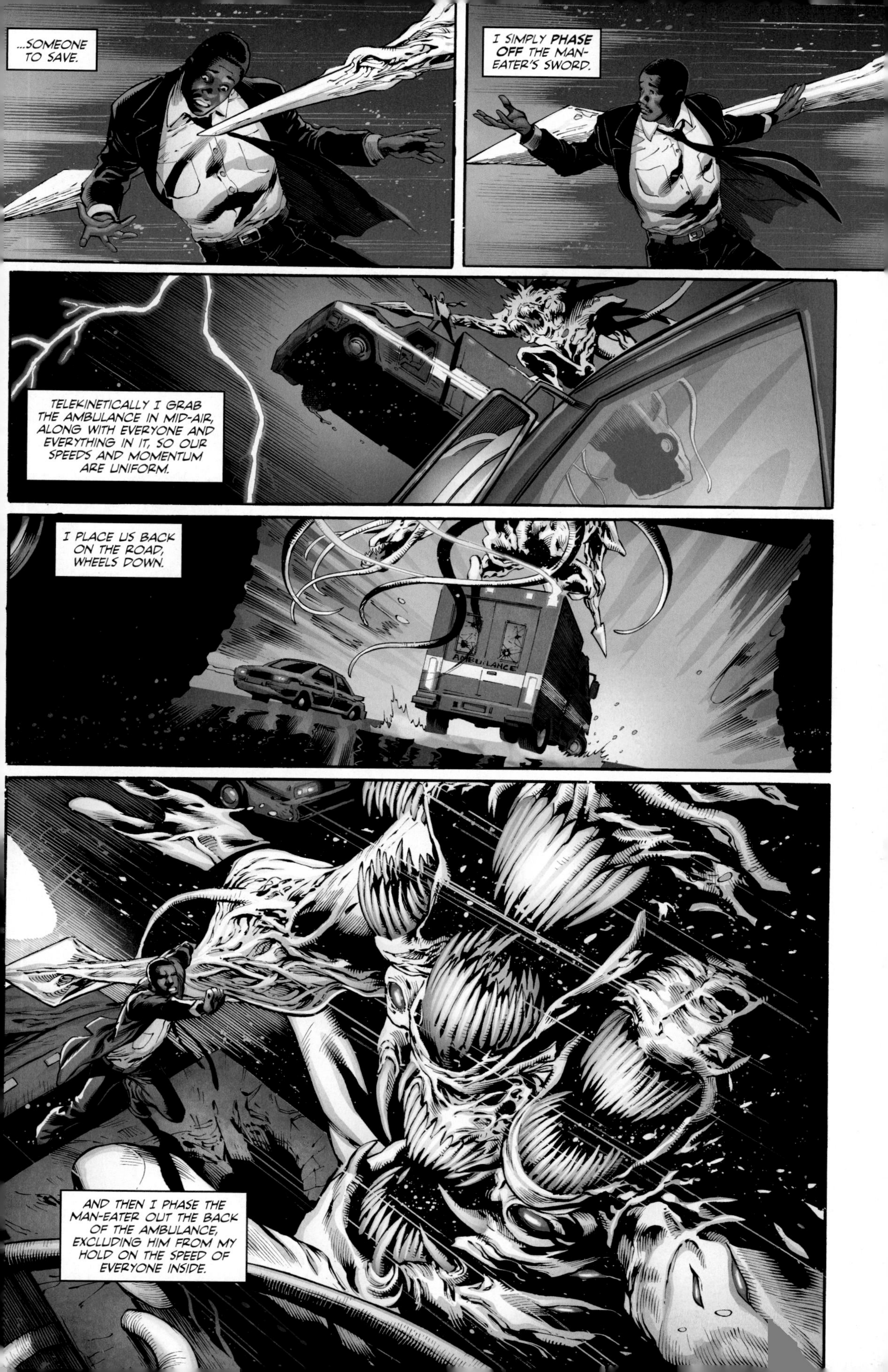

...SOMEONE TO SAVE.
I SIMPLY PHASE OFF THE MAN-EATER'S SWORD.
TELEKINETICALLY I GRAB THE AMBULANCE IN MID-AIR, ALONG WITH EVERYONE AND EVERYTHING IN IT, SO OUR SPEEDS AND MOMENTUM ARE UNIFORM.
I PLACE US BACK ON THE ROAD, WHEELS DOWN.
AMBULANCE
AND THEN I PHASE THE MAN-EATER OUT THE BACK OF THE AMBULANCE, EXCLUDING HIM FROM MY HOLD ON THE SPEED OF EVERYONE INSIDE.

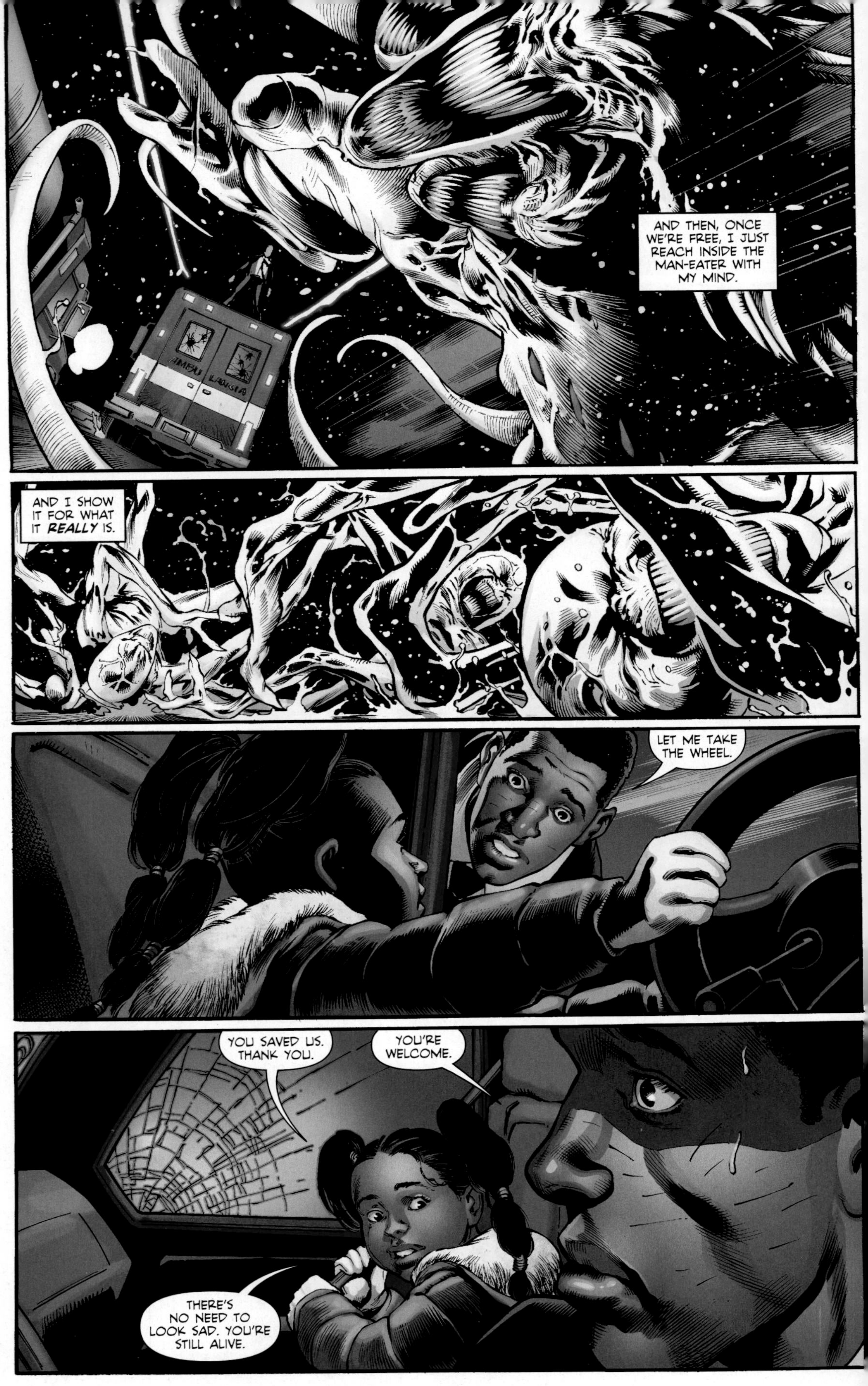
AND THEN, ONCE WE'RE FREE, I JUST REACH INSIDE THE MAN-EATER WITH MY MIND.
AND I SHOW IT FOR WHAT IT REALLY IS.
LET ME TAKE THE WHEEL.
YOU SAVED US. THANK YOU.
YOU'RE WELCOME.
THERE'S NO NEED TO LOOK SAD. YOU'RE STILL ALIVE.

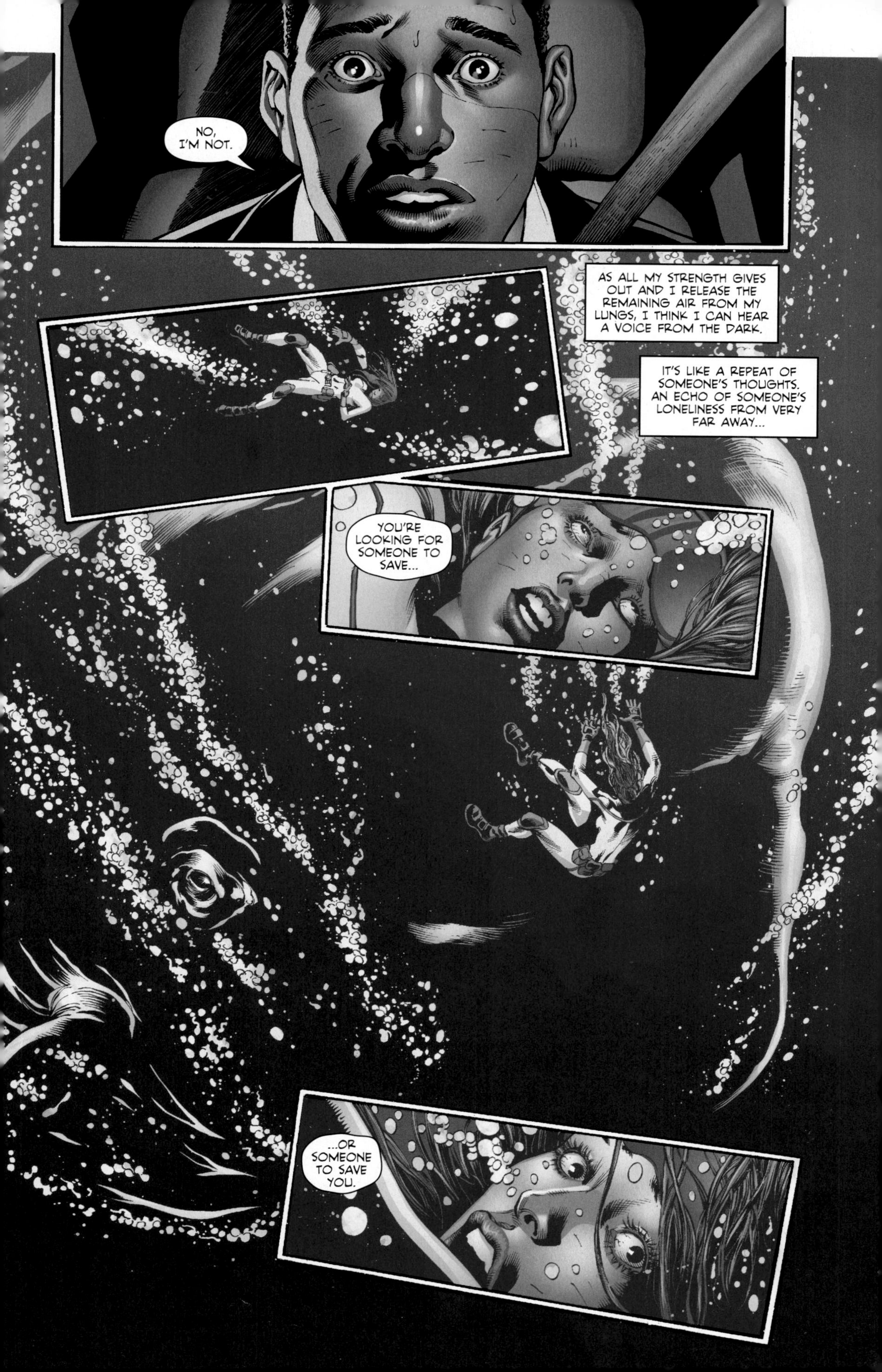
NO, I'M NOT.
AS ALL MY STRENGTH GIVES OUT AND I RELEASE THE REMAINING AIR FROM MY LUNGS, I THINK I CAN HEAR A VOICE FROM THE DARK.
IT'S LIKE A REPEAT OF SOMEONE'S THOUGHTS. AN ECHO OF SOMEONE'S LONELINESS FROM VERY FAR AWAY...
YOU'RE LOOKING FOR SOMEONE TO SAVE...
...OR SOMEONE TO SAVE YOU.

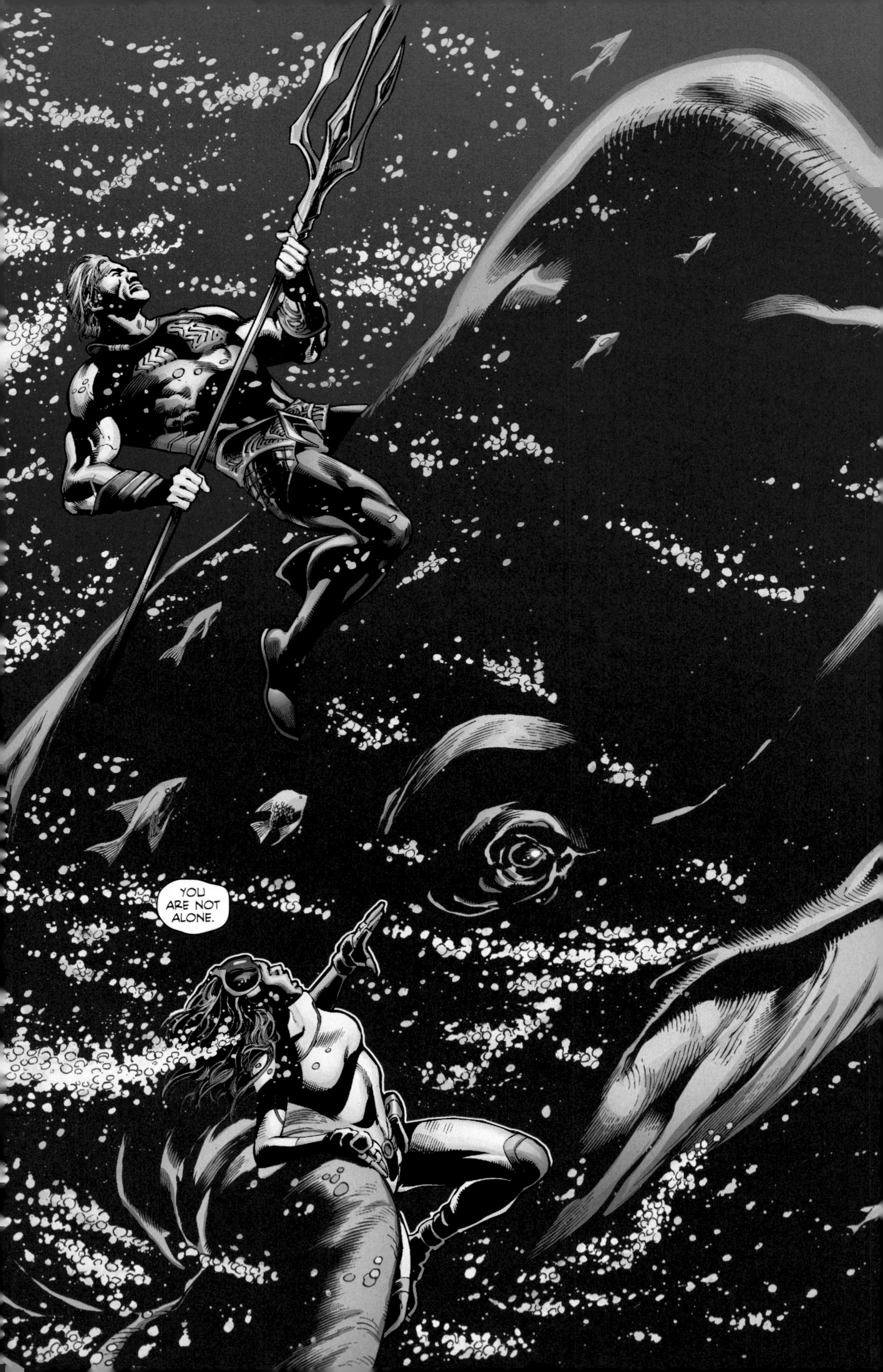
YOU ARE NOT ALONE.

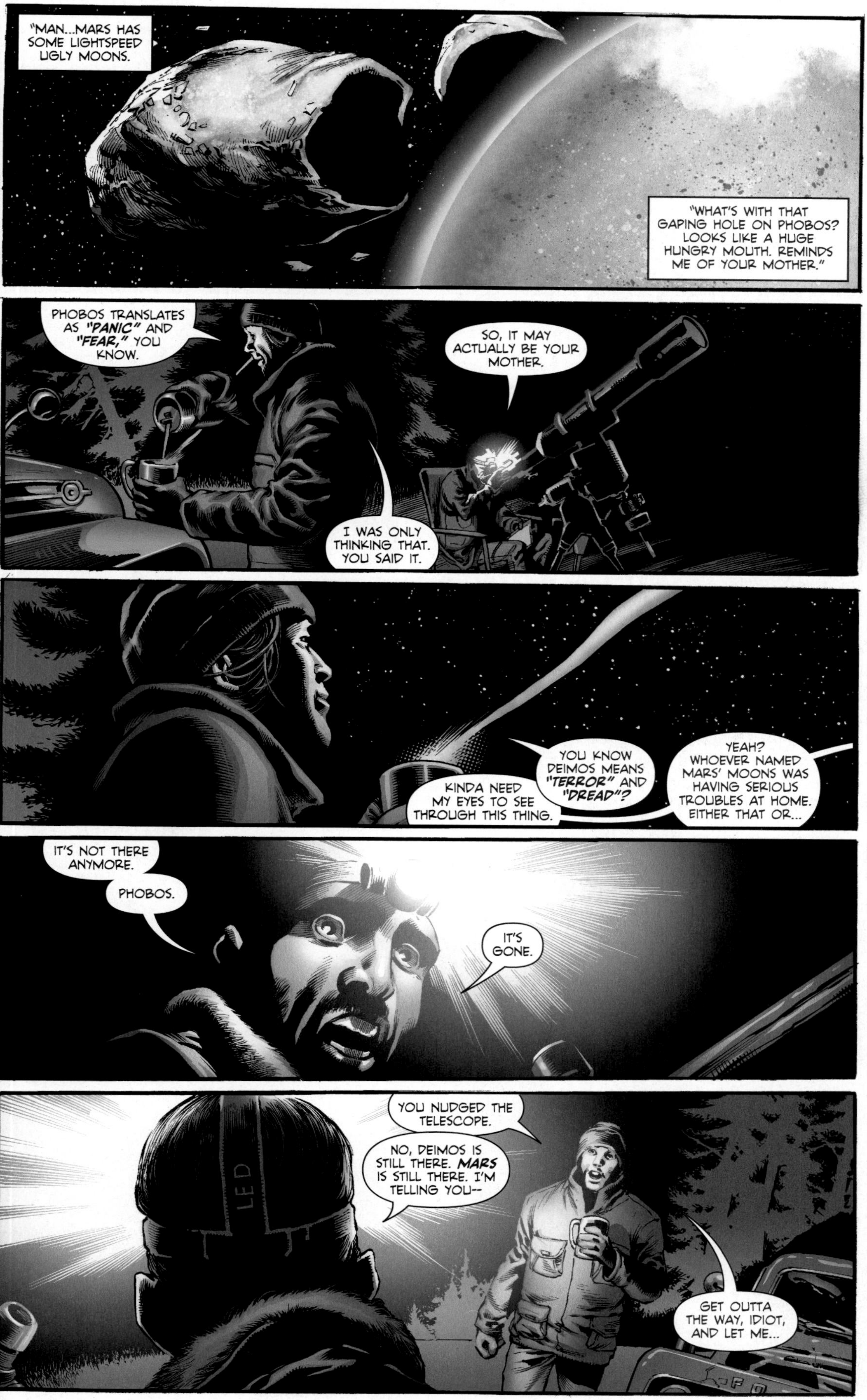
"MAN...MARS HAS SOME LIGHTSPEED UGLY MOONS.
"WHAT'S WITH THAT GAPING HOLE ON PHOBOS? LOOKS LIKE A HUGE HUNGRY MOUTH. REMINDS ME OF YOUR MOTHER."
PHOBOS TRANSLATES AS "PANIC" AND "FEAR," YOU KNOW.
SO, IT MAY ACTUALLY BE YOUR MOTHER.
I WAS ONLY THINKING THAT. YOU SAID IT.
YOU KNOW DEIMOS MEANS "TERROR" AND "DREAD"?
KINDA NEED MY EYES TO SEE THROUGH THIS THING.
YEAH? WHOEVER NAMED MARS' MOONS WAS HAVING SERIOUS TROUBLES AT HOME. EITHER THAT OR...
IT'S NOT THERE ANYMORE.
PHOBOS.
IT'S GONE.
YOU NUDGED THE TELESCOPE.
NO, DEIMOS IS STILL THERE. MARS IS STILL THERE. I'M TELLING YOU--
LED
GET OUTTA THE WAY, IDIOT, AND LET ME...

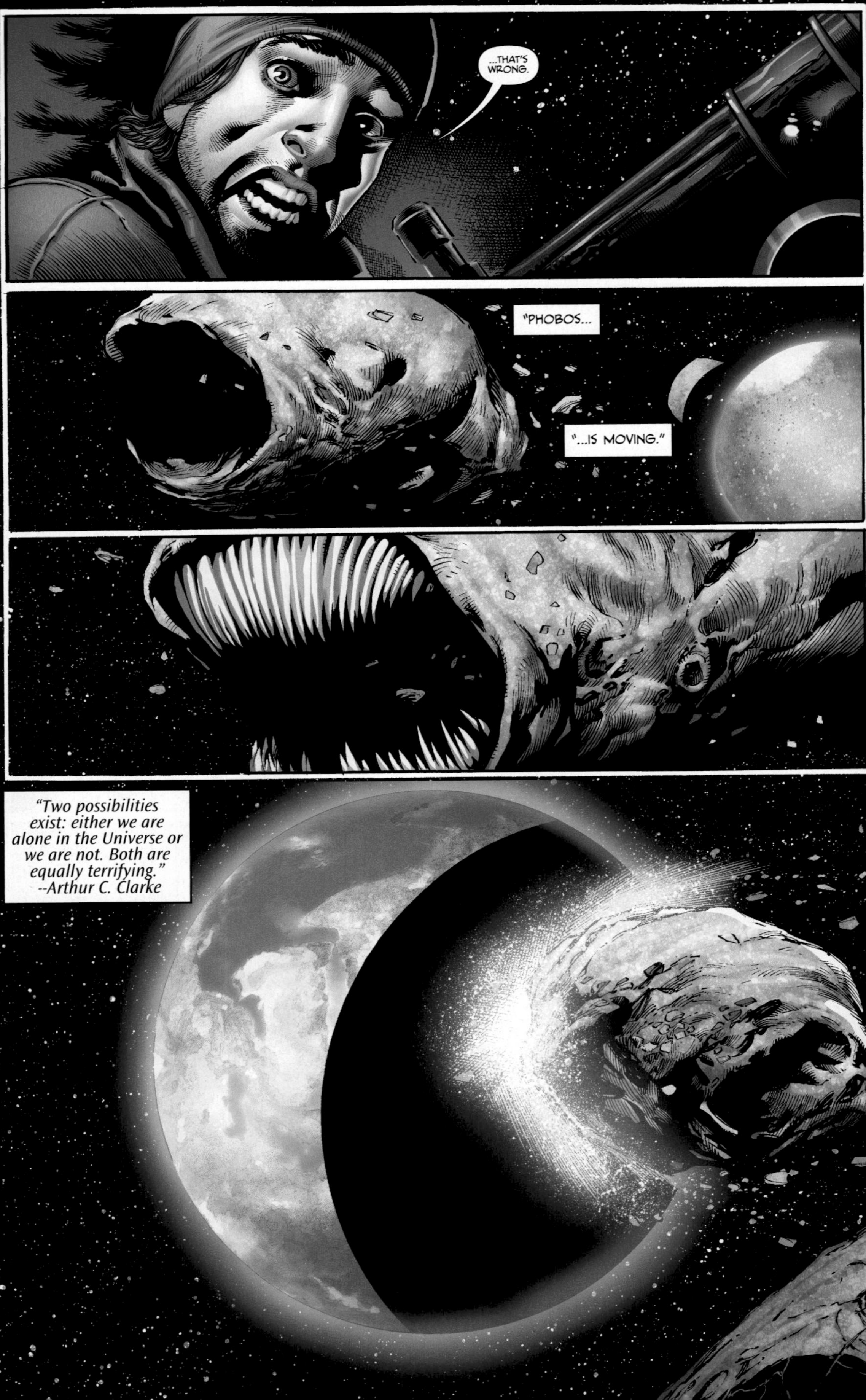
...THAT'S WRONG.
"PHOBOS...
"...IS MOVING."
"Two possibilities exist: either we are alone in the Universe or we are not. Both are equally terrifying."
--Arthur C. Clarke

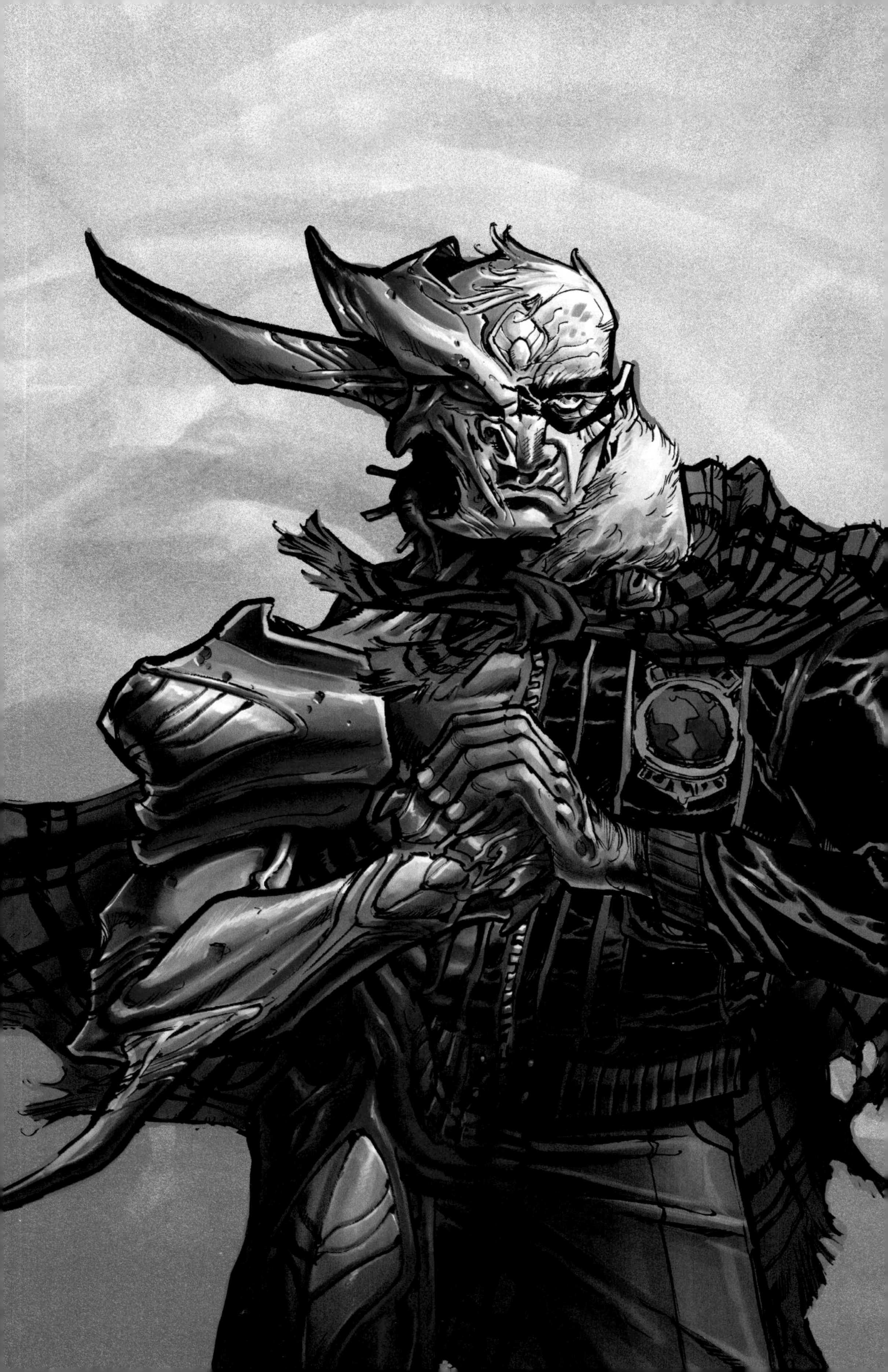

HEART/HEAD
cover by **ERIC CANETE**

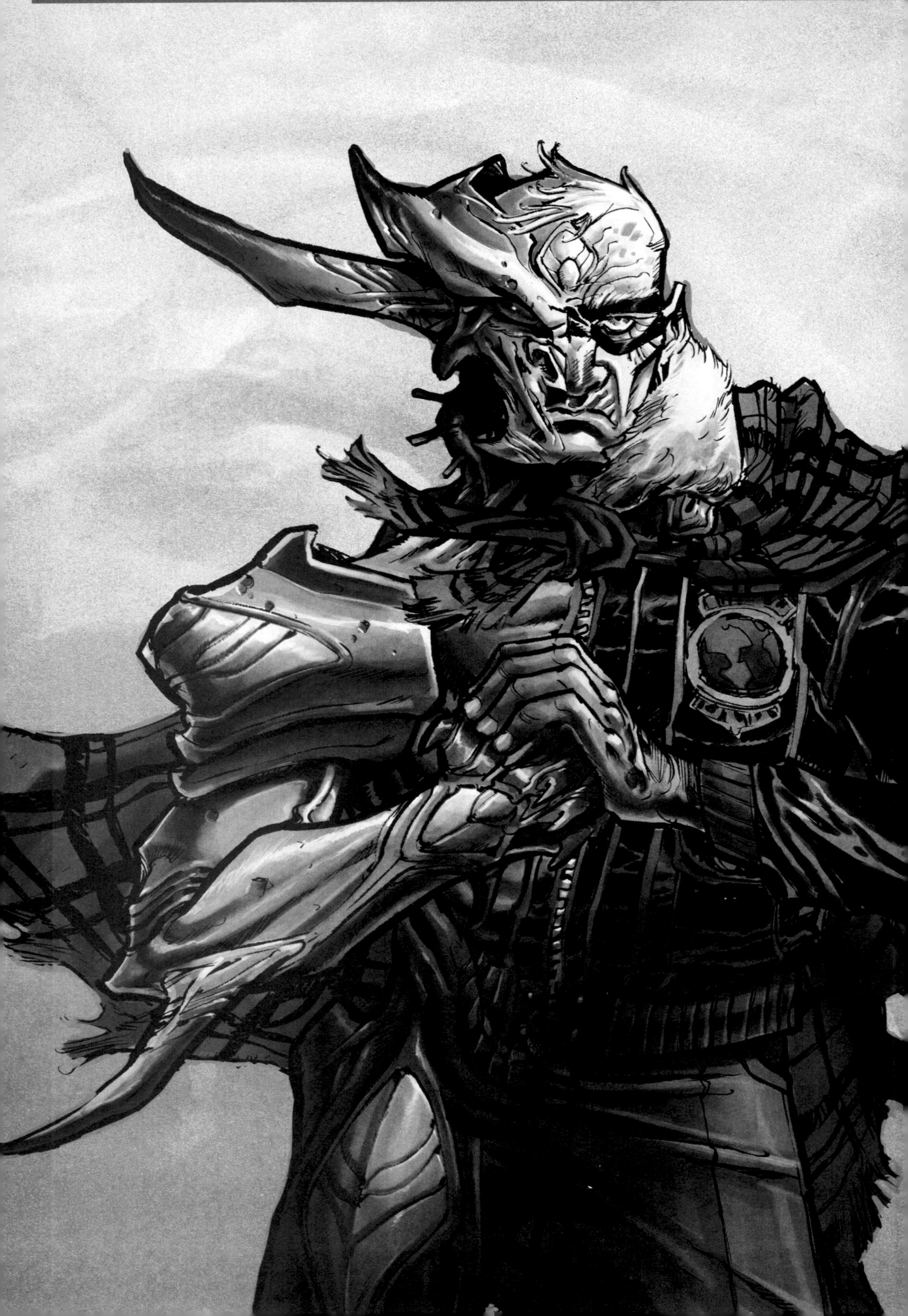

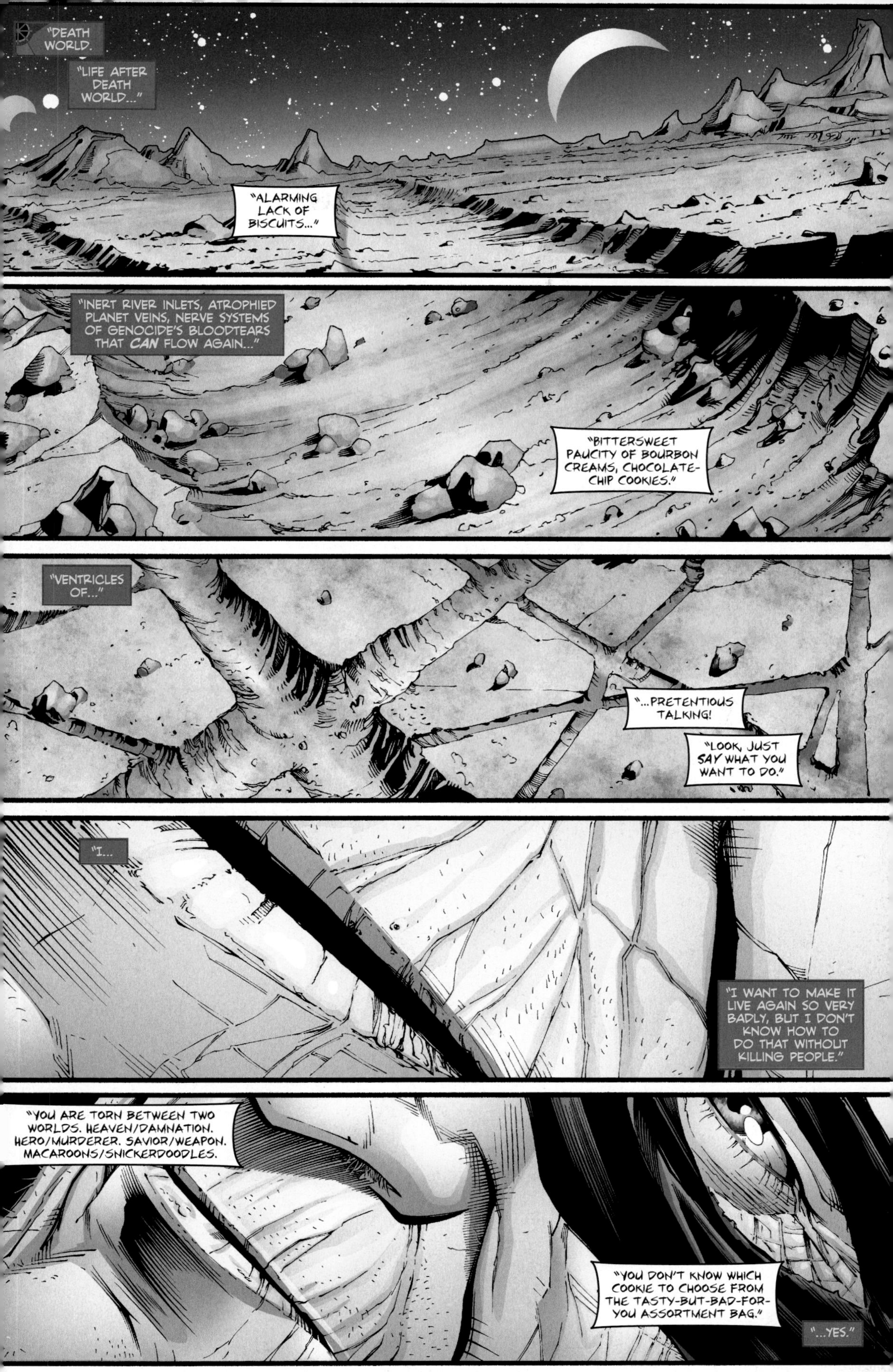
"DEATH WORLD.
"LIFE AFTER DEATH WORLD..."
"ALARMING LACK OF BISCUITS..."
"INERT RIVER INLETS, ATROPHIED PLANET VEINS, NERVE SYSTEMS OF GENOCIDE'S BLOODTEARS THAT CAN FLOW AGAIN..."
"BITTERSWEET PAUCITY OF BOURBON CREAMS, CHOCOLATE-CHIP COOKIES."
"VENTRICLES OF..."
"...PRETENTIOUS TALKING!
"LOOK, JUST SAY WHAT YOU WANT TO DO."
"I...
"I WANT TO MAKE IT LIVE AGAIN SO VERY BADLY, BUT I DON'T KNOW HOW TO DO THAT WITHOUT KILLING PEOPLE."
"YOU ARE TORN BETWEEN TWO WORLDS. HEAVEN/DAMNATION. HERO/MURDERER. SAVIOR/WEAPON. MACAROONS/SNICKERDOODLES.
"YOU DON'T KNOW WHICH COOKIE TO CHOOSE FROM THE TASTY-BUT-BAD-FOR-YOU ASSORTMENT BAG."
"...YES."

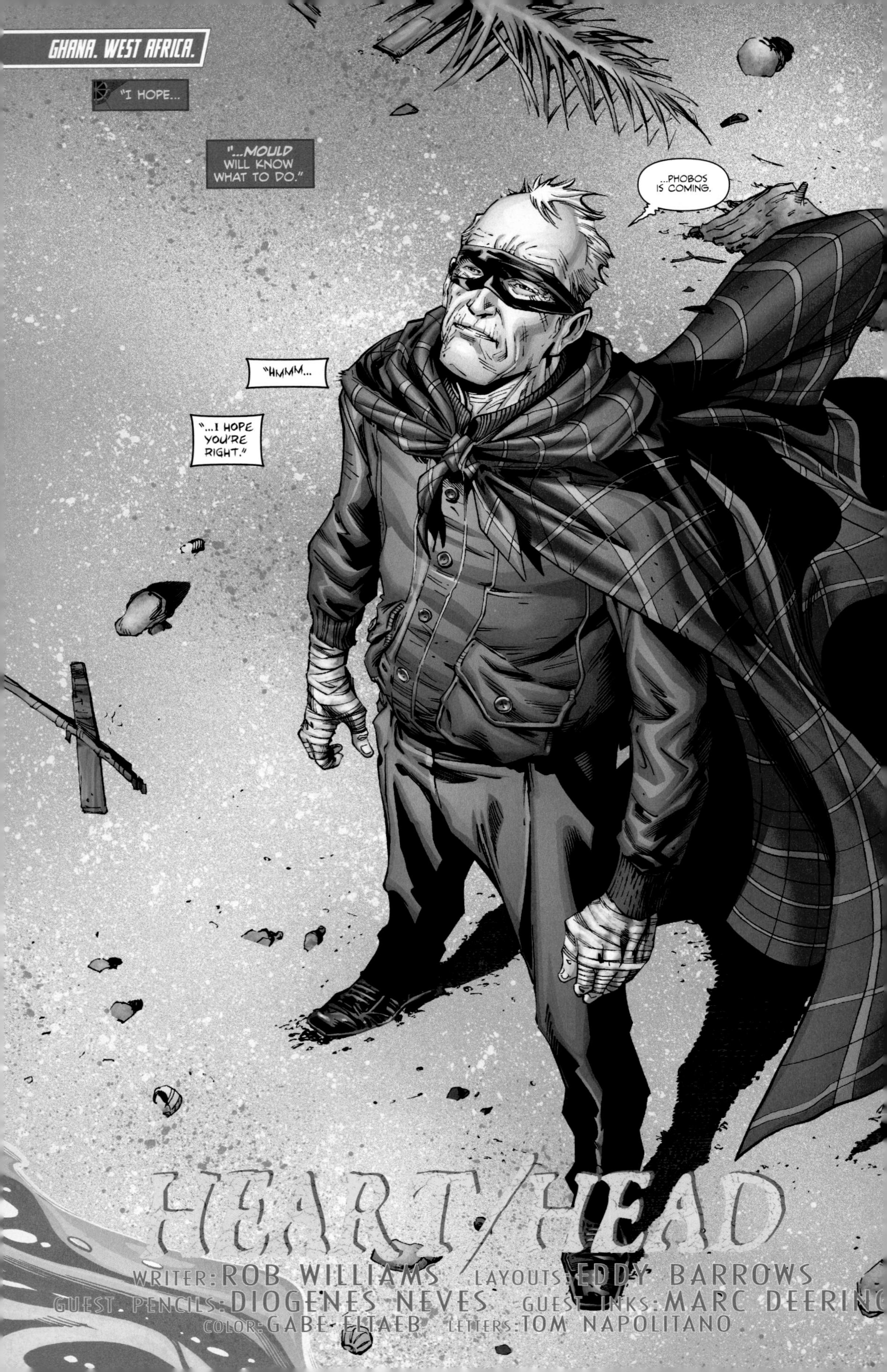
GHANA. WEST AFRICA.
"I HOPE...
"...MOULD WILL KNOW WHAT TO DO."
...PHOBOS IS COMING.
"HMMM...
"...I HOPE YOU'RE RIGHT."
HEART/HEAD
WRITER: ROB WILLIAMS LAYOUTS: EDDY BARROWS
GUEST PENCILS: DIOGENES NEVES GUEST INKS: MARC DEERING
COLOR: GABE ELTAEB LETTERS: TOM NAPOLITANO

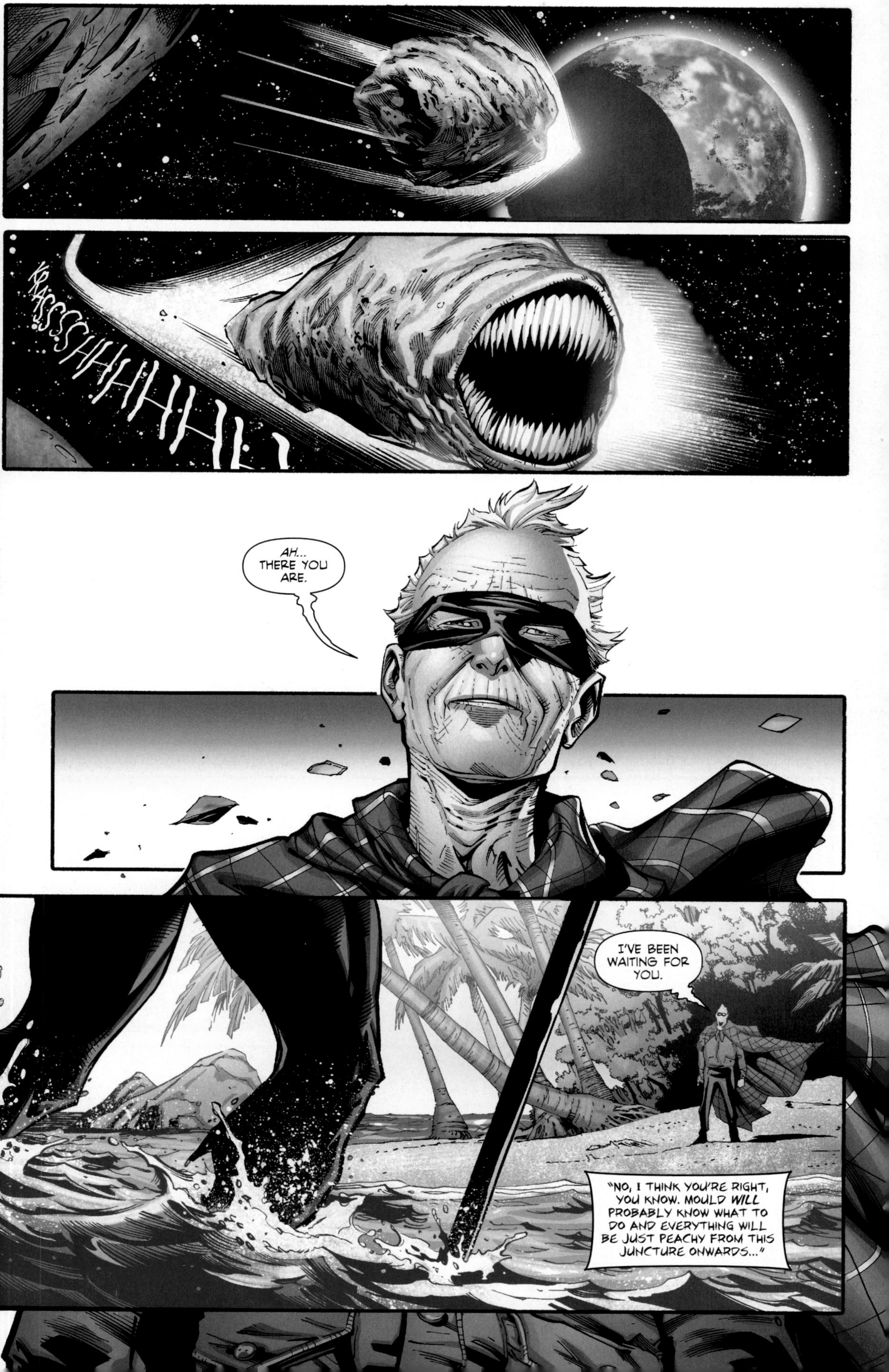
KRASSSSHHHHHHH!!
AH... THERE YOU ARE.
I'VE BEEN WAITING FOR YOU.
"NO, I THINK YOU'RE RIGHT, YOU KNOW. MOULD *WILL* PROBABLY KNOW WHAT TO DO AND EVERYTHING WILL BE JUST PEACHY FROM THIS JUNCTURE ONWARDS..."

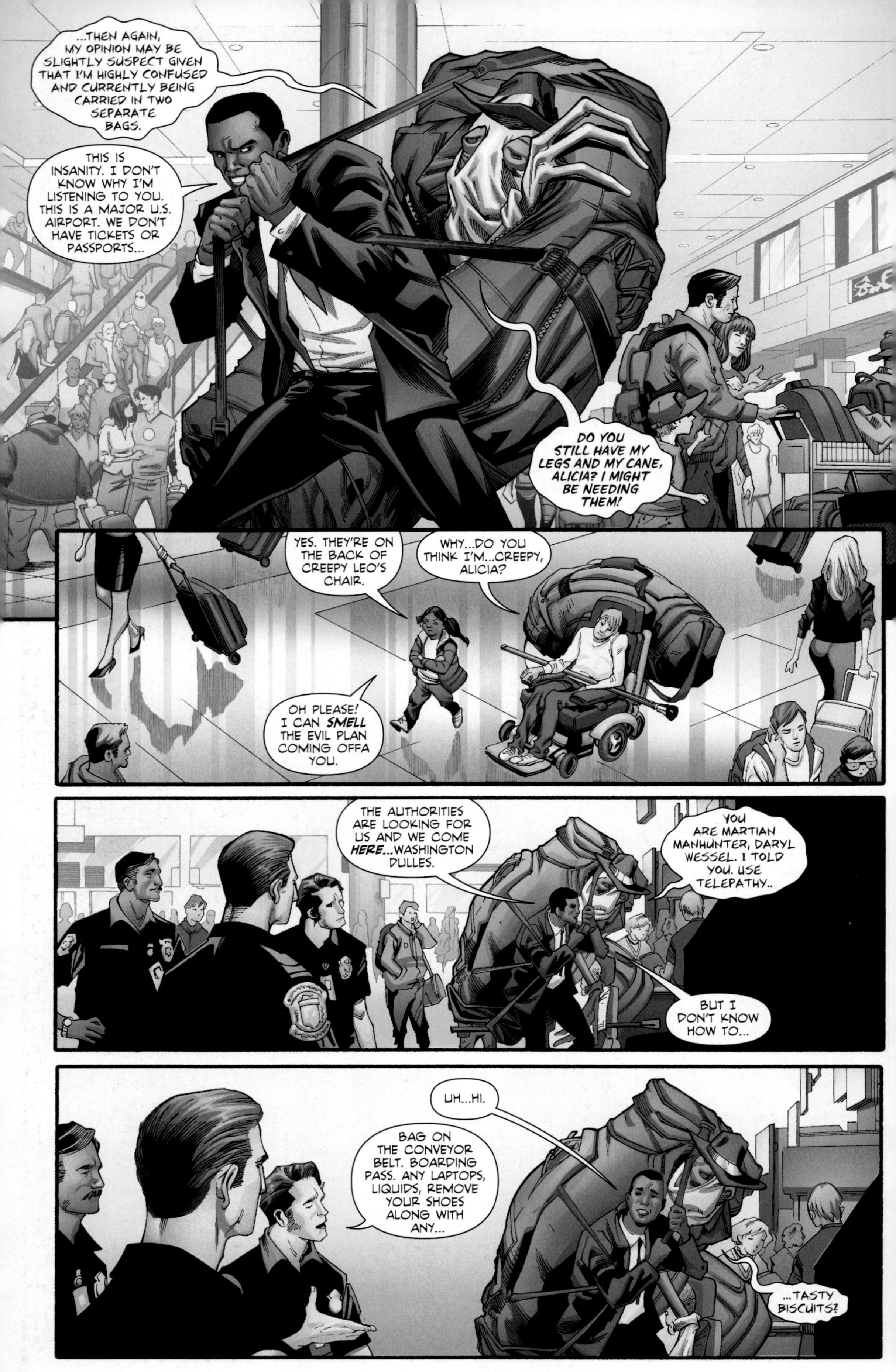
...THEN AGAIN, MY OPINION MAY BE SLIGHTLY SUSPECT GIVEN THAT I'M HIGHLY CONFUSED AND CURRENTLY BEING CARRIED IN TWO SEPARATE BAGS.
THIS IS INSANITY. I DON'T KNOW WHY I'M LISTENING TO YOU. THIS IS A MAJOR U.S. AIRPORT. WE DON'T HAVE TICKETS OR PASSPORTS...
DO YOU STILL HAVE MY LEGS AND MY CANE, ALICIA? I MIGHT BE NEEDING THEM!
YES. THEY'RE ON THE BACK OF CREEPY LEO'S CHAIR.
WHY...DO YOU THINK I'M...CREEPY, ALICIA?
OH PLEASE! I CAN SMELL THE EVIL PLAN COMING OFFA YOU.
THE AUTHORITIES ARE LOOKING FOR US AND WE COME HERE...WASHINGTON DULLES.
YOU ARE MARTIAN MANHUNTER, DARYL WESSEL. I TOLD YOU. USE TELEPATHY..
BUT I DON'T KNOW HOW TO...
UH...HI.
BAG ON THE CONVEYOR BELT. BOARDING PASS. ANY LAPTOPS, LIQUIDS, REMOVE YOUR SHOES ALONG WITH ANY...
...TASTY BISCUITS?

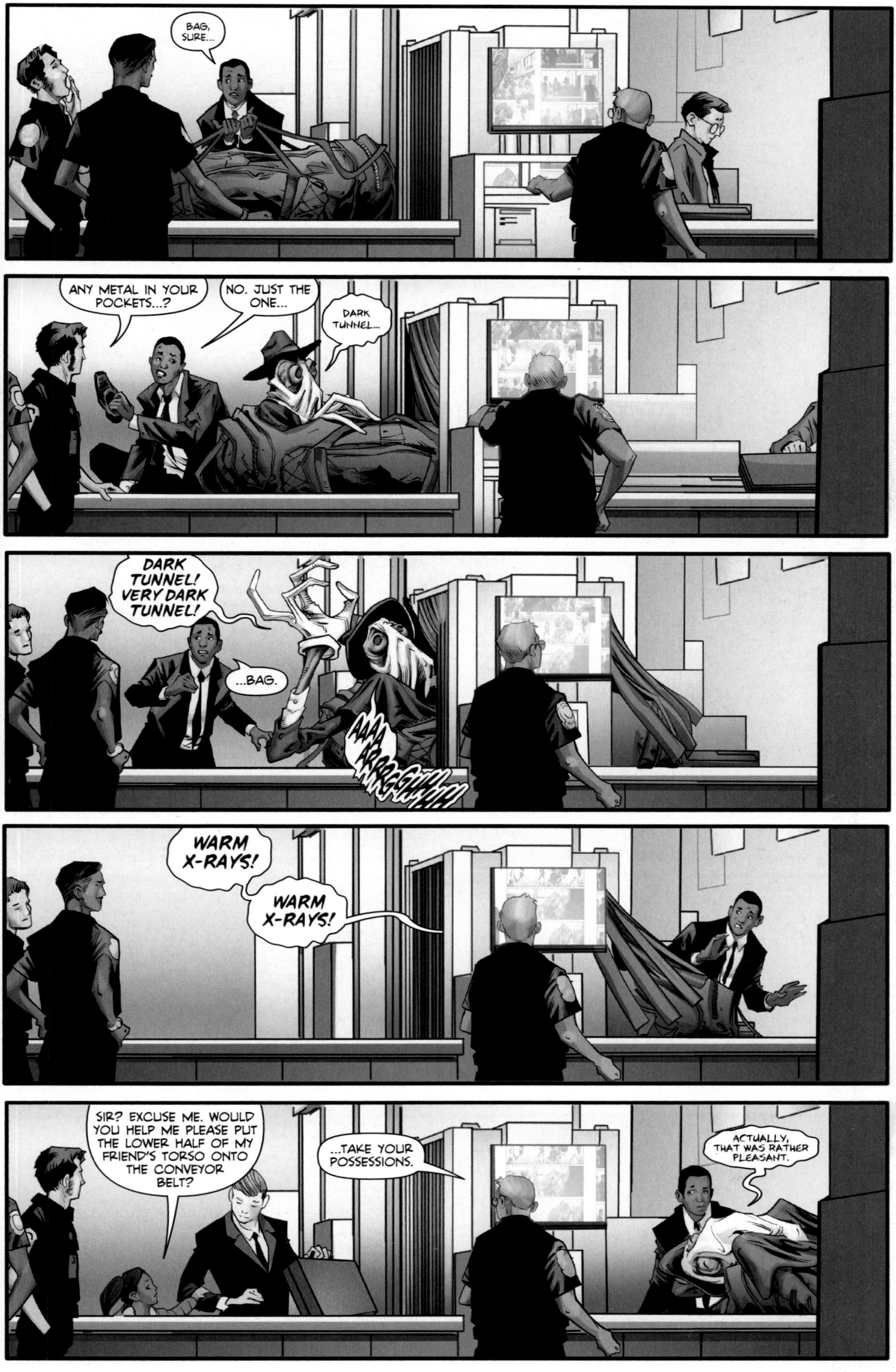
BAG, SURE...
ANY METAL IN YOUR POCKETS...?
NO. JUST THE ONE...
DARK TUNNEL...
DARK TUNNEL! VERY DARK TUNNEL!
...BAG.
AAAA ARRRGHHHH
WARM X-RAYS!
WARM X-RAYS!
SIR? EXCUSE ME. WOULD YOU HELP ME PLEASE PUT THE LOWER HALF OF MY FRIEND'S TORSO ONTO THE CONVEYOR BELT?
...TAKE YOUR POSSESSIONS.
ACTUALLY, THAT WAS RATHER PLEASANT.

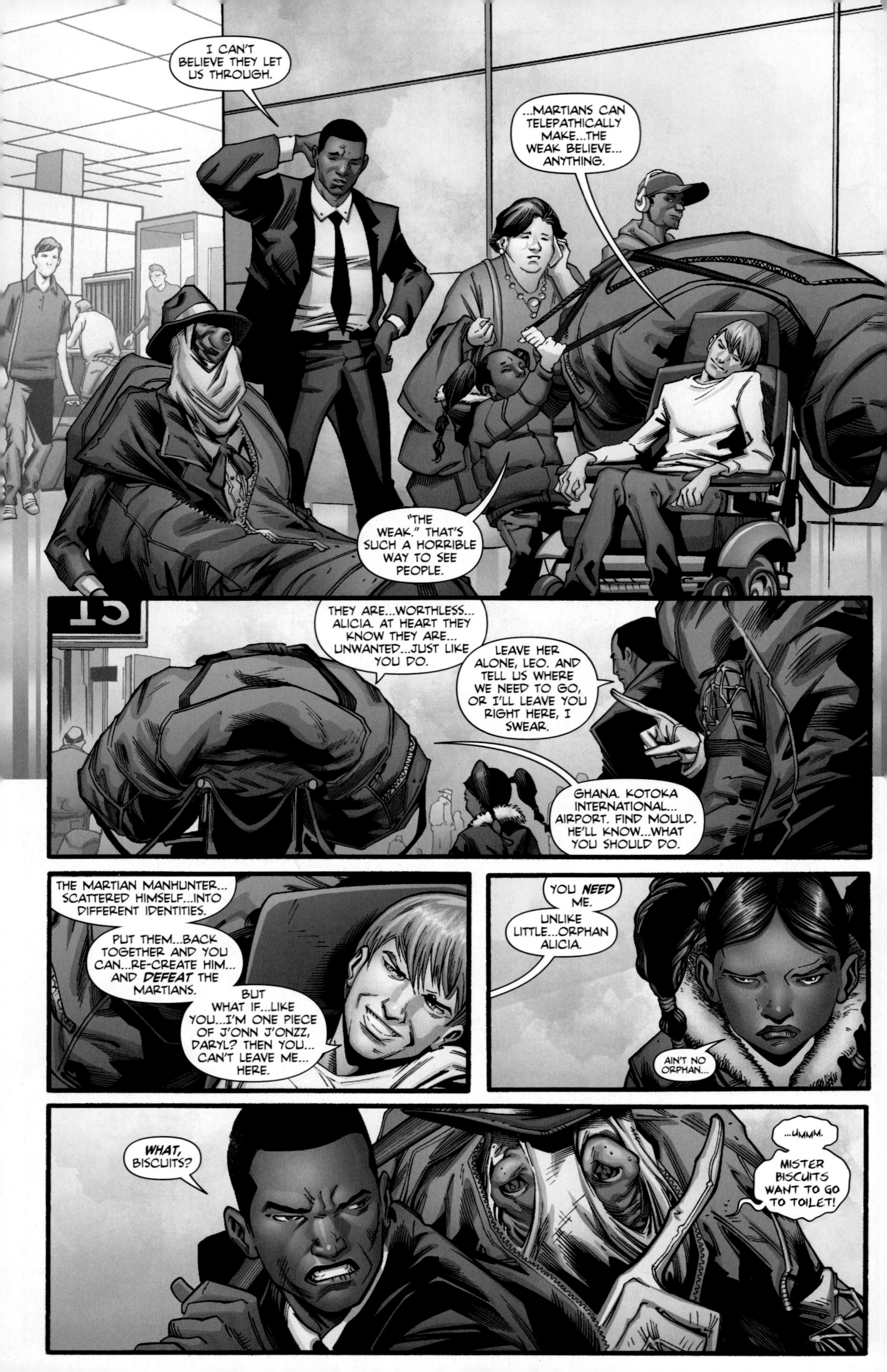
I CAN'T BELIEVE THEY LET US THROUGH.
...MARTIANS CAN TELEPATHICALLY MAKE...THE WEAK BELIEVE... ANYTHING.
"THE WEAK." THAT'S SUCH A HORRIBLE WAY TO SEE PEOPLE.
THEY ARE...WORTHLESS... ALICIA. AT HEART THEY KNOW THEY ARE... UNWANTED...JUST LIKE YOU DO.
LEAVE HER ALONE, LEO. AND TELL US WHERE WE NEED TO GO, OR I'LL LEAVE YOU RIGHT HERE, I SWEAR.
GHANA. KOTOKA INTERNATIONAL... AIRPORT. FIND MOULD. HE'LL KNOW...WHAT YOU SHOULD DO.
THE MARTIAN MANHUNTER... SCATTERED HIMSELF...INTO DIFFERENT IDENTITIES.
PUT THEM...BACK TOGETHER AND YOU CAN...RE-CREATE HIM... AND DEFEAT THE MARTIANS.
BUT WHAT IF...LIKE YOU...I'M ONE PIECE OF J'ONN J'ONZZ, DARYL? THEN YOU... CAN'T LEAVE ME... HERE.
YOU NEED ME.
UNLIKE LITTLE...ORPHAN ALICIA.
AIN'T NO ORPHAN...
WHAT, BISCUITS?
...UMMM.
MISTER BISCUITS WANT TO GO TO TOILET!

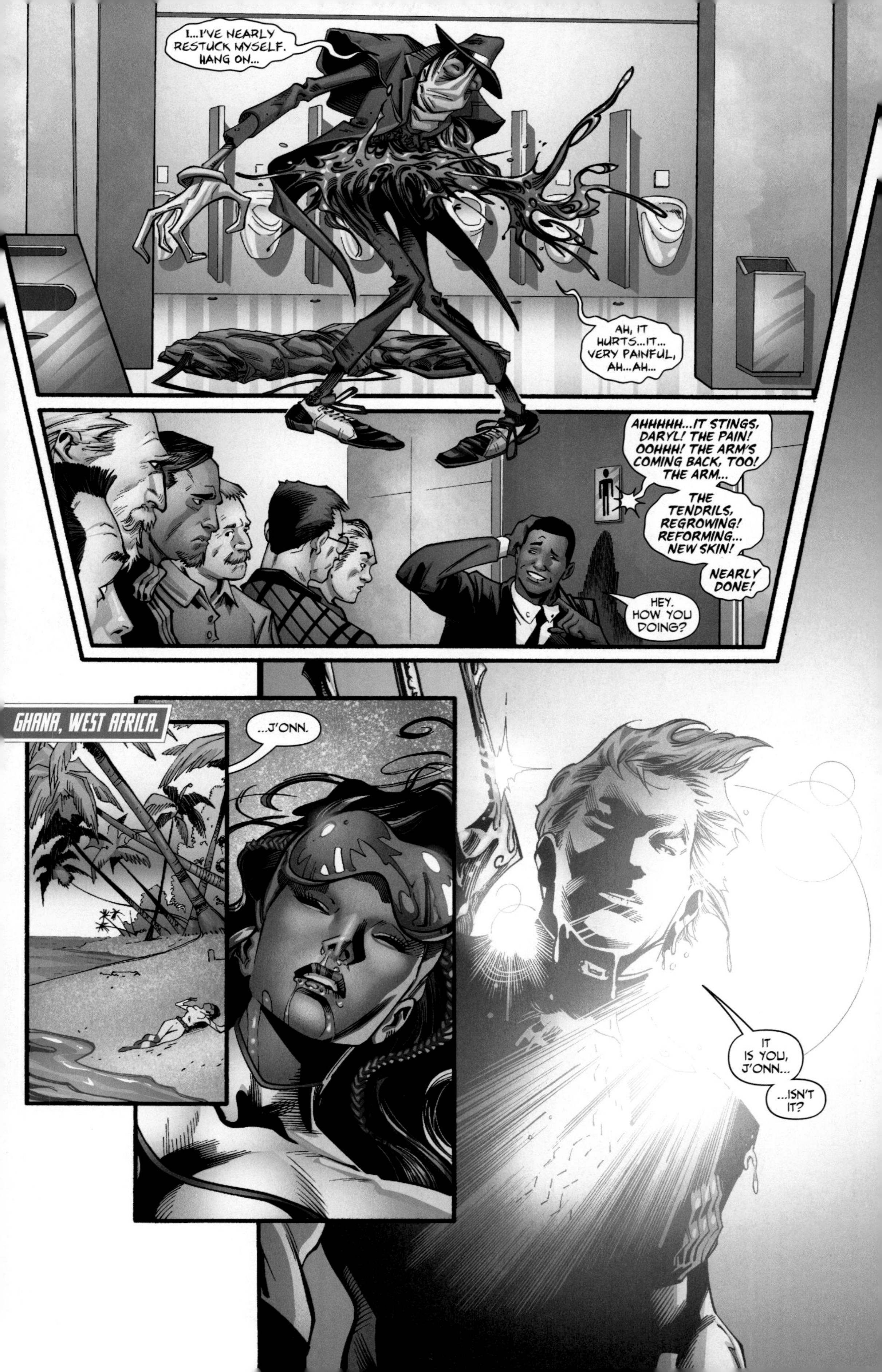
I...I'VE NEARLY RESTUCK MYSELF. HANG ON...
AH, IT HURTS...IT... VERY PAINFUL, AH...AH...
AHHHHH...IT STINGS, DARYL! THE PAIN! OOHHH! THE ARM'S COMING BACK, TOO! THE ARM...
THE TENDRILS, REGROWING! REFORMING... NEW SKIN!
NEARLY DONE!
HEY. HOW YOU DOING?
GHANA, WEST AFRICA.
...J'ONN.
IT IS YOU, J'ONN...
...ISN'T IT?

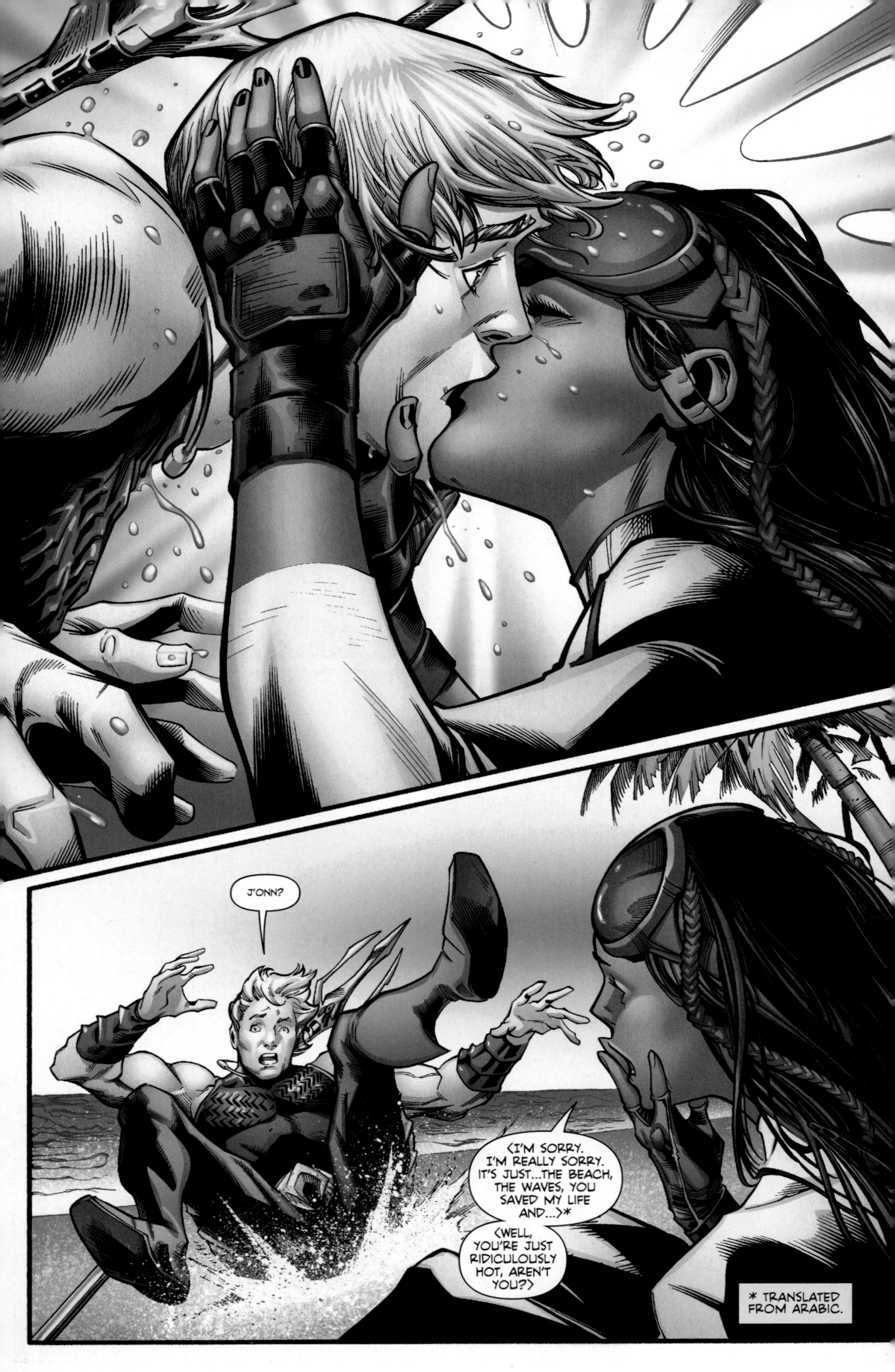
J'ONN?
<I'M SORRY. I'M REALLY SORRY. IT'S JUST...THE BEACH, THE WAVES, YOU SAVED MY LIFE AND...>*
<WELL, YOU'RE JUST RIDICULOUSLY HOT, AREN'T YOU?>
* TRANSLATED FROM ARABIC.

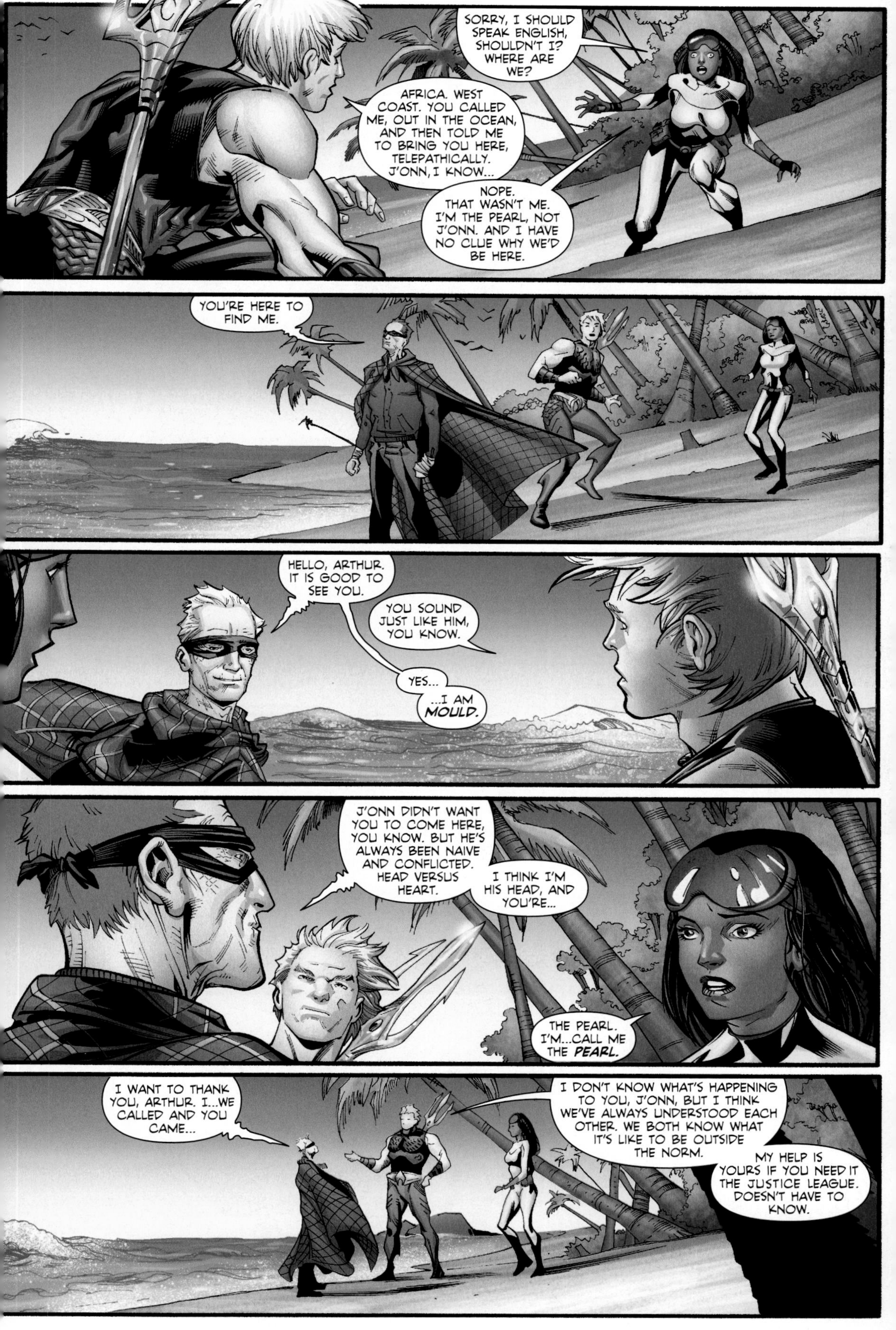
SORRY, I SHOULD SPEAK ENGLISH, SHOULDN'T I? WHERE ARE WE?
AFRICA. WEST COAST. YOU CALLED ME, OUT IN THE OCEAN, AND THEN TOLD ME TO BRING YOU HERE, TELEPATHICALLY. J'ONN, I KNOW...
NOPE. THAT WASN'T ME. I'M THE PEARL, NOT J'ONN. AND I HAVE NO CLUE WHY WE'D BE HERE.
YOU'RE HERE TO FIND ME.
HELLO, ARTHUR. IT IS GOOD TO SEE YOU.
YOU SOUND JUST LIKE HIM, YOU KNOW.
YES...
...I AM MOULD.
J'ONN DIDN'T WANT YOU TO COME HERE, YOU KNOW. BUT HE'S ALWAYS BEEN NAIVE AND CONFLICTED. HEAD VERSUS HEART.
I THINK I'M HIS HEAD, AND YOU'RE...
THE PEARL. I'M...CALL ME THE PEARL.
I WANT TO THANK YOU, ARTHUR. I...WE CALLED AND YOU CAME...
I DON'T KNOW WHAT'S HAPPENING TO YOU, J'ONN, BUT I THINK WE'VE ALWAYS UNDERSTOOD EACH OTHER. WE BOTH KNOW WHAT IT'S LIKE TO BE OUTSIDE THE NORM.
MY HELP IS YOURS IF YOU NEED IT THE JUSTICE LEAGUE. DOESN'T HAVE TO KNOW.

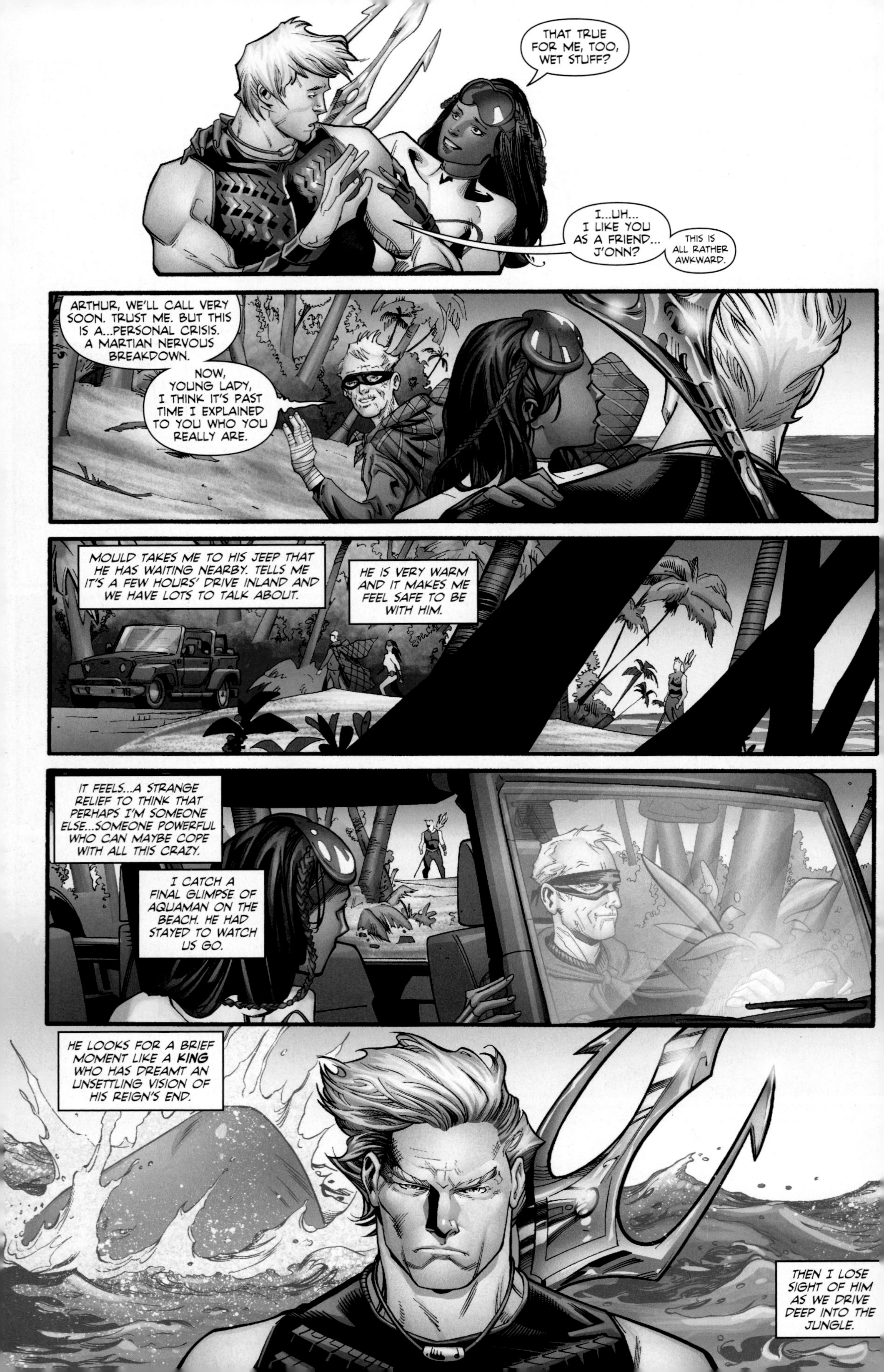
THAT TRUE FOR ME, TOO, WET STUFF?
I...UH... I LIKE YOU AS A FRIEND... J'ONN?
THIS IS ALL RATHER AWKWARD.
ARTHUR, WE'LL CALL VERY SOON. TRUST ME. BUT THIS IS A...PERSONAL CRISIS. A MARTIAN NERVOUS BREAKDOWN.
NOW, YOUNG LADY, I THINK IT'S PAST TIME I EXPLAINED TO YOU WHO YOU REALLY ARE.
MOULD TAKES ME TO HIS JEEP THAT HE HAS WAITING NEARBY. TELLS ME IT'S A FEW HOURS' DRIVE INLAND AND WE HAVE LOTS TO TALK ABOUT.
HE IS VERY WARM AND IT MAKES ME FEEL SAFE TO BE WITH HIM.
IT FEELS...A STRANGE RELIEF TO THINK THAT PERHAPS I'M SOMEONE ELSE...SOMEONE POWERFUL WHO CAN MAYBE COPE WITH ALL THIS CRAZY.
I CATCH A FINAL GLIMPSE OF AQUAMAN ON THE BEACH. HE HAD STAYED TO WATCH US GO.
HE LOOKS FOR A BRIEF MOMENT LIKE A KING WHO HAS DREAMT AN UNSETTLING VISION OF HIS REIGN'S END.
THEN I LOSE SIGHT OF HIM AS WE DRIVE DEEP INTO THE JUNGLE.

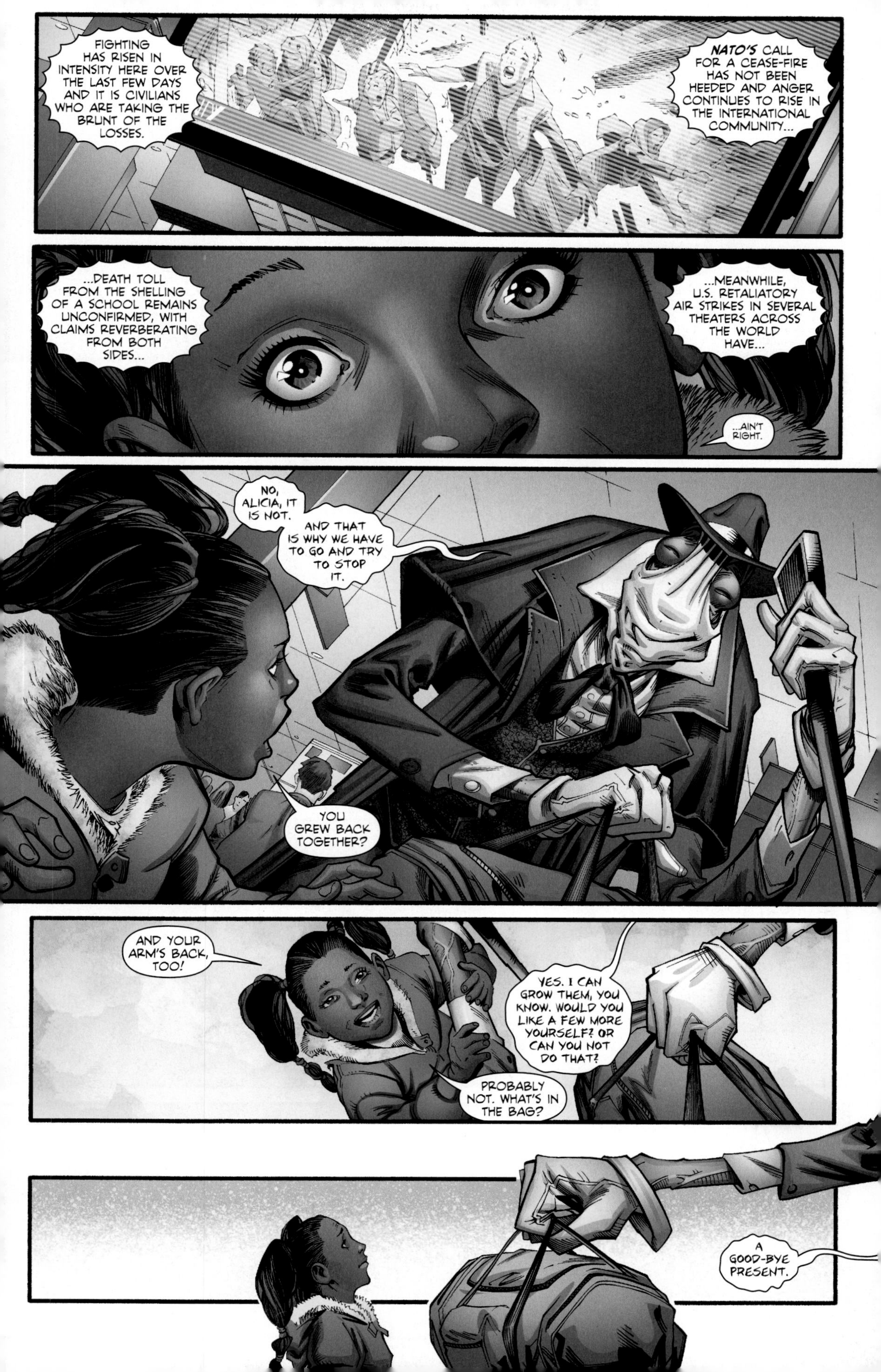
FIGHTING HAS RISEN IN INTENSITY HERE OVER THE LAST FEW DAYS AND IT IS CIVILIANS WHO ARE TAKING THE BRUNT OF THE LOSSES.
NATO'S CALL FOR A CEASE-FIRE HAS NOT BEEN HEEDED AND ANGER CONTINUES TO RISE IN THE INTERNATIONAL COMMUNITY...
...DEATH TOLL FROM THE SHELLING OF A SCHOOL REMAINS UNCONFIRMED, WITH CLAIMS REVERBERATING FROM BOTH SIDES...
...MEANWHILE, U.S. RETALIATORY AIR STRIKES IN SEVERAL THEATERS ACROSS THE WORLD HAVE...
...AIN'T RIGHT.
NO, ALICIA, IT IS NOT.
AND THAT IS WHY WE HAVE TO GO AND TRY TO STOP IT.
YOU GREW BACK TOGETHER?
AND YOUR ARM'S BACK, TOO!
YES. I CAN GROW THEM, YOU KNOW. WOULD YOU LIKE A FEW MORE YOURSELF? OR CAN YOU NOT DO THAT?
PROBABLY NOT. WHAT'S IN THE BAG?
A GOOD-BYE PRESENT.

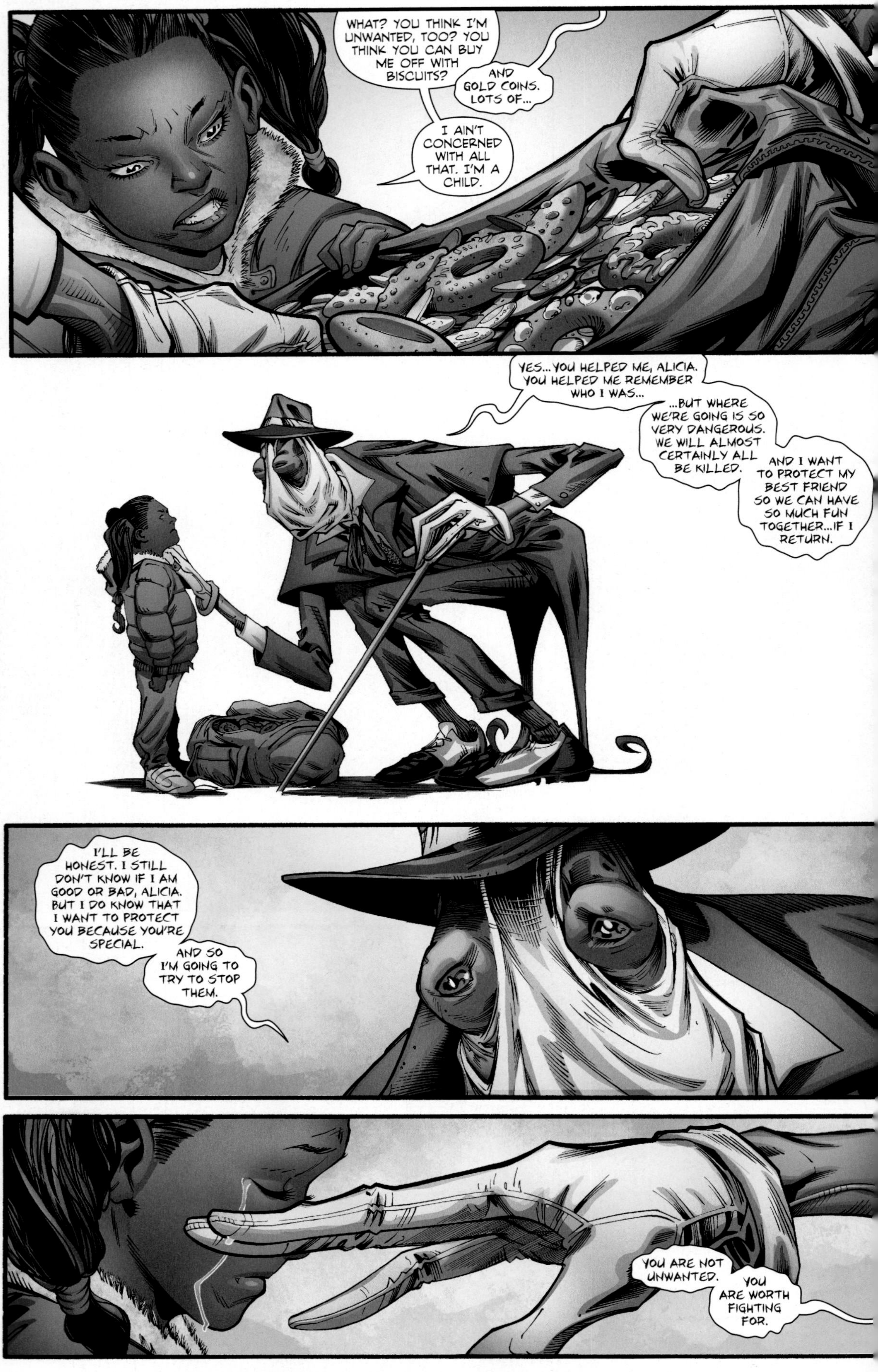
WHAT? YOU THINK I'M UNWANTED, TOO? YOU THINK YOU CAN BUY ME OFF WITH BISCUITS?
AND GOLD COINS. LOTS OF...
I AIN'T CONCERNED WITH ALL THAT. I'M A CHILD.
YES...YOU HELPED ME, ALICIA. YOU HELPED ME REMEMBER WHO I WAS...
...BUT WHERE WE'RE GOING IS SO VERY DANGEROUS. WE WILL ALMOST CERTAINLY ALL BE KILLED.
AND I WANT TO PROTECT MY BEST FRIEND SO WE CAN HAVE SO MUCH FUN TOGETHER...IF I RETURN.
I'LL BE HONEST. I STILL DON'T KNOW IF I AM GOOD OR BAD, ALICIA. BUT I DO KNOW THAT I WANT TO PROTECT YOU BECAUSE YOU'RE SPECIAL.
AND SO I'M GOING TO TRY TO STOP THEM.
YOU ARE NOT UNWANTED.
YOU ARE WORTH FIGHTING FOR.

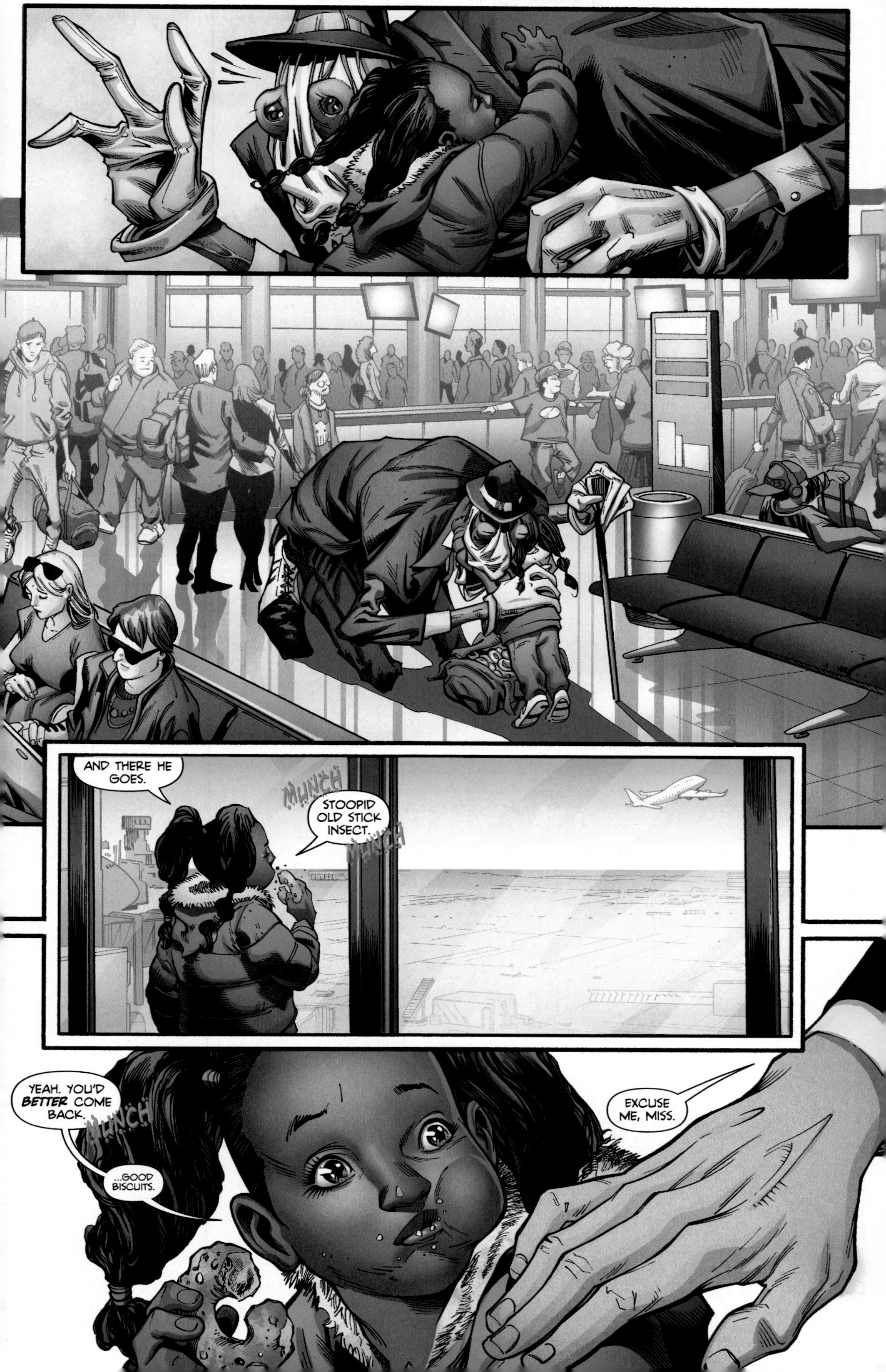
AND THERE HE GOES.
MUNCH
STOOPID OLD STICK INSECT.
MUNCH
YEAH. YOU'D **BETTER** COME BACK.
MUNCH
...GOOD BISCUITS.
EXCUSE ME, MISS.

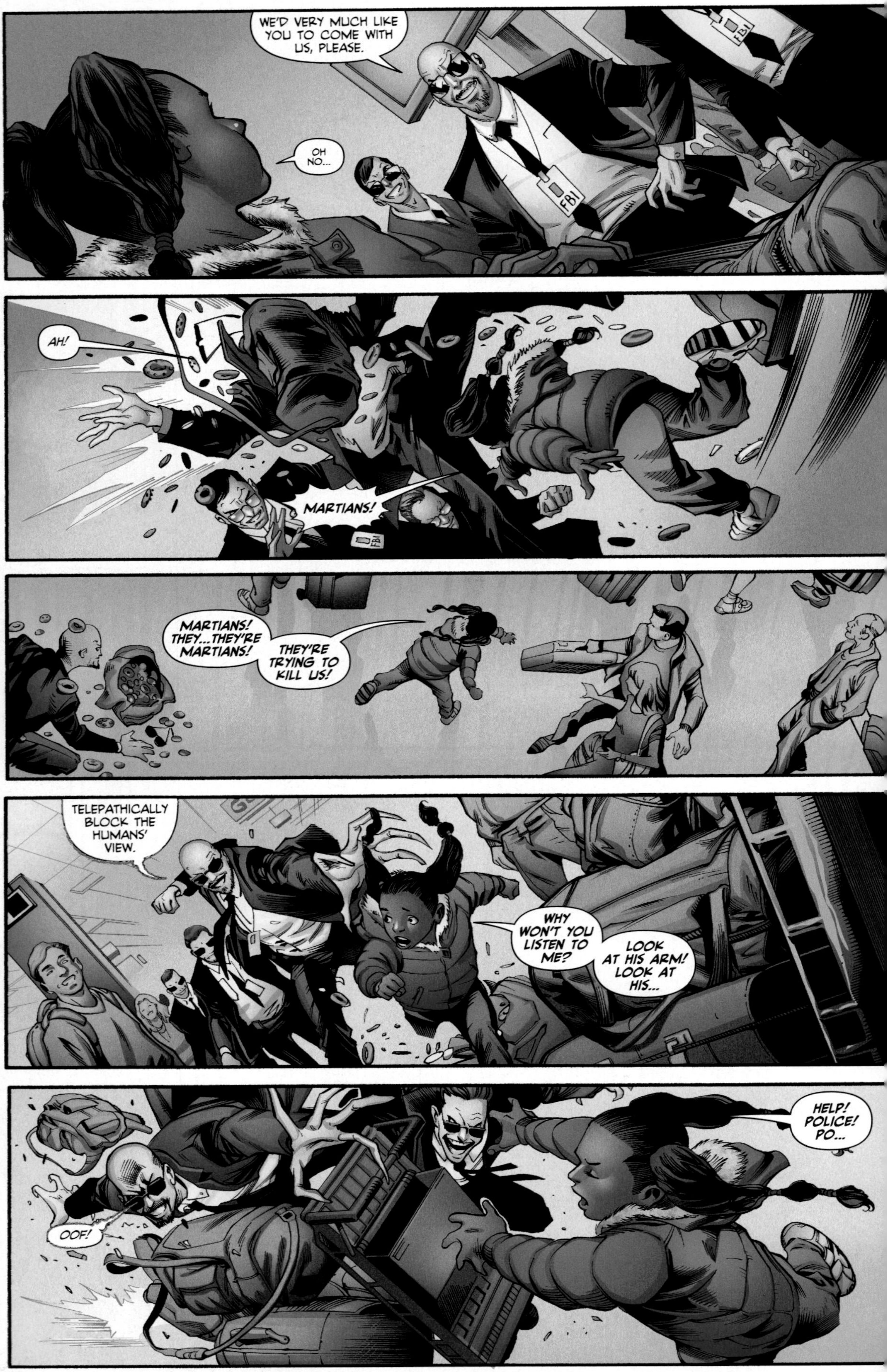
WE'D VERY MUCH LIKE YOU TO COME WITH US, PLEASE.
OH NO...
FBI
AH!
MARTIANS!
MARTIANS! THEY...THEY'RE MARTIANS!
THEY'RE TRYING TO KILL US!
TELEPATHICALLY BLOCK THE HUMANS' VIEW.
WHY WON'T YOU LISTEN TO ME?
LOOK AT HIS ARM! LOOK AT HIS...
HELP! POLICE! PO...
OOF!

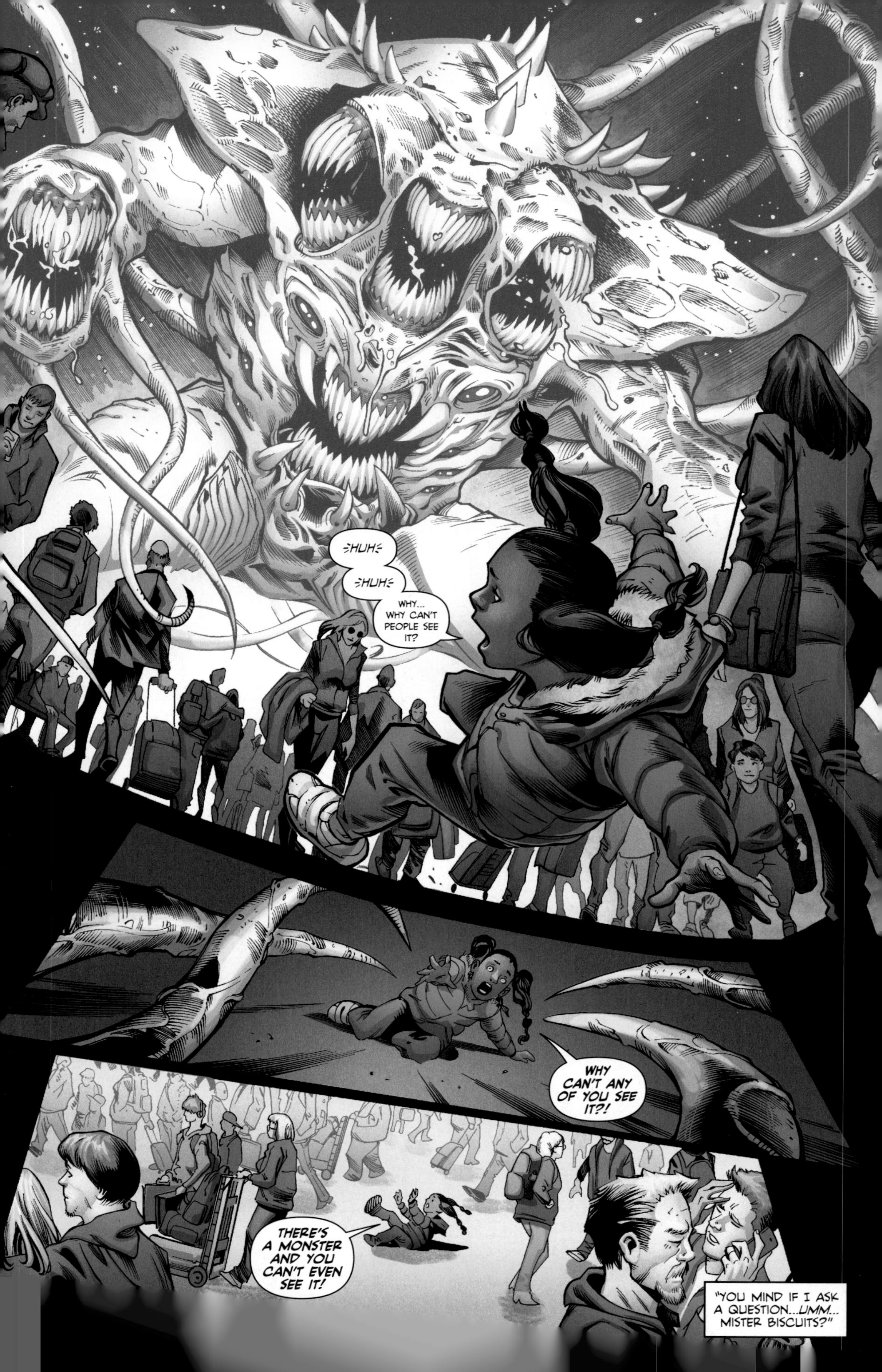
HUH
HUH
WHY... WHY CAN'T PEOPLE SEE IT?
WHY CAN'T ANY OF YOU SEE IT?!
THERE'S A MONSTER AND YOU CAN'T EVEN SEE IT!
"YOU MIND IF I ASK A QUESTION...UMM... MISTER BISCUITS?"

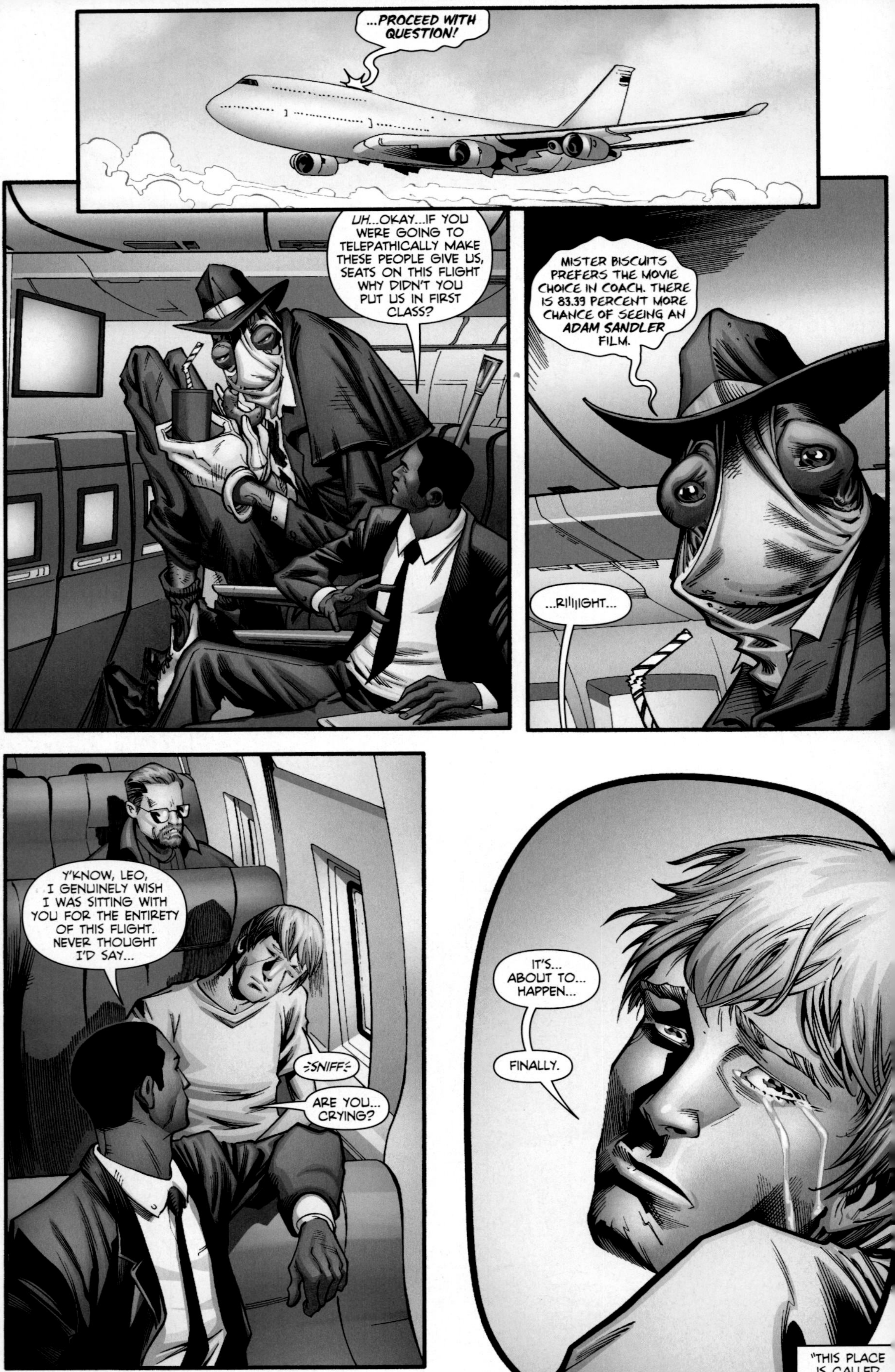
...PROCEED WITH QUESTION!
UH...OKAY...IF YOU WERE GOING TO TELEPATHICALLY MAKE THESE PEOPLE GIVE US, SEATS ON THIS FLIGHT WHY DIDN'T YOU PUT US IN FIRST CLASS?
MISTER BISCUITS PREFERS THE MOVIE CHOICE IN COACH. THERE IS 83.39 PERCENT MORE CHANCE OF SEEING AN ADAM SANDLER FILM.
...RIIIIGHT...
Y'KNOW, LEO, I GENUINELY WISH I WAS SITTING WITH YOU FOR THE ENTIRETY OF THIS FLIGHT. NEVER THOUGHT I'D SAY...
SNIFF
ARE YOU... CRYING?
IT'S... ABOUT TO... HAPPEN...
FINALLY.
"THIS PLACE IS CALLED BOSUMTWI."

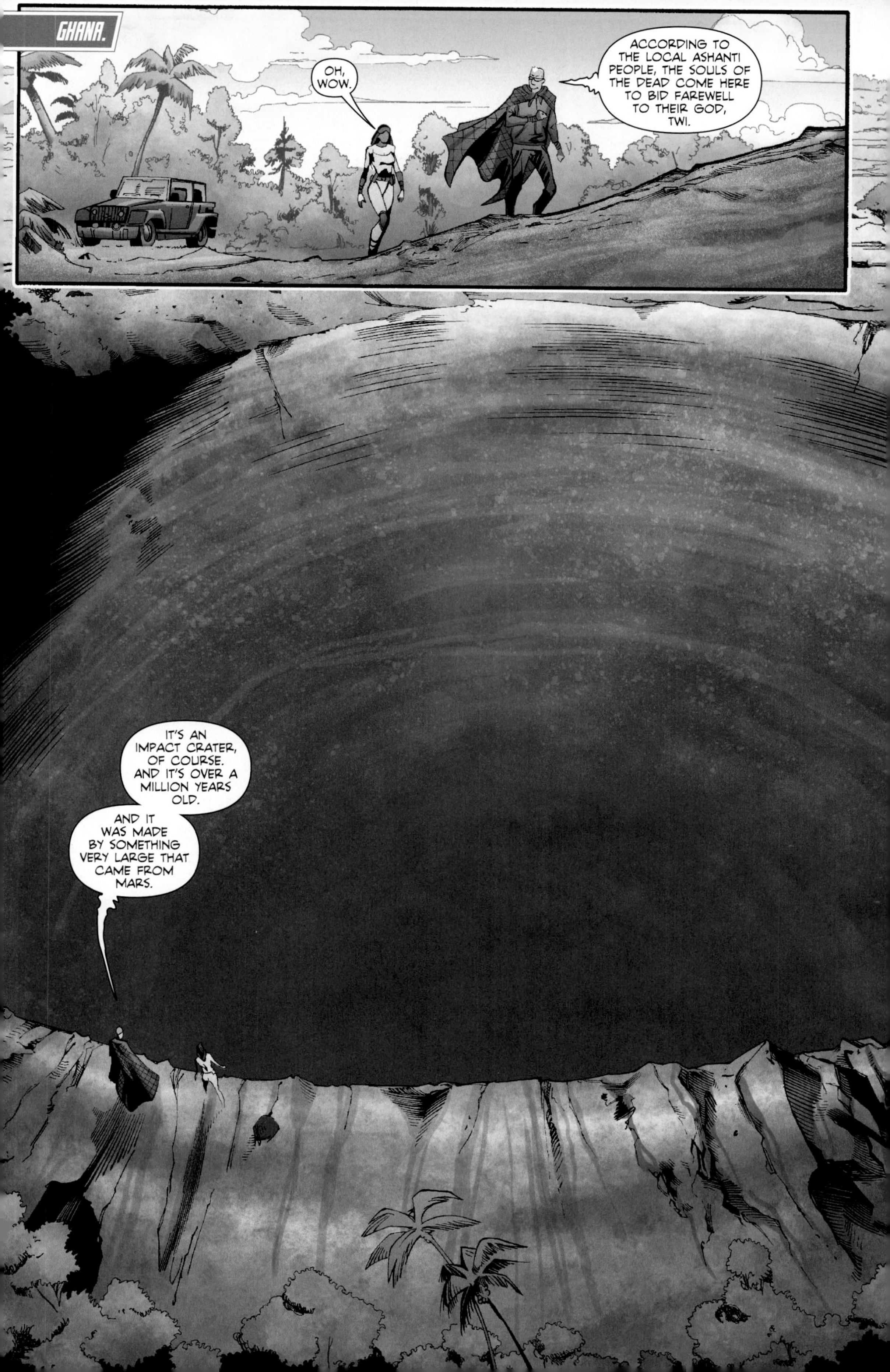

GHANA.
OH, WOW.
ACCORDING TO THE LOCAL ASHANTI PEOPLE, THE SOULS OF THE DEAD COME HERE TO BID FAREWELL TO THEIR GOD, TWI.
IT'S AN IMPACT CRATER, OF COURSE. AND IT'S OVER A MILLION YEARS OLD.
AND IT WAS MADE BY SOMETHING VERY LARGE THAT CAME FROM MARS.

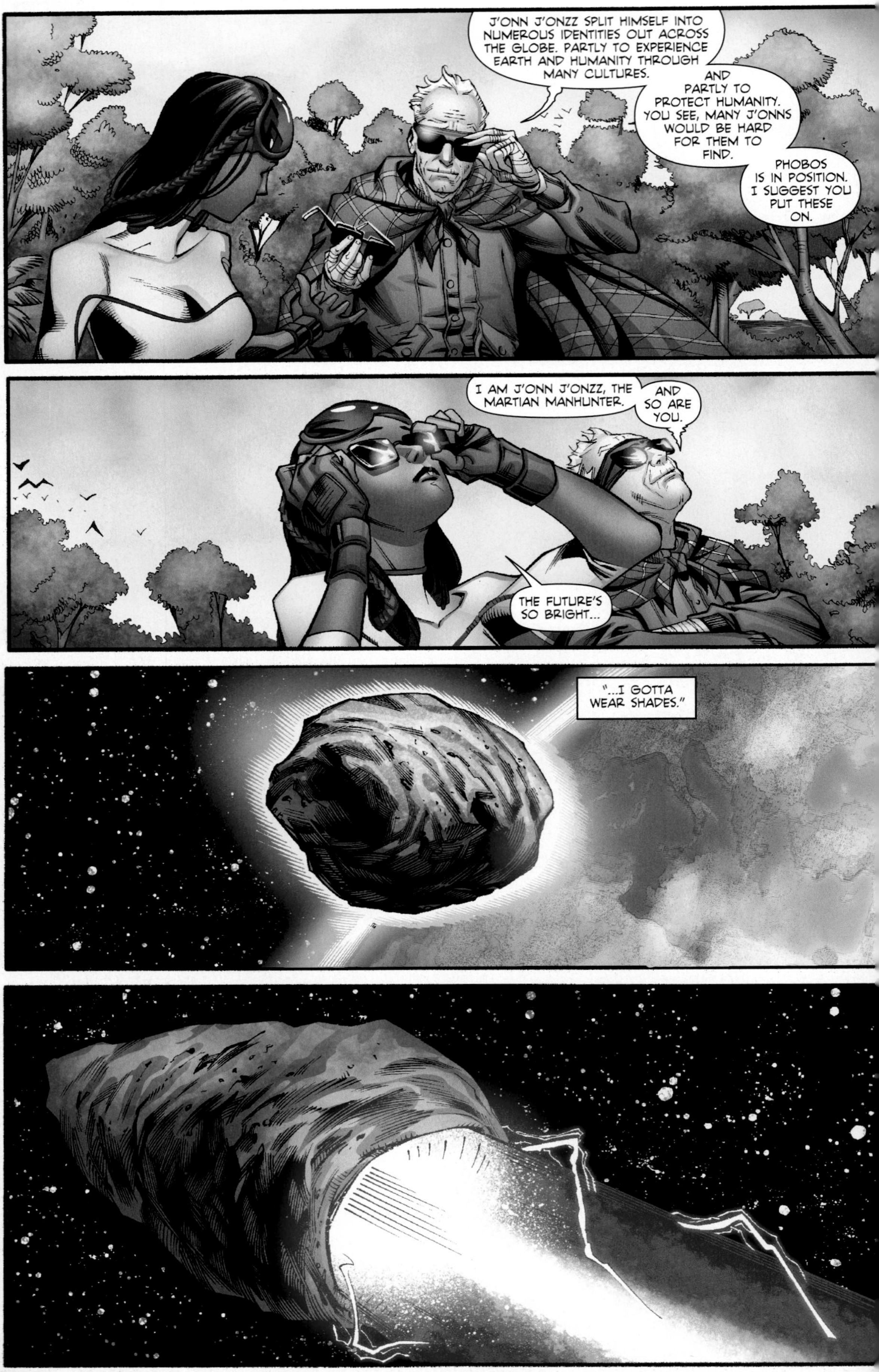
J'ONN J'ONZZ SPLIT HIMSELF INTO NUMEROUS IDENTITIES OUT ACROSS THE GLOBE. PARTLY TO EXPERIENCE EARTH AND HUMANITY THROUGH MANY CULTURES.
AND PARTLY TO PROTECT HUMANITY. YOU SEE, MANY J'ONNS WOULD BE HARD FOR THEM TO FIND.
PHOBOS IS IN POSITION. I SUGGEST YOU PUT THESE ON.
I AM J'ONN J'ONZZ, THE MARTIAN MANHUNTER.
AND SO ARE YOU.
THE FUTURE'S SO BRIGHT...
"...I GOTTA WEAR SHADES."

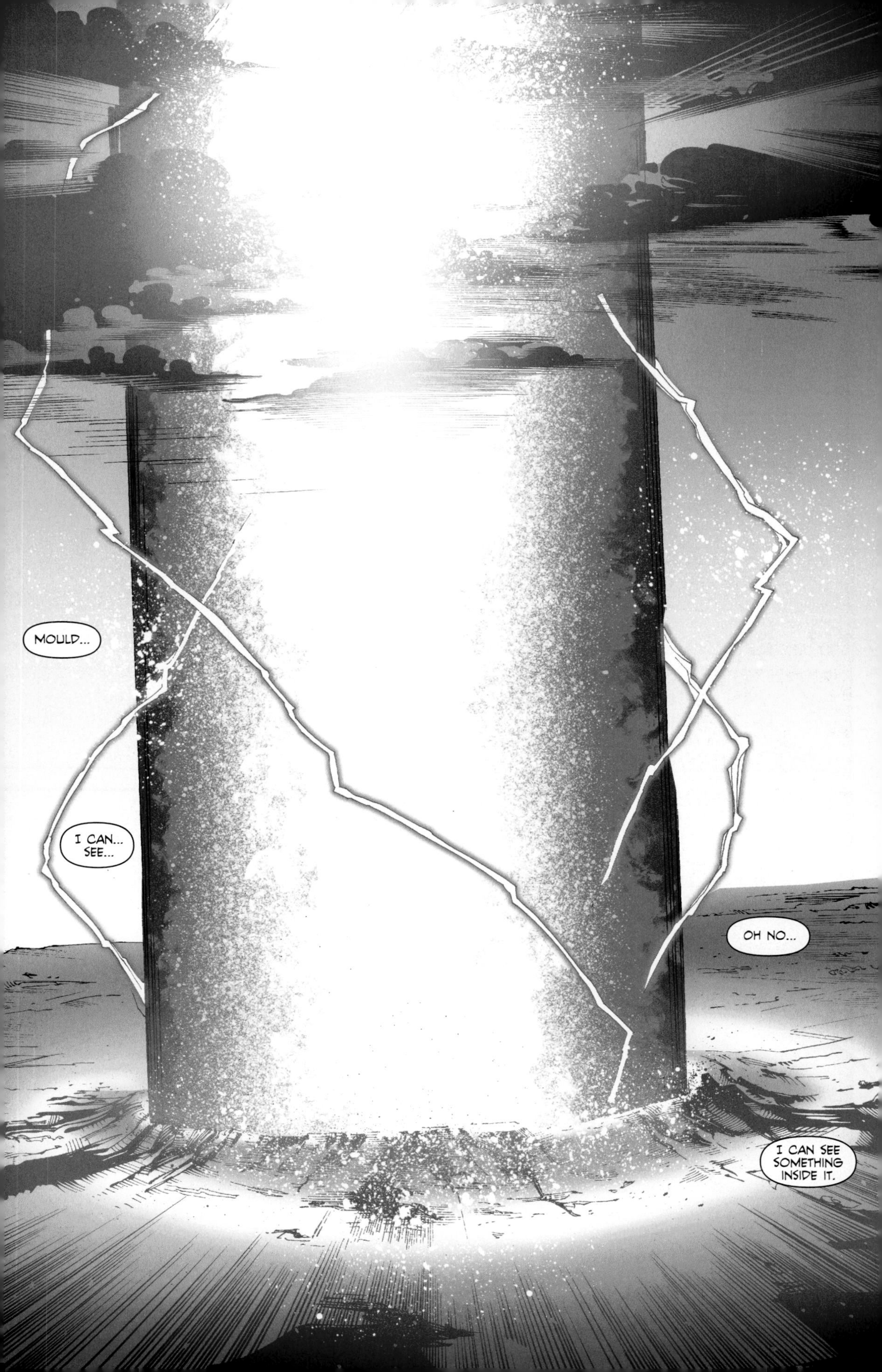
MOULD...
I CAN... SEE...
OH NO...
I CAN SEE SOMETHING INSIDE IT.

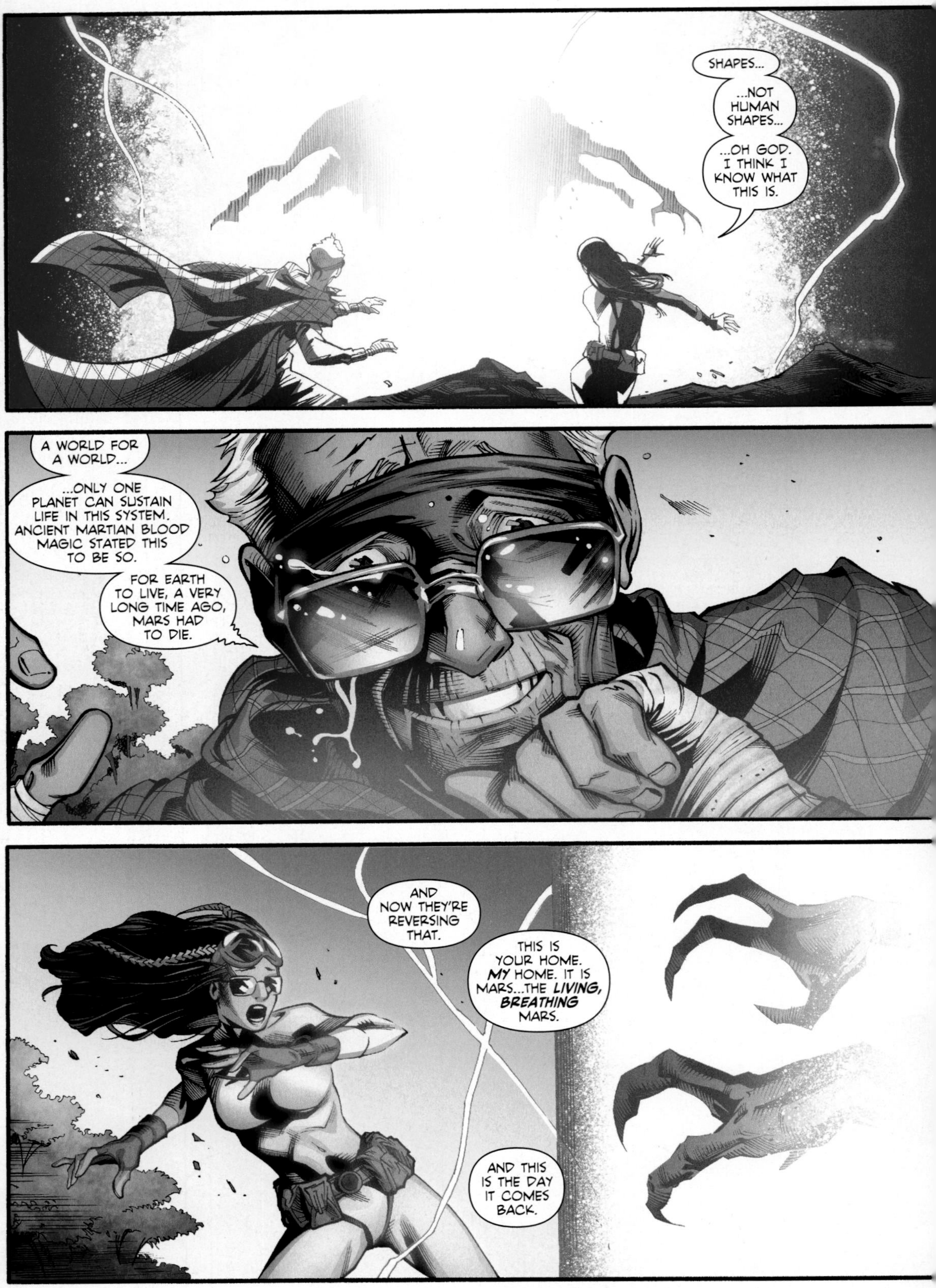
SHAPES...
...NOT HUMAN SHAPES...
...OH GOD. I THINK I KNOW WHAT THIS IS.
A WORLD FOR A WORLD...
...ONLY ONE PLANET CAN SUSTAIN LIFE IN THIS SYSTEM. ANCIENT MARTIAN BLOOD MAGIC STATED THIS TO BE SO.
FOR EARTH TO LIVE, A VERY LONG TIME AGO, MARS HAD TO DIE.
AND NOW THEY'RE REVERSING THAT.
THIS IS YOUR HOME. *MY* HOME. IT IS MARS...THE *LIVING, BREATHING* MARS.
AND THIS IS THE DAY IT COMES BACK.

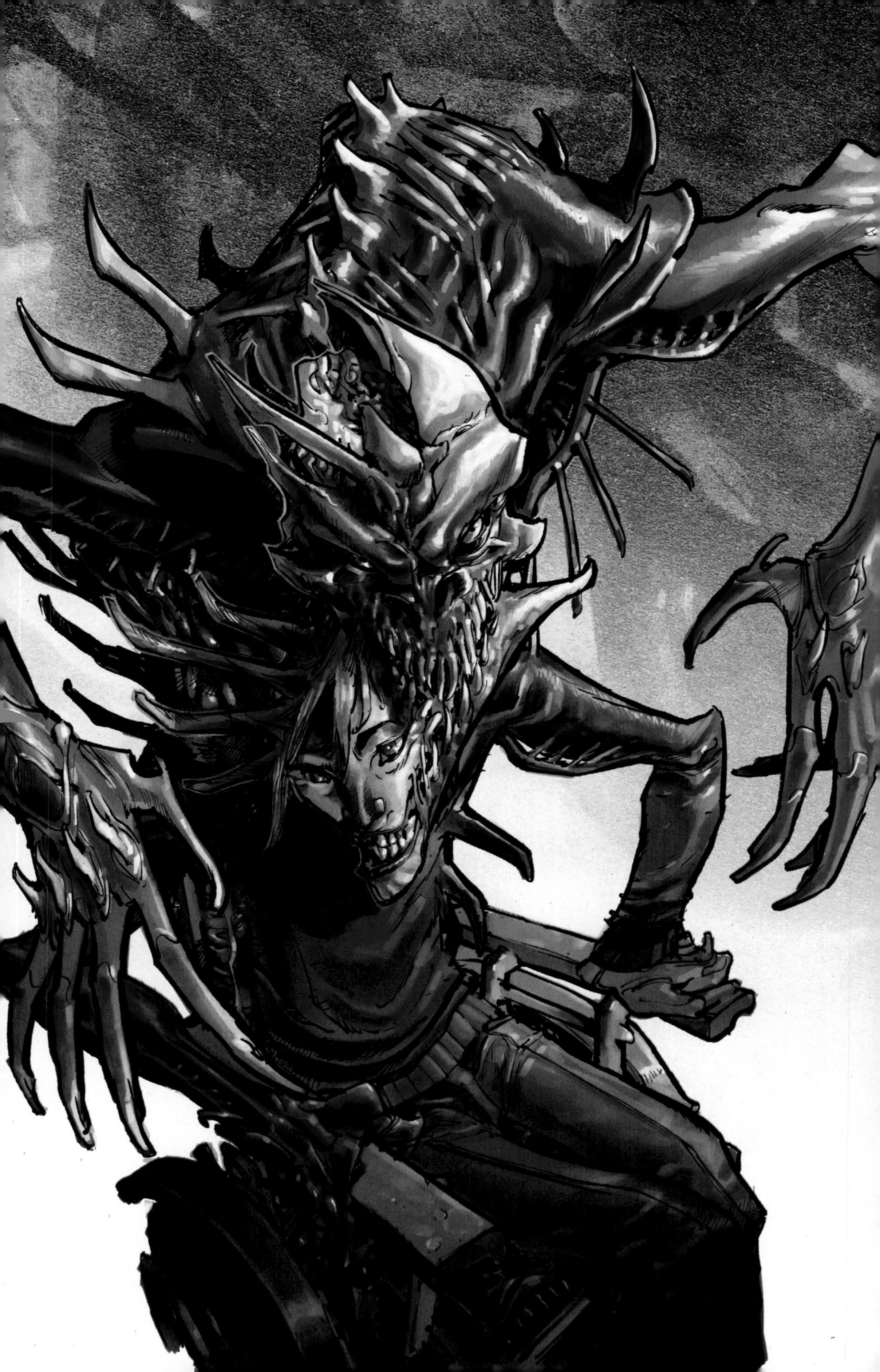

WE ARE ALL DIFFERENT PEOPLE
cover by **ERIC CANETE**

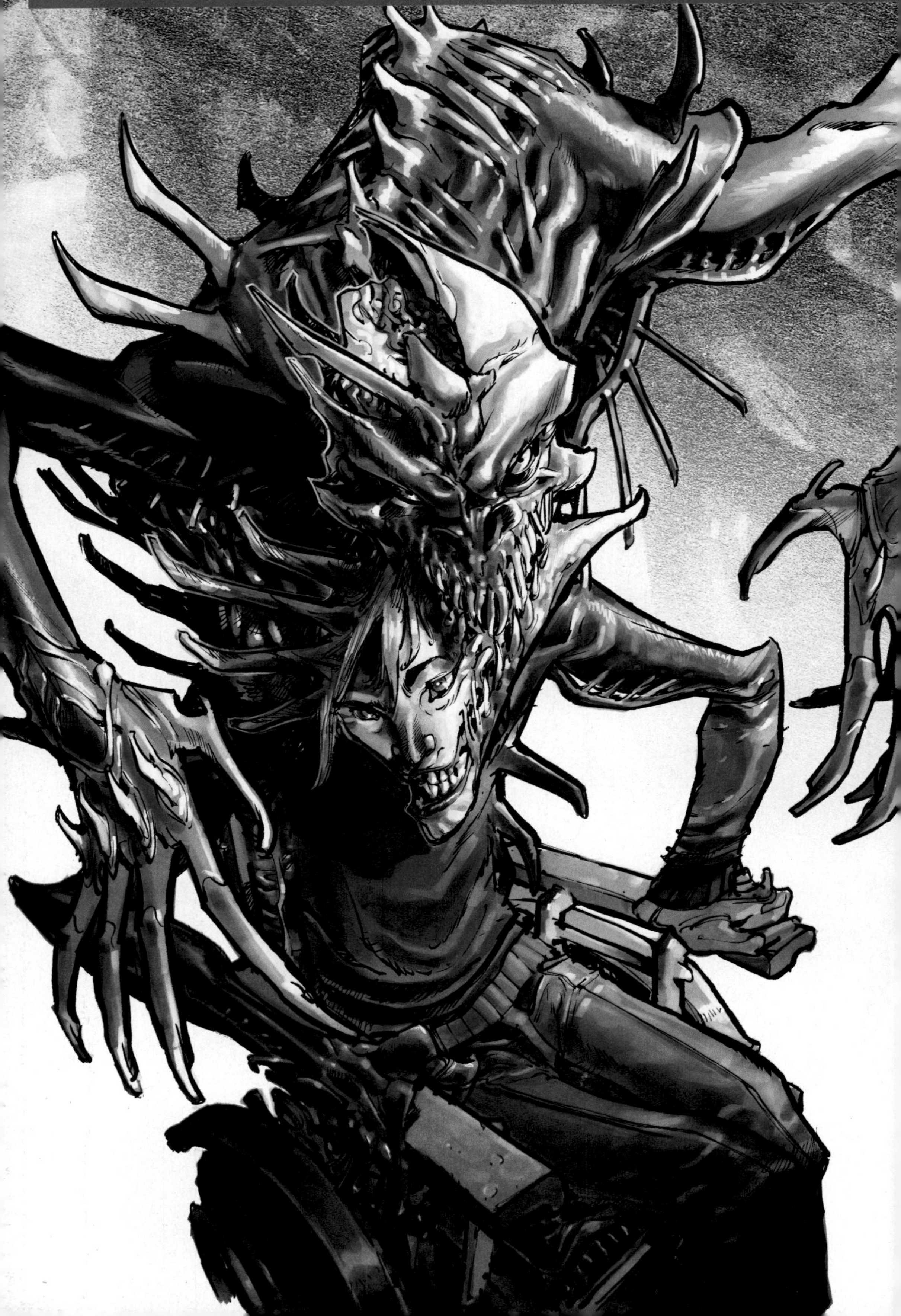

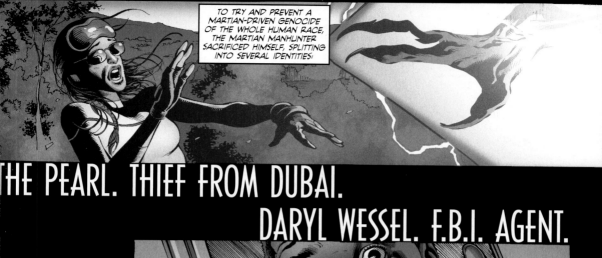

TO TRY AND PREVENT A MARTIAN-DRIVEN GENOCIDE OF THE WHOLE HUMAN RACE, THE MARTIAN MANHUNTER SACRIFICED HIMSELF, SPLITTING INTO SEVERAL IDENTITIES:

THE PEARL. THIEF FROM DUBAI.

DARYL WESSEL. F.B.I. AGENT.

IN ORDER TO PROTECT THESE INDIVIDUALS, J'ONN GAVE THEM **FALSE** MEMORIES. THEY BELIEVED THEMSELVES TO BE TRULY HUMAN. WITH REAL JOBS, TANGIBLE DESIRES, DEEPLY FELT LOVES.

MOULD. J'ONN J'ONZZ'S INTELLECT GIVEN HUMAN FORM.

AND IN DOING SO, HE MADE THEM THREE-DIMENSIONAL. INDIVIDUALS CAPABLE OF MAKING THEIR **OWN** CHOICES.

MISTER BISCUITS. 65% THROUGH **PAUL BLART: MALL COP 2.**

J'ONN J'ONZZ, IT TURNS OUT, DIDN'T GET EVERYTHING QUITE RIGHT...

HA! ROTUND HUMAN FELL OVER.

AMUSING.

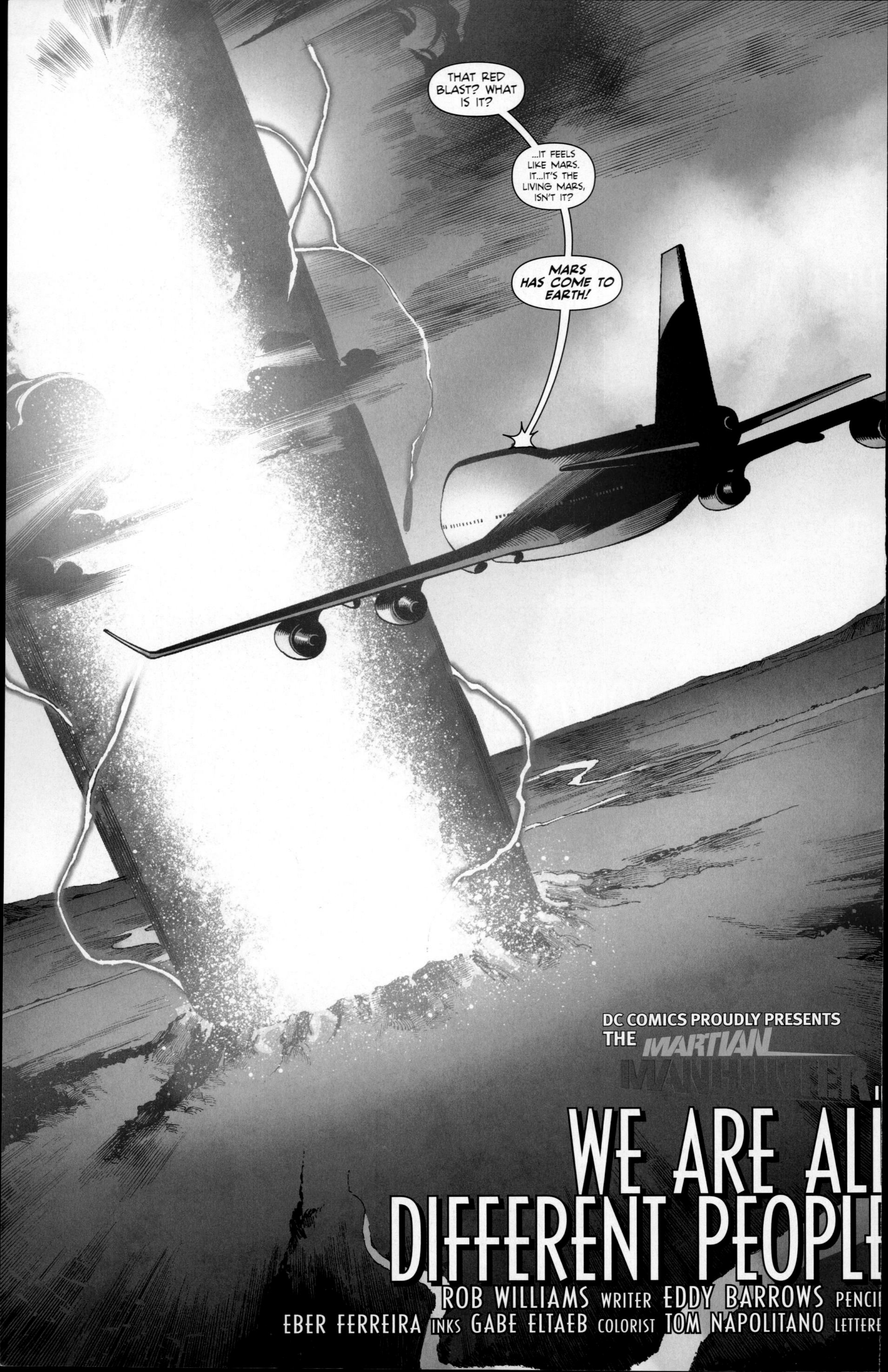

THAT RED BLAST? WHAT IS IT?
...IT FEELS LIKE MARS. IT...IT'S THE LIVING MARS, ISN'T IT?
MARS HAS COME TO EARTH!
DC COMICS PROUDLY PRESENTS
THE MARTIAN MANHUNTER
WE ARE AL
DIFFERENT PEOPLE
ROB WILLIAMS WRITER EDDY BARROWS PENCI
EBER FERREIRA INKS GABE ELTAEB COLORIST TOM NAPOLITANO LETTERE

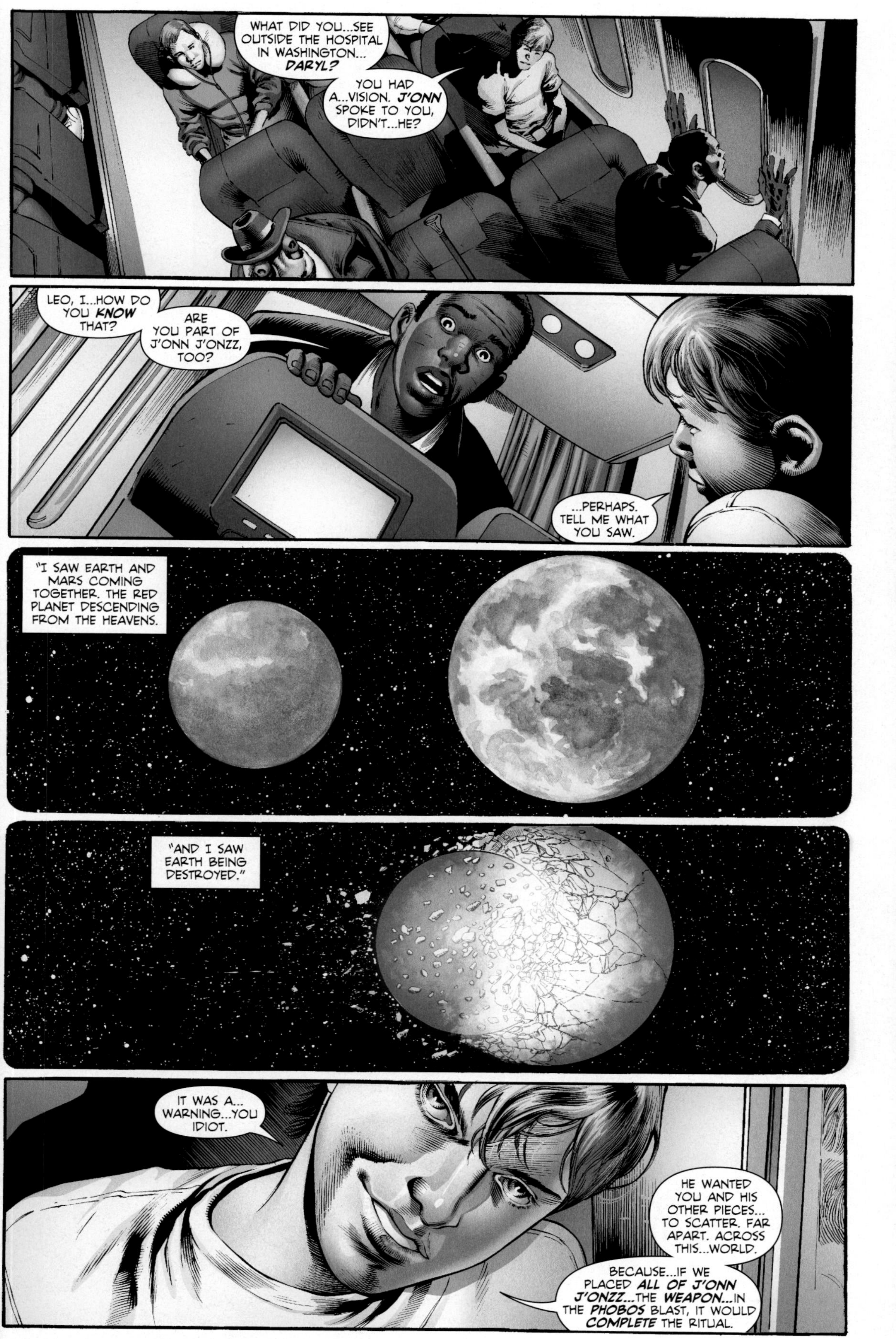
WHAT DID YOU...SEE OUTSIDE THE HOSPITAL IN WASHINGTON... DARYL?
YOU HAD A...VISION. J'ONN SPOKE TO YOU, DIDN'T...HE?
LEO, I...HOW DO YOU KNOW THAT?
ARE YOU PART OF J'ONN J'ONZZ, TOO?
...PERHAPS. TELL ME WHAT YOU SAW.
"I SAW EARTH AND MARS COMING TOGETHER. THE RED PLANET DESCENDING FROM THE HEAVENS.
"AND I SAW EARTH BEING DESTROYED."
IT WAS A... WARNING...YOU IDIOT.
HE WANTED YOU AND HIS OTHER PIECES... TO SCATTER. FAR APART. ACROSS THIS...WORLD.
BECAUSE...IF WE PLACED ALL OF J'ONN J'ONZZ...THE WEAPON...IN THE PHOBOS BLAST, IT WOULD COMPLETE THE RITUAL.

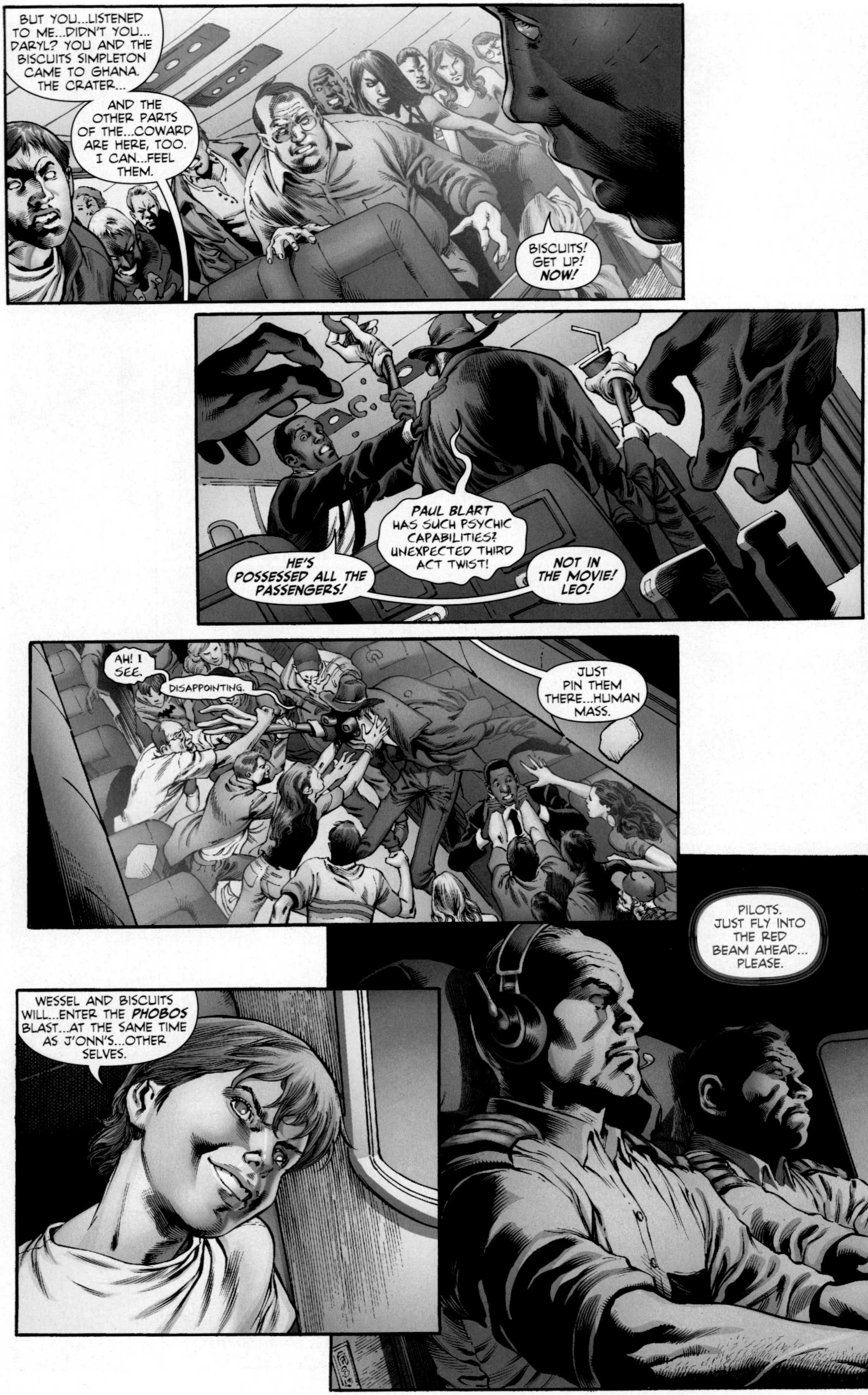
BUT YOU...LISTENED TO ME...DIDN'T YOU... DARYL? YOU AND THE BISCUITS SIMPLETON CAME TO GHANA. THE CRATER...
AND THE OTHER PARTS OF THE...COWARD ARE HERE, TOO. I CAN...FEEL THEM.
BISCUITS! GET UP! NOW!
PAUL BLART HAS SUCH PSYCHIC CAPABILITIES? UNEXPECTED THIRD ACT TWIST!
HE'S POSSESSED ALL THE PASSENGERS!
NOT IN THE MOVIE! LEO!
AH! I SEE.
DISAPPOINTING.
JUST PIN THEM THERE...HUMAN MASS.
PILOTS. JUST FLY INTO THE RED BEAM AHEAD... PLEASE.
WESSEL AND BISCUITS WILL...ENTER THE PHOBOS BLAST...AT THE SAME TIME AS J'ONN'S...OTHER SELVES.

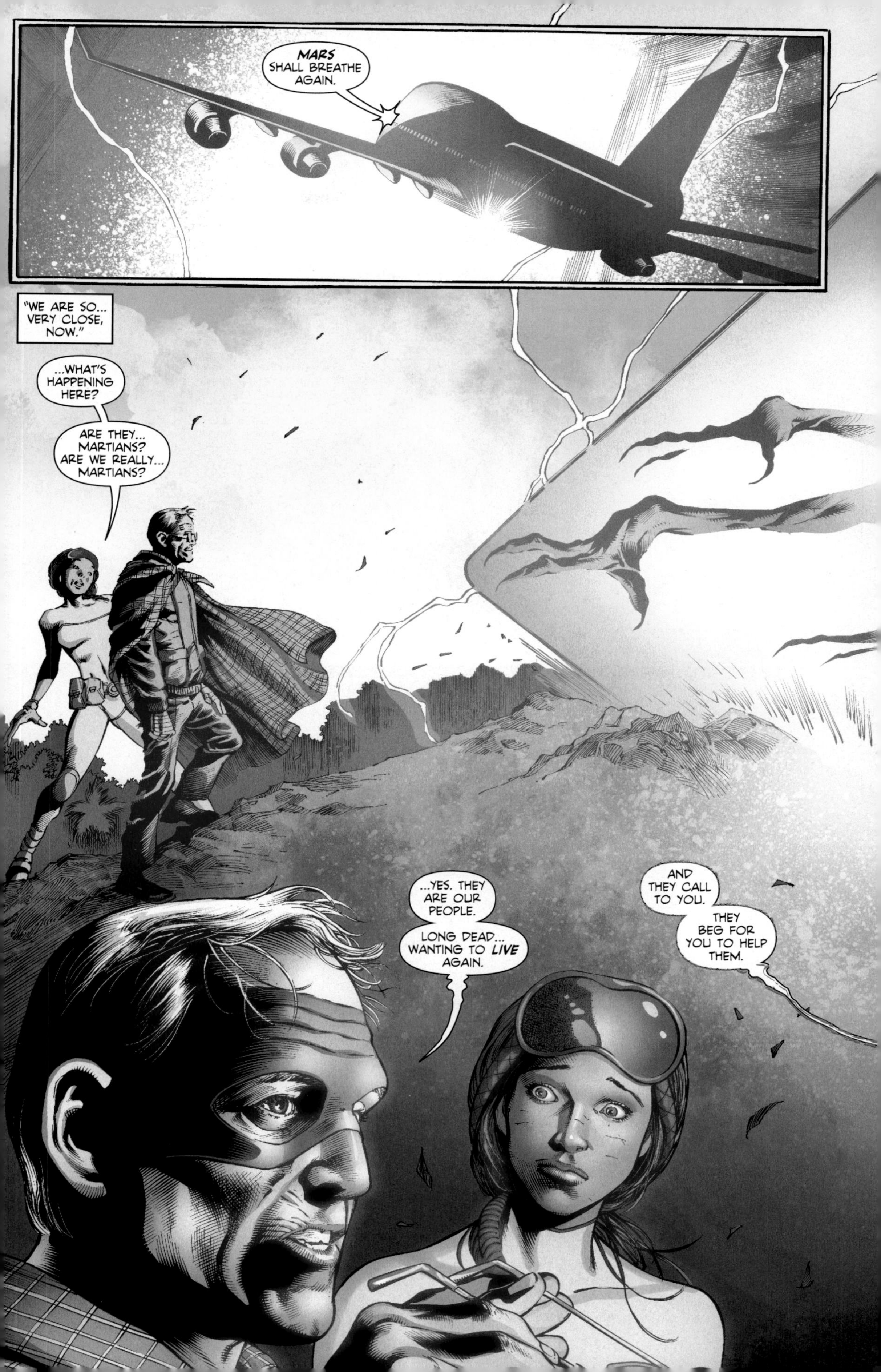
MARS SHALL BREATHE AGAIN.
"WE ARE SO... VERY CLOSE, NOW."
...WHAT'S HAPPENING HERE?
ARE THEY... MARTIANS? ARE WE REALLY... MARTIANS?
...YES. THEY ARE OUR PEOPLE.
LONG DEAD... WANTING TO LIVE AGAIN.
AND THEY CALL TO YOU.
THEY BEG FOR YOU TO HELP THEM.

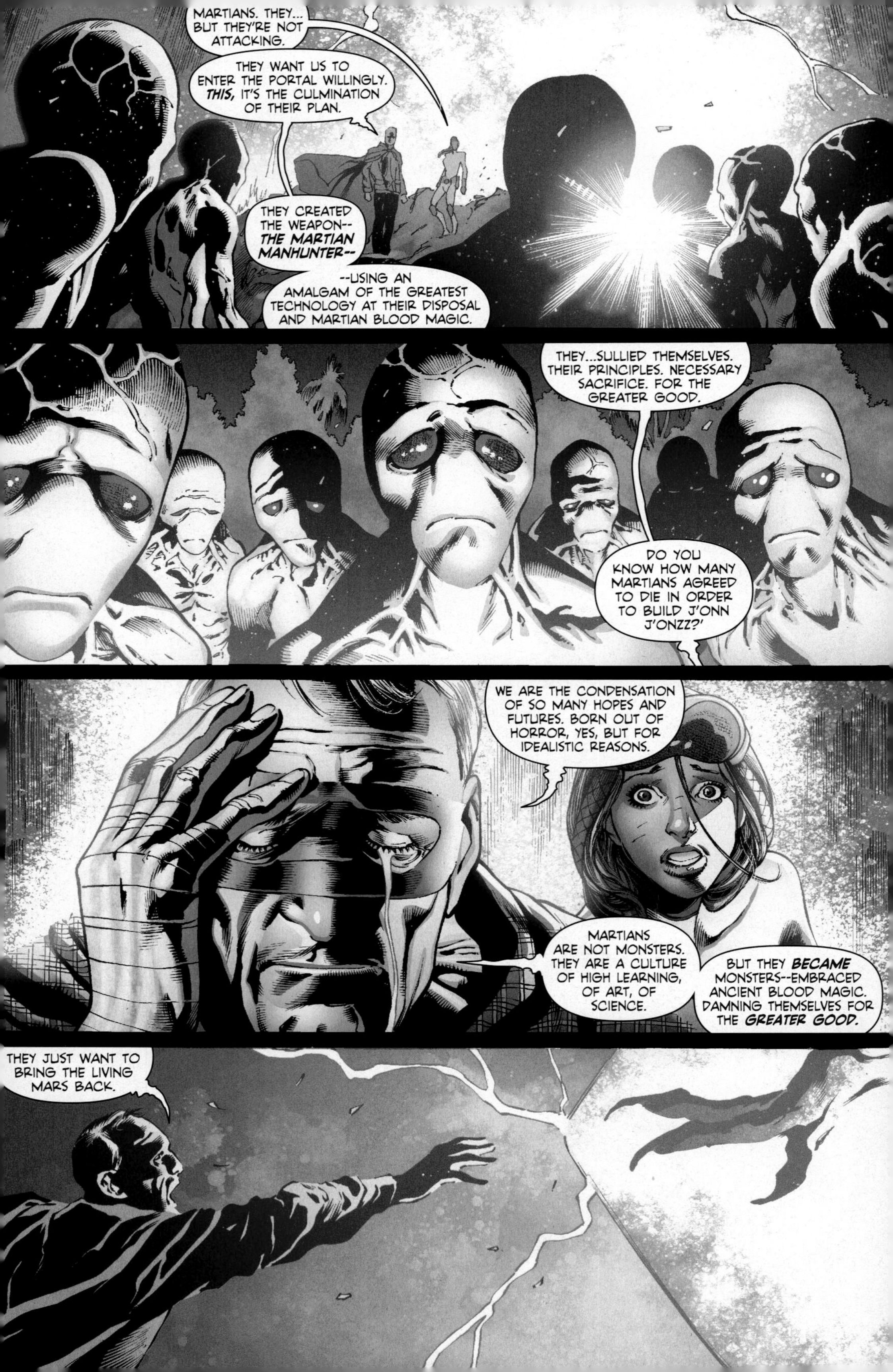
MARTIANS. THEY... BUT THEY'RE NOT ATTACKING.
THEY WANT US TO ENTER THE PORTAL WILLINGLY. *THIS,* IT'S THE CULMINATION OF THEIR PLAN.
THEY CREATED THE WEAPON-- *THE MARTIAN MANHUNTER--*
--USING AN AMALGAM OF THE GREATEST TECHNOLOGY AT THEIR DISPOSAL AND MARTIAN BLOOD MAGIC.
THEY...SULLIED THEMSELVES. THEIR PRINCIPLES. NECESSARY SACRIFICE. FOR THE GREATER GOOD.
DO YOU KNOW HOW MANY MARTIANS AGREED TO DIE IN ORDER TO BUILD J'ONN J'ONZZ?'
WE ARE THE CONDENSATION OF SO MANY HOPES AND FUTURES. BORN OUT OF HORROR, YES, BUT FOR IDEALISTIC REASONS.
MARTIANS ARE NOT MONSTERS. THEY ARE A CULTURE OF HIGH LEARNING, OF ART, OF SCIENCE.
BUT THEY *BECAME* MONSTERS--EMBRACED ANCIENT BLOOD MAGIC. DAMNING THEMSELVES FOR THE *GREATER GOOD.*
THEY JUST WANT TO BRING THE LIVING MARS BACK.

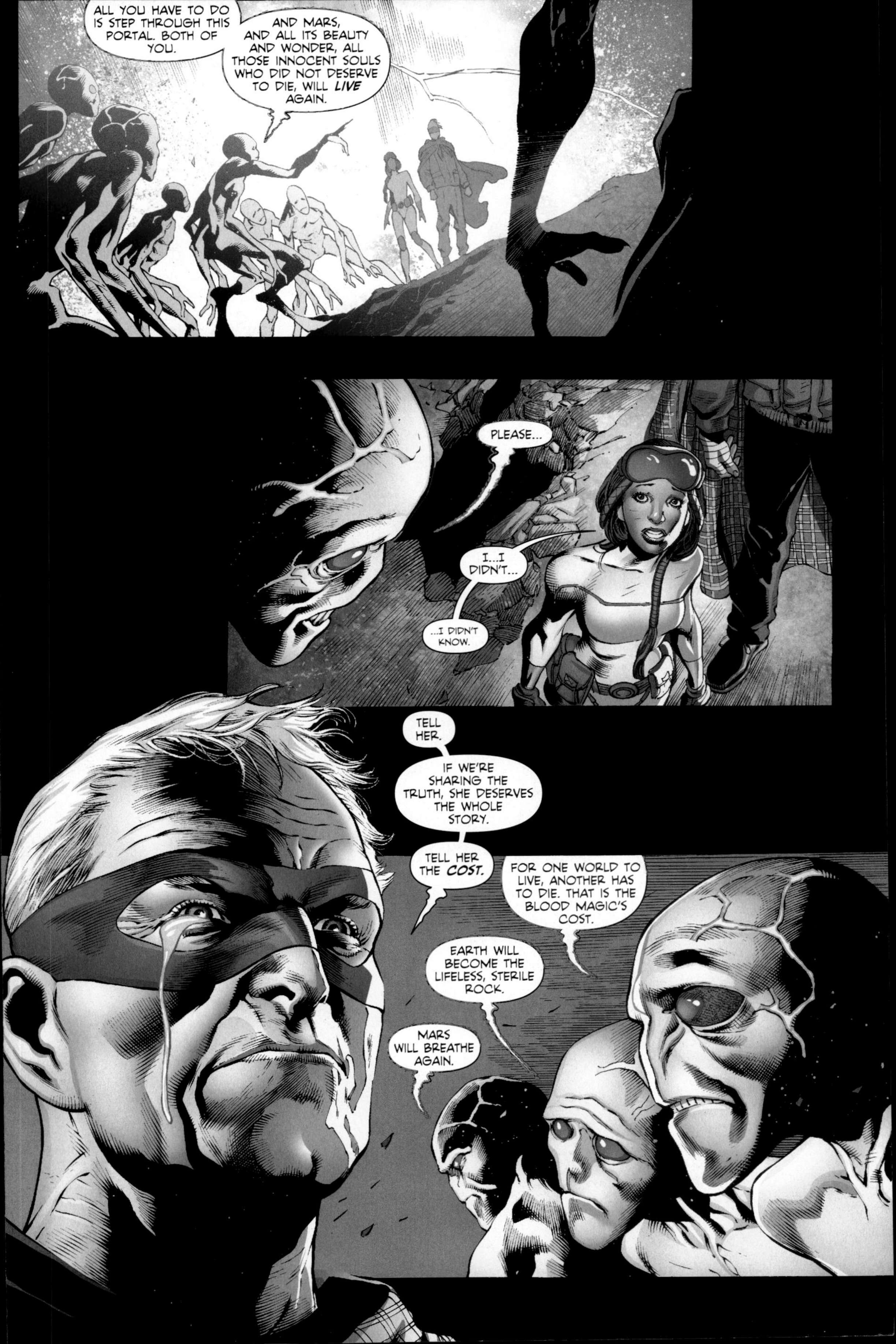
ALL YOU HAVE TO DO IS STEP THROUGH THIS PORTAL. BOTH OF YOU.
AND MARS, AND ALL ITS BEAUTY AND WONDER, ALL THOSE INNOCENT SOULS WHO DID NOT DESERVE TO DIE, WILL LIVE AGAIN.
PLEASE...
I...I DIDN'T...
...I DIDN'T KNOW.
TELL HER.
IF WE'RE SHARING THE TRUTH, SHE DESERVES THE WHOLE STORY.
TELL HER THE COST.
FOR ONE WORLD TO LIVE, ANOTHER HAS TO DIE. THAT IS THE BLOOD MAGIC'S COST.
EARTH WILL BECOME THE LIFELESS, STERILE ROCK.
MARS WILL BREATHE AGAIN.

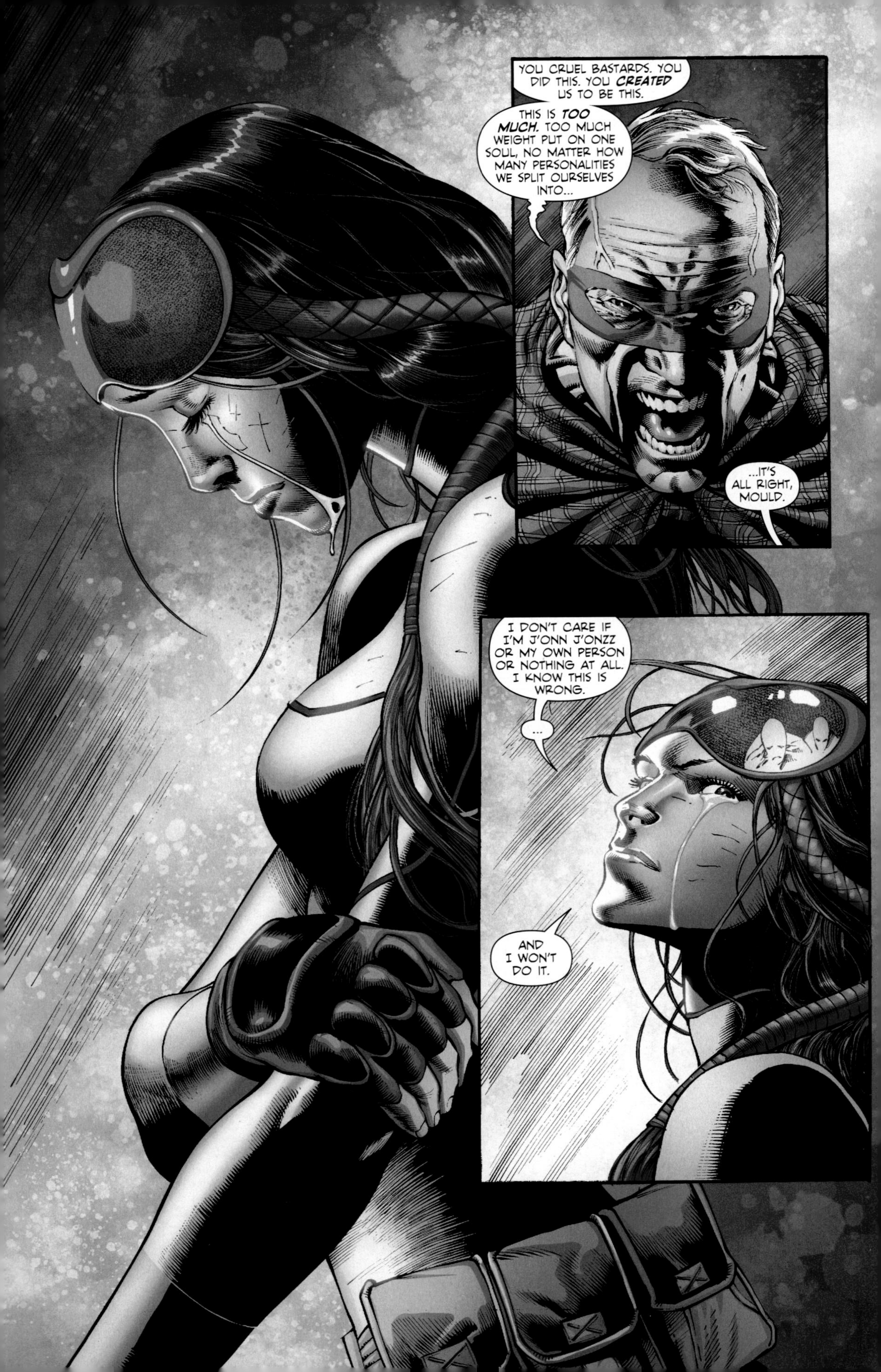
YOU CRUEL BASTARDS. YOU DID THIS. YOU CREATED US TO BE THIS.
THIS IS TOO MUCH. TOO MUCH WEIGHT PUT ON ONE SOUL, NO MATTER HOW MANY PERSONALITIES WE SPLIT OURSELVES INTO...
...IT'S ALL RIGHT, MOULD.
I DON'T CARE IF I'M J'ONN J'ONZZ OR MY OWN PERSON OR NOTHING AT ALL. I KNOW THIS IS WRONG.
...
AND I WON'T DO IT.

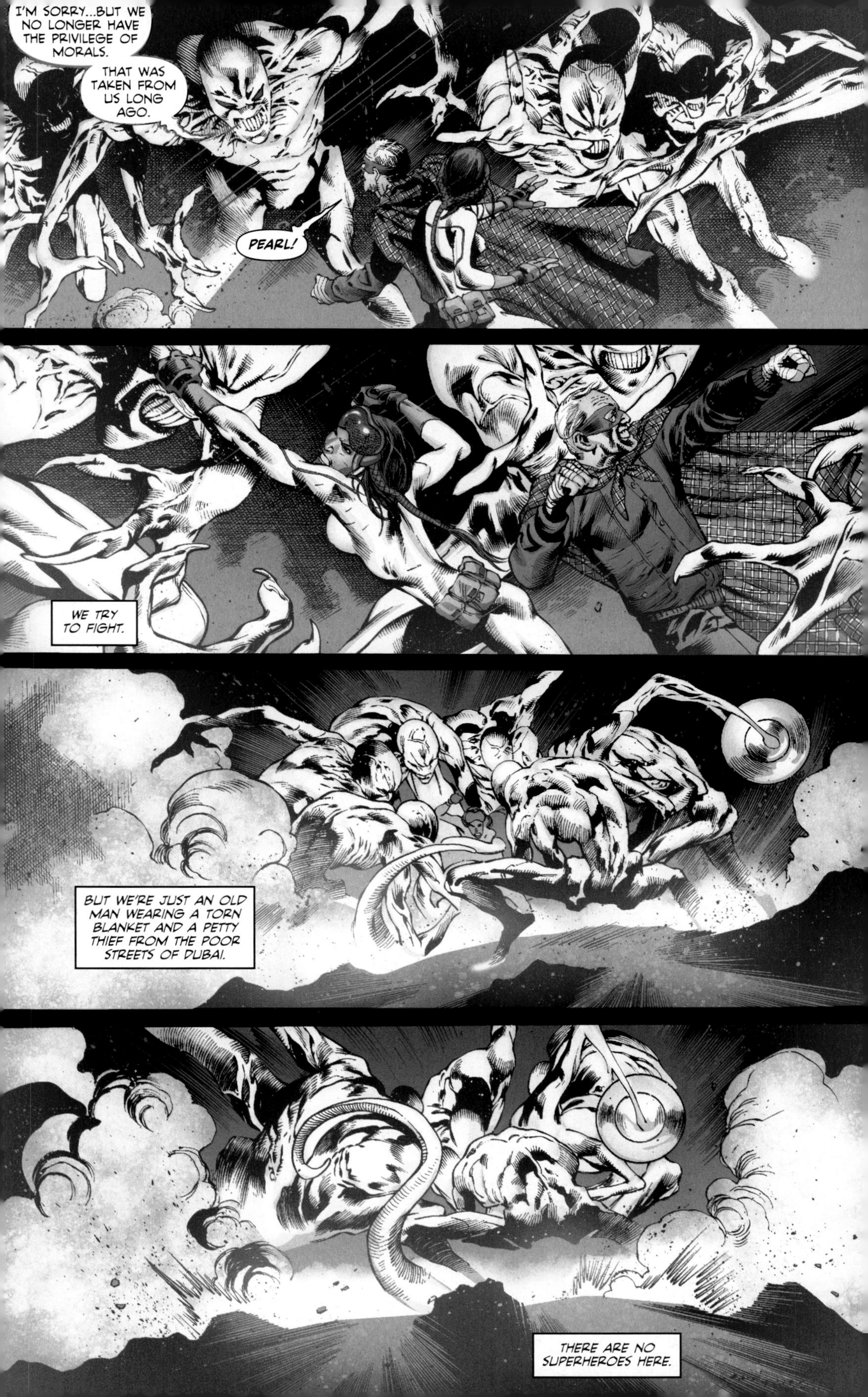
I'M SORRY...BUT WE NO LONGER HAVE THE PRIVILEGE OF MORALS.
THAT WAS TAKEN FROM US LONG AGO.
PEARL!
WE TRY TO FIGHT.
BUT WE'RE JUST AN OLD MAN WEARING A TORN BLANKET AND A PETTY THIEF FROM THE POOR STREETS OF DUBAI.
THERE ARE NO SUPERHEROES HERE.

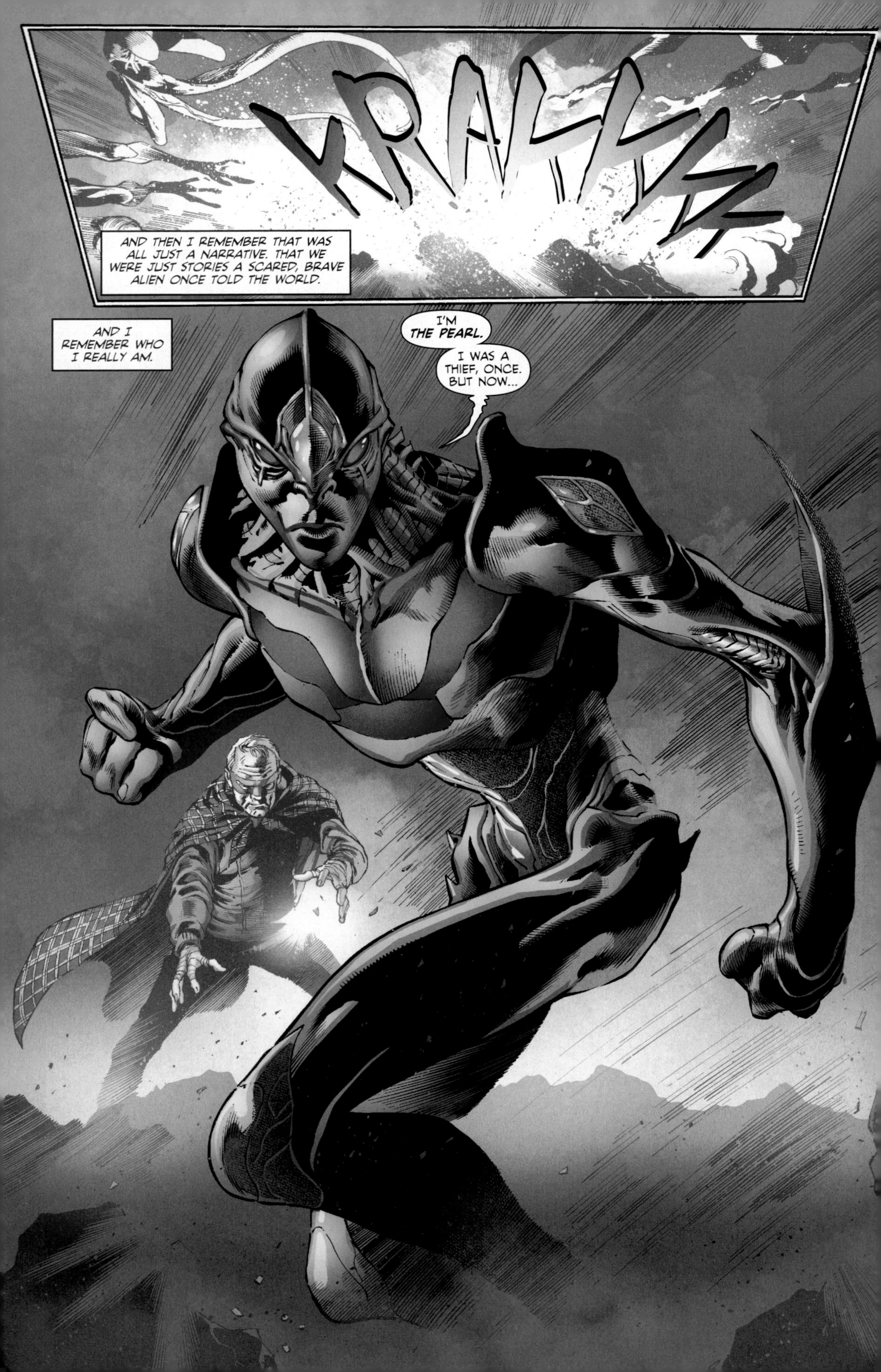
KRAKKKK
AND THEN I REMEMBER THAT WAS ALL JUST A NARRATIVE. THAT WE WERE JUST STORIES A SCARED, BRAVE ALIEN ONCE TOLD THE WORLD.
AND I REMEMBER WHO I REALLY AM.
I'M THE PEARL.
I WAS A THIEF, ONCE. BUT NOW...

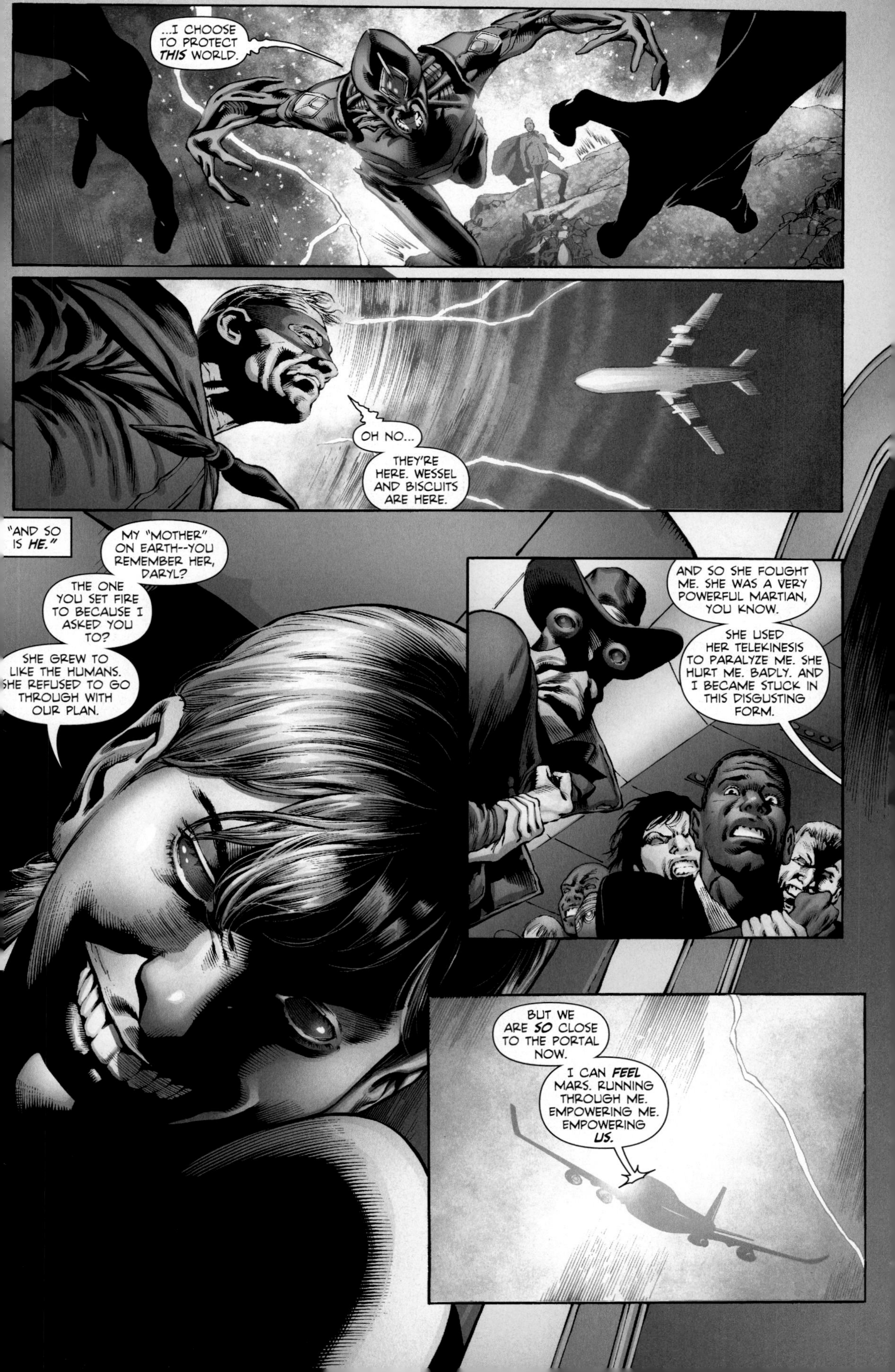
...I CHOOSE TO PROTECT *THIS* WORLD.
OH NO...
THEY'RE HERE. WESSEL AND BISCUITS ARE HERE.
"AND SO IS *HE.*"
MY "MOTHER" ON EARTH--YOU REMEMBER HER, DARYL?
THE ONE YOU SET FIRE TO BECAUSE I ASKED YOU TO?
SHE GREW TO LIKE THE HUMANS. SHE REFUSED TO GO THROUGH WITH OUR PLAN.
AND SO SHE FOUGHT ME. SHE WAS A VERY POWERFUL MARTIAN, YOU KNOW.
SHE USED HER TELEKINESIS TO PARALYZE ME. SHE HURT ME. BADLY. AND I BECAME STUCK IN THIS DISGUSTING FORM.
BUT WE ARE *SO* CLOSE TO THE PORTAL NOW.
I CAN *FEEL* MARS. RUNNING THROUGH ME. EMPOWERING ME. EMPOWERING *US.*

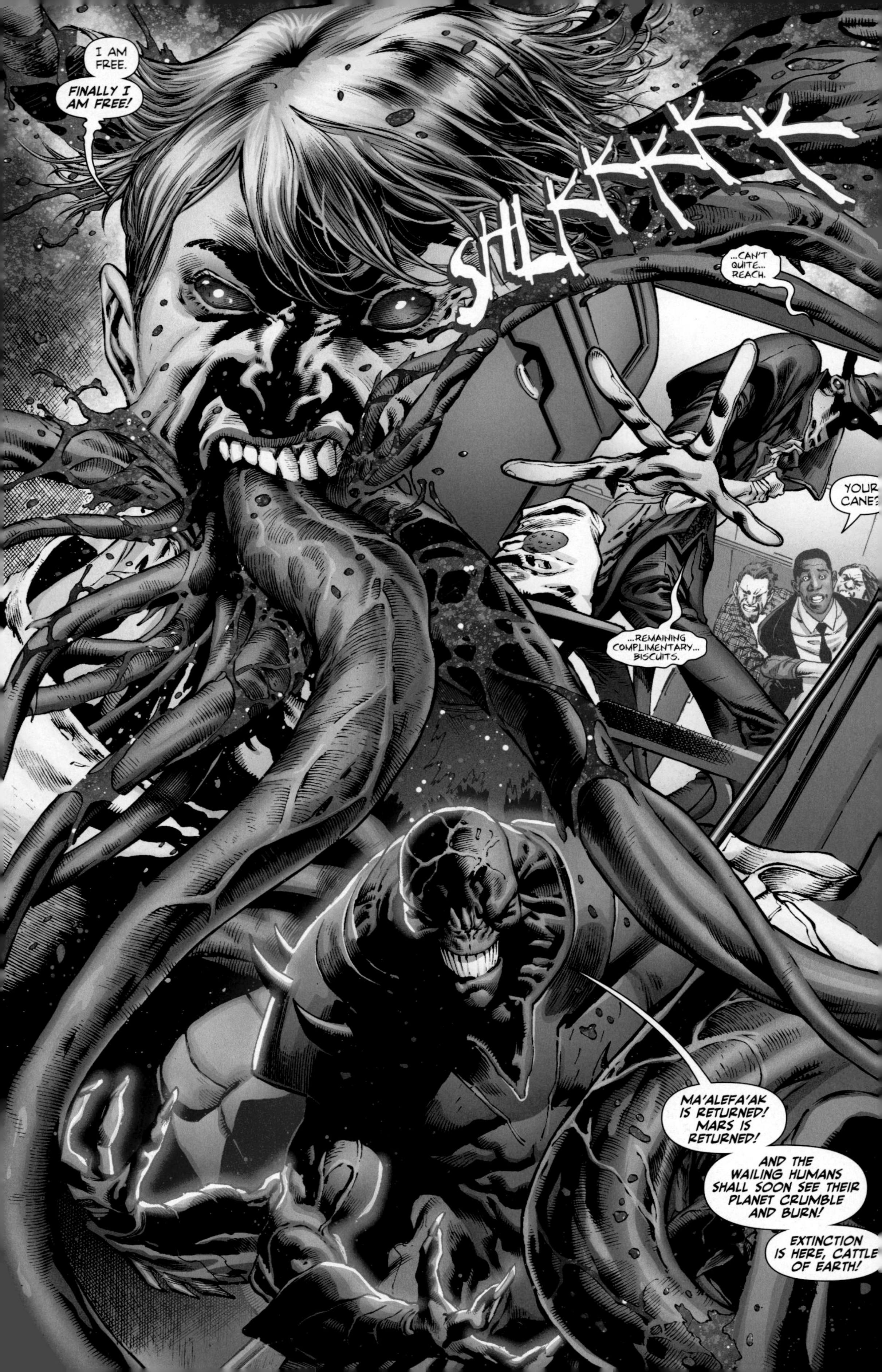

I AM FREE.
FINALLY I AM FREE!
SHLKKKKK
...CAN'T QUITE... REACH.
YOUR CANE?
...REMAINING COMPLIMENTARY... BISCUITS.
MA'ALEFA'AK IS RETURNED! MARS IS RETURNED!
AND THE WAILING HUMANS SHALL SOON SEE THEIR PLANET CRUMBLE AND BURN!
EXTINCTION IS HERE, CATTLE OF EARTH!

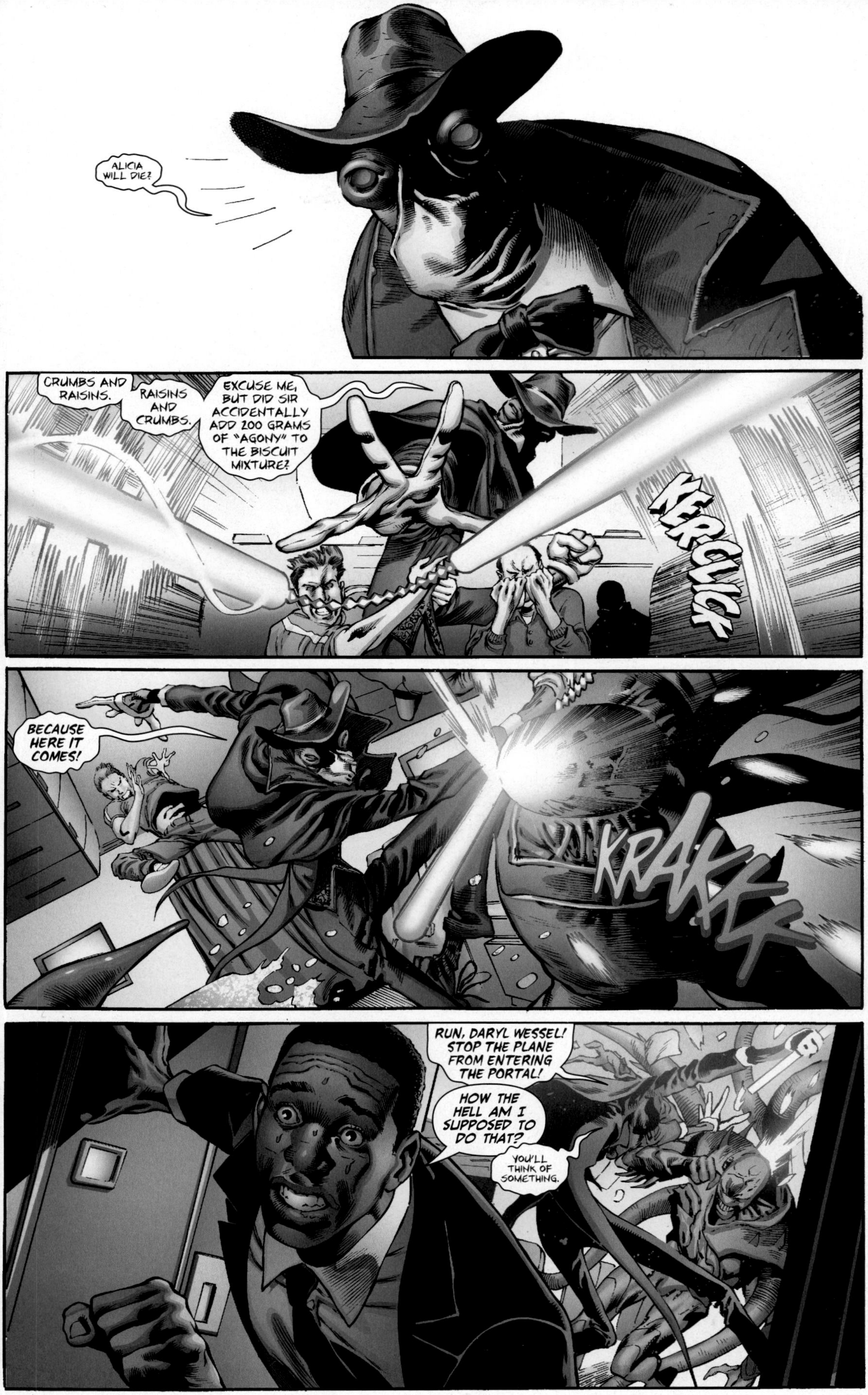
ALICIA WILL DIE?
CRUMBS AND RAISINS.
RAISINS AND CRUMBS.
EXCUSE ME, BUT DID SIR ACCIDENTALLY ADD 200 GRAMS OF "AGONY" TO THE BISCUIT MIXTURE?
KER-CLICK
BECAUSE HERE IT COMES!
KRAKKK
RUN, DARYL WESSEL! STOP THE PLANE FROM ENTERING THE PORTAL!
HOW THE HELL AM I SUPPOSED TO DO THAT?
YOU'LL THINK OF SOMETHING.

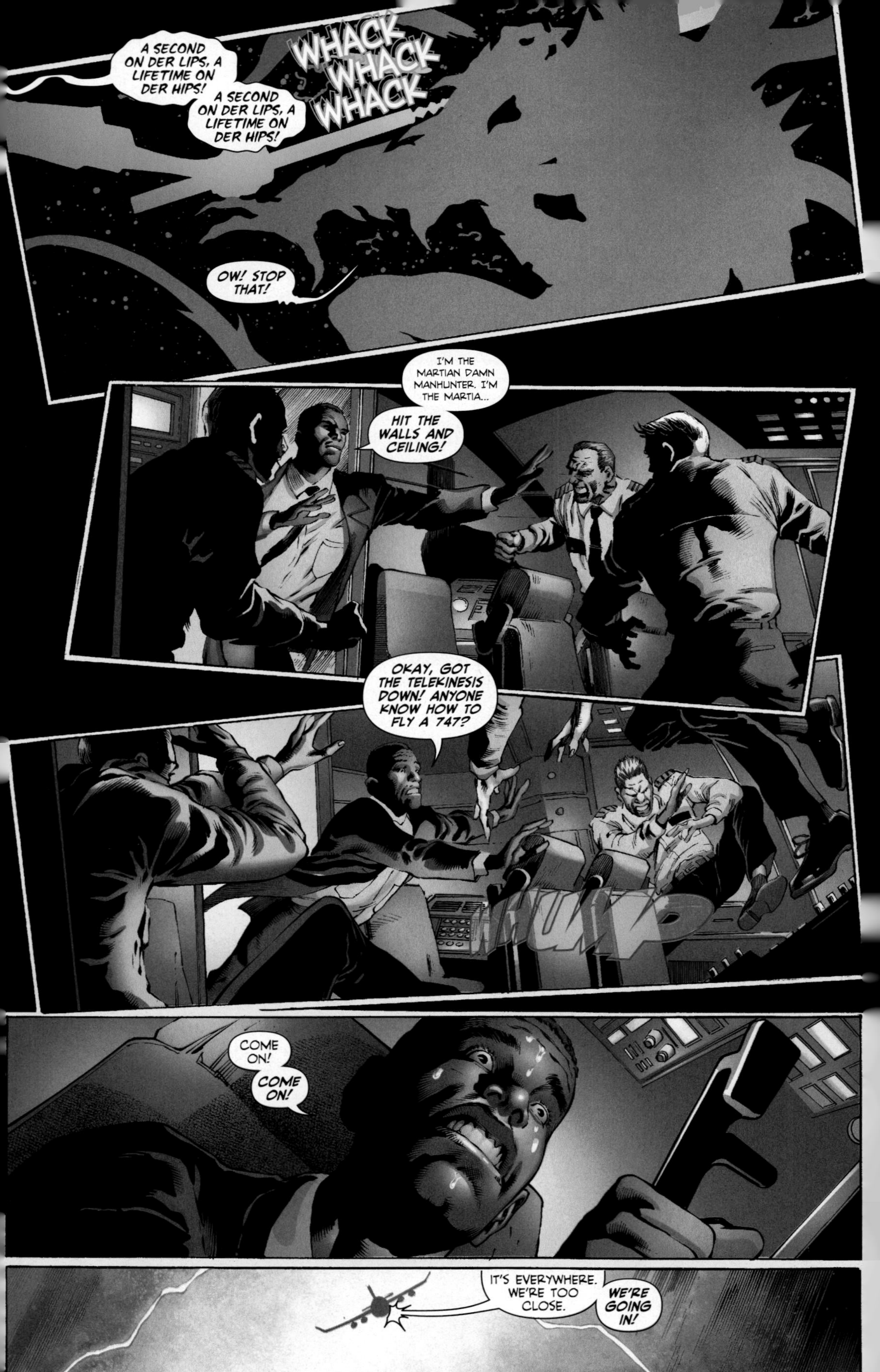
A SECOND ON DER LIPS, A LIFETIME ON DER HIPS!
A SECOND ON DER LIPS, A LIFETIME ON DER HIPS!
WHACK WHACK WHACK
OW! STOP THAT!
I'M THE MARTIAN DAMN MANHUNTER. I'M THE MARTIA...
HIT THE WALLS AND CEILING!
OKAY, GOT THE TELEKINESIS DOWN! ANYONE KNOW HOW TO FLY A 747?
COME ON!
COME ON!
IT'S EVERYWHERE. WE'RE TOO CLOSE.
WE'RE GOING IN!

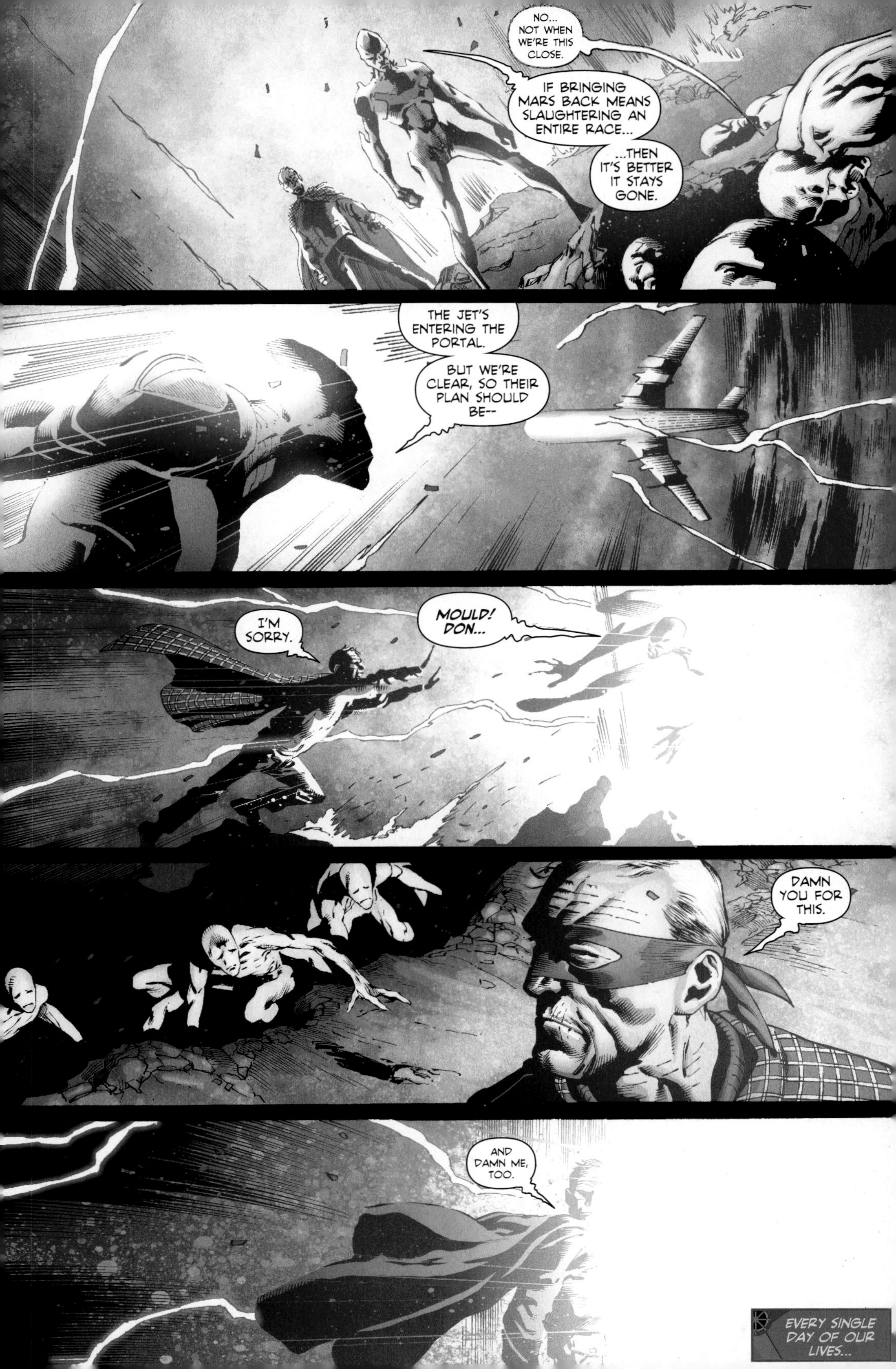
NO... NOT WHEN WE'RE THIS CLOSE.
IF BRINGING MARS BACK MEANS SLAUGHTERING AN ENTIRE RACE...
...THEN IT'S BETTER IT STAYS GONE.
THE JET'S ENTERING THE PORTAL.
BUT WE'RE CLEAR, SO THEIR PLAN SHOULD BE--
MOULD! DON...
I'M SORRY.
DAMN YOU FOR THIS.
AND DAMN ME, TOO.
EVERY SINGLE DAY OF OUR LIVES...

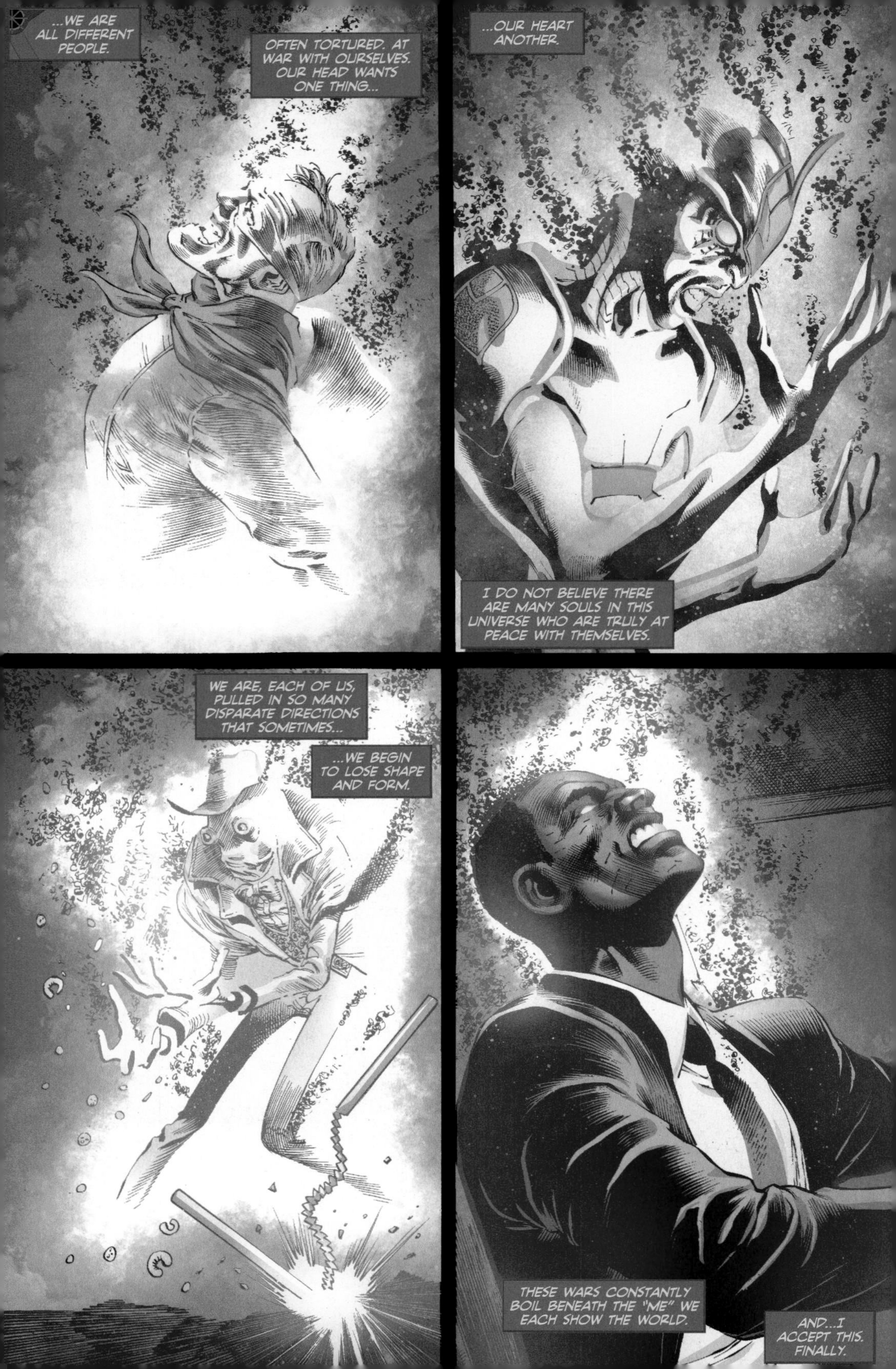
...WE ARE ALL DIFFERENT PEOPLE.
OFTEN TORTURED. AT WAR WITH OURSELVES. OUR HEAD WANTS ONE THING...
...OUR HEART ANOTHER.
I DO NOT BELIEVE THERE ARE MANY SOULS IN THIS UNIVERSE WHO ARE TRULY AT PEACE WITH THEMSELVES.
WE ARE, EACH OF US, PULLED IN SO MANY DISPARATE DIRECTIONS THAT SOMETIMES...
...WE BEGIN TO LOSE SHAPE AND FORM.
THESE WARS CONSTANTLY BOIL BENEATH THE "ME" WE EACH SHOW THE WORLD.
AND...I ACCEPT THIS. FINALLY.

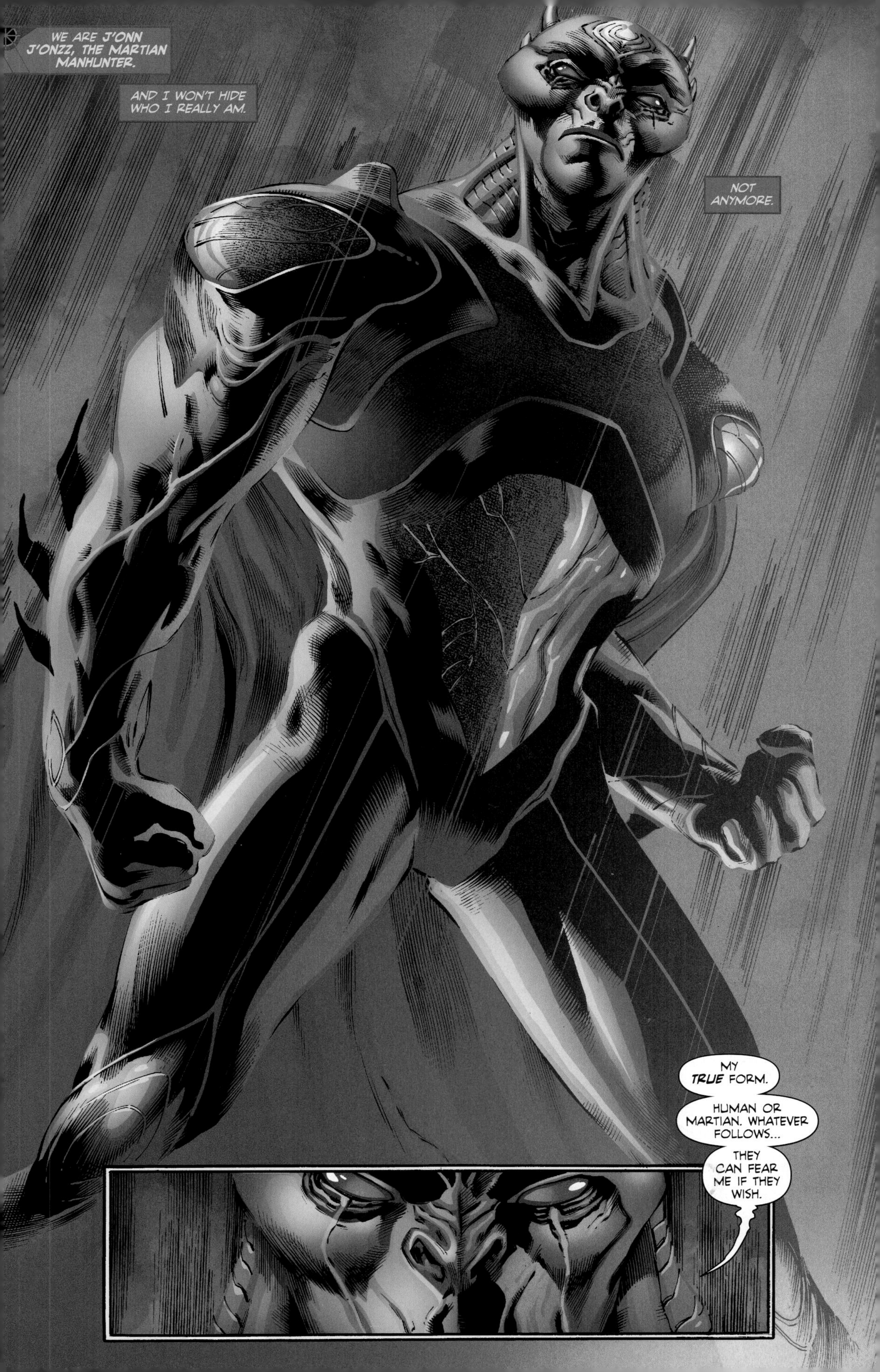
WE ARE J'ONN J'ONZZ, THE MARTIAN MANHUNTER.
AND I WON'T HIDE WHO I REALLY AM.
NOT ANYMORE.
MY TRUE FORM.
HUMAN OR MARTIAN. WHATEVER FOLLOWS...
THEY CAN FEAR ME IF THEY WISH.

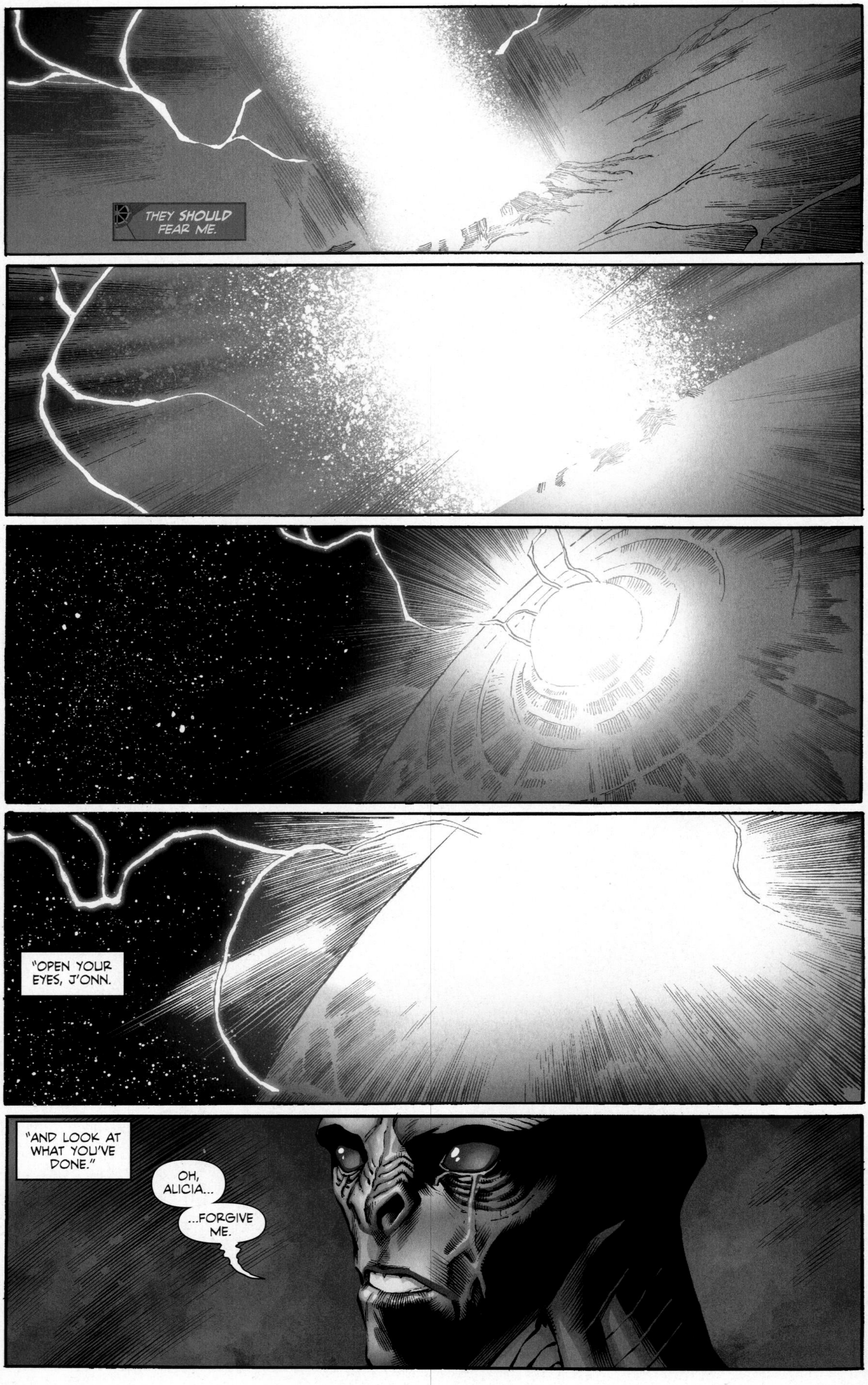
THEY SHOULD FEAR ME.
"OPEN YOUR EYES, J'ONN.
"AND LOOK AT WHAT YOU'VE DONE."
OH, ALICIA...
...FORGIVE ME.

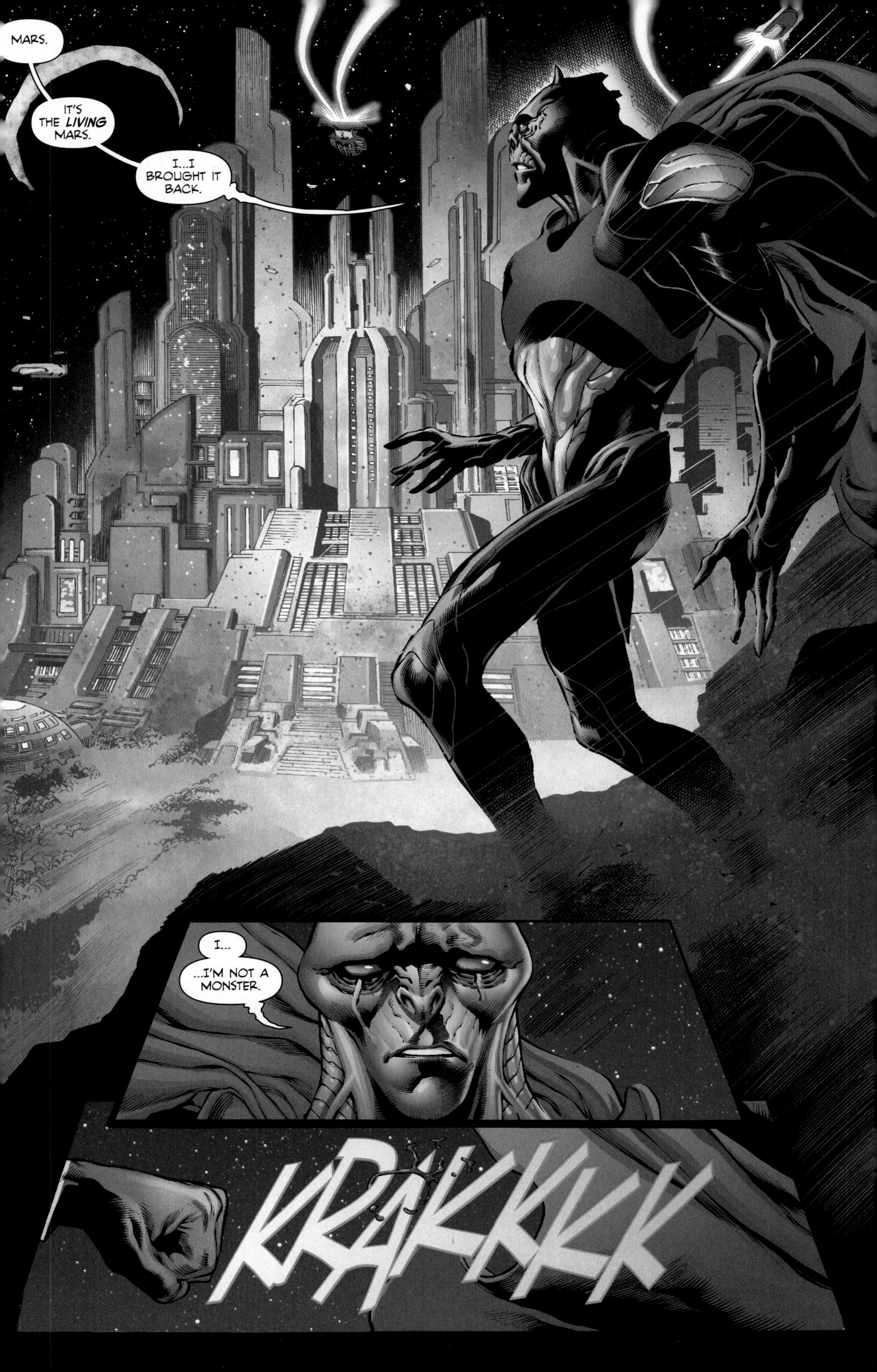
MARS.
IT'S THE *LIVING* MARS.
I...I BROUGHT IT BACK.
I...
...I'M NOT A MONSTER.
KRAKKKK

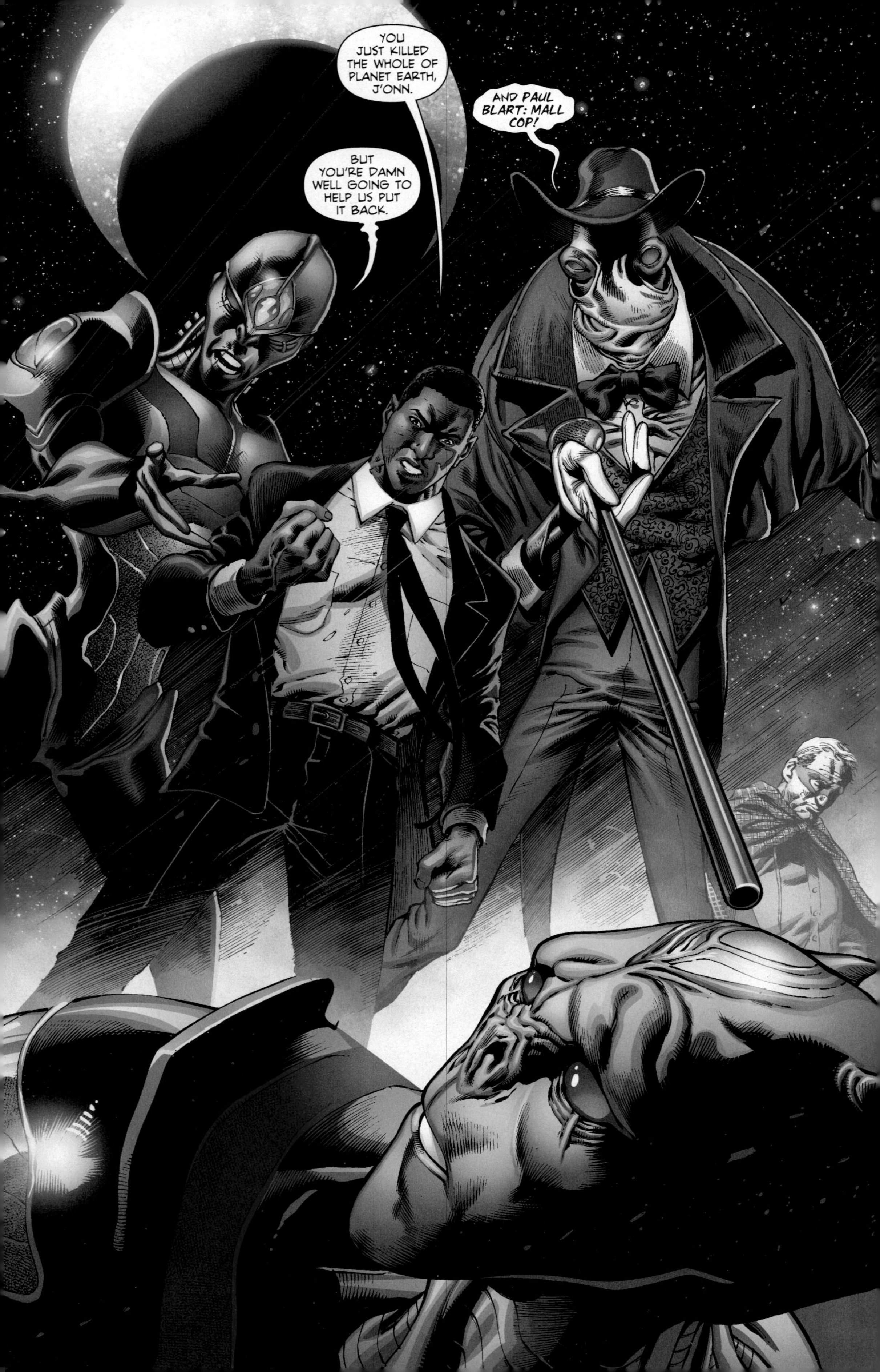
YOU JUST KILLED THE WHOLE OF PLANET EARTH, J'ONN.
BUT YOU'RE DAMN WELL GOING TO HELP US PUT IT BACK.
AND PAUL BLART: MALL COP!

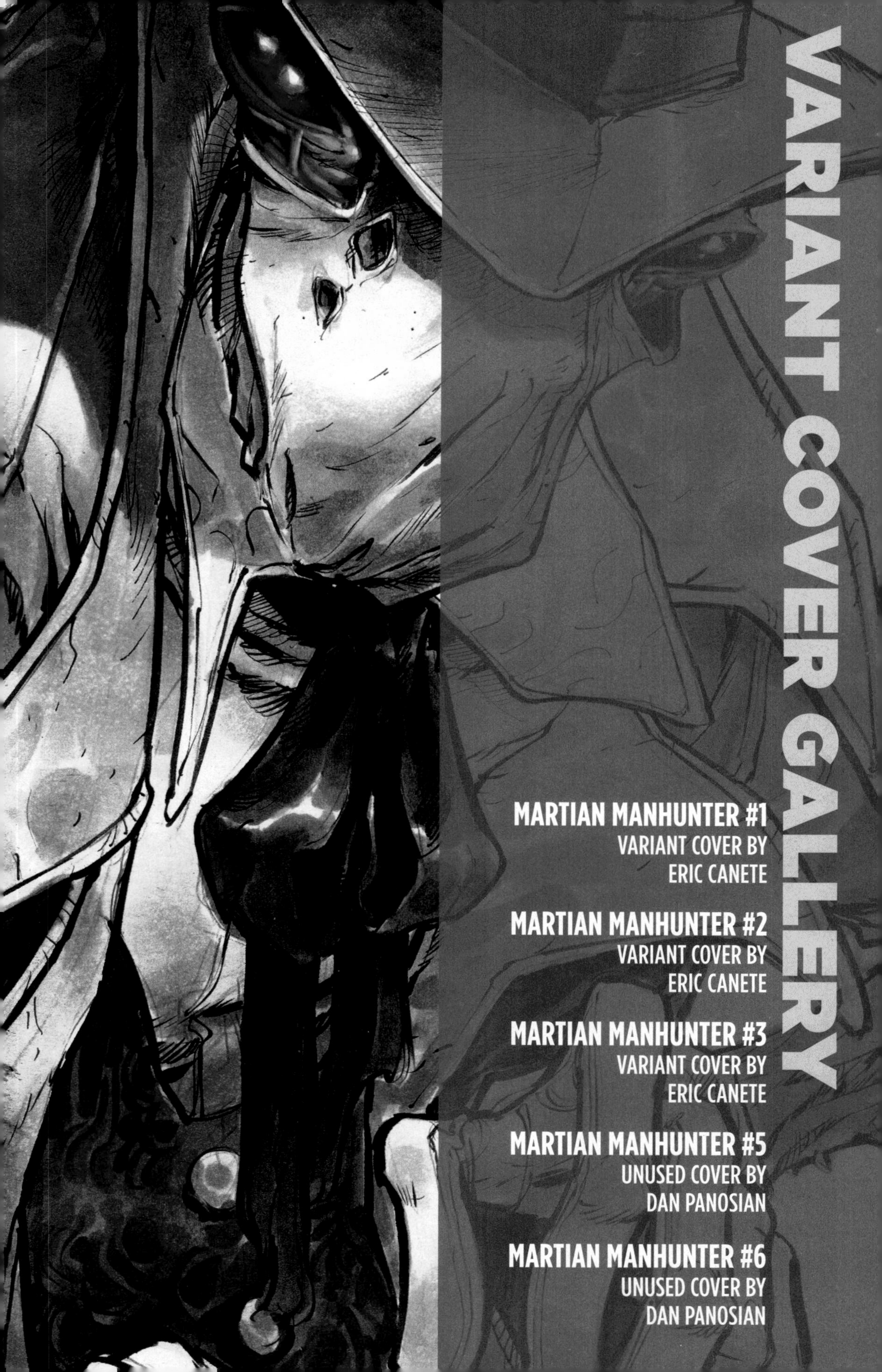

VARIANT COVER GALLERY

MARTIAN MANHUNTER #1
VARIANT COVER BY
ERIC CANETE

MARTIAN MANHUNTER #2
VARIANT COVER BY
ERIC CANETE

MARTIAN MANHUNTER #3
VARIANT COVER BY
ERIC CANETE

MARTIAN MANHUNTER #5
UNUSED COVER BY
DAN PANOSIAN

MARTIAN MANHUNTER #6
UNUSED COVER BY
DAN PANOSIAN

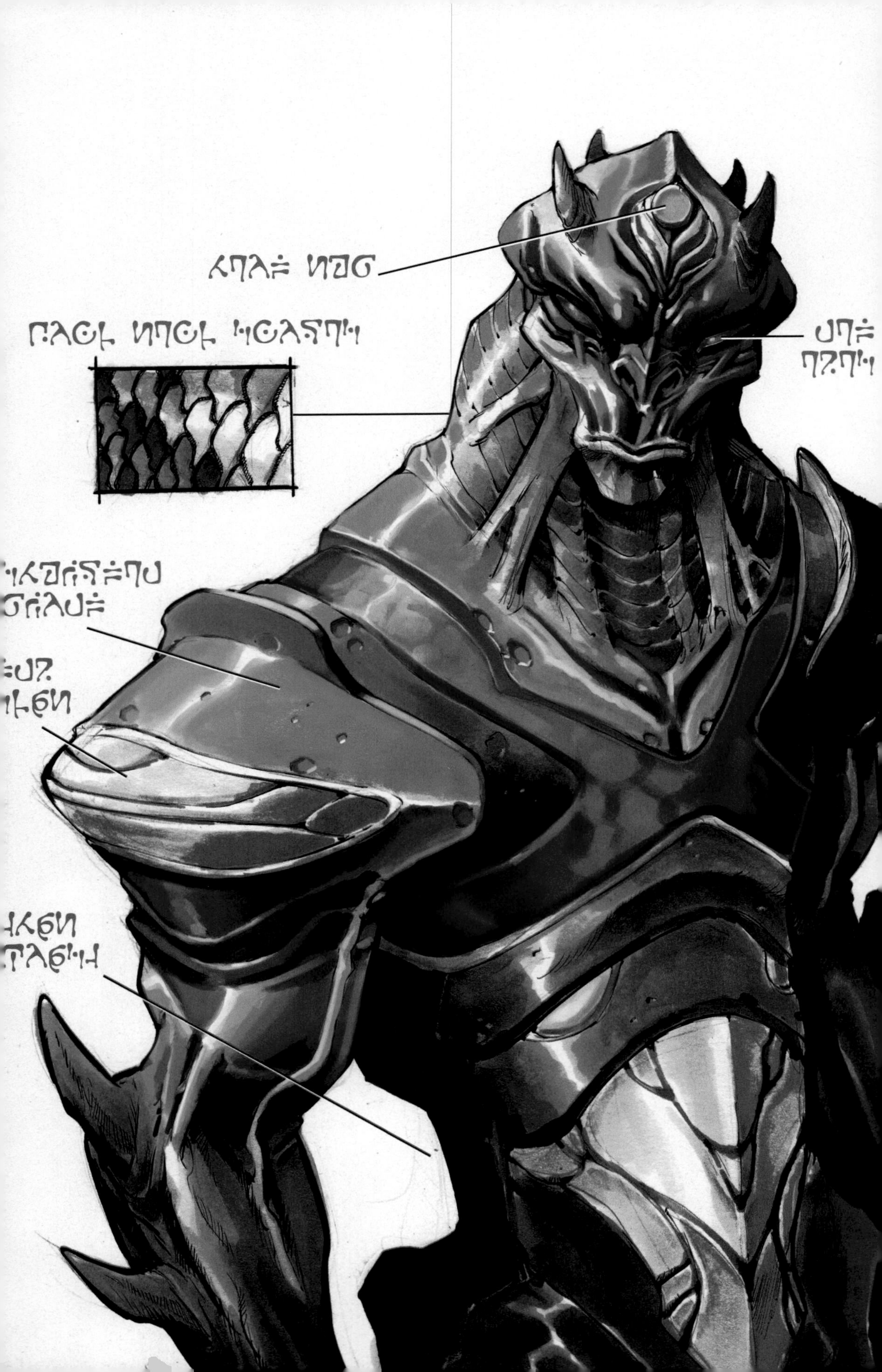

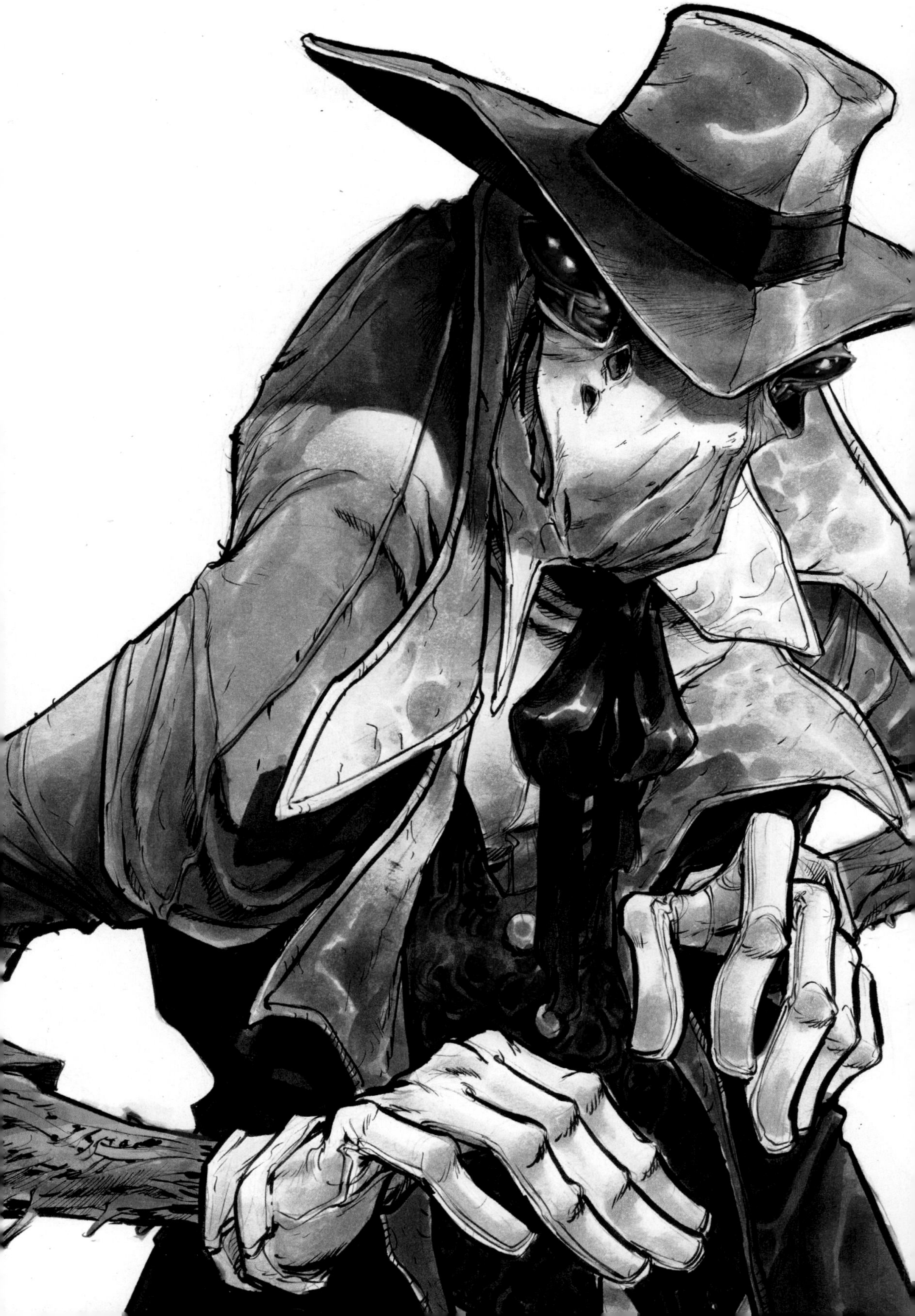

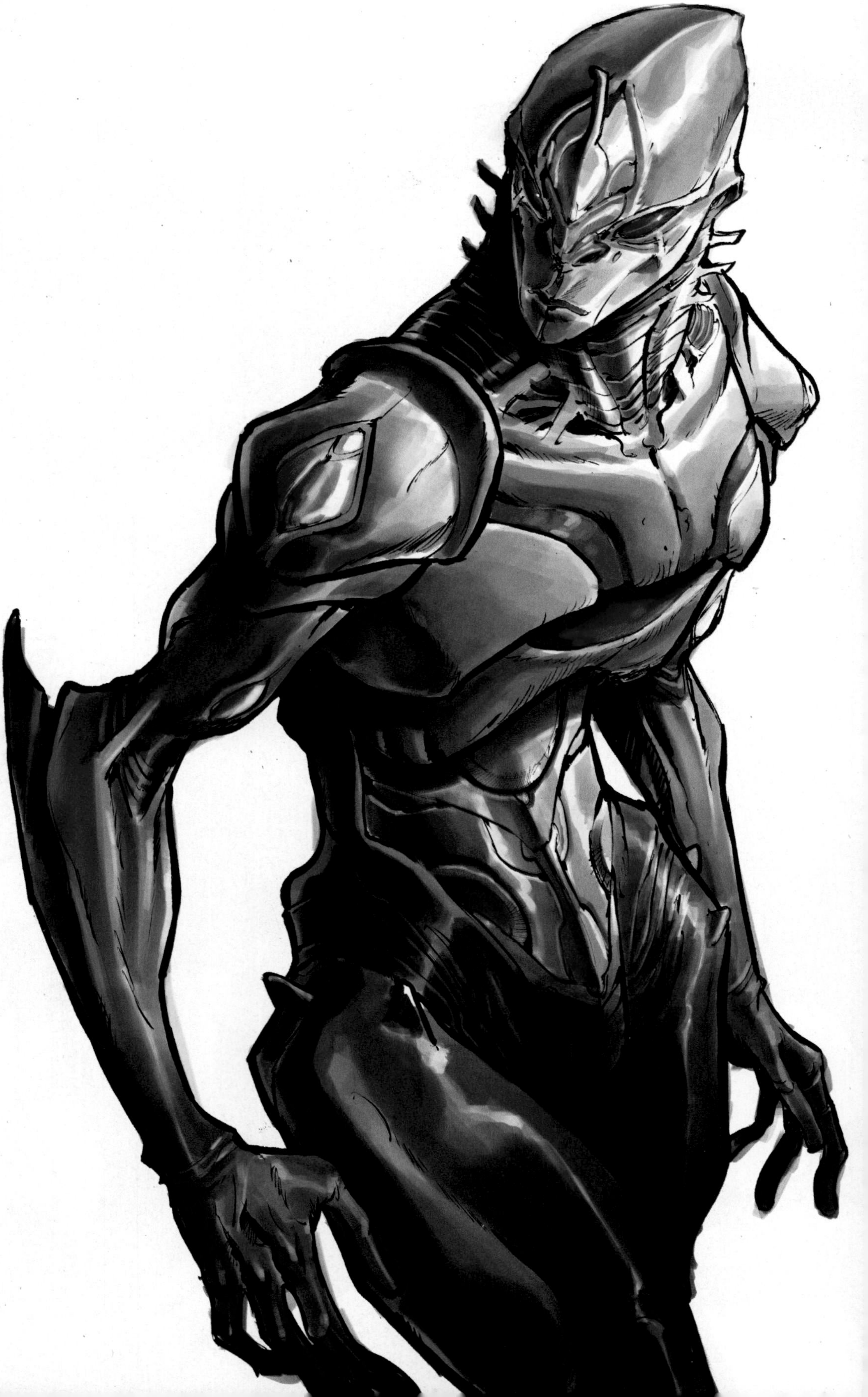

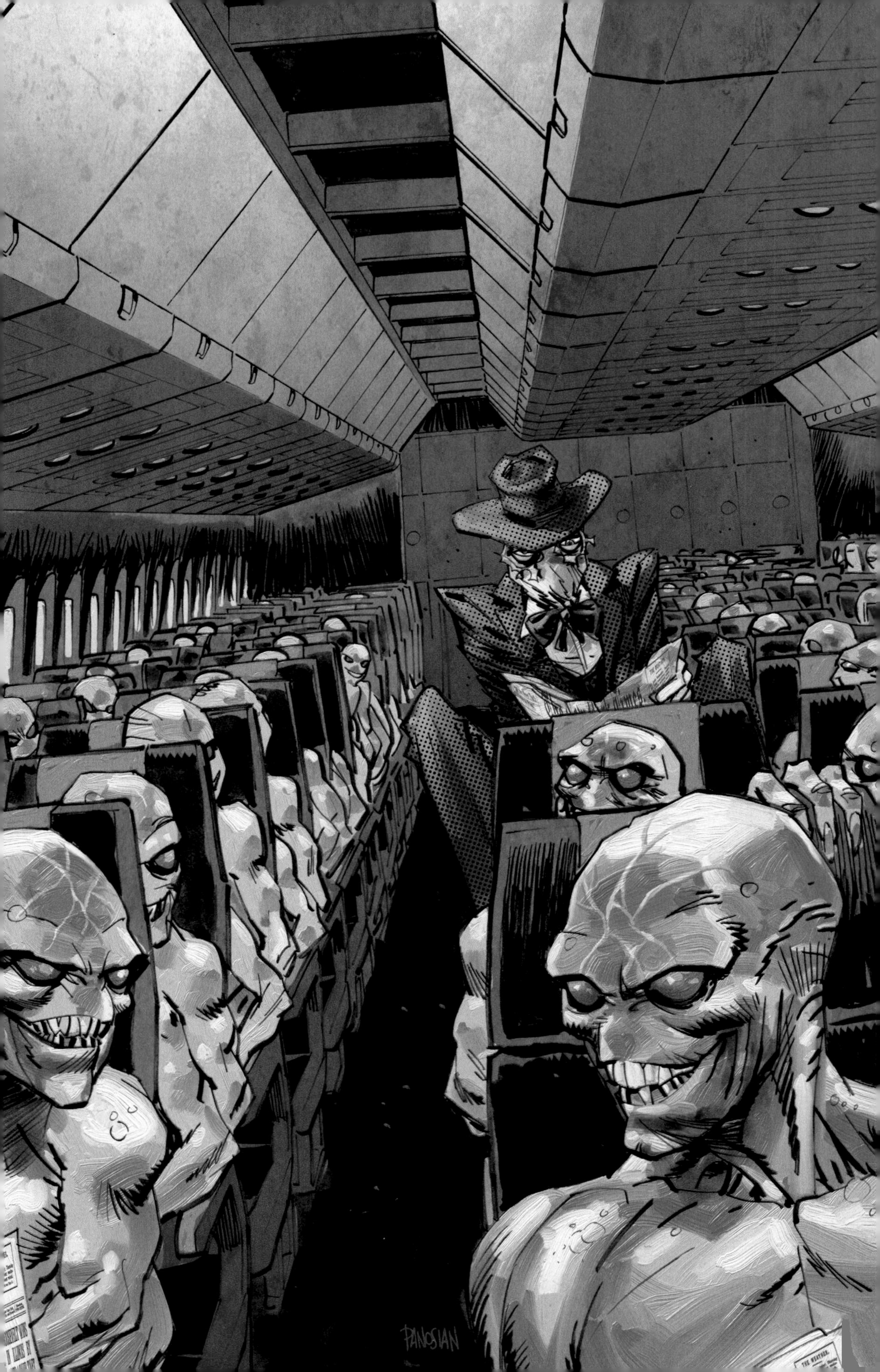
PANOSIAN

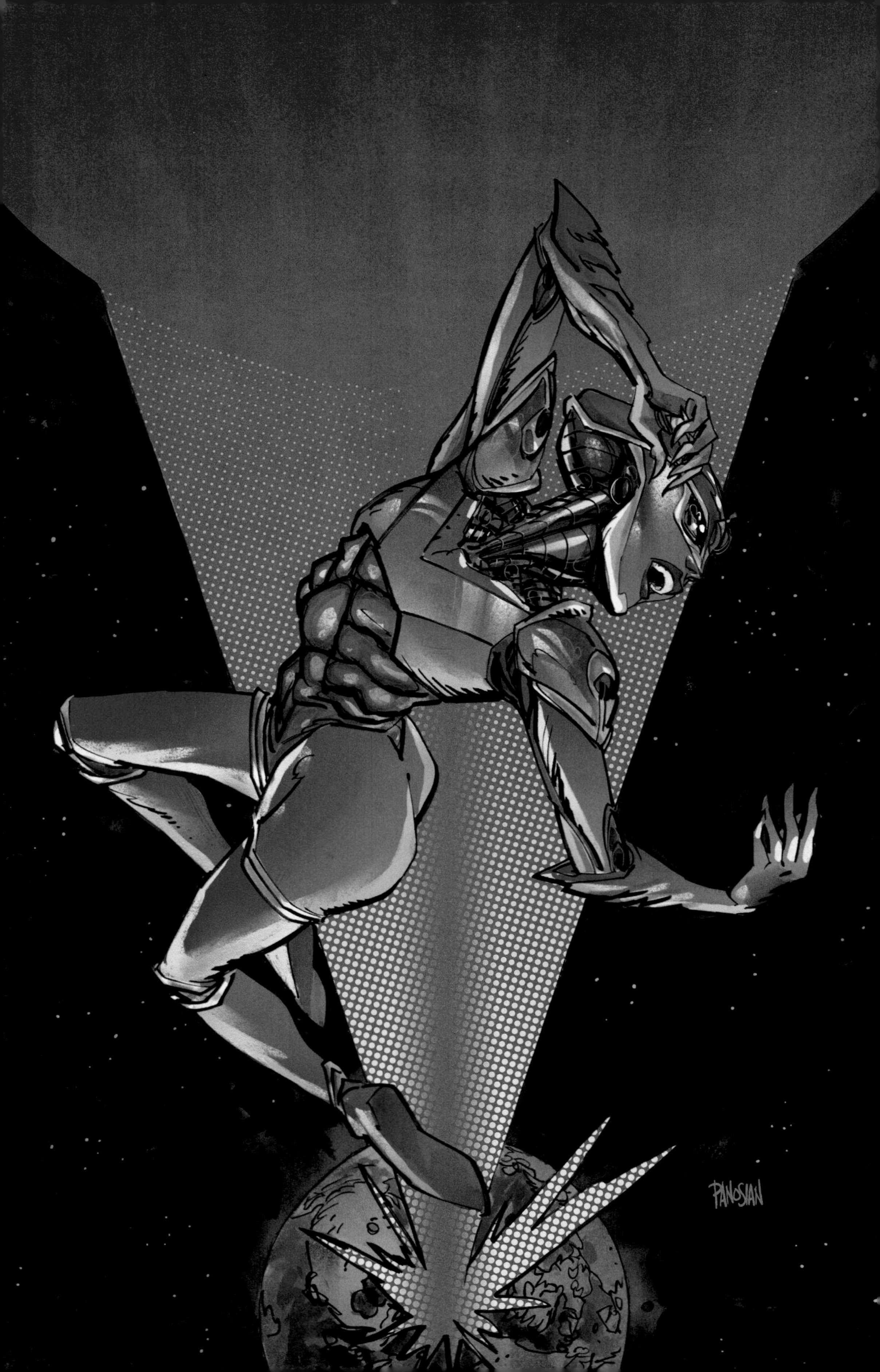
PANOSIAN

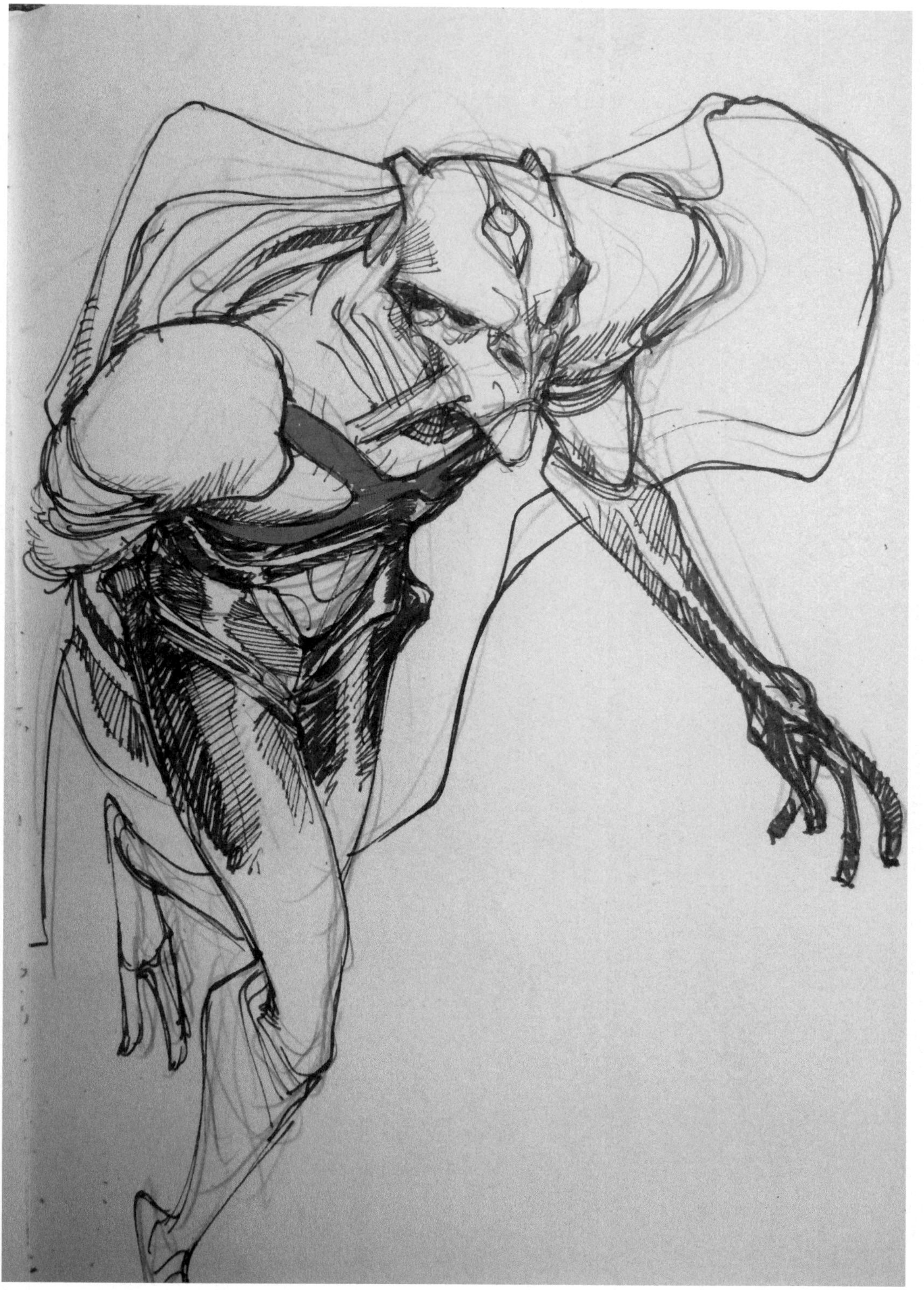

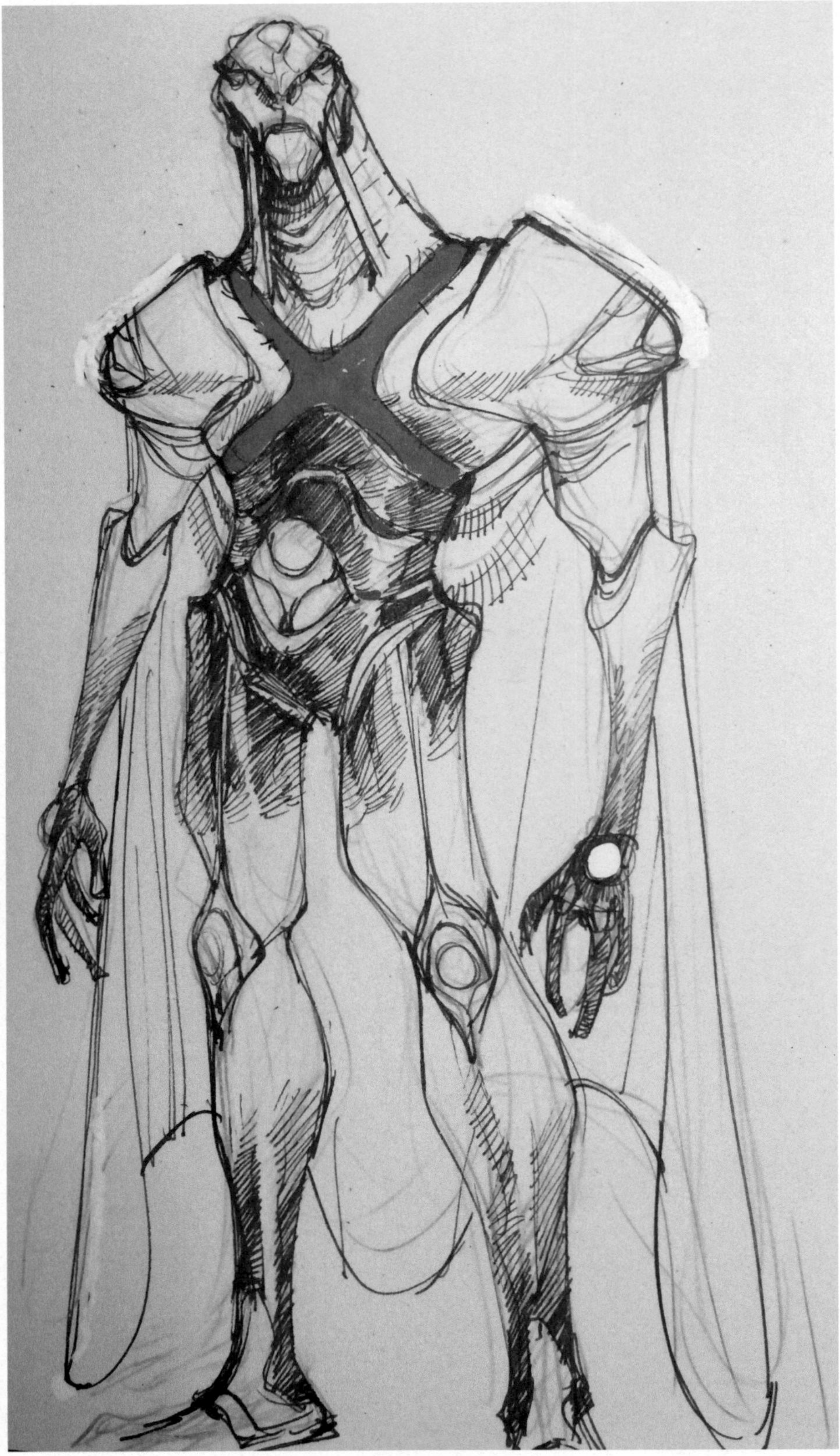

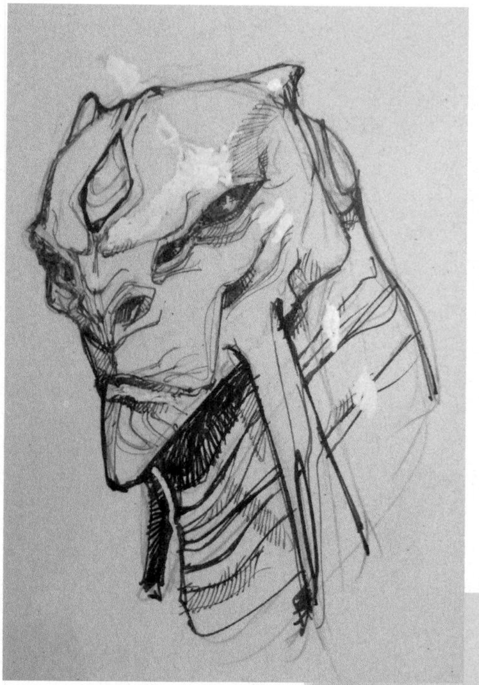
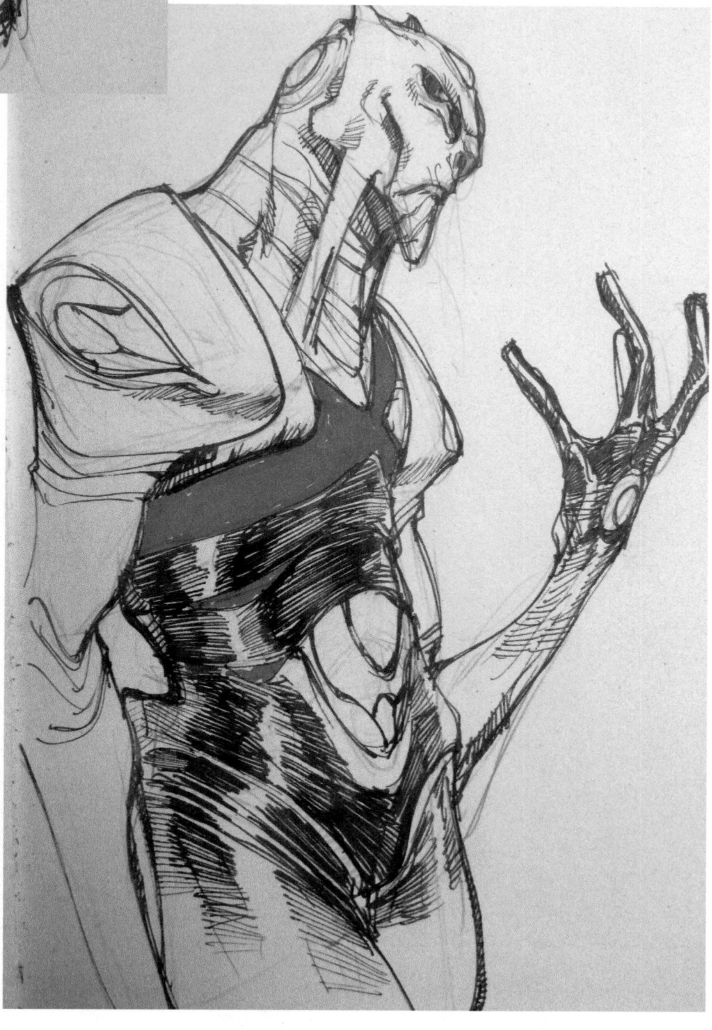

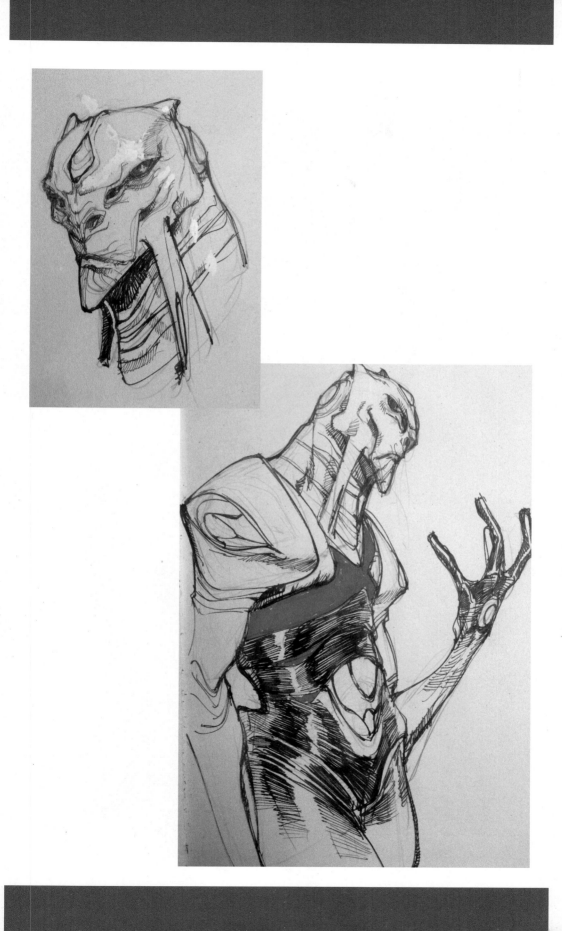

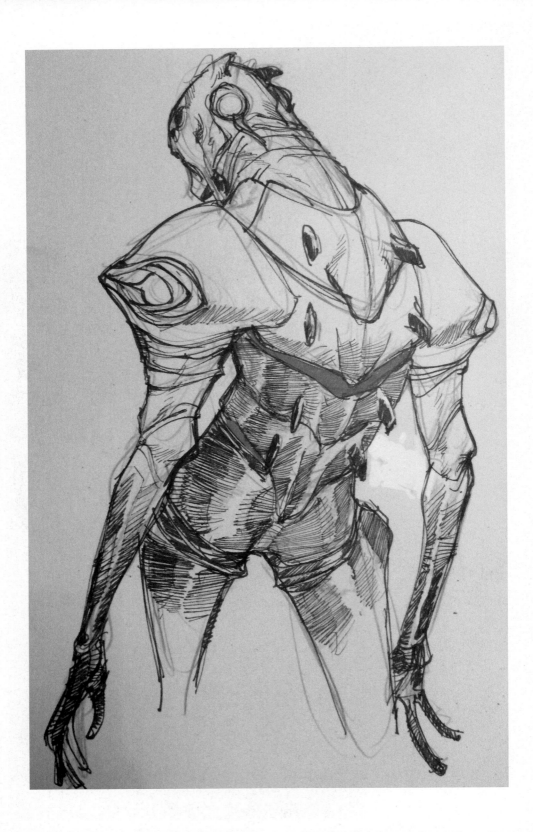

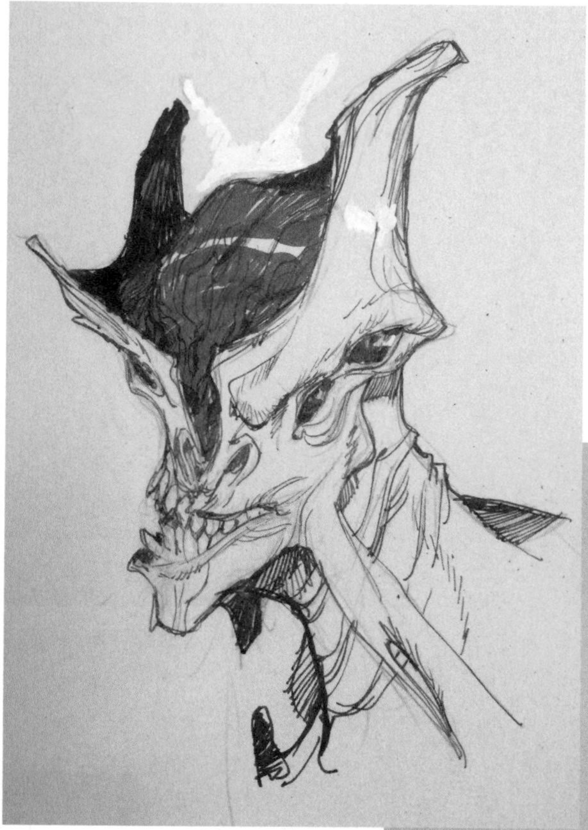
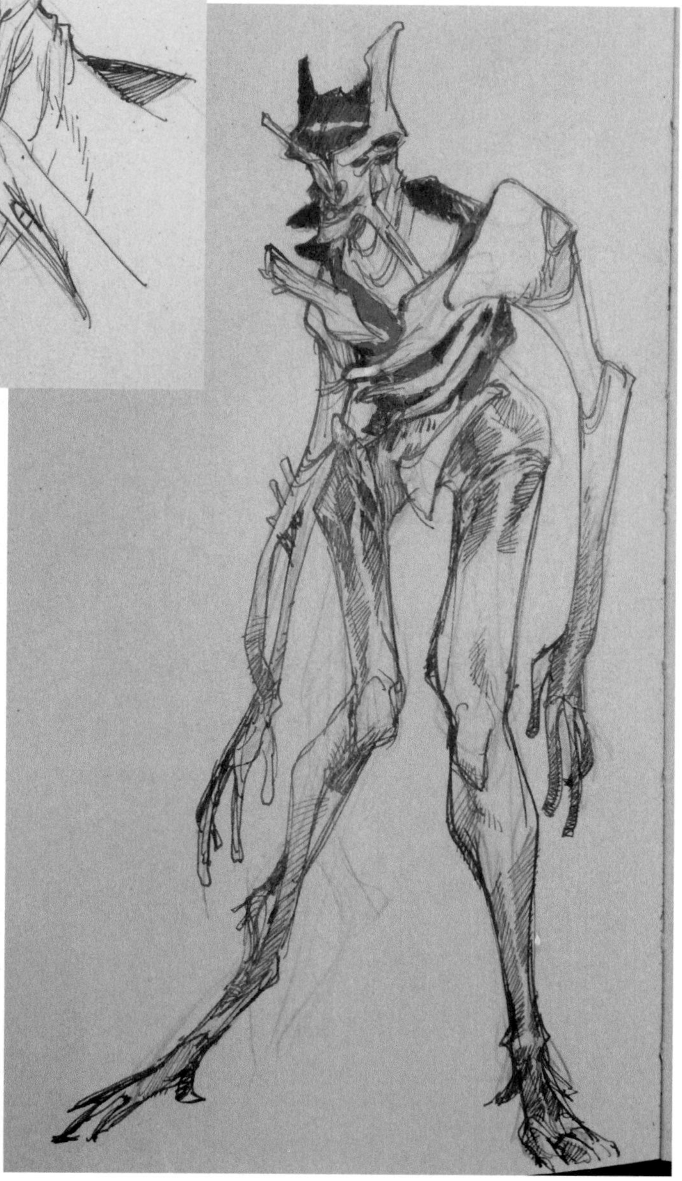

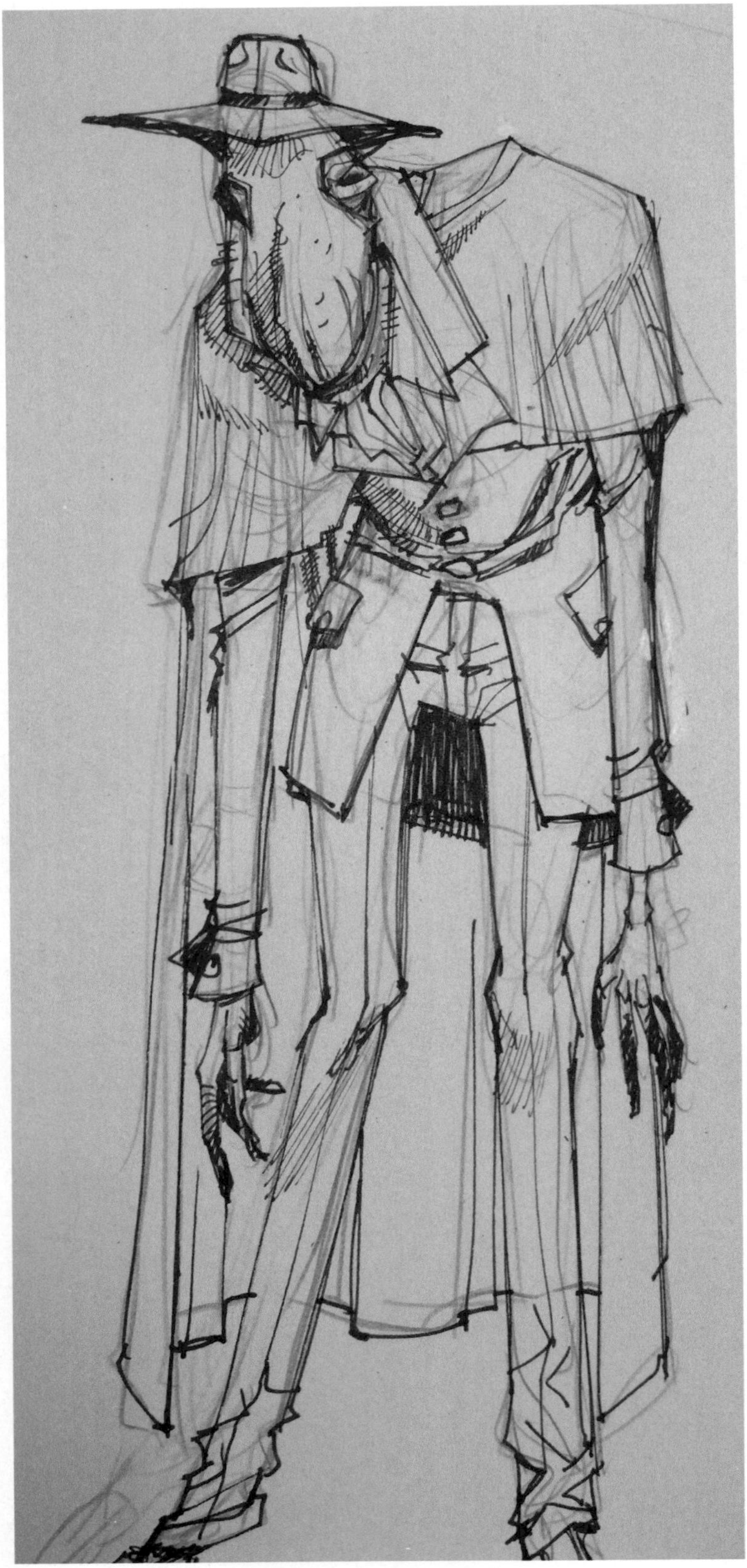